Sebago is a lightweight racing yacht designed and specially built by Bill Lee, one of a series called a Santa Cruz 50. She measures 50 feet overall, 46.5 feet on the waterline, with a beam of 12 feet and a draft of 8 feet. She displaces about 20,000 pounds and has transferable water ballast of two tons.

BOOKS BY HAL ROTH

Pathway in the Sky (1965)
Two on a Big Ocean (1972)
After 50,000 Miles (1977)
Two Against Cape Horn (1978)
The Longest Race (1983)
Always a Distant Anchorage (1988)
Chasing the Long Rainbow (1990)
Chasing the Wind (1993)

HAL ROTH

CHASING THE WIND

A Book of High Adventure

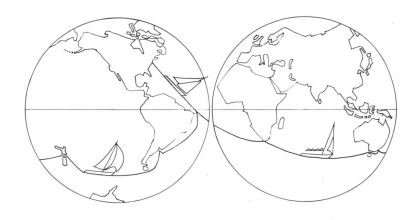

MAPS BY DALE SWENSSON
WIND GRAPHS BY ED BODEN
DRAWINGS BY ERIC SPONBERG

S

SHERIDAN HOUSE

"You can train a man in navigation, seamanship, celestial observation and the computing of tide, current, speed, wind and drift, and yet he will never be a sailor unless, at the moment of truth when he is forced into a corner from which there is no way out except by instant intuitive action, he unerringly makes the right move."

JAN DE HARTOG

Published by Sheridan House Inc.
145 Palisade Street
Dobbs Ferry, NY 10522

Library of Congress Cataloging-in-Publication Data

Roth, Hal.
   Chasing the wind : a book of high adventure / Hal Roth ; maps by Dale Swensson ; wind graphs by Ed Boden ; drawings by Eric Sponberg.
      p.   cm.
   ISBN 0-924486-55-4
   1. BOC Challenge Race.   I. Title.
GV832.R66   1994   93-33596
797. 1′4—dc20   CIP

Maps by Dale Swensson
Wind graphs by Ed Boden
Drawings by Eric Sponberg
Front cover photo: Daniel Forster
Photos by the author, including back cover photo
Cover and design by Jeremiah B. Lighter

Printed in the United States of America

ISBN 0–924486–55–4

Contents

PHOTOGRAPHS

MAPS, TABLES, AND DRAWINGS

Introduction

PERHAPS THE ULTIMATE fantasy is to head off into the blue and to sail around the world in a tiny sailboat with white sails, a shelf of books you always wanted to read, and a vague plan to visit distant places.

> You pick a date.
> You cross an ocean with only the power of the wind on your sails.
> You glide gently into far-off harbors.
> You see new people.
> You make your own decisions.
> You become a sort of first explorer—all on your own.

In the late summer of 1990, I set off to sail around the world in a 50-foot yacht. I was by myself, one of 25 entrants (from 10 countries) in a global sailing race. Twenty-five captains in 25 sleek sailing vessels started from the east coast of the U.S. and sailed southeast in the Atlantic to Cape Town, South Africa. After a stop for repairs and supplies, we headed eastward in the Southern Ocean to Australia, where we gathered in Sydney. Then east across the Tasman Sea, onward in the vast Southern Ocean, around Cape Horn, and north to a little port in Uruguay in the South Atlantic. Finally—by now there were 18 of us left—we aimed our vessels north in the Atlantic and returned to the U.S. where we had started many months before. In all I sailed 30,000 miles.

The winner of the race—who competed in a high-tech 60-footer—made his trip in 122 sailing days, or about four months. My 50-footer was slower and I was not expected to do as well. I took a poky 211 days—about seven months—and came in last after a series of misadventures and rigging problems that plagued me from the start. I got far behind the main fleet and sailed mostly by myself. I must have disappointed my friends and my sponsor because I certainly disappointed myself.

I tried my best to speed up, but the reality of such a race seems to be that once behind, you can never catch up. Nevertheless the voyage was high adventure at its best, and somehow I managed to keep going.

I knew that tens of thousands of schoolchildren were following the race ("Is Cape Horn scary?"), and I learned from their 1,200 cards and letters (and my later visits to schools) that the young people applauded my attempts to stay in the race. Certainly a part of real life is to set a goal and to try to achieve it no matter what happens. It's easy to be discouraged and to give up. It takes a little more grit to continue the chase when things are hard.

Since the race I've heard a thousand questions: What do you do at sea on a long voyage? How do you deal with storms and calms? How do you decide which way to go? How do you manage by yourself? What do you eat? When do you sleep? How do you get by without an engine? How do you fix things? What about weather forecasts? How do you keep up your spirits? Are the oceans full of oil spills and plastic and junk? Are there really whales and porpoises and birds out there? Why in God's name do you do it?

I had already sailed my specially-built Santa Cruz 50 AMERICAN FLAG in an earlier BOC Challenge race during 1986–87. Together we logged 27,597 miles in 171 days as we sailed around the world.* I learned a lot during the race, and the vessel was still in excellent condition. I thought we could do better, so I decided to enter the 1990-91 race.

A Maine company named Sebago, which makes stylish, long-lasting boating and recreational shoes, offered to sponsor me. I felt lucky to represent this enterprising Yankee firm that was so full of enthusiasm for the race. On the day I signed the contract, Sebago's president, Dan Wellehan, waved a bony forefinger at me and said: "Hal, we want you to win, but we want you to come back."

I solemnly promised to do both.

My first move was to hire Art Paine, a superb boat carpenter, who made a sleek spade rudder to replace the old heavy skeg and barn door rudder. Art and Dave Markle, another expert Maine carpenter, then ripped out the interior, glassed in two midship frames, and made all new high-class furniture of wide-planked varnished mahogany. Margaret—my wife—and I then sailed the yacht from Maine to Rhode Island where we took her out of the water at the Hood yard in Portsmouth.

The performance of the Santa Cruz 50 to windward was poor so I hired a naval architect named Rodger Martin to design special

*For an account of this race see the author's earlier book *Chasing the Long Rainbow.*

water ballast tanks. Master mechanic Steve Pettengill and his helper Davis Murray built 400-gallon fiberglass tanks along the port and starboard sides of the after part of the cabin. The idea was that when either the port or starboard tanks (each was 14 feet long) was pumped full of saltwater, the extra 3,400 pounds would tilt the yacht 10° one way or the other.

When sailing to windward (which made the yacht heel), I could pump all or part of the 3,400 pounds to the high side to straighten up the yacht. This made the vessel more powerful, able to stand up to a given amount of sail, and hence faster. A moment before tacking I opened a valve which allowed the water to run from the tank on the high side to the low side. After tacking, the water was then on the new high side.

While the tanks were being constructed (a complex, incredibly messy job) I worked out some of the plumbing and hunted up valves and special 12-volt one-quarter horsepower pumps. As soon as a carpenter had part of the interior back together I asked Herb Weiss, an old friend and electrical engineering whiz from MIT, to work on the wiring. We moved the electrical panel to a new location and Herb started in. He put in gel cell batteries and a high-tech voltage regulator. We mounted a big alternator on the little inboard diesel engine. Meanwhile I had the rudder shaft sonic-tested for possible cracks and replaced the upper rudder bearing. I hired naval architect Eric Sponberg to design a taller, lighter mast, which Paul Rosenfield at Metalmast in Connecticut agreed to build.

We discovered that an earlier epoxy coating on the bottom of the hull and keel had contracted an acute case of chicken pox and had thousands of tiny blisters. We tried various corrective schemes, but nothing worked, and we finally had to grind off the defective coating, a terrible job. We then rolled on five coats of West epoxy which had to be applied according to a complicated time schedule. The bottom job alone took five people three weeks of backbreaking work. While the ground crew rested for a few days the yacht was hauled into the painting shed where the topsides were sprayed with glistening coats of white Awlgrip.

All this time Margaret cheerfully worked 12-hour days along with the men. She sanded, mixed paint, rolled on epoxy, held wrenches, measured wire, ran errands, and dealt with the bills and payments. She was a marvel.

As soon as SEBAGO was out of the paint shed, we stepped the new mast, and the boat began to look like a yacht again. I worked with the riggers to install new 1x19 wire for the shrouds and stays. We put up two sets of new Schaefer roller-furling gears for the headsails. Meanwhile a local artist carefully positioned the name and red and blue vinyl decorations (designed by the Sebago company) on the beautiful white hull. Finally we rolled on blue Awlgrip bottom paint and put the yacht in the water.

The carpenters spent another week in the cabin while Herb Weiss worked on the wiring. Steve Pettengill and I mounted a vertical pole on the after deck for the radar antenna, and we bolted a new Edson bilge pump in place. Fred Cook from Schaefer brought a new stem fitting and a hefty mainsheet traveler system. Tripp Estabrook from Harken arrived with new masthead sheaves. One morning the sailmaker delivered 15 bags of sails.

We bent on a mainsail and jib and went for a test sail to try the water ballast tanks. The transferable water system worked to perfection. SEBAGO was now stiffer, sailed more upright, and on some points of sailing went half a knot faster. She seemed like a new vessel.

We moved to Newport and began to go sailing every day. Now that we were operational, the press began to take an interest in us, and the Sebago advertising people sent a film crew to make a short video film. Meanwhile we installed a weatherfax machine, a Raytheon Global Positioning System (GPS) receiver, a 406 MHz emergency position-indicating radio beacon (EPIRB), and checked the two autopilots. We put a powerful new single sideband radio on board, but the performance was marginal. The radio company decided to add more copper grounding strips inside the hull.

By now months had passed. The focus of my life was my daily work list, a roll of electrical tape, a 15mm end wrench, a bosun's chair, and a box of cotter pins. I had no time to read the newspaper and scarcely time to wash my face in the morning. The start of the race was coming up, and I was still immersed in technical baloney. Would I ever be ready? Was there a light at the top of the mast? I needed to think about *the sailing itself.*

My long-time friend Ed Boden, an expert sailor and super-mechanic, arrived from North Carolina and took charge of small and large jobs. A half dozen others joined our volunteer force including Kim Roberts, who made an impressive bracket for the antenna of the Standard C satellite radio which had finally come from Japan. A few days before the race we hauled SEBAGO out of the water. I removed the propeller, strut, and shaft while Ed and a helper wet-sanded the bottom. Margaret and Ed then rolled on a last coat of Awlgrip bottom paint. Hank and Marie Bernhard threw a big party. Were we ready? I hoped so. Maybe now I could think of the course and my sailing schemes.

A newcomer to the sea might think that you sail from Port A to Port B by simply heading from one to the other. Sometimes this is possible, but generally not, because prevailing winds and ocean currents (and tidal streams near the shore) push you first one way and then another. Often it's much faster (and easier on both you and the vessel) to sail far to the right or left of your target so that you get help from a favorable wind that blows in a specific area at a certain season. Or to avoid an unfavorable ocean current.

The longer the distances you have to sail, the more important it is to pay attention to prevailing winds and currents. In addition, sailors try to avoid calms and storms and to stay away from steamer, fishing, and regulatory traffic.

The French Vendée Globe race and the BOC Challenge race are round-the-world singlehanded races that start in the North Atlantic and go east-about by way of the Southern Ocean and Cape Horn. The 24,000-mile Vendée race is nonstop (best time so far: a phenomenal 109 days, or an average of 220 miles per day). The 27,500-mile BOC Challenge is a little longer because of three publicity, rest, and refitting stops that require the yachts to detour slightly from the main sailing routes (best time: a remarkable 122 days, or an average of 225 miles per day).

Since wind and weather information are all important, sailors with more facts on board and the wisdom to use them have an advantage. During the race described in this book there were no restrictions on shore-based weather forecasts or routing advice.* This meant that captains with the deepest pockets had professional weathermen sending advice once or twice a day. And of course we all heard the joke: "Is it smarter for a sponsor to teach a captain about the weather or to teach a weatherman how to sail?"

A sailing vessel goes faster with winds from certain directions relative to its course. (A wind from the side—the beam—for example, makes a yacht speedier than a wind 35° or 45° forward of the beam.) The performance of a yacht relative to the strength and direction of winds can be determined by calculations and sailing trials with great accuracy, plotted on a graph, and programmed into a computer. These figures are called *Velocity Prediction Programs* (or VPP's).

A weatherman researches historical wind directions, wind strengths, and storm patterns for an area. He gets the latest figures from the five-day weather models in Europe and the U.S. He looks

---

*Outside private weather and routing are no longer allowed in these races. Instead the captains get a general forecast. This equalizes the events somewhat and helps preserve the spirit and tranquillity of singlehanding.

at approaching storms and reads reports from ships and weather buoys. He tracks satellite weather data and draws charts of nearby high and low pressure areas. He thinks about wave heights and ocean swell. By radio or telex the weather expert may ask the captain about the conditions on board (winds, clouds, the dew point, air and water temperatures, barometric pressure). The weather expert then shakes all these things together and uses his judgement to serve a weather cocktail. Sometimes the drink is sweet; sometimes it's sour.

It's the greatest help to the captain to know what weather is coming. If it's going to be nasty he can think about smaller sails or a hot meal. He may postpone a deck job or decide to get a few miles of extra clearance from a dangerous island or headland. If the winds are predicted to decrease, he can prepare his light-weather sails, think about that repair aloft, or maybe cut a navigational corner a little closer.

If the weatherman concerns himself with his client's VPP figures and tries to keep the yacht on her speediest point of sailing consistent with making fast tracks toward the target, he becomes a *router*. He devises a general strategy to head for the target. He works out VPP tactics to keep the vessel clicking off the knots. Some of a router's directions are only idealized dreaming, but often they work and work very well. Percentage-wise, outside routing is always beneficial because it's something your opponent may not have. Big ships have been routed into easier and fairer weather and current patterns for years. The results? Oil tankers and merchant ships arrive earlier, save millions of dollars in fuel bills, and have less damage and breakage on board.

Or said another way, suppose you head for a distant port and take the weather as it comes. Suppose that the chances for favorable weather are one in two, or five chances out of ten. If you pay nominal attention to weather forecasts, your odds might increase to six in ten. If you pay particular attention and study other factors, your chances could jump to six-and-a-half or seven out of ten. With professional forecasting and routing, the odds could go to eight or eight-and-a-half out of ten. My figures are arbitrary, of course, and may be exaggerated, but the message is clear: Each increment of improved weather forecasting and routing advice brings a corresponding increase in speed.

Many of the yachts in the 1990–91 BOC Challenge race had routers or some arrangement to get outside weather information. A few competitors discussed weather and routing openly and passed along data to other captains. Other contestants filed their fingernails and pretended they had never heard of such things.

Nevertheless, just before the start, the telephone booths outside race headquarters were jammed. Competitors were seen scribbling down courses to sail and expected winds.

I made an arrangement with Bob Rice, a weather expert in Bedford, Massachusetts, to send me information. I planned to coordinate Bob's data with an excellent set of VPP figures provided for SEBAGO by Peter Schwenn of Design Systems in Annapolis. Since my radios were untested and it was the first time I had worked with Bob, I arranged to pay for the information on an "as received" basis. The day the race started Bob drove to Newport and personally handed me a forecast. We arranged a radio schedule. I hoped that all these unpracticed disciplines would work. I would find out.

The pages that follow are from my logbooks and tell of the small triumphs, the annoyances, the shattering disappointments, the trials, the pleasures, the delights—all the stuff of high drama on the narrow stage of a tiny ship far out at sea.

EDITOR'S NOTE: The author has provided an extensive glossary of sailing terms which can be found at the end of the book.

The start.

CHAPTER ONE

South to the Equator

SEPTEMBER 15, 1990. (SATURDAY). DAY 0.

<u>2200.</u>   Hooray, hooray! The great race started today at 1200, and SEBAGO and I are out in the Atlantic rushing along a little south of east. This morning at ten o'clock—two hours before the start—a low, dark line of heavy squalls passed over Newport. The sky was a sickly yellow, and the weather people were all yelping about disaster. The race director—whose face was gray and drawn and who looked as if he was about to have a heart attack—ran up and down the dock screaming at each captain: "You have to make your own decision whether to start or not. It's up to you! It's up to you!"

All the shouting was for naught, however, because the line squalls quickly passed to the east. By noon a SW wind began to fill in, and 24 yachts started as the cannon boomed at the beginning of a lovely afternoon.

The race began on an arm of Narragansett Bay called East Passage, which runs along the western shore of the city of Newport. Partway down the shore was the SE end of the starting line which was marked by a flag, the cannon, an official party, a tent full of champagne bottles, and thousands of spectators.

A few seconds after the cannon boomed, SEBAGO and I crossed the line. By chance I was at the SE end of the line and closest to Newport, so everyone on shore could see us. Philippe Jeantot in CRÉDIT AGRICOLE was immediately to my right; then Isabelle Autissier in ECUREUIL, and José Ugarte in BBV. I sailed close to shore and tacked, followed by Philippe, Isabelle, and José, as we danced our way toward the sea. Earlier in the morning, just before the towboat plucked us from the dock at Goat Island (at 1030), hundreds of people wished me good luck and showered me with small gifts. There were handshakes and bright smiles from every side. I must have autographed 100 books and SEBAGO posters. I seemed to have friends everywhere. I was very touched.

The starting area at Newport was well patrolled by the Coast Guard, and the spectator fleet stayed at a distance. It was nice to

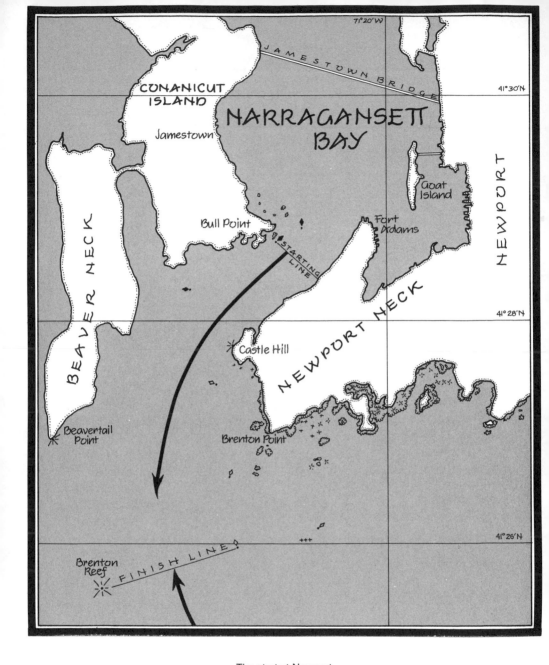

The start at Newport.

begin the race without fighting for room with the spectator boats as we did in 1986. Tacking these big boats close to the other competitors is hazardous enough.

Shortly after the start of the race, Philippe Jeantot and I got stuck in a light wind area for a few minutes before we managed to sail out of the Newport channel. I was surprised at the speed of Alain Gautier's vessel, which was slightly ahead and well heeled to starboard. Perhaps she had a favorable gust of wind. It was fun to see the other yachts under sail. Soon we'll be spread across the Atlantic and far from one another.

After I got clear of the land I filled the starboard water ballast tank, which increased our speed by half a knot and helped us sail more upright. A lot of people motored out with the fleet, and the sea was sloppy from powerboat wakes. Again and again people called across words of encouragement. All my helpers—Margaret, Ed Boden, Spence Langford, and Evelyn Jones—were on a launch which accompanied SEBAGO and me for half an hour. I felt desperately alone when they left.

Yesterday was a disaster because of work on the Standard C satellite radio. The radio company waited until 24 hours before the start of the race—after weeks of fiddling—before sending an expert. Even then the engineer, Jim Medlock, had a tough time. Some of the circuit boards had bad plug contacts which needed re-soldering. The work was spread all over the cabin, and three radio men ran in and out all day. I've never been able to get electronics people (or other specialists) to understand that they're only one part of a complex project. Each of these people thinks that he's Jesus Christ Superstar, and that everything else must stop while he does his act.

After the engineer and his helpers left, Ed Boden, Margaret, and I were up almost all night finishing the stowing and other jobs which were impossible to do while the radio people jammed up the cabin. (My hope of a good night's sleep vanished.) The engineer gave me complicated hand-written instructions for the laptop computer that runs the Standard C. I hope I can make it work, but I have no confidence at all. The radio installation should have been completed weeks ago so I could have made trial calls.

I'm extremely tired and need to sleep. What a day! What a week! The start of a major ocean race is certainly not for the faint of heart.

How nice it is to be at sea again. I've been taking deep breaths of lovely clear air and looking up at my old friends in the night sky—the Big Dipper, Scorpio in the south, Arcturus down from the arm of the Dipper, Cassiopeia, and all the other stars.

2229.   I had just stretched out for a nap when the wind shifted to the WSW. The autopilot tried to deal with this, but the sails got backed and stopped the vessel. Then the NNW wind (13 knots) returned. A fishing boat to port. We're crossing the Nantucket shoals. Lowest depth so far is 4.1 fathoms. I'm steering for the Pleiades, one of my favorite constellations.

Sebago's moment of glory as she leads some of the fleet at the start in Newport.

<u>2300.</u>   Wind down to 8 knots from almost dead astern (WNW). A number of fishing boats around. Lightning crackling in the sky to the east. We're rolling a lot in the ground swell.

SEPTEMBER 16, 1990. (SUNDAY). DAY 1.

<u>0108.</u>   When the night was really black outside my grandfather Ferdinand Knapp used to say "It's as dark as a shovel of coal at midnight." There's no moon tonight and except for two nearby fishing boats we're suspended in a black void. While rolling in the swell I heard the clatter of something falling on deck and rushed out to find pieces of plastic batten hardware at the foot of the mast. A very bad sign.

<u>0349.</u>   Eight fishing boats in sight. Wind almost nil. Autopilot acting up. The light wind is dead aft.

<u>0819.</u>   Two sonic booms from a Concorde airplane overhead. I have been up the mast examining the broken hardware at the front of each of the five full-length mainsail battens. The problem is that the forward thrust and side-to-side motion of the battens in a big swell in light winds put a bending strain on the thin plastic side plates. All ten have broken and allowed the battens to push forward. The adjustment screw (to vary the fore-and-aft tension on the long battens) at the front of each batten now bears against the

Isabelle Autissier on *Ecureuil-Poitou-Charentes* alongside *Sebago* at start of race.

mast. These screws are not only scratching the mast, but restrict the movement of the sail. In other words, the hardware that holds the front of the battens has disintegrated. The battens are effectively jammed against the mast. I cannot use the sail properly. What to do? (1) go back to Newport? (2) fabricate new side plates of metal? (3) put up the spare mainsail?

I certainly don't want to return to Newport. If I had some ¼" thick aluminum I could possibly make new side plates, but there's no material on board. I don't think plywood would do. I can put up the spare mainsail, but it's 100 sq. ft. smaller.

The batten hardware should all be made of metal, not flimsy, brittle plastic that reminds me of Crackerjack box prizes. Certainly no one has ever used this plastic hardware on a sail of this size (585 sq. ft.) or tried it at sea. How sailmakers can send people to sea with such junk is mind-boggling. Especially in such a highly publicized race. However I suppose it's my fault because I should have tried the sail in stronger conditions than the trifling winds around Newport. For the moment I will continue with the new mainsail and watch the battens closely.

We (SEBAGO and I) are on Georges Bank about 160 miles east of Newport. Very light winds from the north. Fishing boats, lots of seagulls, and an upset sea because of the shallowness. I just spent an hour tidying up the cockpit—putting away lines and repairing the fog horn. I'm a little disappointed at the food stores on board.

No milk and no fruit. What happened to all the oranges and grape-fruit? I need to sleep.

<u>0840.</u>   Two more loud bangs and the distant sound of an air-plane. The Concorde en route to Saudi Arabia? The autopilot stops working after running for only a few minutes. I can get it going again if I turn the power off and on. What can be wrong?

<u>0940.</u>   We're abeam of PATRIOTS, from New Bedford, a red and white steel trawler. Five men on deck. All waved and indicated they would rather sail than fish. We're on a course of 114°M at about one knot with the wind dead aft.

<u>1000.</u>   My strategy for Leg 1 of the race—which is roughly 7,000 miles—is to sail at the highest possible speed even if I sail additional miles. This leg is by far the most complex of the four because we go through seven wind zones. We begin in the wester-lies of the northern latitudes. Next come the northerly variables between the westerlies and the trade winds. Then the NE trades, the doldrums, the SE trades, the southerly variables, and finally the westerlies of the southern latitudes. We also come under the influence of the Azores high-pressure area and the South Atlantic high. And to cap it off we're starting on a bad month for hurri-canes in the North Atlantic.

Ocean Passages for the World recommends a long initial slog to the east so a vessel will have plenty of clearance after she turns south and gets near the hump of Brazil (where both the wind and current are contrary). However Bertie Reed (on GRINAKER) and I discussed this at length before the start and decided to head straight for the shoulder of Brazil because our yachts sail so well to windward. We can save a little distance, but we must be careful to maintain enough easting. Once around the hump of Brazil and past Recife, I'll head south for the island of Trindade*(20°30'S., 29°20'W.) which is 620 miles east of the coast of Brazil. Then south until the westerlies and east to Cape Town.

To recap, the general course from Newport to the Equator is SE. Then south to 34–35°S. to pass below the South Atlantic high-pressure area. Finally a left turn and onward to the tip of Africa. Since most of the sailing course is S or SE, any winds from the SE or E are headwinds. And the faster the yacht, the more the appar-ent wind pulls ahead.

People who write about the BOC Challenge race as a simple off-the-wind lark that's full of beam reaching and spinnaker runs

---

* Not to be confused with Trinidad in the Caribbean.

CONTESTANTS (25) AT THE START OF THE 1990–91 BOC CHALLENGE ROUND-THE-WORLD SINGLEHANDED RACE

CAPTAIN	COUNTRY	SHIP NAME	BEAM	DISPL.
CLASS 1 (thirteen 60-footers)				
David Adams	Australia	*Innkeeper*	14'7"	24,250
Christophe Auguin	France	*Groupe Sceta*	19'0"	25,000
Isabelle Autissier	France	*Ecureuil-Poitou-Charentes*	11'3"	20,500
John Biddlecombe	Australia	*Interox Crusader*	12'3"	26,000
Kanga Birtles	Australia	*Jarkan*	15'6"	25,760
Nandor Fa	Hungary	*Alba Regia*	16'0"	20,943
Alain Gautier	France	*Generali Concorde*	19'0"	26,000
Philippe Jeantot	France	*Crédit Agricole IV*	18'3"	25,353
John Martin	South Africa	*Allied Bank*	19'7"	23,529
Enda O'Coineen	Ireland	*Kilcullen*	14'7"	18,500
Mike Plant	U.S.A.	*Duracell*	15'0"	27,500
Bertie Reed	South Africa	*Grinaker*	15'0"	27,000
José Ugarte	Spain	*BBV Expo '92*	15'4"	26,455
CLASS 2 (six 50-footers; one 42-footer)				
Jack Boye	U.S.A.	*Project City Kids*	11'4"	18,500
Yves Dupasquier	France	*Servant IV*	13'1"	12,125
Josh Hall	Great Britain	*Spirit of Ipswich*	13'9"	24,000
Don McIntyre	Australia	*Sponsor Wanted*	12'0"	17,500
Hal Roth	U.S.A.	*Sebago*	12'0"	19,000
Yukoh Tada	Japan	*Koden VIII*	13'7"	11,023
Jane Weber	Canada	*Tilley Endurable*	13'2"	22,000
CORINTHIAN CLASS (five entries)				
Robin Davie	Great Britain	*Global Exposure* (40')	11'8"	17,920
Bill Gilmore	U.S.A.	*Zafu* (44'5")	13'7"	20,600
Robert Hooke	U.S.A.	*Niihau IV* (44'3")	14'1"	20,000
Minoru Saito	Japan	*Shuten-dohji II* (50')	12'0"	19,000
Paul Thackaberry	U.S.A.	*Volcano* (49'11")	11'6"	16,000

simply don't know what they're talking about. Measured at the Equator, Cape Town is 5,400 miles *east* of Newport. Since a majority of the winds have easterly components, this means bashing to windward or close to it most of the time.

SEPTEMBER 17, 1990. (MONDAY). DAY 2.

<u>0246.</u>   The wind (and weather front) finally arrived at 0130. The night looked thick and nasty. I put one reef in the big mainsail and unrolled 90% of the jib. I had trouble getting water in the port water ballast tank and had to prime the electric pump. Now we're hard on the wind and going at 8.5 knots. The water ballast makes an enormous difference in sailing. I'm very sleepy.

<u>0358.</u>   We're pounding along at 8.5 knots with the single-reefed mainsail and most of the jib. Wind 19 knots apparent at 31°. We need another reef.

<u>0930.</u>   A long hard night, but we've been sailing well. Squalls and gusty weather. The autopilot drive unit broke away from its mount. I steered for an hour until I got the wind vane gear hooked up. The next project is to get past the Gulf Stream. For a time last night we were slogging along at 6 knots with just the single-reefed mainsail.

     The food stores are a mess. Can't find anything. What could have happened to the box of oranges and the box of grapefruit that I saw in the cockpit before I left Newport? Also I am trying to find the clock and a stapler. Where do things get to? I am reading *The Blond Knight of Germany*, a biography of Erich Hartmann (by Toliver and Constable). About Germany's great fighter pilot. A laudatory account but entertaining.

<u>1826.</u>   A struggle to change the autopilot drive, which has a broken wire caused when the unit dropped after the main mounting bolt worked loose. Lots of wind this afternoon, and we have been making good time. Mostly with the partial genoa and single-reefed mainsail. I spoke with Don McIntyre on SPONSOR WANTED—whose position was 37°56'N., 65°58'W. I finished the last of the stew that Dorothy Carey cooked for me. Big seas outside. A NE gale across the Gulf Stream certainly makes a mess of the ocean.

<u>2238.</u>   Wind NE at 27 knots. A good nap and more to eat. I still need a few days to collect my wits. I continue to be amazed when I think of all the kindness and good wishes on the dock in Newport.

     I can't imagine where the citrus fruit is hidden although various things are beginning to turn up. I'm finding cheese everywhere. Certainly there's enough on board for a kingdom of mice.

SEPTEMBER 18, 1990. (TUESDAY). DAY 3.

<u>0337.</u>   Wind down, but we're surrounded by squalls and heavy rain.

<u>0615.</u>   When the wind is on the beam, the luff of the mainsail trembles and vibrates. A terrible noise caused by too much spacing between the luff slides.

I can't seem to get everything together, and I'm a bit disheartened by the long voyage ahead. I've never had this feeling before. I think my general malaise is due to lack of energy. I am going to make a big breakfast.

<u>1636.</u>   Drama on the foredeck. I put up a new asymmetrical spinnaker, but after the sail was flying, the wind increased to 20 knots. We were clearly overloaded. When I went to pull down the sock to douse the sail, the sock line got wrapped around the eased sheet. In an instant both lines were locked together with a dozen twists and snarls. The sail itself whipped around the midstay several times while the sock whirled around the headstay and jammed. It took an hour to get the sail down. I cut both the sheet and tack lines, and finally had to disconnect the midstay at the base so I could slide the wire stay out of the tangled mess. I think the sail is OK, but I had to uncouple the furling sock from the sail. What a relief to slide the spinnaker down the front hatch and see it safely disappear.

This morning I discovered that I had entered an equatorial waypoint of 8°N. into my GPS receiver for my turn southward to Trindade. I should have entered 8°S. No wonder I have not been getting south!

<u>2103.</u>   I woke from a nap because the yacht was rolling heavily on a windless sea. I looked outside and saw a big squall coming. I had the genoa poled out to port so I started to roll it up. However as the first step I should have dropped the outboard end of the spinnaker pole because with the clew of the sail held high, the sail doesn't roll up evenly. The sail began to flog a little, a noise that sailors hate because it means possible damage.

By now, however, I had another more urgent problem. We were up to 10 knots, the wind was increasing, and I needed to get the mainsail down. I rushed forward and let the halyard go. The wind jammed the long battens against the mast, spreaders, and lee shrouds, and it was hard to claw down the stiff 10-oz. Dacron cloth. As soon as I got one tie around the lowered mainsail I hurried forward to the genoa. The sheets were fouled with one another; pulling and tugging were pointless. Back in the cockpit I cranked the furling winch, but it didn't help. I rushed forward again and stood on the pulpit to try to reach the fouled area of the sail, but I could do nothing except untangle the sheets a little. The wind grew stronger, and the noise and vibration from the flogging sail were increasing. What to do? Throwing off the halyard was no good because most of the sail was tightly furled. The upper leech of my beautiful new genoa was being ruined. I could have reached up and cut the sheets away, but then how could I have controlled the sail?

The night was black. As usual I had a flashlight jammed in my mouth so I could see. Again I stood on top of the pulpit and tried to do something while the sail flogged above me. I jumped down and rushed back to the cockpit and tried the furling winch again. This time I cranked harder and managed to roll up more of the sail. There was less flogging, and now the clew was loose. Could I untie the sheets and free them? It was risky. I untied one, unwound it from the sail and re-tied it. Then the second! A minute later we were sailing nicely under the partially unwound genoa! Wonderful!

The yacht is an absolute shambles, but tidying up comes second. We must keep going toward the target! In the morning I will examine the main, slides, and battens. What a voyage so far! Poor navigation, a bad spinnaker wrap, fouled furling gear, mainsail problems, and two autopilot changes. What we really need is a new captain.

SEPTEMBER 19, 1990. (WEDNESDAY). DAY 4.

<u>0701.</u>   A good sleep , but we have been rolling heavily with the mainsail down. In the daylight I discover that not only has the batten hardware shattered into dozens of pieces, but the battens have broken as well. All five of them. In many places. The battens are as flimsy as the hardware. It seems so futile, so pathetic, and so frustrating to make an efficient, well-designed, high-performance product and then to ruin all the good work by using bad fittings. What's so galling is that I gave North Sails positive, explicit instructions ("Write this down.") to use French battens and hardware, and the loft manager agreed. ("I've got it.")

I must hoist a mainsail to ease the rolling, although we're hurrying along before a NW wind with just a jib up. The yacht is a shambles with piles of gear everywhere. The new lee cloths for the pilot berths need to be shortened and remounted. The galley needs an hour of work. However the first job is the mainsail. Can I repair the larger fully battened sail or must I change to the spare?

<u>1241.</u>   A victory of sorts. I put up the spare mainsail. It's 100 sq. ft. smaller, and already has 10,000 miles of use, but at least it's up and drawing. It seems a shame to use a less efficient sail in a race, but there was little choice. I still have to fasten two slide guards alongside the mainsail track above the gooseneck so the slides can't escape from the mast track, but I can do that later.

The broken ends of fiberglass battens on the new mainsail were splintered, jagged, and thoroughly lethal. Dangerous weapons! I realize now that the sides of the batten fixtures at the luff were bearing heavily on the mast whenever the sail was eased to starboard.

I have spare battens for the new mainsail on board and in time could fit them. The only way to extract the broken battens, however, would be to cut open the batten pockets, carefully remove the broken pieces (with gloves and pliers), and then re-sew the pockets. However the new battens would only break in turn because they're so weak. And I have no luff end hardware for the battens.

It's tricky for one person to deal with a fully battened sail at sea because it's impossible to slide the foot of the sail from the

Sebago heading eastward at 8 knots on Day 1.

boom without removing the battens. Since I couldn't remove the battens without a great deal of work, the only thing I could do was to lower the sail, bundle it up parallel to the main boom with many ties, and then go along the boom and cut away the boom slide lashings. I then dropped the luff slides from the mast, removed the three reefing lines, and unshackled the tack and clew fittings. The next step was to maneuver the bundled sail to the port side of the coachroof and to lash it down. So far the job had taken two hours.

The spare mainsail was below in the forward cabin. I hoisted it on deck with a halyard, wrestled the sail along the deck, and maneuvered it into position. Then I fed the boom slides along the main boom, and put in the four short battens. I then sewed shut the ends of the batten pockets, reeved the reefing lines, fed the luff slides into the mast track, tied the main halyard to the head, and hoisted the sail.

The old sail is performing OK, but is four feet short on the hoist and the leech seems straight and lacking in area. My secret weapon is gone! I am not feeling very kindly toward the sailmaker.

1911.   Wind very light. A change to the south is predicted. I spoke with Spence Langford and Herb Hilgenberg on the SSB (barely working) this evening. The yacht is still a mess, but there may be hope.

2015.   News from the fleet (via the SSB receiver): The three high-tech French yachts with carbon fiber masts (GENERALI CONCORDE, GROUP SCETA, and CRÉDIT AGRICOLE) are leading Class 1. SERVANT IV (Yves Dupasquier) is leading Class 2. VOLCANO (Paul Thackaberry) lost one of his twin rudders on a lobster pot warp at the start of the race. Paul returned to Newport for repairs and began again a day later. The Irish yacht KILCULLEN (Enda O'Coineen) is to start today after many problems.

2143.   The wind shifted exactly as Herb Hilgenberg predicted. It's amazing how these weather people can call shifts.

SEPTEMBER 20, 1990. (THURSDAY). DAY 5.

0617.   An easy night with no wind and a long sleep. The sky was clear in the middle of the night, and the stars were lovely. Auriga was just above us, and I could see Capella and the nearby yellowish star of Aldebaran. I have been force-feeding myself plenty to bring up my energy level after all the recent sail wrestling. I whipped the ends of half a dozen lines, partially picked up the cabin, and tucked away the mass of lines on the cockpit floor. I need to figure out the length of the spinnaker sheets, and to reeve a new line on the starboard side.

<u>1355.</u>   At noon our position was 35°19′N., 59°27′W. or about 780 miles east of Cape Hatteras off the coast of North Carolina. The wind has been 3–7 knots from the south all day. I have been trying to keep going to the ESE. Only 79 miles in the last 24 hours. Terrible.

I was debating whether to change to the 165% genoa when a little more wind came up. I pumped up the windward water ballast tank, and the speed increased one knot. Wonderful.

<u>2109.</u>   Tried tacking south but no good. Wind almost nil. Back to the starboard tack. Very dark. Sleepy. Talked to four or five of the competitors tonight.

<u>2400.</u>   I have put up the 165% headsail and we're gliding along slowly. The ocean is quite calm. Bright stars again, but a little foggy in spots. Fog isn't the right word. Misty?

SEPTEMBER 21, 1990. (FRIDAY). DAY 6.

<u>0742.</u>   A poky night. A trace of wind from the south. I have put up an asymmetrical spinnaker, but there's scarcely enough wind to keep the sail full. How are the others doing?

So far I have seen 3 pairs of white-tailed tropicbirds. Dainty, unmistakable all-white birds with black markings around the eyes and on the wings. Very rapid wing beats, yellow-orange bills, piercing calls, and long streaming tail feathers. Wingspan 3 feet or a little less.

No ships since Newport and no sightings of other BOC vessels, although several are nearby. I am still on the hunt for the fruit. This morning I discovered a head of lettuce in a plastic bag underneath two loaves of bread.

Today I will try the Standard C radio again. This involves switching on the big set, the thermal printer, and the laptop computer. Then typing 20 commands to see if I can get through to Bob Rice in Bedford, Massachusetts. I am trying to receive weather information (for which I pay a daily fee if I get the report). Actually I'm not so concerned about calling Bob, but for him to contact me with weather forecasts and suggested waypoints. It's easy for me to send messages to the Atlantic ground station in England, but I can't seem to get beyond England. The ground station sends me routine service messages, but nothing comes from Bob. Before the race I implored the radio people to sort this out, but I was told to be quiet (the dumb captain) while they (the experts) fixed things.

All the leading boats are receiving daily weather routing from shore stations (carefully plotted to make the most of each yacht's sailing characteristics), which means they have big tactical advantages. In addition to Bob Rice, I was offered weather routing from Bermuda, but I am unable to contact Herb Hilgenberg on the SSB radio. My batteries are up and I call right on schedule, but hear nothing. Isn't the technical world wonderful?

I need to solder a wire on the autopilot drive unit that I pulled out the other day so I can use it as a spare. Also I must check over the spinnaker that got wrapped and install the furling sock over the sail. However these are all secondary jobs. My main business is to keep the yacht going as fast as I can in these poor conditions.

1017.   The sky is almost clear of clouds. The sea is a deep turquoise punctuated with clumps of bright yellow gulfweed (or sargasso) that look like stars in the sea. Earlier this morning I happened to glance in the mirror in the head and scared myself when I saw a strange tanned and unshaven face peering back. To shake all this I took a sponge bath, put on clean clothes, shaved off my whiskers, and combed my hair. I feel much better.

Robin Davie on GLOBAL EXPOSURE and Don McIntyre aboard SPONSOR WANTED are within VHF range—20 to 30 miles—and we exchanged a few pleasantries. Much grumbling about the weather from Don who wears me out with all his talk. At times the best thing about the radio is to be able to switch it off so I can have some peace and quiet.

1228.   Down spinnaker. Then I unrolled the 800 sq. ft. genoa. Next I eased the genoa halyard and dropped the sail on deck. Then I folded the sail (one hour on the sweltering deck). Finally I hoisted the 915 sq. ft. light genoa. An amazing sail. We're going 2.5 knots on a course of 150°M. in 1.5 knots of true wind from the SW.

Good news! The missing fruit has turned up in the bottom lockers in the forward cabin, a place I never thought to look.

1947.   More straightening up in the cabin. I heaved some old broken engine parts and pieces of angle iron over the side. I can't imagine how such junk got left on board.

I have been sitting outside in the cool of the night while the big 165% genoa pulls us along magically. What a great sail in light airs on a quiet sea. What is so ironical is that now I am using two 1986 sails on the 1990 mast. The extra height of the new mast is a complete waste because the old sails are shorter—$12,000 for nothing!

I have finally stopped seeing Margaret around every corner and am getting settled. I miss her cheerful presence, but I am enjoying the sailing. Just think, we have been married for 30 years and have been sailing together for 28 years (except for the last BOC race). She's my best friend, and I love her a lot.

I will like it much more if I can get some wind so that I can chase the leaders. Those ahead are speeding away while I slat in calms. At noon today I showed only 75 miles in the last 24 hours.

<u>2024.</u>   While changing sails on the foredeck I had 12–15 dolphins around the bow. Each was 6–8 feet long, and gray with a white belly. They were in groups of two or three and lay on the surface or just below and came up to breathe every minute or so. A strong fishy smell. From time to time I could hear them talking to one another in their high-pitched squeaky language. Some of their dorsal fins seemed damaged—from nets? It was grand watching such good swimmers at close range. Although I've seen lots of dolphins I've never had a group around me in a calm before.

SEPTEMBER 22, 1990. (SATURDAY). DAY 7.

<u>0612.</u>   We're surrounded by cumulonimbus—enormous, towering, cylindrical clouds shaded with delicate blues and grays. There's more swell, and we're rolling a lot which makes writing hard. The wind comes and goes. I suppose we're in the transition area north of the trade wind zone. The best hours are at dawn, before the sun floods the world with heat and glare.

I must make another effort with the satellite radio. Also I need to try the weatherfax receiver this morning. Each of the function keys has two operations, and trying to work out the instructions (in poor Japanese English) is like breaking a code.

Yesterday I got the twisted spinnaker sorted out and back into its furling sock. I'm worried that the lightweight genoa will get torn or rub itself to death on the spreaders in the calms.

I fret about those ahead, and that I am getting behind. My only hope is to exploit SEBAGO's best points of sailing. Now is the time I could use the big mainsail.

<u>1541.</u>   Genoa down this morning for small repairs when the wind rose to 17 knots as a small weather front passed.

I went to reef the main, and discovered that the sail wouldn't come down. I tried everything. I finally climbed to the top of the mast—the steps are certainly handy—and found that a new Kevlar slide at the bottom of the headboard formed a jamming couple with the stainless steel slide above. The two slides would go up but not down. I cut the slide lashing of the lower slide and knocked it loose with a screwdriver. There should never be two different kinds of slides on a headboard.

Very sleepy. A south wind at 16 knots and a couple of good hours at 8.5 knots. What a difference the water ballast makes in our performance!

SEPTEMBER 23, 1990. (SUNDAY). DAY 8.

<u>0022.</u>   I forgot to write that when I was up the mast yesterday, a merchant vessel came close and did a half circle around us. I don't think the ship saw the yacht and was merely altering course. Perhaps the crew watches were being changed. I was glad to see the ship go. No dramatic rescues please.

News from the fleet: KILCULLEN (Enda O'Coineen) lost her mast in a collision with a fishing boat and is out of the race. The mast broke in three places, and KILCULLEN's bow was badly damaged. Poor Enda, who was so excited about the race, had terrible weather problems when he crossed the Atlantic before the start. Then to lose the mast on the first day of the race was ill fortune indeed.

ZAFU (Bill Gilmore) also dropped out. "The race ceased to be fun," he said from Morehead City, North Carolina. I was a little surprised at Bill because a good many sailors would have done anything to have competed. Bill made the decision to go, paid his entry fee, spent months preparing his yacht, and completed a 2,000-mile qualifying voyage. He passed the troublesome scrutineering, and actually started the race.

Once the competition was underway, the entrants that I spoke to talked of relief and pleasure and excitement ("It's the payoff for all the work."). How different were the stories of Enda (who was so keen and thrilled by it all), and Bill Gilmore (who seemed weary and blasé).

The official race program lists 28 sailors. Three did not start, and two have now dropped out which leaves 23 still in the race— 21 men and 2 women. The characters and personal identities of the competitors are beginning to emerge. Each is so different.

GRINAKER (Bertie Reed) hit a whale this morning. Bertie—a chain smoker and often found with a bottle of beer in his hand—is

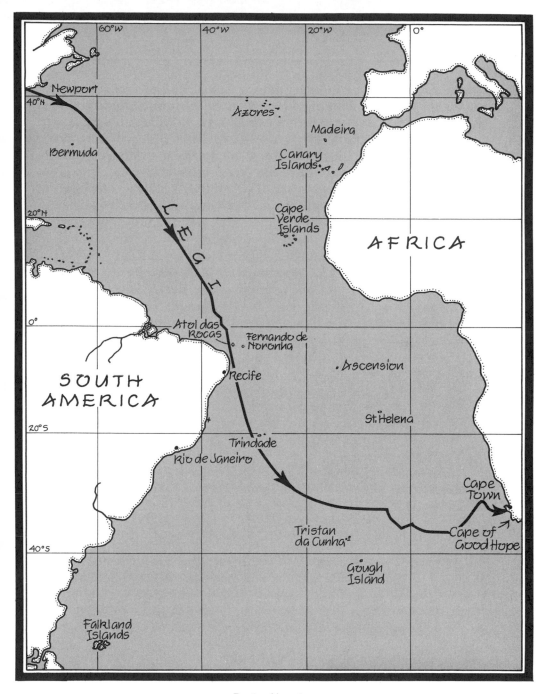

Route of Leg 1.

genial, upbeat, and friendly. He likes to talk and is always helpful with advice. Nandor Fa, aboard ALBA REGIA, reported a broken main boom fitting. Nandor, who speaks in a rather frail and breathy voice, is the only Hungarian sailor I have ever met. It seems a miracle that he was able to design, build, and find the money for his sleek-looking 60-footer in a Communist-bloc country. He is determined and wildly eager to win, although his rig and sails show many signs of cost-cutting. John Biddlecombe on INTEROX CRUSADER has autopilot problems. John seems very laid back and doesn't appear to have the drive of the others.

John Martin's million-dollar ALLIED BANK is an awesome sailing machine, and John is one the leaders. Since the last race he has let his hair grow long, has put on a lot of weight, and now wears wild clothes. Both he and Bertie Reed are from South Africa where they're big names. I've never heard anything said, but I think they're both keen to outdo one another. Jack Boye on CITY KIDS has been sailing well and moving up in the fleet. Jack, a retired stockbroker from Wall Street, is always pleasant and courteous, but keeps to himself. A true singlehander, I guess.

The two women sailors are in a class by themselves. Isabelle Autissier on ECUREUIL appears to be an excellent sailor and is quite at ease in her skinny 60-footer. She is a bit overwhelmed by all the publicity. The Canadian, Jane Weber, aboard TILLEY ENDURABLE, seems much less a sailor and organizer than Isabelle. Jane's yacht was scarcely ready, she is already far behind, and from listening to her complaints on the radio I don't think she will get far. I hope I'm wrong.

Anyway, there we are. All 23 of us. Each a different character in this novel of high adventure. Different, except that we all want to win the race.

<u>0600.</u>   A night of squalls, rain, wind shifts, tacking, and winch cranking.

<u>1100.</u>   I just cooked a spectacular breakfast of tea, toast, and a three-egg western omelet filled with a diced onion, a sliced potato, some chopped green pepper, and bits of chunk turkey. Margaret would be proud of me. Now I'm drinking coffee.

<u>1207.</u>   I despair of ever getting south.

<u>1345.</u>   Jesus, sailing is hard work. South wind 14 knots. Course 125°M. Furl genoa. Out jib. Change sheet lead block. Adjust leech cord (twice). Reef mainsail. Fill windward ballast tank. Adjust mainsheet and traveler. Now she's going nicely, but it took 90 minutes of string pulling. While I was at it I reeved the second reefing pendant. I climbed the leech by pulling myself up the third reefing pendant. Not bad for an old man. Careful, don't get too cocky!

<u>1554.</u>　　Message on the radio from Fred Cook at Schaefer: "Check the tightness of the four Allen screws at the bottom of the jib furling gear."

<u>2111.</u>　　Wind SSW 8–10 knots. I shook out the reef in the mainsail, unrolled the big genoa, and eased off 10°. Now we're doing a steady 8 knots (8.44 just now) only 13° off course. The main thing is to keep her going toward the target.

SEPTEMBER 24, 1990. (MONDAY). DAY 9.

<u>0104.</u>　　I sent another message to Bob Rice via the Standard C radio and asked for a weather forecast. The heat is increasing as we sail south.

<u>0450.</u>　　A ship bound SE. A big squall so I furled the genoa. Before I set the sail again I put more turns of the furling line on the drum.

<u>1113.</u>　　I don't understand how the true wind (17 knots) can remain in the SSE so persistently. I am trying to steer a magnetic course of 164°, and the wind is varying between 135° and 180°. In other words, right on the nose, which means tacking back and forth as the wind shifts. It's been squally all night together with rain, inky darkness, no moon, and damp heat. (The remnants of the bread are growing rainbows of mold.)

At one time I woke to find us heeled 35° and racing eastward. I couldn't get the yacht to bear off until I furled the jib. At the moment we have one reef in the main and most of the jib set. We're on the port tack and heading a little west of south. Earlier the seas were quite lumpy, but are smoother now.

My hands are swollen and sore from all the line handling during the past nine days.

Again nothing has come over the Standard C radio. I can only conclude that my messages to and from the U.S. are blocked at a technical level beyond my control.

A problem on east-west voyages is that I pass through a time zone (15° of longitude) every few days and am forever changing the ship's clock. Some sailors operate on GMT all the time. I am thinking of doing this, but will I have trouble getting used to dawn coming at noon?

<u>1805.</u>　　The SSB radio is not working properly, and to contact a shore station takes an hour or more. I am told that my signal is very weak. I finally got through to Bob Rice for weather informa-

tion, but he was not expecting my call. He asked me to phone later. Apparently he has not received any of my Standard C communications. It's all very discouraging.

About an hour ago I started the generator to charge the batteries. Suddenly there was a lot of banging, so I shut off the little diesel and found the mounting bracket for the big alternator broken (bad welding). I will have to repair the bracket somehow. This means no power for the Standard C radio. Is someone trying to tell me something?

2030.   I'm looking at a trade wind sky—little puffs of perfectly spaced cotton floating high overhead. However we should have E or NE winds, not SSE.

2200.   A Polish ship came close and gave us a friendly toot.

SEPTEMBER 25, 1990. (TUESDAY). DAY 10.

1026.   A hot bangety-bang night which seemed to go on forever. In the middle of the black night the wind rose a little, and the pounding got to me. I rolled up the jib, reefed the mainsail, changed the water ballast (which transfers quickly), and tacked. Then I unrolled less of the jib. I reckon we are on the fringe of the Azores high which is north and east of us. Much of the fleet is hundreds of miles ahead. There's nothing I can do except to try to get south. I am eating very lightly with all the heat and pounding.

I finished the biography of Erich Hartmann, the WW2 German flying ace. An extraordinary pilot who shot down 352 Allied planes before he was captured by the Russians and held prisoner until 1948. I wish the American biographers had praised their subject less and told more about Hartmann's motivations and feelings.

What can I use for a metal strap to repair the alternator bracket?

1304.   Too rough to cook or boil water. Lunch of smoked sturgeon (a gift from the Zapf family) and bread carefully sliced clean of gray, yellow, and blue mold. Surprisingly a head of lettuce is still in good condition. I am hunting for mayonnaise.

1801.   We were right on course and hurrying SSE until we met a line of heavy squalls. At first I thought we had hit the NE trades. I found an easterly wind and tacked (change water ballast, runners, and sheets). But the wind has been changing from SW through to S to E. Still lots of dark squalls around. Jib rolled up because of high winds. Had a nice shower, put on clean clothes, and cooked a hot meal. Come on steady easterly winds! Where are you?

<u>2101.</u>   More rain and squalls. Wind south 24 knots. Gray skies. Lumpy seas.

SEPTEMBER 26, 1990. (WEDNESDAY). DAY 11.

<u>0516.</u>   The screw on the latch of one of the settee drawers came out and dumped the cameras and various goodies all over the place. I put in a longer screw. I must check all these fastenings when I get to port. Why do carpenters use such dinky little screws?

It's dark and hot as we crash along. Will we ever get away from these S and SE winds? Where are the trades? Do the trade winds exist?

<u>1054.</u>   Crashing and banging across the sea at 8 knots with the yacht heeled to 30° and the stowed leeward spinnaker pole making ominous noises. No doubt adrift. I thought of heaving to under the main and backed jib, but when I tried it we heeled ominously to leeward because of the full ballast tank. I then rolled up the jib and gybed the vessel around. With just the reefed main we made 4 knots or so. I lashed the spinnaker pole carefully, put a stanchion pipe back in its socket, and hoisted the little storm jib. Now we're making 6.5 knots on 180°M. The wind is ESE at 16–22 knots, but the weather is very squally. I got soaked and cold putting up the little jib. How dumb not to put on oilskins!

Hauled out in Portsmouth, Rhode Island for new Awlgrip bottom paint before the start of the race. Margaret and Ed Boden in charge.

If I'm careful I can run the autopilot, SSB radio, GPS receiver, and interior lights with the output from the four solar panels. At the moment, the batteries are down about 50 percent because of all the Standard C radio trials.

<u>1202.</u>   To save electricity I want to shut off the autopilot and use the wind vane steering device. However the two bevel gears in the mechanical linkage of the wind vane often slip past one another, which allows the pendulum movement to swing to one side instead of staying in the middle.

<u>1502.</u>   I'm still trying to use the wind vane, but I need to deal with the mis-aligned bevel gears. The solution involves leaning over the transom with two wrenches, loosening two nuts, and adjusting a vertical rod. Since hanging over the back of the yacht is risky, I put on my safety harness and clip myself to the back-stay. However there's a big load on the water blade at 8 knots, water is flying all over the place (the wind is ESE at 18 knots), and it's hard to adjust anything.*

The ride is bumpy today, and it was a real achievement to heat something for lunch.

<u>1631.</u>   A northbound merchant ship to port. I am beginning to worry about my easting and getting past the hump of Brazil.

SEPTEMBER 27, 1990. (THURSDAY). DAY 12.

<u>0056.</u>   I've been hearing a lot of creaking from the mast shrouds. When I went out for a look I found the after lower shrouds were quite slack, not a good sign.

<u>0614.</u>   Until the middle of the night, I thought we would have a 200-mile day for sure. All day we scooted along at 8, 8.5, and 9 knots. Then a few hours ago, when I shortened sail for a squall, I noticed that the after lower shrouds were *very* slack. What's happened? Has the mast step collapsed? Have the mast fittings started to creep down the mast? Have the wires begun to pull apart?

The last squall has gone on for an hour, although the wind is finally easing off. We're near a tropical depression that is supposed to be moving toward the NW. Also I have been troubled by a stiff neck. Altogether it's not been a good night. Will daylight ever come?

---

*After the race, Hans Bernwall, the manufacturer of the Monitor wind vane steering gear, made a design change that corrected this problem.

<u>1353.</u>   A busy morning. As I feared, something is wrong with the rig. As soon as it got light, I saw a big bend to starboard in the mast. The Navtec U-bolt that connected the port after lower shroud to the deck sheared on one side of the U. The rest of the U-bolt bent and was still attached to the turnbuckle and holding the wire shroud, but only barely. I immediately rigged a tackle between the rail and the shroud and ran the hauling part to a winch, which straightened the mast a little.

Fortunately I had a spare U-bolt on board. I was so anxious to get to work that I foolishly neglected to put on a jacket and got soaked (and chilled) by a wave. First I removed the remnants of the old U-bolt. Then I caulked the two 7/16″ dia. holes, installed the new U-bolt, and put on the washers and nuts underneath in the cabin. After I tightened the nuts I couldn't see any caulking oozing out so I removed everything and added more caulking before tightening the nuts again. There's a little water around the area inside, but if there's a leak it's not serious. The job took two hours.

<u>1402.</u>   It took a while to wash the salt water from the tools and to oil them and then to eat. I must start work on the broken alternator bracket. I put a second reef in the mainsail, which was hard work because I got the lead of the reefing pendant wrong when I bent on the sail. Now we're sailing better and have less heel. It's amazing how this vessel goes faster with less sail. I am falling asleep.

<u>2108.</u>   I spent the afternoon making a bracket for the engine alternator from a scrap of angle iron. Cutting, filing, drilling, and bolting. Not a perfect job, but I got the alternator mounted and the charging plant working. The Makita battery-powered angle drill is simply a miracle tool for sailors. I will have the bracket welded when I get to Cape Town.

SEPTEMBER 28, 1990. (FRIDAY). DAY 13.

<u>1232.</u>   We crash along day after day. The wind (SE 16 knots) is still from ahead, and we're leaning to starboard. Today my big project was to shave. Also to try to rest my sore hands. I wish SEBAGO and I were 150 miles farther east. I suppose we will cope somehow.

I think the Brookes & Gatehouse speed indicator may be over-reading. I slept a lot last night, but am sleepy again. With all

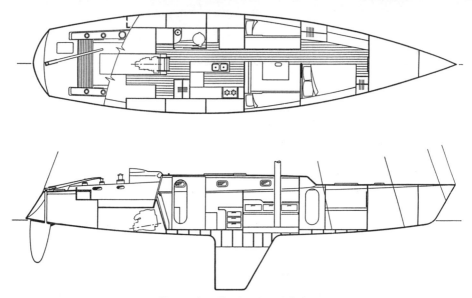

Plan and profile drawing of *Sebago*.

the sun on the solar panels I don't have to worry about electricity. The radio reported that oil prices have doubled and that Japanese stocks have plummeted. The business world seems far away.

Today in Class 1 the leader is GENERALI CONCORDE, with CRÉDIT AGRICOLE 77 miles behind. In Class 2, CITY KIDS is in first place, 39 miles ahead of SERVANT IV. The Corinthian class is led by GLOBAL EXPOSURE. VOLCANO is 214 miles behind.

2137.   Less wind. Hurricane Josephine has upset the trade wind pattern. Three kinds of clouds are around us. I will be glad to get south of all the tropical disturbances. Can you imagine starting a race in the middle of the hurricane season?

How nice it is to stand in the cockpit in light weather (SE 9 knots) with the yacht sailing well. For once no spray is flying over the cockpit. The clouds, an occasional tropicbird, easy swells from the east, the sails pulling nicely—all these things add up to heaven.

2145.   John Biddlecombe (INTEROX CRUSADER) lost his autopilots and plans to stop in Recife for replacements. Jack Boye (CITY KIDS) is sailing on the edge of hurricane Josephine. Jack is also troubled with leaks.

Everyone reports fickle winds farther south. All, I note, are making spectacular times despite their grumbling. Yesterday I logged 196 miles, and made good 179 miles.

SEPTEMBER 29, 1990. (SATURDAY). DAY 14.

1129.   Two weeks today. What a marathon! I am sailing faster than in the earlier race, but the others have improved even more.

Can you imagine that one of the Frenchmen on a 60-footer is 1,000 miles ahead of me?

1145.   In such a long race, the project breaks down into a series of problems (or battles or chess games). The problem of the rigging, the problem of the sails, the problem of what course to keep, the problem of how hard to drive the yacht, the problem of steering, the problem of electricity, the problem of storms, the problem of calms, the problem of the autopilots, and so on. It's fix, fix, fix and decide this and decide that all day long! Such a list immediately suggests that the simplest vessel is the most reliable.

Is an 18,000-pound 60-foot cat ketch with 3 identical masts and 3 identical self-tacking sails the answer? Lightweight freestanding carbon fiber masts and an end to the dozens of lines that complicate my life? In light winds you would fly all three sails. When it breezed up you could drop the middle sail. When it got really nasty you could hoist the middle sail and drop the front and back sails. The flip side is a simple rig x 3 = a complicated rig. A light mast x 3 = a heavy rig. There are no easy answers.

1210.   A run of 164 miles today. So far I have come 1,795 miles. This morning I realized that I was getting hungrier and hungrier because most of the galley drawers and bins have swollen shut in the warm moisture of the tropics. There is plenty of food on board. I simply couldn't get to it. I finally got out my woodworking tools and began to break into long-closed storage places and found all sorts of goodies. While I'm writing this I am eating from a tin of smoked fish. Delicious!

1248.   Wind ESE 7 knots. Full genoa. Squalls all around us.

1300.   I cleaned the galley this morning. This included spooning two pounds of melted butter from the bottom of the ice box into a plastic jar. What a greasy mess. I am falling asleep.

1827.   CITY KIDS continues to lead in my class and is 464 miles ahead of me. SEBAGO has been sailing well all day in 7–8 knots of ESE wind and flat seas. The big 165% genoa is perfectly suited to these conditions.

Many chores today. I soldered the broken wire inside the autopilot drive assembly, adjusted the B&G speedometer with the GPS readings, straightened out the chart table stowage, and sorted various cans of fastenings. It's very hot, and I have the galley hatch and one portlight open. SPONSOR WANTED reports that she is in the middle of Josephine, which has been downgraded from a hurricane to a tropical storm.

<u>2312.</u>   By far the best night of the race. Going well on a smooth sea with maximum sail. Moon, sparkling water, stars. It's all lovely. Like a song by a beautiful singer.

SEPTEMBER 30, 1990. (SUNDAY). DAY 15.

<u>0221.</u>   Can there be a touch more east to the wind or is it an aberration? I have actually eased the sheets a little.

<u>0230.</u>   False hopes. The wind is heading us again. I reckon we are 1900 miles north of the mouth of the Amazon river.

<u>0957.</u>   It's a problem to fill the windward water ballast tank when the yacht is heeled. I finally pulled off the hose to the pump and primed it after letting go the sheets to bring the yacht horizontal. Some of the snatch blocks are getting loose (and quickly become lethal weapons) because the springs that hold the disconnect pins are too weak.

<u>1231.</u>   Wind ESE 10 knots. A lovely day. We're going well. I've been working on chafe problems along the starboard side deck. The difficulty is the running backstay control line which rubs on everything in sight. I rove a new line and added an extra fairlead block. A good meal of barbecued pork, rice (at last cooked correctly), and tea (made with bottled spring water measured out one cup at a time, like gold, since the water from Newport has turned horrible).

<u>1958.</u>   I was worried that the tired old starboard jib sheet would break so I replaced it with a new line. It's a little dicey standing on the lifelines and leaning out to tie the sheet in place.

<u>2024.</u>   Earlier today I spoke with José Ugarte on BBV. He told me that he changed his mainsail because of a three-foot rip in the Kevlar material. José has been repairing a water ballast tank that suddenly burst and dumped two tons of saltwater in his cabin!

<u>2147.</u>   I am encouraged by the excellent sailing. We're logging a steady 8.6 knots hour after hour. Spray is flying around so I have closed the portlights and hatch.

OCTOBER 1, 1990. (MONDAY). DAY 16.

<u>0145.</u>   Heavy rain. I rushed out and had a shower and feel great. I continue to worry about easting. The 60-footers ahead all logged

runs of 220–240 miles yesterday. I wonder what sort of winds they had? Saw a meteor—super white—fall into the sea ahead.

<u>0620.</u>   A rough night bouncing all over the place. The wind is back to ESE (18 knots), and we're strapped in again.

<u>1021.</u>   A poor night. I got up for a squall, only to find that when the wind rose to 24 knots, the increase stayed with us. I eased the jib sheet (perhaps too much) and was cranking the furling line winch when suddenly the line jammed. The furling line somehow got fouled in the self-tailer on the winch. I tied a short line to the furling line forward of the winch, led the short line to a second winch to take the load, and straightened things out. Then I furled the sail. By then, however, the two loose sheets had whipped themselves into a frenzy of knots which compounded themselves into a giant snarl the size of a man's head. Really! It took me an hour on the foredeck to unwind all the knots.

<u>1300.</u>   The sky is clearing and looks better.

<u>1700.</u>   The wind has been moving between the south and east and blew up to 34 knots for a few minutes. It's now 17 knots from the SSE.

A little earlier while we were sailing under the main alone (on the port tack), the east wind shifted to the south. Since the autopilot was steering a course a little east of south, the wind pushed us off on the starboard tack. I forgot about the water ballast, and it heeled us way over to port. I gybed (turning to port) with the tiller, transferred the water ballast (from port to starboard) by gravity, and then—turning to port—tacked through the eye of the wind so that we were finally on starboard tack with the water ballast to windward. Complicated, eh?

<u>1852.</u>   SEBAGO should be more to the east, and I can see the wisdom of getting easting farther north in the westerlies. As I sail south into a position NW of Cabo de São Roque at the bulge of Brazil, the fickle SE winds (which are supposed to be E or NE) and the adverse South Equatorial Current are both working against us.

Bertie Reed and I worked out this strategy before the race. The straight line distances are a little shorter, but the winds and current are wrong. Bertie and I had good intentions, but our plan was bad. We should have listened to the captains who contributed to *Ocean Passages for the World*.

<u>1950.</u>   I have been out in so much rain today that I got chilled and put on a clean shirt, underwear bottoms, and oilskin trousers.

For dinner I had a powerful meal of chicken cacciatore and rice. My rice is quite good now—light and fluffy. I have cut down a small plastic cup that holds exactly the amount of rice I like for a meal. I take one measure of rice and two measures of water which I cook for 20 minutes or so (plus some steaming). I still have a few small bottles of spring water on board which I am using to make tea. The water in the tanks is not nice.

I finished *The Good Soldier* by Ford Madox Ford, supposedly one of the great novels of this century. I found it well written, but a middling yarn much too shy of action for my taste. The pace reminded me of Henry James. "A novel of passion," says the jacket. Baloney.

OCTOBER 2, 1990. (TUESDAY). DAY 17.

<u>1157.</u>   The one truth about sailing is that if you don't like the weather, just wait a while. Yesterday the wind blew up to 33 knots with lumpy seas of 12 feet. Today we've had seven hours of calms, and the ocean is flat. I had a good breakfast, tidied up the interior a little, and have been working on various deck jobs. The yacht is damp and steaming inside from being closed up in the tropics. What a relief to open the front hatch and a few portlights. A while ago I was in the lazarette checking the autopilot and found a plastic bucket, which I have tied to the main boom to catch rainwater.

<u>1315.</u>   Nine knots of wind from the east. We're right on course. How nice to hurry along at 8.3 knots with eased sheets and no pounding. I keep finding loaves of bread—bright with mildew—in the lockers.

<u>1443.</u>   A gorgeous day with an easterly breeze of 11 knots. We're logging a steady 8.5 knots. When I reef, I secure each luff cringle with a short piece of line. (I do not use hooks which, as a singlehander, I find unsatisfactory.) After tying down the luff reefing pendants, I put the leech reefing line on a #52 two-speed winch and crank away.

OCTOBER 3, 1990. (WEDNESDAY). DAY 18.

<u>0200.</u>   Wind 19 knots from the east. We're tearing through the night with big strains on everything. I tied the second reef in the main and rolled up more of the jib. Almost the same speed but a better ride. I must reeve ¼" dia. lines on the luff of the main so that if necessary I can use a winch to pull down the luff of the sail.

In the tropical Atlantic, red-billed tropicbirds often flew round and round the yacht at high speed while they chattered excitedly. Unlike terns or petrels, the tropicbirds flapped their wings at high speed and seemed to have the metabolism of nervous hummingbirds. I could never understand why the tropicbirds didn't wear themselves out with all their chattering and scolding and high speed wing movements.

It's a real terror to need a reef and not be able to get the sail down because it's jammed against the rigging by the wind.

<u>0747.</u>   Going 7–8 knots with just a tiny mainsail and a scrap of jib. The air in the cabin is stuffy with the yacht mostly closed up. We're at 12°N., about 930 miles east of the island of Grenada in the West Indies. I am studying the charts of the Brazilian coast.

This is the second time I've done this passage, and I've had very little wind with any north in it. The operative wind for a voyage from the east coast of the U.S. to the southern tip of Africa seems to be east through south.

<u>0902.</u>   A great discovery! I've found that I can use a pair of scissors to trim mold from a slice of bread. It's like cutting out paper dolls.

<u>1803.</u>   I really felt weak this afternoon. I cranked one sail in, let another out, and then went back to the first. I had to move the sheet a little because of a chafe problem. Suddenly I felt all in. The heat of the tropics, the days of pounding, and the work must be getting to me.

<u>2140.</u>   Reading *Billy Bathgate* by E. L. Doctorow, a stunning novel that seems to have won every award. I find this one relies a good deal on shocking the reader. However the yarn of Dutch Schultz is good. The people are as real as a dog's bark.

<u>2200.</u>   I thought I did well with a run of 189 miles today, but
SPONSOR WANTED logged 235, KODEN 216, SERVANT IV 213, and
SPIRIT OF IPSWICH 218. Some competition! Jack Boye in CITY KIDS
has overtaken Yves Dupasquier in SERVANT IV for the Class 2 lead.
CITY KIDS is more than 10° east of SERVANT. In Class 1, Philippe
Jeantot is leading, narrowly ahead of John Martin.

I have saltwater sores under my wristwatch strap so I have
switched the watch to my other arm.

OCTOBER 4, 1990. (THURSDAY). DAY 19.

<u>0420.</u>   A good sleep and an easy night except for a few small
squalls at 0100. Up to clean the galley and sinks and to reorganize
the cooking pots. I feel much better today.

Yesterday on the radio Bertie Reed spoke of monumental
rains. "I've got the cleanest ship in the fleet," he said.

Just now I'm sailing through a forest of towering cumulonimbus clouds. The wind has dropped, and the full moon is shining
down on the clouds which have a thousand changing ridges and
valleys and domes—a whole mountain range in the sky. The
clouds look milky in the moonlight and often glow with a pearly
light. Then they block the moon and it's dark. Ten minutes later
the moon is back and so bright that I can count the squalls in the
distance.

<u>1158.</u>   Wind and sea down. Cabin 82°F. Hatch and three port-
lights open. A nice breakfast of two soft-boiled eggs, two slices of
oatmeal bread (still good) with butter and jam, and a cup of tea
made with pure water. Busy repairing reefing pendants.

<u>1403.</u>   I have a splendid print of an old French fishing boat
tacked up in the cabin. Unfortunately mildew has grown on the
print, and the mounting has become a little wavy from moisture. I
cleaned the print and put in some extra fastenings to hold the
edges better. All this heat and humidity are not good for artwork.

<u>2126.</u>   A heavy squall and rain for two hours. Very black out-
side. We're going at 7.25 knots under the mainsail alone. I need to
set a scrap of jib. A good dinner of macaroni, Salisbury steak,
vanilla pudding, and tea. Finished *Billy Bathgate*, the wonderful
novel by E. L. Doctorow who certainly has an inventive mind.

<u>2131.</u>   The monumental rain continues. I would like to bucket
some of it into the water tanks, but I don't like the idea at night
on a lumpy sea.

OCTOBER 5, 1990. (FRIDAY). DAY 20.

<u>0021.</u>   As soon as it's light I must tighten the after lower shrouds, which again seem dangerously slack. When the yacht rolls, the wires get slack and then tighten with a jerk.

<u>0030.</u>   Wind SW 10. According to the Brazilian pilot charts, it never blows from the SW here.

<u>0043.</u>   Atol das Rocas is 947 miles on a magnetic bearing of 155°.

<u>0913.</u>   Gray and overcast and slightly cooler. Layered stratus down low. Cumulonimbus towers in the distance ahead.

<u>0936.</u>   Wind dying. Light rain.

<u>0940.</u>   During the rush to store the vessel, my helpers put a dozen loaves of bread on board "just in case." Practically all the loaves turned moldy, and I have been heaving one over the side every couple of days. A loaf of dark brown pumpernickel kept reasonably well. However a loaf of oatmeal bread has kept perfectly fresh (a miracle) and is still soft and delicious 19 days after departure. How nice to have a whole slice with butter and jam.

<u>1418.</u>   When I went to tighten the starboard after lower shroud, I discovered that the U-bolt was broken. Just like on the port side eight days ago. The twang I heard yesterday must have been it. What to do? The problem is to anchor the lower shrouds.
    There were unused U-bolts alongside the deck connections for the middle and upper shrouds so I decided to move the after lower shrouds forward to them. (I could have taken the U-bolts out and moved them aft, but since two have already broken, why do it?). This moved the after lowers forward to an in-line position with the middle and upper shrouds. I had to shorten one wire with the big Felco cutters and to put in a new wire end fitting. I tightened the shrouds enough to keep the slack out of the lee shrouds. I'm well aware that there's a danger of overtightening.

<u>1430.</u>   While becalmed I heard an ominous knocking. I looked in the lazarette and found that the engagement plate on the autopilot quadrant was about to fall off. Two of the four bolts were gone and two were loose. After I dealt with this problem I sat down at the chart table with a cup of tea only to discover that the GPS bearings on distant points have changed from *magnetic* to *true* bearings. The automatic variation correction device in the

receiver is not working. Perhaps the software needs to be repro-grammed when you near the Equator and go from north to south latitudes. It's no big problem, but I'm glad I noticed the change. Henceforth I will use true bearings and work accordingly. The Raytheon GPS, by the way, has worked perfectly so far. Fortunate-ly I have a spare GPS (not hooked up), and my trusty Plath sextant together with this year's almanac, and sight reduction tables.

<u>1940.</u>   In 20 days I have seen a greater shearwater, two or three Wilson's storm petrels, and six or eight white-tailed tropicbirds. Also one shore bird (misplaced). Pathetically few birds for 2,750 miles of ocean.

<u>1953.</u>   We're becalmed, and the rigging has been snapping and clicking as we roll in the swell. I considered tightening the lower starboard shroud, and looked at it long and hard. However the wire seems OK. I don't know which is worse, the rig or my worry-ing about it.

OCTOBER 6, 1990. (SATURDAY). DAY 21.

<u>0800.</u>   A steady light wind all night. We have been sailing nice-ly with the full main and the big genoa. The sea is perfectly calm, and we slip along effortlessly. Will the altered rig stand up? I hope so. Because of the rig problems I am anxious to get into Brazilian waters where I can stop if necessary. However the city of Recife is still 960 miles away.

<u>1024.</u>   A group of noddies is nearby and busy fishing, their thin black tern wings contrasting against the sea as the birds twist and turn.

<u>1400.</u>   I put a shut-off valve in the starboard freshwater tank outlet line and looked into the port tank, which is almost full. A small amount of sediment is floating in the bottom. The water smells OK. The tank hold-down straps were loose so I tightened them.
    Becalmed again. Where is the wind? I am beginning to feel that I am in orbit in outer space. Margaret is flying to Cape Town on October 29th, according to a relayed message from Newport.

<u>1655.</u>   We passed an orange-colored spherical float about one meter in diameter overlaid with heavy rope netting. Two stainless steel identification plates. Too neat and tidy to be a fishing float. The ball was only about 6–7 meters away, but there was no wind and no way to get it unless I jumped in with a line. My guess is

that the ball has something to do with submarines or one of the space programs.

<u>2100.</u>   A shock. I looked out and saw a brightly lighted cruise ship about one mile to port. People are still alive out there!

OCTOBER 7, 1990. (SUNDAY). DAY 22.

<u>0321.</u>   A busy night. Calms, then light airs, followed by a big squall with a fair wind. I caught two gallons of water which I poured into the port tank.

<u>1051.</u>   A bit of the blues this morning because the winds are so fleeting and transitory. Will I ever get around this corner of South America?

<u>1513.</u>   Bertie Reed took GRINAKER so close to the St. Peter and Paul rocks (510 miles NE of the corner of Brazil) that he almost hit them.

<u>1619.</u>   I'm a little tired of how Biddlecombe and McIntyre—two of the Australians—keep congratulating themselves on how great they are. Maybe they're just joking and putting the rest of us on.

This equatorial heat is staggering. I try to keep inside during the day and spend the nights outside.

<u>1657.</u>   Sailors are such hopeless romantics! As soon as the knotmeter touches 7 or 8, we convert that reading to miles per day (or week) and glorify in tremendous runs, generally not achieved. I think it's an intelligent policy *not* to discuss wind and weather with fellow competitors.

<u>1800.</u>   A ship to starboard changed course for me. Erratically, but he did change. A large (15,000-ton?) bulk ore carrier with seven compartments judging by the deck cranes. We have a south wind of 12 knots so I am trying to make easting. A good dinner of cannelloni. All I needed was some Italian opera and a glass of Chianti.

<u>2113.</u>   I discovered a tin measuring cup in the galley. Now I can measure accurately. I inspected the four forward settee lockers, which are always wet from bilge water. There are two solutions: (1) fiberglass the lockers into watertight boxes or (2) use large, deep plastic boxes to store things. Certainly any gear must be put in heavy plastic bags.

OCTOBER 8, 1990. (MONDAY). DAY 23.

<u>0129.</u>   Wind SSE 13 knots. We're on a course of 120°M., but no matter how I trim the main and jib, I can't get more than 7.5 knots. The west-setting current is killing us.

<u>0853.</u>   We have sailed all night at 6–7 knots. However close-hauled on a flat sea with 11–13 knots of wind, we should be going 8 knots. I grind my teeth when I look at the big mainsail with the broken battens that sits bundled up on deck. If I ever needed that big sail, it's now. Yesterday I took a long look at the 5 broken battens and the batten pockets to see if I could make repairs, but the job is hopeless because the spare battens are identical to the broken ones.

<u>1131.</u>   I took down the 165% genoa and put up the smaller one (139%) because it has better shape and the area is nicely suited to the current wind (SSE 14). The change took 90 minutes. The biggest problem is feeding the luff tape into the groove at the bottom of the aluminum extrusion on the headstay. The tape must run up smoothly, but if the feeding angle is too acute, the tape catches at the bottom of the extrusion and jams. I must have made 20 trips between the halyard winch on the mast and the extrusion at the bow to straighten out the luff of the sail. The tape pulled out of the extrusion four times. Each time I had to lower the sail and start over. A frustrating business. Now—finally—the sail is up and drawing.

<u>1230.</u>   125 miles in the last 24 hours. We're at 5°54'N. and 37°03'W.

<u>1622.</u>   Less wind. I have a hatch and a portlight open. Lovely cool air inside where I am shaded from the great yellow candle burning in the sky.

<u>1629.</u>   Debating whether to tack south. How steady will the wind be?

<u>2034.</u>   We must continue eastward before tacking because all the expected winds farther south are from the SE, E or S.
     I am fuming over the instructions for the video camera, which are in Japanese. The camera is complicated—with many new features—and I need help to figure out how to run it. That, along with the Standard C radio fiasco, makes two excellent items useless because of faulty instructions.

I am reading *The Logbook of Grace*, the story of a 1912 whaling trip written by Robert Murphy, a naturalist who went along to collect birds and mammals. The half-brig DAISY hailed from New Bedford. She was 123 feet overall and had a crew of 34. DAISY was an old-time whaling ship and really belonged to the era of Herman Melville and the 1840s. (In 1846 there were 736 Yankee whaling ships roaming the oceans; DAISY was the last.) Murphy tells it all. From the first sighting of the whales to the last cask of oil. (He also mentions sea leopards, creatures I've always been curious about.)

Whaling's too awful and bloody for me, and I can't imagine living closely with three dozen men for a year. Nevertheless Murphy's writing is good, especially his descriptions of the Norwegian whaling station on South Georgia in the South Atlantic. The slaughter of the whales was horrific but part of life a century ago. Today most people are against killing whales and dolphins. Yet there are many parallels with slaughtering beef cattle. Where does society stop? With beef cattle? Pigs? Chickens? Pumpkin seeds?

<u>2154.</u>   How wonderful it is to sail through the tropical night just after the sun is gone and before the moon has risen. Just now SEBAGO seems in a groove, and with only 6 knots of true wind is going 7 knots. Our course is not too good. We're headed for Fortaleza on the north Brazilian coast, too far to the west, but we have hundreds of miles in which to make a little easting. Nevertheless I must be careful because the adverse current is shoving us sideways toward the Caribbean at 1–2 knots.

OCTOBER 9, 1990. (TUESDAY). DAY 24.

<u>0121.</u>   A long session in the cockpit. Squalls, wind. Genoa furled; jib out. One reef. Course not ideal, but we'll see how things look when it's light.

<u>1136.</u>   I've sorted through all 100 charts and conclude that the plans of Trindade, Martin Vaz, and Fernando de Noronha are not on board. I've been trying to get in touch with Durban and St. Helena, but the stations are blocked by hams who prattle on and on about nothing and use 200 words to pass a message of 10 words and then repeat everything.

<u>2055.</u>   While furling the jib in a squall, I noticed that the furling line was almost chafed through. Not a good line to lose. To replace the line on a Schaefer 3000 gear requires removing the sail, or at least sliding the sail up a little so the drum assembly at the

bottom of the headstay can be taken apart. Too bad this happened when it's windy, and water is flying all over the foredeck.

What to do? I finally got the idea of furling the sail and continuing to haul on the furling line until all the furling line was unwound from the drum (this merely wound the sheets a few extra turns around the furled sail). I then cut and whipped the end of the 10mm dia. furling line about two feet from the drum and bent on a new line (I used a carrick bend and seized the ends.) Would it work? Of course, and the job was easy. While all this was going on, I ran off to the east. A lot of rain, lines in the cockpit, and general confusion. I collected 4 gallons of water.

It's often hard to get the Argos positions of the yachts in the fleet. The operators on the U.S. marine station WOM read the reports at normal speed, which makes it impossible to copy the numbers, particularly if the reception is marginal. The reports should be read at dictation speed, and each set of numbers should be read twice. The real way to communicate numerical material is by telex, and I suppose that will be the scheme of the future.

Robin Davie on GLOBAL EXPOSURE reported that when he was near Bermuda he saw 10 whales at one time. Aboard VOLCANO, Paul Thackaberry is having trouble with water in his forward watertight compartment. Don McIntyre had the unnerving experience of seeing a freighter with apparently no one on watch cross within 500 meters of SPONSOR WANTED. Don called the vessel on VHF but got no answer.

2229.   Wind south 22 knots. One squall after another. I'm resting up after dealing with the furling line. At the moment the yacht is on the starboard tack and jogging along at 4–5 knots while warm rain pours down.

OCTOBER 10, 1990. (WEDNESDAY). DAY 25.

0152.   Although the compass (120°M. or 100°T.) shows that we're making 10° toward the south, the current is shoving us toward the northwest. *We're actually gaining north latitude.* Terrible! I must tack and go south again.

0930.   Bashing and pounding. The wind is unsteady and goes back and forth between SE and SSE. When it's SE we sail south. When it's SSE we sail ESE. In the last eight hours we have made good 35 miles to the east and 10 miles south.

1054.   A westbound ship to starboard, headed 240°M., toward the mouth of the Amazon. Wind SE 17, a clear sky, and a surprisingly rough sea. The sky is a light bright blue; the sea a deep inky cobalt.

More chafe on the jib furling line. Since the line is long and moves in and out, it's hard to find the cause. I have threaded bits of yellow yarn along the chafed area to serve as flags to mark the offending block or whatever. I suspect the stanchion guides may be the problem, but I'm not sure.

I just ate half a small can of corned beef with mayonnaise. Pretty strong fare for these rough seas. Yesterday a black noddy with a white forehead patch perched on my shoulder for a minute or two in the cockpit. It reminded me of the time that a noddy flew into Margaret's hands on one of our Pacific trips. I miss Margaret and my friends a lot.

<u>1640.</u>   Going well. Fairly rough, and we pound and crash on one wave in six or seven. Yet it's amazing how the yacht can get in a groove once in a while and track at high speed with apparent ease. I feel like staying on this course (215°M.) all the way to the Brazilian coast and then taking my chances at Cabo de São Roque. Maybe there's a strong countercurrent close in. Let's try something different instead of slavishly following the others. I need to outsmart SERVANT IV, CITY KIDS, and SPONSOR WANTED.

<u>1918.</u>   We go back and forth. Just now the wind has backed to the SSE so I've gone on the starboard tack. My game plan for Leg 1 has been dumb. I should have gone way east early on as Jack Boye did in CITY KIDS. Here I am out in the ocean tacking back and forth against a foul current and an adverse wind. It's madness. Meanwhile Jack is 700 miles ahead.

OCTOBER 11, 1990. (THURSDAY). DAY 26.

<u>0500.</u>   The course (123°M.) is poor, but the seas are comfortable. A clear night with lots of stars. Orion is overhead. I should have been a shepherd.

<u>0848.</u>   I fret about getting past the bulge of Brazil. I suppose the first thing is to get to the Equator.

<u>1106.</u>   No more grapefruit. The last apple went several days ago.

<u>1250.</u>   At noon we were 130 miles north of the Equator. During the last 24 hours we logged 166 miles but made good only 106 because we tacked 4 times.

<u>2102.</u>   Going nicely up to 8 knots. However the course was SW—disastrous—and I know that current is setting us westward. I tacked to make easting again. Will we ever get out of this? The current is definitely a factor because the speeds are different on opposite tacks.

I know it's crazy (and I've only been at sea for 26 days), but when we go to windward, the surface of the sea sometimes seems to slope very slightly one way or another. It's almost as if the world were sliding down on me. I have the definite feeling that we're sailing across hills and slopes. I read somewhere that with satellite instruments, scientists have found that the level of the oceans is much more variable than they formerly thought. Could this be what I am seeing? Or has my head gone soft?

I rested a lot today and read *Sweet Bird of Youth* by Tennessee Williams. A good play.

OCTOBER 12, 1990. (FRIDAY). DAY 27.

<u>0109.</u>   Wind south 17 knots. Course 120°M. When we're on the starboard tack we seem to be exposed to more of the prevailing ocean swell. The ride is bumpier than the port tack.

<u>0638.</u>   Tacked to port. Course 220°. A smoother ride (because of the SE swell), and we're going half a knot faster.

<u>0910.</u>   Heeled 20° and pressed very hard. The cursed southerly winds have been blowing for more than a week. Hot and stuffy below—76 miles to the Equator.

<u>1244.</u>   Large cumulus clouds ahead. Wind south 18 knots. The wind is low and close to the sea. The higher clouds seem stationary.

John Martin in ALLIED BANK is now in first place in Class 1. CRÉDIT AGRICOLE is second, 159 miles behind. GENERALI CONCORDE is third, 212 miles from the lead. In Class 2, CITY KIDS is first. SPONSOR WANTED is second, 319 miles from the leader. SERVANT IV is third, 497 miles behind. SEBAGO is back 825 miles.

In the Corinthian class GLOBAL EXPOSURE is first. VOLCANO is second, trailing by 157 miles. NIIHAU IV is third, 409 miles behind.

<u>1538.</u>   Philippe Jeantot during the chat hour: "The noise of my wind generator is so strong that I thought it was a helicopter."

<u>1622.</u>   I put a second reef in the mainsail and increased the area of the jib a little, which has made a surprising difference in the heel of the yacht and her motion. We're going faster with less effort.

John Biddlecombe on INTEROX CRUSADER is about 480 miles south of me. His aluminum-hulled vessel has a big crack around the rudder post. "I went back to adjust the Aries wind vane gear and saw cracks which I simply couldn't believe," John said on the radio. "The upper bearing on the deck has torn away."

<u>1815.</u>   Earlier I spoke with Robin Davie who complained that he had been plagued by headwinds "practically all the way so far."

<u>2025.</u>   We're finally across the Equator! I rushed out to see the yellow line, but I must have just missed it. During the last four days we have logged 602 miles and made good 368 miles because of tacking.

CHAPTER TWO

The South Atlantic

OCTOBER 13, 1990. (SATURDAY). DAY 28.

<u>0056.</u>   Heavy squalls. Over on our ear. I've rolled up most of the jib, and we're still tearing along at 7–8 knots.

<u>0102.</u>   I reckon it's 264 miles to land. Not much luck sleeping. I can't seem to get involved in a book.

<u>0740.</u>   Another rough night. It's hard to believe that SEBAGO hasn't fallen to pieces from the pounding. No wonder ships disappear at sea.

Just before dawn I watched the edge of a band of altostratus change from gray to a ribbon of glistening silver as the moon rose above the clouds. If a painter had done it he would have been called a fake. Nature is spectacular sometimes.

The wind continues unsettled from the S and the SSE, with dense banks of clouds, and squalls here and there. One is blowing a gusty 25 knots just now.

<u>0900.</u>   The motion threw a cup of tea off the stove even though the stove clamps were around the cup. I have been sitting under the cockpit dodger reading *Tess of the d'Urbervilles* by Thomas Hardy. It's one of those titles I've always heard about but never read. About 18th-century rural England. Life before computers, police sirens, and credit cards must have been peaceful. So far the book is surprisingly good.

I hope the wind will be less strong and not so contrary along the coast of Brazil. During the 1700 hours broadcast of the Argos positions, SERVANT IV was put on alert as the closest vessel to INTEROX CRUSADER (9°18'S., 29°49'W.) which is disabled with rudder problems. SERVANT IV's position was 8°06'S., 31°52'W.

OCTOBER 14, 1990. (SUNDAY). DAY 29.

<u>0046.</u>   Wind a little less. I am working eastward whenever possible. This puts us closer to the wind, drops our speed from 8.5 to

7.5 knots, and increases the pounding, but we must get around the bulge of Brazil which is 97 miles ahead. The GPS is marvelous because (1) we can keep track of our position and (2) see how the longitude is changing with the west-setting current.

0253.   We're 55 miles west of Atol das Rocas and 96 miles from Cabo Calcanhar on the Brazilian coast.

0920.   A masked booby, a large brown bird with white wingtip patches, is circling SEBAGO. Boobies are old friends from the tropics, a sure sign of land, and sometimes harbingers of a weather change. I am tired of living heeled over at 20° and 30°.

I tossed out half a dozen rotten carrots which I accidentally stored in a closed locker.

1003.   Wind SSE 20. Course 210°M. Tearing along at 8.5 knots hard on the wind with a big reef in the jib and a double reef in the mainsail.

1019.   I wonder how John Biddlecombe is doing with his rudder problems? I'm looking at a large, plump, dark-brown bird with white wing patches at the ends of short, wide wings. I think it's a south polar skua.

1500.   José on BBV complains that his vessel will only do 9.5 knots. He said that he was getting weather information from Spanish ham operators who predicted westerlies for today at his position (21°00′S., 22°11′W).

1939.   Shook out the second reef. We're going well at almost right angles to the swells. No hammering. Again we increased our speed when I rolled a reef in the jib. It's wonderful the way this hull slips through the water. No sign of land. Lots of heavy banks of clouds in the distance. Directly overhead I see lovely swirls of cirrus—ice crystals six miles up.

2348.   I can plainly see the loom of city lights. Brazil!

OCTOBER 15, 1990. (MONDAY). DAY 30.

0012.   We're 22 miles offshore at Cabo Bacopari. We have finally weathered the hump of Brazil.

0335.   It's lovely out tonight. The clouds are gone, and the great vault of the sky seems huge and endless. I begin to feel its dimensions only because of the hundreds of stars up there. Who was it who said that the stars are only holes in the sky that lead to heaven?

The seas are easier, and we're rushing through the night to windward at 8–8.5 knots. To starboard I can just see the faint loom of lights of cities along the coast, about 35 miles to the west. We've left the adverse south equatorial current and should be in the fair Brazil current which sets SSW parallel to the land.

No sign of ships. I presume they're farther in toward shore. Nevertheless I've turned on the navigation lights for the first time in a month. We have 3,332 miles to go to Cape Town.

The water ballast system is a complete success, and our windward performance is much better than during the 1986–87 race. So far my rig repairs have held, although I'm nervous every time I look aloft. I admit that I'm not pushing the yacht as hard as I would if I weren't concerned about the mast coming down.

I wonder about the amount and quality of water in the fresh-water tanks. How good is the little emergency watermaker?

I'm enjoying *Tess of the d'Urbervilles*. A wonderful picture of pastoral life in England during the early 1800s.

<u>1029.</u>   I opened up the starboard freshwater tank and found 16 or 17 gallons. I have 3 gallons of spring water in jugs, which gives me a total of 20 gallons, plus whatever is in the port tank. If I figure my needs at half a gallon per day I have enough for at least 40 days. The problem is that the tank water tastes terrible. Either I got bad water in Newport or saltwater has leaked into the tanks. A leak is doubtful because the filler caps have excellent, well-greased O-ring seals. My mistake was not having a couple of empty plastic jugs on board for the rainwater I caught. I put the rainwater into the regular tanks which of course spoiled the rainwater.

<u>1500.</u>   Wind less. ESE 9 knots. Genoa up. A run of 188 miles at noon today.

<u>2148.</u>   Wind SE 6–7. A beautiful evening, by far the best of the trip. How nice to relax in the cockpit with a cup of tea. Finally no banging and crashing. I finished *Tess of the d'Urbervilles*.

OCTOBER 16, 1990. (TUESDAY). DAY 31.

<u>0130.</u>   A very smooth ocean. We're going well, but it would be nice to ease the sheets a little and speed up. I have been hard on the wind—or very close to it—for 4,000 miles.

<u>0334.</u>   A busy few hours. A ship 8 miles to starboard headed NNE. Squally and a light rain. Jib up in place of the genoa.

I finally got a call through to Margaret today (her birthday) after about 50 tries during the past week. She is planning her trip to Cape Town. I wished her happy birthday and asked her to bring a few bits of gear. She raised another $7,000, and we discussed further funding efforts. She was surprised at me being so far west and asked about my weather information.

Something is wrong with the SSB radio. Although my batteries are up and run everything else with ease, the SSB apparently needs higher voltage. The WOM operator told me to start my generator. ("The difference is like night and day," he said.) No wonder I haven't been getting through.

Overcast out. Stars gone. Wind fluky. Time to sleep.

<u>0854.</u>   I've been trying to get the small genoa to set without the top vibrating when I have a small reef rolled in the sail. The design of the sail apparently makes reefing impossible.

<u>1029.</u>   I hear ominous creaking noises somewhere amidships on the port side, near the chainplates, I'm almost afraid to say.

Dolphins and sunlight near the Equator.

2002.   GENERALI CONCORDE made 328 miles toward Cape Town today. Some run for a singlehander.

I have fired off more than a dozen messages to Bob Rice on the Standard C radio. I have never received an answer, but I regularly get routine service bulletins from Inmarsat, the company that runs the satellite operation in England (which handles all Atlantic traffic). The radio works perfectly, but I can't seem to get past England. I think my problem is procedural, and the radio was not commissioned properly.

OCTOBER 17, 1990. (WEDNESDAY). DAY 32.

0400.   The night is black, and I can see nothing outside. A couple of big flying fish (7–8" long) in the cockpit. You know they're on board by their oily smell. Wind SSE 13 knots. Where, I wonder, is that easterly that John Biddlecombe talked about so much? The best I can do is SSW, so I'm making no easting at all.

I'm stunned by the 328-mile run of Alain Gautier. Imagine 13.6 nautical miles an hour! All congratulations to him, but I feel discouraged. A race format that links 60-foot gold-platers and smaller, less advanced yachts is hopeless. It's great for the stars at the head of the fleet (the heroes), but terrible for the bit players who are far behind (the losers).

The four leading Class 1 yachts (ALLIED BANK, CRÉDIT AGRICOLE, GENERALI CONCORDE, and GROUP SCETA) represent a new generation of light-displacement yachts with extreme beam (19 ft.), deep draft (12–13 ft.), and large sail area (2,500 sq. ft.) set on lofty (82 ft.) carbon fiber masts. These yachts are extremely powerful because they carry 7,000 pounds of water ballast when going to windward. This means they have lots of sail-carrying ability and can maintain high average speeds. Their all-up costs are from $600,000 to $850,000.

The other eight Class 1 yachts are hopelessly behind, and any comparisons with the Class 2 and Corinthian class vessels are ludicrous.

1214.   A day's run of 176 miles at noon today. We're 320 miles east of the coast, on a line between Salvador and Ilhéus. The best we can do is 8.3 knots. The race has been underway for 5 weeks. Alain Gautier (GENERALI CONCORDE) is 88 miles ahead of Philippe Jeantot (CRÉDIT AGRICOLE). Third place is John Martin, 190 miles out of first.

Jack Boye (CITY KIDS) leads Class 2 and is 347 miles ahead of Don McIntyre (SPONSOR WANTED). Third is Yves Dupasquier (SERVANT IV), 484 miles behind Jack. SEBAGO is 957 miles out of first.

In the Corinthian class, Robin Davie (GLOBAL EXPOSURE) is leading Paul Thackaberry (VOLCANO) by 158 miles. Third is Robert Hooke (NIIHAU IV), back 327 miles.

1927.   At 1600 I decided to go on the starboard tack because the ESE wind backed to the south.* While I was forward dealing with the running backstays, I noticed a big bend in the mast. I immediately rolled up the jib which slowed us to two knots. Since there was no more take-up room on the turnbuckle for the lower starboard shroud, I cut the wire and moved the Sta-Loc wire end fitting up a few inches. I then tightened the lower shroud and both intermediate shrouds. I'm glad I have 1x19 wire and not rod rigging so I can deal with such problems on board. All the delays and repair time because of the broken rigging have certainly ruined my chances for this leg. At least I'm still going, however.

A beastly headache all day. I seem to have run out of radio links with the rest of the world. Still no reply on the Standard C from Bob Rice. I know the system works because I've received more routine messages from Goonhilly, the station in England that runs the system for the Atlantic. Apparently there is no link between Goonhilly and Bob. I give up.

OCTOBER 18, 1990. (THURSDAY). DAY 33.

0025.   A good sleep. I feel much better. My headache is largely gone, and I'm hungry. The night is a bit cooler (we're at 15°S.), and the air has more the feeling of the temperate zones that I like. It's incredible how constant the direction of the SE trade wind is. The Pilot charts show various other directions, but true SE is what we've experienced. I must keep looking at the mast and adjust the shrouds to keep the spar straight.

0213.   A beautiful night. I feel much better. I think my trouble was mental confusion from satellite radios, high electricity demands, weatherfax machines with impossible directions, and high-tech weather advice that doesn't come. In other words too much technology heaped on the shoulders of a dumb sailor. I

* In the southern hemisphere a backing wind moves clockwise when viewed from above. A veering wind moves counterclockwise.

think I'm better off without any of it except the weatherfax machine if I can figure out how to program the double function keys.

<u>0510.</u>   The weather is definitely cooler. Thank heavens I'm out of the doldrums, the terrible *pot au noir* (the pitch-pot) as the French call it.

<u>0702.</u>   Course due south at 8.3 knots. Flat sea. Wind SE 12–13 knots. We're heeled 30°.
    I heard on the radio that John Biddlecombe put into Recife, Brazil to get the mounting of his top rudder bearing fixed. Unfortunately the repairs were "totally unsatisfactory." John decided to withdraw from the race and has notified the committee. He and I talked many times on the radio, and I'm sorry to see him go. I have trouble believing that he couldn't have cobbled up something in Recife to have made it to Cape Town. I suspect that he was disappointed by his performance in comparison with the leaders. In any case John is out of the race.
    This leaves 22 competitors.
    The Hungarian Nandor Fa aboard ALBA REGIA reported that he has blown out his genoa and is sailing with his mainsail alone. One of the two Japanese competitors, Minoru Saito, on his 50-foot cutter SHUTEN-DOHJI II, radioed that he has a severe toothache that he is attempting to relieve with saltwater rinses.

<u>0827.</u>   Life aboard is much easier with one reef in the main and three or four turns in the jib furling gear. Almost the same speed. And smaller loads on the rig.

<u>1324.</u>   I opened up the port water tank and found it half full, say 9½ gallons. The starboard tank is almost full, so in 4.7 weeks I have used 9½ gallons plus 4 gallons of rain water and 3 gallons of spring water, which add up to 16½ gallons. This works out to be half a gallon per day. However I have been careful. Enough to drink and for cooking. A little for personal washing, and I always wash my hands with soap and water after going to the head (no hepatitis, please). I do the dishes in seawater with a little freshwater rinse of boiling water. I generally rinse off my hands with a few drops when I come in from working on deck and handling lines.

<u>1703.</u>   A big swell from the south every 10 seconds. A mighty storm is blowing somewhere in the Southern Ocean.

OCTOBER 19, 1990. (FRIDAY). DAY 34.

<u>0025.</u>   Tomorrow will be five weeks. I must work hard and see how soon I can reach Cape Town.

<u>0041.</u>   The finish line is 2,878 miles on 120°T. The island of Trindade bears almost SE (129°T.). Distance 238 miles. It's fascinating (and slightly hypnotic) to watch the numbers (hundredths of a nautical mile) flicker past one another on the face of the GPS set.

<u>1031.</u>   Banging along as usual. Sea a bit rougher. Some swell from the SW. Bright and sunny. I splurged with water and had a sponge bath and put on clean clothes.

<u>1200.</u>   179 miles today. The barometer has risen to 1018 mb.

<u>1648.</u>   I woke up at 1430 because we were heeled way over to starboard. A lot of sail up with 16 knots of wind. I reefed the main and then realized the wind was from the east. "This is it," I said, and immediately eased the sheets. False! Soon the wind was back in the SE and less. I unreefed the main and jib only to have the wind increase again. I hung on for a while but had to reef once more.

A gorgeous day. A thin veil of high stratus. Lower down are some extra-puffy cumulus clouds. A few gentle rain showers, different from the gusty squalls of the doldrums. We're in the transition zone between the SE trades and the horse latitudes. Maybe I will see Trindade tomorrow.

OCTOBER 20, 1990. (SATURDAY). DAY 35.

<u>0239.</u>   When will the wind shift? Or will I go to the South Pole on this course?

<u>0811.</u>   The wind has veered a little to the east (110°), a good sign. We don't have a clear shot for Cape Town (141°M.), but 155°M. is the best course for a long time. As usual we're on the port tack and going to windward with small sails and the water ballast pumped to the high side.

A complex sky with a few low cumulus clouds. At mid-altitude are random swirls of thin stratus. At the top of the scene are mares' tails—high cirrus—that contrast strongly with the deep blue sky above. All are strongly sidelighted by the yellowish rays of the early morning sun. It's all so beautiful.

<u>0820.</u>   I have tried again and again to telephone Herb Weiss in the U.S. to set up a ham schedule on 10 meters. No luck getting

through to a shore station even though I am careful to have my batteries at full power. I hear Cape Town radio talking with other vessels in the fleet, but my signal is either too weak or off frequency. The SSB radio is maddening.

<u>1008.</u>   It's a nice change to have the rising sun over the starboard bow.

<u>1233.</u>   Noon to noon—178 miles. We're almost to 22°S. latitude. Heeled to 30° with a lot of pounding so I eased off 10° to 165°M.

<u>1502.</u>   Barometer 1017 mb. We're beginning to fall under the influence of the enormous South Atlantic high-pressure area. I reckon we're in the NW sector and should get easterlies.

<u>1613.</u>   An easterly wind! (I can hardly believe it after writing about easterlies only an hour ago.) I have eased the jib sheet a touch, and set more of the mainsail. The wind has dropped to 12 knots, and the seas are more abeam. Actually the east wind—090°—is a magnetic compass reading which is really 090° minus 25° of westerly magnetic variation or 065° true. In other words the true wind is ENE.

     The radio is working a little. I spoke with SPONSOR WANTED and BBV. CITY KIDS has been becalmed (barometer 1020 mb.) for 12 hours in the middle of the South Atlantic high (Jack Boye is having fits.) I tried to identify a bird for José Ugarte on BBV (probably a noddy). Don McIntyre spoke of telephoning the weather people in the Falkland Islands to check on the movements of the high-pressure area. I believe Don called via WOM in Florida. Some ambitious and costly telephoning.

     I must keep pushing south before I head east to Cape Town. Both CITY KIDS and SPONSOR WANTED began to go SE too far east in my judgement. I want to get down to 34°S. and then head east with fair westerly winds.

<u>1843.</u>   With a free wind and close-reaching, we're going along at 8–9 knots on a course of 165°M. or 140°T. Say SE. However, we're farther west than the others. At these speeds in the lumpy seas that are running, the genoa puts a severe strain on the rig.

<u>2102.</u>   What an improvement in my outlook and the sailing conditions since yesterday. We crossed 23°S. and finally got east of 30° west. The radio has worked enough for me to talk with several yachts. The leading Class 1 sailors will finish in a few days.

2304.   I'm worried about the rigging, in particular the shrouds which have been so troublesome. The slack lee shrouds are making a lot of noise.

OCTOBER 21, 1990. (SUNDAY). DAY 36.

0325.   I was walking along the deck when a flying fish whizzed out of the sea and smacked me on the shoulder. No damage except that my shirt no longer smells like a rose garden.

Down genoa, up jib. Speed almost the same and far less strain on the rig and the passenger's nerves. I could sail this yacht a very long way with just the mainsail and the 110% jib (and water ballast) and do quite well.

1142.   One squall after another. Long, dark horizontal lines. I'm reading *Piece of Cake* by Derek Robinson. A novel about the RAF and the phony war of early 1940.

1210.   Day's run, 211 miles. I climbed up in the cockpit without a jacket on for a quick look around. A wave broke aboard and drenched me.

1546.   Wind ESE 20 knots. Lumpy seas. I have been in the cockpit trying to get the yacht to do 10 knots and steer a reasonable course. No luck, and the vessel is all over the place. I tried letting out half the water ballast, but it didn't help. I considered putting up an asymmetrical spinnaker, but came to my senses just in time.

1925.   The wind is down to 12 knots. With only 60 percent of the earlier windspeed we're going almost as fast and she's steering a perfect course. I've noticed that when the wind shifts or changes in strength, it takes the yacht a while to settle down and find her groove. It almost seems that she's human.

It's getting cooler each night. I've put my shorts away, and I'm wearing trousers.

2000.   The setting sun is golden yellow beneath a bank of stratus. Our position is 25°49'S., 27°20'W. or 2,411 miles to Cape Town on 113°T. We've had a couple of good days, and I'm pleased with our progress. If the 5 yachts ahead of us have some of the sail and rig problems and poor winds that SEBAGO and I had earlier and we continue to hurry along, maybe we can improve our position.

2127.   A big squall has gone on for an hour. Wind NNE up to 28 knots. We're logging 7 knots under the single-reefed main. Can this wind be a weather front going east?

2200.   Unrolled a scrap of the genoa to go with the mainsail.

2346.   I'm surprised at this strong wind out of an almost clear sky. Good-bye trade winds. I expect this sort of thing in the Southern Ocean, but not here.

OCTOBER 22, 1990. (MONDAY). DAY 37.

0053.   Nasty out. So far the wind direction is steady and 26–28 knots. The new moon set early. Black and ominous outside. At least we're getting pushed south and east.

0526.   Wind NE 21. Need to pole out the jib, but the night is incredibly dark.

0530.   We're heading a little north of Tristan da Cunha, an unlighted group of four islands. Tristan, Nightingale, Inaccessible, and Gough. A good question for a quiz show.

1000.   I managed to call in my position to Cape Town radio. However to get through I had to run the generator. With a strong beam wind, the yacht tends to round up and steer an uneven course. Still we're doing well, and I think I'll leave her alone. We're touching 11 knots from time to time.

1200.   Day's run, 221 miles.

1404.   High thin clouds and bright sunshine.

1742.   Winds up to 33 knots from the NE. Beam winds and big seas are a disaster. Water is flying everywhere and we are crashing and banging.

I spoke with Don McIntyre at 1500. He said this gale was part of a small intense low and suggested that I head south to 30°S. prior to the wind shift to the SW(?). This sounded reasonable so I changed course to 190°M., and now we're running at high speed. The yacht is under no strain at all. When she takes off at 14 knots and starts down a long wave slope I wonder whether she's going to dive to the bottom of the sea. However she always comes back up. At least so far. (Maybe I should be writing with waterproof ink.) An amazing vessel.

It's astonishing how comfortable the yacht is when she's running fast. What a difference from the windward tacking nightmare at the hump of Brazil.

I had a hard time getting the port pole and lines organized for the running rig. I hadn't set the pole for ages (this shows what sort of winds I have had), and I knew I would have problems, especially with the spinnaker pole end fittings. The latches were jammed with salt and corrosion and needed a lot of oil and attention.

I got soaked while doing all this. Sweat from the inside and lots of water from the outside. These rigs are complicated with all the downhauls, lifts, sheets, and guys. Some big seas broke right over the vessel (and me). I was glad that I had my safety line clipped on.

I am enjoying *Piece of Cake* a lot. An intriguing group of characters. Some likable, some hateful. World War II and Hurricane flying seem a long time ago.

1835.   Outside for a look. I believe the front is passing. However, the barometer has only dropped to 1010 mb. from 1013.5, not much of a dip. Low stratus, driving rain, gray and gloomy. Squalls on top of the wind. I cranked in the headsail until only about eight or nine feet of the clew are left. Our speed has stabilized at 8-9-10. Oops—11. I wonder how the other four yachts near me are doing?

1857.   More wind and squalls. I can see a little setting sun through thin clouds in the west.

1913.   Weather worse. The poled-out headsail began to flog, and I thought we might lose the rig. I managed to roll up the sail. Wind NE 44 knots. Damn! I shut both storm doors and am letting her take care of herself. I wish I had the third reef tied in. The leech of the main is vibrating and making a hell of a noise, but that's why we have 10-oz. cloth. The cloud layers seem to be thinning and dissipating.

While I was writing, the wind suddenly dropped to 34 knots. Now it's going back up. Things are flying around the cabin. The wind is down to 28 knots. Everything seems quiet except when we roll, and loose gear crashes across the cabin sole. How can there be such foul weather in the temperate zone in spring? Shocking, simply shocking. There's 40 knots again.

2123.   The motion below is not too bad now. A little rolly. For dinner I managed to cook some noodles and ate an orange.

OCTOBER 23, 1990. (TUESDAY). DAY 38.

0023.   I was standing on the companionway steps with the top half of the storm door open and had just reached outside to the autopilot control to change the course a little when a big wave thundered on board. Cold water suddenly filled the cockpit, exploded into my arms and face, and carried on below to flood the electrical panel.

<u>0955.</u>   Last night about 0300, SEBAGO was tearing along to the south at 10–11 knots in front of the NE gale when the autopilot died. The boat gybed, and suddenly we were sideways on to 35-knot winds. The headsail was flapping violently. The reefed main was backed but held by the vang tackle. I quickly rolled up the headsail. I then disconnected the autopilot and tried to shove the tiller to windward to get the vessel to gybe back on course. Impossible.

The scene in the cockpit was daunting. Waves were breaking right over us; I was already soaked and soon trembling from the cold. We were headed west, and the wind blew over the starboard quarter. During a lull, I shoved the tiller to windward, held it with a couple of turns of line to a winch, and got the yacht to gybe and swing around on course. The main was double-reefed, but made a mighty crack when it swung across. Once on course I connected the autopilot. We immediately gybed. I repeated the procedure several times before I realized the autopilot was dead.

I ducked below and put on an oilskin jacket. I was wet, but I knew I would get some warmth from more clothes. I gybed the yacht again and began to steer by hand. I lashed the tiller, got her to steer about 090°, and we hobbled along with the mainsail. Meanwhile I thought of the wind vane steering gear. Unfortunately the bevel gears in the vane mechanism had slipped past one another again. To deal with the gears (by now I had special names for them) I had to climb over the stern pulpit and down on the transom to the vane mount. I got two wrenches and, carefully harnessed, went over the pulpit to see what I could do.

Imagine the scene: the middle of the night, a shrieking gale, waves breaking over the yacht, spray everywhere. We were thumping along slowly to windward and fell off every second or third wave with a knock that threatened to pitch me off the transom and into the ocean.

In order to see I held a small flashlight in my mouth. I was sure I was going to lose my two wrenches, but I was in luck and managed to align the gears. I quickly climbed back to the cockpit, hooked up the vane, and headed SE under the mainsail. I went below, stripped off my clothes, and wiped myself with a dry towel. Then I put on clean clothes, made something to eat, and stretched out on a bunk. Sleep was heaven.

<u>1110.</u>   Wind down to 16 knots from the NE, and a big leftover sea from the gale. GENERALI CONCORDE has finished Leg 1 of the

race. Three more Class 1 yachts are supposed to reach Cape Town today. The four super yachts won easily.

1426.   Course SSE. The wind (16 knots) has veered to the NW, and the swell from the gale has eased off. I just finished gybing the downwind rig for the first time since Newport. A one-hour project. The cursed mainsail (with the broken battens) that's stowed on the port side deck is terribly in the way. The vane is steering reasonably well. I should have a spinnaker up, but the wind vane is not up to it. I must sleep.

1806.   No time for sleep. I have been trying to adjust the steering vane which has assumed a new importance in my life. I can't seem to get the gears set to utilize the full side-to-side travel of the water blade. I think I could fix the mechanism if we were stopped, but we're sailing at 7 knots. This puts a big load on everything, and it's dangerous to slip the bevel gears a cog or two to adjust the position of the water blade relative to the air blade. Nevertheless I've adjusted the tiller lines carefully, and we seem to be going OK.

2248.   I have been sleeping on the cabin sole on one of the settee cushions. Comfortable and quite a good place really. No way to fall out of bed. I'm almost at the end of the bottled water, which I have reserved for drinking and tea.

OCTOBER 24, 1990. (WEDNESDAY). DAY 39.

0610.   My speed has dropped—I've had to reduce sail because the vane can't handle high speeds (8–9 knots). I must try to repair the autopilot. The motor is probably burned out. A spare motor should be in the aft locker of the starboard quarter berth. The wind is north, 17 knots. I'm going to gybe and see if I can get on a reaching course. Then I'll hunt for the motor.

1400.   Reports of 45 knots this morning from SPONSOR WANTED. I must sleep a little.

1639.   The wind has veered to the NW. I've reset the vane for a course of 110°.

1959.   Freshly cooked spaghetti with butter and a little cheese is delicious.

OCTOBER 25, 1990. (THURSDAY). DAY 40.

<u>0106.</u>   Wind north 11 knots. The barometric pressure is creeping upward (1020.5 mb.). Tristan da Cunha is 501 miles to the SE.

<u>0552.</u>   There's no reason to change the motor in the autopilot drive unit because the motor works when I put 12 volts into it directly. It does not work when it's hooked up through the control box. So the problem must be in the box or in the input to the box from the compass. Since I have already used my spare control box the only thing I can do is to change the compass and the compass amplifier.

<u>1105.</u>   I learned that SERVANT IV had a run of 279 miles in 24 hours during the gale two days ago. Some run for a 50-footer!

I changed the compass and the compass electronics unit of the autopilot but, as expected, got no action in the drive unit. The trouble is in the control box, because the output voltage is always negative even when I move the control knob from one side of the course to the other.

The old control box runs for 5 minutes and then some electronic goodie inside quits. I'm afraid both control boxes are useless. I will have to rely on the wind vane steering gear, a lashed tiller, or hand steering to get to Cape Town.

<u>1152.</u>   I had a sudden idea and tried reversing the polarity of the wires to the autopilot drive unit to see if that would help. No response.

<u>1230.</u>   Day's run, 129 miles. 1,856 miles to go. So far the four super yachts of Class 1 (GENERALI CONCORDE, GROUPE SCETA, CRÉDIT AGRICOLE, and ALLIED BANK)—"the aircraft carriers" as they are called—have triumphed, and finished within 10 hours of one another. The winning time was 37½ days which beat the Newport-Cape Town record by 4½ days.

In Class 2, Yves Dupasquier in SERVANT IV is now only 45 miles behind Jack Boye in CITY KIDS, who has 1,096 miles to go. SPONSOR WANTED (Don McIntyre) is third, 169 miles out of first. SEBAGO is 1,864 miles from Cape Town.

In the Corinthian class the first two places are a toss-up between VOLCANO and GLOBAL EXPOSURE (2,102 and 2,115 miles to go). Third is Minoru Saito in SHUTEN-DOHJI II , 2,896 miles from Cape Town.

Canadian Jane Weber, one of the two women in the race, has headed for Barbados in the West Indies because of torn sails, a broken generator, and pains in her back. She's probably out of the race. That leaves 21 competitors.

1501.   Ten knots of wind on the port quarter. We're running nicely at 5–6 knots under the main and poled-out jib. I rolled out the genoa behind the main and thought we would pick up some speed, but we didn't.

1601.   Green and white spinnaker up. The vane is steering with wide swings in the course. Speed 7–8 knots. Today I had the pole against the headstay when I opened up the spinnaker. The big sail pulled us way over sideways until I grabbed the tiller and cranked in the spinnaker guy to haul back the pole. Some business setting a big spinnaker by yourself without an autopilot. A mixture of terror and fright until the damned thing is up and settled.

Some of the yachts ahead are stalled out in the South Atlantic high (INNKEEPER reports 1030 mb.). Will I be able to catch up?

1921.   I had the giant green spinnaker up for two hours. A lot of work, but more speed. About an hour ago I noticed dark clouds rolling up astern so I took down the sail. The wind vane is coping, but the side-to-side travel is not right. I steered for a while, and our speed picked up at once. What a pity both autopilots quit. I have the small genoa poled out.

The radio is full of complaints from the becalmed 60-footers ahead. GRINAKER (Bertie Reed), BBV EXPO (José Ugarte), and INNKEEPER (David Adams) are in a little group about 650 miles from Cape Town and have completely run out of wind. "A 5-day loss is almost impossible to make up," said Bertie.

OCTOBER 26, 1990. (FRIDAY). DAY 41.

0303.   Wind NNE 11. I changed from the running rig to the fore-and-aft rig. Not so easy without the autopilot. I put down the spinnaker pole, pulled in the mainsheet, and switched the headsail, but I couldn't get the vane to handle the helm. With the 800 sq. ft. genoa and full main, the vessel kept rounding up and racing along at 9 or 10 knots. I finally reefed the genoa and kept shortening the windward steering vane line until I got some balance with the vane. If I had full travel with the vane, the control would be easier. I am soaking wet from perspiration.

A lovely night with Orion overhead. The moon set about 0100. I am about out of good drinking water and am wondering how to enjoy my last cup. Straight? With brandy? Or in tea or coffee?

<u>0444.</u>   Running rig back up.

My right forefinger has a bit of infection at the end. Yesterday—or the day before—I nicked the finger on a fragment of sharp fiberglass in the lazarette. I put some antibiotic ointment on the finger. Today it was very sore. I examined it under a magnifying glass and squeezed out some white stuff. A little more squeezing and a sliver of fiberglass about 3/16 of an inch long slid out! I have rubbed in more ointment.

I made a cup of tea with tank water. Absolutely undrinkable.

<u>1211.</u>   I rolled up the genoa and slowed the yacht so I could slip a tooth on the steering vane gears. Then some adjustments on the rod between the air and water blades. Genoa up again. I believe the main part of the vane is centered better.

<u>1707.</u>   The conditions were ideal for a spinnaker, but I had no autopilot. However the vane gear seemed to be working OK, so I put up the green chute. Yesterday it filled on the leeward side so today I winched the spinnaker pole 45° to windward before I set the sail. I presumed the chute would fill in front of the yacht and all would be well. Alas, I neglected to secure the sock furling line under a snatch block. When I winched the spinnaker pole aft, the sock shot up—furling line and all—and I watched with my mouth open. There was nothing to do except to go ahead and sail with the spinnaker, which I did for several hours.

When it was time to douse the chute I let the guy fly, and rushed forward and madly pulled in material from the leeward clew. I also let the halyard go. But too quickly. Suddenly the sail was in the water, a gigantic green sea anchor. It took half an hour to get it aboard.

With a 15-knot wind we can sail at 5 knots under the main. With the poled-out genoa and main we can log 6–7, maybe 8.5 at times. With the spinnaker we can sail at 7–8–9 and sometimes 10. (We surf at 12–14 knots for a few seconds from time to time.) But spinnakers for singlehanders—as we've seen—have built-in problems. At the moment we have one bent stanchion and a very wet spinnaker up the mast in the sock, draining and drying out.

<u>1720.</u>   There's an enormous cloud bank 15–20 miles south of us that extends for miles in an east-west direction. Also lots of cirrus overhead. Don McIntyre told me that he had a spinnaker over the side yesterday. I suspect this happens to everyone in the race. The three 60-footers—BBV, INNKEEPER, and GRINAKER—are still becalmed. The captains are chewing their fingernails. While I was

hunting for the emergency water purification device I found two bottles of wine, a pleasant discovery.

<u>2247.</u>   Mid-altitude clouds are overtaking us from the NW. The SE sky is clear with lots of stars. A fine evening with a smooth sea and a light NW wind.

OCTOBER 27, 1990. (SATURDAY). DAY 42.

<u>0218.</u>   A big weather change. Squalls, low rolling clouds, and light rain.

<u>0913.</u>   Another long night. The wind shifted to the SSW and blew hard (at the moment it's 33 knots). My problem is that the wind vane gear in its present condition will not steer in strong winds. I sat up most of the night steering or helping the vane gear. I was caught with one reef and had a dodgy time running forward to put in the second reef while helping the vane gear. After some fiddling, I got the vane gear to steer a poor course and had a short nap. This morning the wind increased, and the overtaking clouds began to look ominous, so I put in the third reef with the usual struggle. I tore the luff along one panel of the main, and the halyard is fouled around a couple of the mast steps.

SERVANT IV has taken the lead from CITY KIDS. SERVANT's runs the past few days have been 221, 225, and 279. Very impressive. There is a nasty sea running all out of proportion to the time the wind has been strong.

Without an autopilot I am losing about 50 miles a day. I must try to do better.

<u>1024.</u>   I poled out about ¼ of the small genoa (the pole was already in place) which balances the triple-reefed mainsail. Last night we passed a couple of miles south of a large northbound ship. A tanker or bulk carrier.

<u>1326.</u>   At noon we showed 160 miles in the last 24 hours— 1,500 miles to go to Cape Town. The current wind is SW 22. Our course is poor—about 100° instead of 130°, but there isn't much I can do. The poor vane is hard pressed. The next step is to put up the double-reefed main, but the halyard is fouled. It's impossible to think of climbing the mast in these seas. I had better let her go (ENE true) and make up the southing later. The seas look a little easier, and I have unrolled more of the genoa. A black-browed albatross is circling us.

<u>1345.</u>   We're down to 32°S. and the weather is getting cooler. Last night I wore a shirt, trousers, boots, sweater, and oilskins. Many birds. Pintado petrels (with their unmistakable black and white spotted wings) and two small albatrosses.

<u>2217.</u>   A brutal night with water flying all over the place.

OCTOBER 28, 1990. (SUNDAY). DAY 43.

<u>0209.</u>   Wind SW 26 knots. The mother and father of all squalls just went through. I've stopped wearing some fancy foul-weather trousers I was given because the zipper jams on the fly every time I use the zipper. I wonder who designed such clothing? Back to old faithful yellow Helly-Hansen.

Considering the wind, we're doing well on our latitude and have held the same figure since noon yesterday. We still have 108 miles of southing to make to Slangkop Point south of Cape Town, but we have 28°08′ of longitude to do it. The weather is getting colder all the time.

<u>0700.</u>   Unrolled more of the genoa and put a half tank of water ballast to windward.

<u>0756.</u>   Hard going. We're reaching to the east across large seas from the SW. We're not pounding, fortunately, but the motion is severe. I wear my oilskins while cooking so I won't scald myself. Speaking of cooking, I'm not doing much. In any case, after 43 days at sea my menu choices are limited.

Last night I got cold so I put on thermal underwear tops and bottoms and the light Musto foul-weather bottoms. The modern clothing is wonderful, and I soon warmed up. For breakfast I had a cheese and onion omelet although it would hardly have passed *Cordon Bleu* standards. I'm down to 6 or 8 large crackers which I would like to eat but am trying to ration (one per day). The perfect seagoing cracker is a toasted wheat "crispbread" called Wasa. From Sweden. Excellent stuff.

I'm reading a book called *25 Centuries of Sea Warfare* by Jacques Mordal. Well done, but the battles are often so vast and hazy that the reader never gets close to the officers and sailors, which makes for somewhat sterile reading. Of course the writing job for the historian is not easy because he probably has only limited second- or third-hand material. Certainly the naval battles of the ancient world seem impossibly remote. I'm beginning to realize that Greece and Rome were really very small civilizations. I know almost nothing about early Japan, China, or Africa. I wonder how the Roman empire compared in size with the Incas or Aztecs, or even the Indian nations of North America? A nice subject for a book.

<u>1042.</u>   Wind SSW 18–22 knots. Course 95–120°M. I ran off downwind for a few minutes to put away the starboard spinnaker pole. Now we're reaching across big seas with a reefed main and part of the jib. Heeled 20°–30° with a half tank of water ballast to starboard.

I've been looking at pintado petrels, soft-plumaged petrels, Elliot's storm petrels, and a few black-browed albatrosses. Trying to identify a large brown bird with a yellow beak and white around the eye. Either a sooty albatross, a northern petrel, or a white-chinned petrel.

SERVANT IV is now in the lead by 61 miles. Fourteen yachts are still out.

<u>1310.</u>   I've been listening to the fellows (and Isabelle) talking about broken autopilots, repairs to rigging, a collapsed gooseneck, instrument failures, ripped sails—everyone in the race has something wrong. The winner has the best solutions, but even to finish you need to be clever. We're a bunch of ragtag mechanics.

<u>1326.</u>   Wind dropping. Seas less. Barometer very high—1029 mb. I suspect that in a few hours the wind and seas will be gone. Then up the mast to deal with the main halyard.

<u>1521.</u>   I spoke to Will Oxley on KNOTS, a new Swan 53 on her way to Sydney via Cape Town. KNOTS was at 33°28'S., 28°39'W. Will and his brother are taking the new family yacht to Australia. With steaks, booze, and pretty girls.

<u>1709.</u>   The sky is covered with low puffy stratus. Wind south 17 knots. Going 7.8 knots with 3 reefs in the main and a partially reefed jib, plus a full ballast tank to windward. Still a sizable sea running from the SW. We continue to struggle south. The wind is cold.

I've been watching a black-browed albatross as he flies around and around the yacht. He hardly ever flaps a wing, yet has splendid control over his flight. About his only wing movement is a bit of trembling when he does a vertical bank and wheels close to a wave top. Sometimes the big white bird comes within 10 or 15 feet of the ship as he circles low. Then we both look at one another. Each studies the stranger. Who, I wonder, is the smarter or wiser? No doubt the albatross because he is home. I'm the intruder.

<u>1827.</u>   I can see the most delicate shade of blue—the palest turquoise—through a small opening in the clouds. I had a long talk with Robin Davie, who sounded a little lonely.

OCTOBER 29, 1990. (MONDAY). DAY 44.

<u>0044.</u>   A marvelous sleep. Seas down. Wind south 16 knots, but fitful and gusty. We have been logging 7.7 knots for some hours, but have slowed to only 3.3. I'm putting up more canvas.

<u>0146.</u>   Wind south 10–16 knots. Jib down. Genoa up. Cool, settled weather except for the fluky wind (in speed, not direction). Keeping headed a little south is a problem because when the vane eases off we creep northward. The sky is covered with stratus except for a few chinks that let moonlight through.

<u>0800.</u>   Becalmed. A marginal breakfast of eggs (poor), Vienna sausage (terrible), and sauerkraut (abysmal).

<u>1300.</u>   Still no wind; 143 miles at noon. At daylight I tried to lower the mainsail to clear the halyard, but I discovered that the loose slide below the headboard was jammed between the headboard and the mast. It was impossible to lower the sail. I didn't want to take off all the slides so I climbed the mast, knocked the jammed slide loose with a big screwdriver and—to keep it out of mischief—lashed the loose slide to the next slide lower down. Doing this aloft was hard because I needed one hand to hold on. After what seemed an eternity aloft, I managed to tie the two slides together. Even in the dying wind the yacht rolled heavily, and I bashed my forehead on a mast step and bled all over the place. What a business!
 When I get to Cape Town I will have a sailmaker remove the headboard and replace it with a stainless steel ring. Headboards are nothing but trouble and expense.
 During the calm was a good time to change the leads of the mainsail reefing pendants. Before the race we rove the pendants so that both parts came down on one side of the sail. This seemed a better lead, but the lines tended to jam on the boom, and chafe at the clew was a problem. I have changed the pendants so that one part is on each side of the sail. In other words a line goes up one side of the sail and comes down on the other.
 The shape of the mainsail is poor. What used to be "my beautiful spare mainsail" is now simply "the old main."

<u>1800.</u>   Still becalmed. Busy cleaning the galley. I took up the filthy galley floorboards and scrubbed and sanded them. One needed a little planing for a better fit.

My hands are sore from 45 days of line handling and saltwater exposure. I use Neosporin ointment on every little cut and a lot of hand lotion. I must keep my hands in shape.

OCTOBER 30, 1990. (TUESDAY). DAY 45.

<u>0153.</u>   Wind west, 6 knots. We're gliding along on a perfectly flat sea. Never have I trimmed the sails and adjusted the steering vane so carefully.

<u>0212.</u>   We've made 6 miles south since the wind came up. Amazing that the water gurgling along the hull woke me. A mother with her child! Yesterday I switched water tanks, hoping that the starboard tank water would be good for tea, coffee, and general drinking. Alas, the water has the same bad taste as the port tank.

Yesterday (after many attempts) I got through to the West Virginia radio station for the schoolchildren broadcast, but the telephone was apparently set for fax receptions. Nobody answered.

<u>0611.</u>   I notice that when I wake up from a deep sleep and rush out to the cockpit and need to make a decision, I usually do the wrong thing. It's better to wait a few minutes before doing anything of consequence.

Just now we're at 32°31'S. I hope to stay on this course until I get to 34°09'S., another 98 miles. This will put me directly west of my landfall target in South Africa.

<u>0652.</u>   I have begun to notice a swell from the SW. I tuned into the African Mobile Maritime ham net and could dimly hear Alistair Campbell's wife and catch a word now and then. No one heard me when I called. I intend to hook up the spare ICOM-M700 single sideband radio (stored in a locker beside me) in Cape Town.

<u>0805.</u>   A little more wind. When I eased the main halyard to put in the first reef, the sail came down easily (hooray), now that the headboard is free. Also the reefing pendants no longer jam in the boom sheaves.

Sky gray and overcast. Low stratus with jagged edges. Cooler and a temperature that suits me (60°F. in the cabin—a number hard to believe). Nevertheless when I'm outside, a jacket and warm trousers feel good.

I have been over-tensioning the main halyard. With less tension, the shape of the mainsail is better.

<u>1210.</u>   Only 66 miles at noon today because of yesterday's calms. Wind backing. Now NW 17 knots. I repaired and re-rove the three reefing pendants on the main boom to finish yesterday's efforts.

I heard on the radio that DURACELL (Mike Plant), JARKAN (Kanga Birtles), and ECUREUIL (Isabelle Autissier) have arrived in Cape Town. Seven Class 1 yachts have now finished. Isabelle reported that her generator failed the first day out of Newport. Her solar panels produced only enough electricity for her autopilot for 12 hours a day so she steered the other 12 hours.

<u>1411.</u>   Wind north, 20 knots. I put a new self-pricking needle in one of the burners on the Primus stove.

<u>1530.</u>   I spoke to the bulk ore carrier ENSOR, an orange-colored Belgian ship bound from Brazil to Japan with a load of iron ore. A friendly officer on watch. A crew of 25.

<u>2119.</u>   About 1700, the wind began to blow hard from the north. I gybed the rig and headed SE (continuing a little south as advised by everyone). A line of squalls was coming toward us, and already we were overpowered. I put in a second reef, and at 30 knots I rolled up the headsail entirely. I know it's a crazy statement, but the winds south of 30°S. seem extra solid and strong and often wail in the rigging.

While I was kneeling behind the mast, cranking the reefing winch, a wall of water about two feet high roared down the side deck. I was wearing the blue and red Lirakis safety harness that Eric Swenson gave me after the 1979 trans-Atlantic race. The harness kept me tied to the yacht, and at that moment I felt very kindly toward Eric for his gift.

OCTOBER 31, 1990. (WEDNESDAY). DAY 46.

<u>0128.</u>   A squally night with light rain. The wind vane started out nicely, but as the wind (NE 25–30) and seas built up, the yacht would get swung around by a sea, and the vane wasn't strong enough to pull the vessel back on course. I had to help the vane every 10 minutes or so. I began to get wet and cold and gradually put on more and more clothing.

Since we're a little south of Cape Town, I'm trying to head more east. While I was writing just now, I realized that the vane brought the yacht back on course. Maybe my tinkering with the vane lines is paying off.

The local wisdom is to go a little south to stay out of the calms of the South Atlantic high-pressure area. All the yachts that have finished so far have come in from 35° or 36°S. At the moment we're at 34°22'S.

<u>0811.</u>   A long night with a lot of hand steering. We were down to just a double-reefed mainsail, but the vane couldn't handle it. Water was flying all over the place, and I had my hands full. At dawn—when I could see something—I began to plan how to drop the mainsail and still keep control of the yacht. Unfortunately it blew harder than ever (NE 36 knots). I hooked up the vane, ran forward, and pulled down the third reef (which leaves a tiny sail because the reef is extra deep). The difference in SEBAGO was hard to believe. The intractable, impossible-to-control vessel suddenly became docile and responsive. Her speed at the moment is 7.3 knots. Will I ever learn that this yacht cannot stand to be overcanvassed?

I think the weather will improve because a heavy squall and hard rain (a weather front?) passed us an hour ago. Everything is wet including the captain who is also very sleepy. I can hardly believe that I've used the third reef twice on this passage.

<u>1030.</u>   The wind has veered to the NNW and dropped to 19 knots. I've shaken out the third reef and poled out half of the genoa.

<u>1215.</u>   The French are exuberant because of their placings in the first leg of the race. In Class 1, GROUPE SCETA is first, GENERALI CONCORDE is third, and CRÉDIT AGRICOLE is fourth. (John Martin of South Africa in ALLIED BANK was second.) Yesterday Yves Dupasquier finished first in Class 2 in SERVANT IV, so the French have done very well.

In Class 1, Alain Gautier in GENERALI CONCORDE actually finished first, but was dropped to third because he was given a 16½ hour penalty for arriving late in Newport prior to the start. The rules clearly stated that all contestants had to be in Newport at a certain date in order for the yachts to be checked. Everyone had arrived on time except Gautier.

At the skippers' meeting before the race he argued that the rule about the time limit was illegal and unfair and that the race was between boats, not rules. Gautier was clever, and his arguments were spirited. However I thought his logic was unreal, and the other captains must have thought so too because when a vote was taken whether to support the rules (which had been published three years earlier), Gautier lost 24–1.

<u>2011.</u>   Wind up and down all afternoon. Third reef in and out again. Storm over, and a clear sky at last. Wind WNW 17 knots. I'm pooped after the gale and the steering difficulties. The lack of an autopilot cost us a lot of miles. One of the vane mounts has lost its mounting bolt. I tried to fit a new bolt, but darkness overtook me. I will try in the morning. I have just eaten (macaroni and cheese, half a grapefruit, tea) and now must sleep. I hope tonight will be peaceful.

<u>2244.</u>   Squall. Handed jib. Full moon. Less than 1,000 miles to go. Many white-chinned petrels around us.

NOVEMBER 1, 1990. (THURSDAY). DAY 47.

<u>0142.</u>   More wind (west, 32 knots). Gybed to starboard tack. Third reef. Vane barely coping. Ominous clouds astern. I'm falling asleep.

<u>0919.</u>   A bright sunny day. Big seas and a variable WSW-SW wind of 18–26 knots. I had a good sleep and dealt with the bolts in the steering vane mounts. One bolt was gone, and 3 others were loose. Took down the port spinnaker pole, tidied up the lines, and put up the starboard pole. I have 3 reefs in the main and about 10 feet of the clew of the genoa poled out to weather. A fair wind, and I was down to only 6 knots!

<u>1543.</u>   Had a nap, ate some wretched packaged macaroni and cheddar cheese, and have been picking up the cabin. The other night during a crisis, one of the tool drawers came out and upset. At the time all I could do was to put the tools in the wastebasket. I have finally sorted and oiled the tools and put them away.

Yesterday I was not only tired but wet, cold, hungry, and dispirited. I kept making stupid mistakes. Tying lines wrong and taking ages to change lead blocks, etc. I forced myself to put on warm clothing and to eat a hot meal. Today I am 100% better, but of course I have slept, eaten, and have both the sun and a fair wind.

<u>2300.</u>   The outer end fitting of the spinnaker pole opened and the sheet came adrift. Suddenly there was a great flapping. I wound up the sail, dropped the pole, rove the sheet, and set everything again. The moon was almost full, and I was able to see surprisingly well.

NOVEMBER 2, 1990. (FRIDAY). DAY 48.

<u>0906.</u>   I am so frustrated I could scream. Fair winds and no way to use the wonderful running qualities of SEBAGO. In desperation I have been looking over the autopilots to see if I can put one together from the wreckage of two. The barometer is rising (1019 mb.).

<u>0925.</u>   In spite of a few squalls, the air is incredibly clear, and I can see for miles. The blue of the sky to the south has the most delicate tint of azure. Simply lovely. Albatrosses, white-throated petrels, and storm petrels are flying around us.

<u>1205.</u>   A little excitement. Hoping to get an autopilot working I installed a new electric motor in one of the drive units. The disassembly is tedious and greasy, but I eventually got the old motor out and found that it didn't work! I quickly put in a new motor and rushed to install the unit. As soon as I connected the last wire I switched on the unit. Nothing. What a disappointment!

<u>1213.</u>   Day's run, 146 miles. The weather is gorgeous again—a deep blue sky and puffy clouds. The temperature is pleasantly cool (two blankets when I sleep). The wind is dead aft, and I'm steering south of my target. I'm afraid of getting stuck in the high-pressure area that trapped three of the Class 1 boats. I've been warned by everyone to stay south. But how far south? I'll go to 35°S. (another 6 miles) and then gybe for the target.

<u>1553.</u>   On deck for 4 hours. I gybed the rig, reeved a new #1 reefing pendant, dealt with a chafed jib sheet, and reefed the main.

<u>2053.</u>   The poor wind vane is pressed to its limit and the water blade thumps against the vane mount with great bangs. I leaned over the transom and tightened the mounts, which appear to be OK. The problem is that the vane copes with the steering demands, but when the vessel gets knocked off course by a wave, the vane doesn't have enough power to return the yacht to her proper course.

<u>2321.</u>   Squalls and hand steering. I am beginning to feel a bit daffy after 7 weeks at sea. It's cooler tonight, and I've put on the second layer of Musto clothing. We're rolling heavily with a light wind from almost dead astern. I will change course a little.

NOVEMBER 3, 1990. (SATURDAY). DAY 49.

<u>1100.</u>   Only 620 miles to Cape Town. I gybed early this morning and did a few rigging chores. Several rain showers upset the

wind, but now it's back, and the sky is clear except for a few small puffy cumulus clouds. Read Somerset Maugham yesterday. Surprising how Maugham and Graham Greene resemble one another in their novels *The Narrow Corner* and *The Quiet American*. Great stuff. I tried a cup of hot chocolate, but the taste of the bad water even comes through the chocolate.

<u>1237.</u>   My hands are sore and swollen from line hauling. I am trying to wear gloves when I work on deck.

<u>1647.</u>   In 7 weeks, sailing mostly to windward, I reckon that 85% of my sailing has been with the mainsail and jib. I've used spinnakers for a day or two, the 165% genoa for three days, and the small genoa (currently bent on) for perhaps three days. I've not had the heavy forestaysail up at all because of the water ballast and the easy-to-reef jib. The asymmetrical spinnakers and the 165% genoas are close in area, but the genoa is much easier to use because it's on a roller furling gear. Also the genoa is useful for both a wider sailing angle and wind range because its luff is on a wire and the material is heavier (3.8-oz. vs. ¾-oz.). I can carry the sail in up to 16 knots of apparent wind, which means we can go to windward at 7 knots in 9 knots of true wind. Plus the genoa is effective poled out. Additionally, the large genoa is preferable to a spinnaker in light winds because the genoa won't wrap around the various headstays (a constant hazard with spinnakers and a terrible problem for singlehanders). We could do without the forestaysail, two asymmetrical spinnakers, and one jib (we have three on board) which would get rid of four heavy bags.

I've been speaking with Robin Davie on GLOBAL EXPOSURE. Robin has 35-knot easterlies (at 36°S. 6°W.), about 600 miles west of us. I spoke with KNOTS which has easterlies in the same area.

<u>1847.</u>   I put a new burner on the stove. Complicated because the burner (threaded on the inside) screws on to an externally threaded nipple. The scheme should be changed to an internally threaded nipple because the present scheme automatically shuts off the fuel if you tighten the burner too much. Dumb!

NOVEMBER 4, 1990. (SUNDAY). DAY 50.

<u>0308.</u>   Cooler, and a wind shift to the south. Starboard pole down. One reef in the main and the full jib. We're gliding along on a flat sea with the Southern Cross high in the sky to the south.

The moon is high and to port, a giant searchlight on everything. The wind strength is not steady, and as it changes, the wind vane heads up or bears off.

0707.   The sky is almost clear of clouds, and the sun is warm and yellow. A slight westerly swell, and not a whitecap in sight. Occasionally we pass two or three white-throated petrels (cape hens) resting on the water and clucking softly to one another. Am I sailing into the windless high? The barometer reads 1022 mb. We have 535 miles to go to Cape Town.

1100.   Both KNOTS and GLOBAL EXPOSURE behind me to the west report easterly winds up to 45 knots, which suggests that they're on the NW quadrant of a high (the big South Atlantic high?). I'm afraid we're going to be overtaken by this problem. What we want is to be on the S, SE, or E quadrant of the high, which should bring NW, W, or SW winds. The high should be north of us, definitely not south.

At the moment our wind is SE 4 knots. The barometer is unchanged. The cloud base is thickening. I suppose I should cook something before the banging starts.

1725.   Wind SE 12–14 knots. One reef in the main, and the jib instead of the genoa. A wandering albatross with a wingspan of about 11 feet circled around while I dealt with the sails.

1813.   A lot of low stratus around the horizon. I just had a meal of rice and tomato chicken, which was excellent. I like the pouch meals prepared by Yurika.

2100.   Wind SSE 18–21 knots. Second reef in main; I wound up much of jib. To get hit with the north end of a high-pressure area this far south is unthinkable. This high should be hundreds of miles north. Famous last words.

NOVEMBER 5, 1990. (MONDAY). DAY 51.

0212.   Not a nice night. Heeled 20°–25° with a SE wind of 23 knots. Two reefs in the main and much of the jib rolled up. I strained my right shoulder a little, and whenever I reach high for something—ouch! The vane is holding the course OK.

0518.   It's chilly, so I have put on more clothes.

0839.   A howling southeaster. No doubt Table Mountain in Cape Town has a white streamer on its summit. Here on SEBAGO, water is flying everywhere—even inside the cabin entry. I think the storm is going to get worse, so I rolled up the 110% jib and hoisted the hanked storm jib. This little sail is well made, with wire pendants at the head and tack, and sets nicely. The day is bright and sunny and the barometer is climbing (1027 mb.) so I hope the high moves north. If only the wind direction would change. We have 381 miles to go to Cape Town.

I made some hot noodles (ramen) for breakfast. The fresh water is ghastly, with large bits of gray stuff floating around. I'm still alive so the contamination must be non-fatal. Where has the bad water come from? When I filled the tanks in Newport? From the plastic tanks? From the plastic hoses connecting the system? From saltwater contamination?

My hands are much better after wearing gloves for several days. I discovered a perfect apple (oh so juicy and delicious!) in one of the galley lockers. This morning I saw a different sort of albatross. Large. Brown on top. No eye bands. Grayish-white underneath the wings, with black wing tips. A juvenile wandering albatross, according to the Harrison bird book.

0943.   The wind dropped to 19 knots. The yacht pivoted on a sea and hove herself to. I pulled on my oilskins and started to set more sail, but by the time I had SEBAGO back on course, the wind was up to 26 knots. I set about 6 feet of the clew of the jib. We now have part of the jib, the storm jib, and the double-reefed main. I see that Yukoh Tada (KODEN VIII) has only 55 miles to go. to Cape Town.

1401.   I am on the latitude of Cape Town trying to go east into strong southeasterlies. The best course I can make is about 090°M. or 067°T. or ENE. However, with leeway and the Benguela Current (which sets NW at a rate of 0.5 to 2 knots), I am probably going NE (or worse). The knotmeter reads 6.5.

1430.   Wind SE 32 knots (prediction 40). Barometer 1027 mb. A bright sun and a sparkling, bubbling sea. In spite of the water ballast we're over at 30°. I have dropped the storm jib and am essentially hove to, although this sort of vessel always keeps going at 2–3 knots. I decided that bashing into the big seas generated by the SE gale was not only stupid but dangerous, because waves were breaking right over the vessel and she was pounding heavily. If stopped we would continue to be set north, but at a slower rate. I'll wait for an improvement in the wind direction or wind strength. I'm trying to minimize any miles made to the north so I don't have to work south against the Benguela Current.

<u>1830.</u>   SE wind 22–29 knots. Seas perhaps less. Storm jib up and we're pressing on. The little storm jib pulls surprisingly well. The yacht seems to be standing up to the pounding, although I must admit that I have reviewed the liferaft options, the ditch kit, and the rubber survival suit. Now for some sleep. SEBAGO will have to look after herself. Good night world.

<u>2008.</u>   In 1½ hours, we've gone 4½ miles north and 10 miles east. Is it worth it?

<u>2047.</u>   Wind SE 33 knots. Jib down again. A big difference in motion and strain on the vessel.

NOVEMBER 6, 1990. (TUESDAY). DAY 52.

<u>0402.</u>   A small leak appeared around the portlight above the oilskin locker and threatened the electrical system. Between waves I opened the portlight, quickly smeared Vaseline along the neoprene seal of the portlight, and screwed it shut.

<u>0629.</u>   Two large waves broke heavily on board. A good thing I was not on deck. I must wear my safety harness when I go outside.

<u>1056.</u>   The forecast from Cape Town predicts more SE weather. The wind is the same (SE 29). The sky has cleared somewhat, and now and then I can see the sun. The motion is severe, and when I move around the cabin I lurch from handhold to handhold. I gave myself a partial sponge bath and managed to shave. The narrow head compartment is good in this weather because I can wedge myself with my body and knees while I use my hands to wash or brush my teeth.

Every once in a while a wave breaks over the vessel. Fortunately none have been as nasty as those two early this morning when water even squirted through the portlights. This passage has certainly been different from 1986 when I had light westerlies.

<u>1233.</u>   Bright sun. Wave period 8–9 seconds.

<u>1538.</u>   Message from Will Oxley on KNOTS: "We now have N and NE winds." Will's weather chart suggests that the high is moving SE, so I should get a northerly airflow.

<u>1818.</u>   Wind SE 35 knots. Noise and motion terrible below. Time to reduce sail. I dressed in oilskins, put on body and soul lashings, slipped into my safety harness, and went outside. I estimated the seas to be 20–22 ft. I turned the vane so we swung to port (I helped with the tiller).

As soon as the vane had control, I hurried forward and eased the main halyard. (The yacht was close to gybing, but the port vang tackle held the boom.) I hauled down on the luff line, belayed it, put a tie through the luff reefing cringle to the mast, and began to crank in the leech reefing pendant. A long pull with the sail full of wind. Then I tidied up the lines, rushed back to the cockpit since we were tearing along downwind *away* from Cape Town, and swung the yacht back on the wind. The motion of the vessel is immeasurably easier. I hope this extra spurt of wind is the last gasp of the gale.

Outside there are long cigar-shaped rolls of clouds running north and south like lines on a chart. The clouds remind me of pampero clouds in the Rio de la Plata in Argentina.

NOVEMBER 7, 1990. (WEDNESDAY). DAY 53.

<u>0137.</u>   Wind south 26 knots. I can stand in the cockpit without water flying into my face.

<u>0240.</u>   Progress! I hoisted the storm jib, and we're going along at 5.3 knots on a course of 100°M. It's funny how hesitant a sailor is to put up canvas after heavy weather. "Just a lull," he will say, or "I had better wait a while." This just masks apprehension. You've got to get sail up right away. This improves the drive of the vessel and helps her motion. Once she begins pushing toward her goal again, the crew is reassured, and life gets back to normal.

At the moment our course is rotten (100° instead of 150°), but at least we're headed for South Africa. A clear sky with a waning moon to port; the Southern Cross is high to starboard.

<u>0813.</u>   Barometer 1014 mb. Big improvement in the weather. I have handed the storm jib, set the double-reefed mainsail, and unrolled half of the jib. Wind SE 18 knots, but there's still a big sea running. We may have to tack to get south. For the moment we will continue toward the ENE. I must not forget the Benguela Current.

<u>1018.</u>   Second reef out. Heavy chafe on the #2 reefing pendant. I pulled through more of the pendant and retied the running bowline farther up the line. Then I trimmed off the ruined part and whipped the end.

<u>1104.</u>   Clear and sunny. Hazy toward the NW. Tiny puffy clouds toward the north. According to a Cape Town forecast I should have NW winds of 10–20 knots at noon.

<u>1139.</u>   The speedometer reads 5 knots. Yet with this wind (SE 16) we should be going 7–8. I checked the impeller, which was OK. Are we dragging a fish net? I wish I knew our true speed over the bottom.* The sky astern looks strange. Sort of a hazy white.

<u>1423.</u>   Sailing well with the full jib, one reef in the main, and a tank of water ballast to starboard. The wind is south 12–13 knots, and our heading is 125°M. The apparent wind is 17 knots. Normally we would be making about 7.5 knots. I reckon we have a 1.5-knot current against us because we show only 5.8–6 knots over the ground.

   We have 221 miles to go, but we're never going to make it on this tack with this wind. Should we tack now or go closer inshore? Normally current along a coastline increases toward shore unless you are very close, when there is a counter-current (and rocks). The wind was supposed to have gone around to the NW at 1200 today. What to do? The starboard tack—the one we're on—is the better tack, and we may get a favorable wind shift. All this shows the wisdom of keeping 50 or 100 miles to the south when approaching Cape Town from the west.

<u>1744.</u>   I've been watching a sunset of six long streaks of clouds that drift together, float apart, and then slowly merge again. When separate, these layers of low stratus are golden-orange; when together, they're blood-red. So lovely to see; so hard to describe.

   The wind is dropping, and the sea is gradually smoothing out. The full main is up, and I'm about to set the genoa. Some difference from yesterday.

<u>2000.</u>   Can you believe it? We're becalmed. I've got the hatches open to air things out. I'm cooking a big meal.

NOVEMBER 8, 1990. (THURSDAY). DAY 54.

<u>0100.</u>   A trifling zephyr from the north, but not enough to make her go in this swell. A ship to starboard.

<u>0418.</u>   Only 191 miles to Cape Town. Wind north 17 knots. I have set up the running rig, and we're sailing at 7.5 knots on a course of 140°M. I replaced the lower starboard mounting bolt on the wind vane gear and tightened the port bolt. These bolts should be wired in place.

---

* The GPS instrument should have given the speed over the ground (SOG), but the readouts were unsatisfactory. I suspect the software was not perfected at that time or it could have had something to do with the satellites, which were just coming on stream.

I'm holding my breath that this wind will hold. No more gales, please.

<u>0858.</u>   A busy morning. The wind veered to the NW and increased to 21 knots. I put in one reef and then gybed the rig. The vane couldn't handle the yacht when we surfed ahead on a wave, so after we rounded up 4 or 5 times I put in a second reef. Now we're on course (150°M.) and going nicely.

Unfortunately I had to climb the mast to free the mainsail luff from a mast step. (A sail slide had come off and when the halyard was eased to reef, the loose luff hooked on a step.) During a lull I hurried up the mast. Never have I gone up and down so quickly.

The failure of the vane to handle the yacht in these conditions is maddening. However with a reef in the poled-out jib and two reefs in the main we're going OK. At least there's no pounding. I've headed a little more south than east. We must reach the latitude of Cape Town before the SE winds and current defeat us.

<u>1312.</u>   The weather is gray and murky; wind NW 12 knots. Full main and jib. Although I can receive perfectly on the SSB radio, I'm unable to transmit to Cape Town from a distance of 150 miles.

<u>1500.</u>   I finished *25 Centuries of Sea Warfare* by Jacques Mordal. Well written and impeccably researched. A good book.

<u>1604.</u>   I'm seeing cape gannets which are found only in the seas around South Africa.

<u>2118.</u>   A little more wind, so I put in the first reef. Watching this hull slip along at 7–8 knots always amazes me. Particularly with small sails. I am convinced this yacht can be a winner. What she needs is a more easily handled mainsail, one that can be reefed without all the pendants and cranking. If I were starting over again I would take a long look at the Hood roller-reefing boom system. I considered it and rejected the scheme because of the luff arrangement above the tack of the sail. However I haven't lived with the system, which may be OK or capable of being improved. Perhaps one could carry a second mainsail as a backup.

<u>2130.</u>   We're 48 miles offshore and 91 miles NW of Cape Town. I have been watching a fishing trawler two miles to port.

NOVEMBER 9, 1990. (FRIDAY). DAY 55.

<u>0505.</u>   Suddenly lots of birds. Black-browed albatrosses in little groups on the water. Two northbound ships—one named

MARABOUT—and three fishing boats in sight. Low clouds and rain showers. My target is SE and the barometer is rising, so I am trying to get south as fast as possible. To reach the latitude of the finish line I need to go to 33°53'S. I am at 33°31'S, so I need 22 miles of southing.

0626.   The course to the finish line is 135°M. I am trying to steer 140° because of the north-setting current.

0642.   CAPE PRINCE, a sleek cargo vessel, passed inshore going north. Lots of cape gannets flying around. Big, comical-looking birds.

0830.   I called the BOC office at 0815. An answering service operator took my message: "SEBAGO will arrive today at 1230Z."

I just saw a seal, and cape gannets are everywhere. Low clouds and a chilly wind. When I called Cape Town radio on the VHF radio, an operator answered instantly. How nice to have a radio that works!

0843.   I'm getting excited about finishing and have put on some clean clothes. What a shock to wear a good shirt and to run around the deck without bulky oilskins. I feel like a Sunday sailor.

1500.   As I approached Cape Town I put up an asymmetrical spinnaker to starboard. However the wind kept veering aft, and I eventually took it down. I started to put up a big red, white, and blue conventional spinnaker and realized that the wind had gone around to the WSW so I hoisted the pole to starboard and hoisted the chute to port.

I was thrilled to see Cape Town come into view. First the tops of Table Mountain, Lions Head, and the peaks of the Twelve Apostles to the south. Then green hills, the tallest buildings, houses and shorelines, and finally dots and ants that grew into automobiles and joggers. The air was clear, and the city sparkled in the warm sun. My wind grew lighter and veered until I had the pole against the headstay.

About a mile from Cape Town the breeze went around to the south. Just as I was dropping the spinnaker, a photographer's launch came rushing up. There were 20 people on deck. I recognized Margaret, Mark and Michele Schrader, Don and Margie McIntyre, Kanga Birtles, and Josh and Laura Hall. Everyone was waving. I dropped the spinnaker and the pole, tidied up the lines, and—sailing nicely with the mainsail and genoa—hurried across the finish line at about 1340. Everybody cheered and clapped. The moment was wonderful.

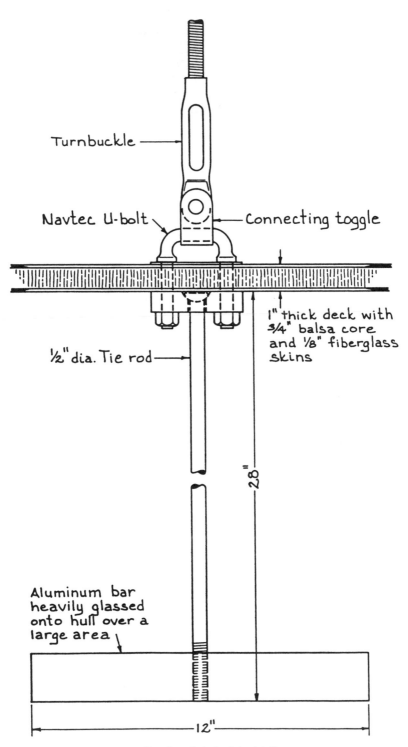

Turnbuckle

Navtec U-bolt

Connecting toggle

1" thick deck with ¾" balsa core and ⅛" fiberglass skins

½" dia. Tie rod

28"

Aluminum bar heavily glassed onto hull over a large area

12"

Drawing of chainplate detail.

CHAPTER THREE

Fifteen Days of Repairs

I was in Cape Town for 15 days. The Sebago company had given Margaret an airline ticket, and it was wonderful to be with her. We stayed with some dear friends—Ken and Fay MacLachlan—at their lovely home in St. James, a little town on the south coast that faced False Bay and the Southern Ocean. At night from our bedroom we could see the winking light on Cape Point—the extremity of the Cape of Good Hope. The next stop south was Antarctica.

St. James was a 40-minute drive from Cape Town, so we rented a little car to get around and to go shopping. Every day we drove to the Royal Cape Yacht Club on the Cape Town waterfront where the 21 BOC yachts were tied up.

My first job was to deal with SEBAGO's chainplates and to get the sailing rig in order.

The mast received its side support from the shrouds—three wires on each side that were connected to large upside-down U-bolts (see sketch). The two threaded fingers of each U-bolt went through the deck and were held underneath with nuts tightened against aluminum blocks. Tie rods (½″ dia.) 28″ long ran from the aluminum blocks downward to anchor points on the hull. Each anchor point was a 1¾″ dia. 12″ long horizontal aluminum bar that was fiberglassed to the hull over a large area. The arrangement was designed so that in theory the decks "floated" while the real shroud loads were taken by the hull anchor points. All of this had been set up and arranged by designer-builder Bill Lee in California. I had never touched any of it.

Before the race I asked Lee whether the chainplates were strong enough for the additional loads from the water ballast system. Lee replied that he regularly sailed with 15 people (say 2,400 pounds) sitting on the weather rail. Although the water ballast tank loads (3,500 pounds) were 45 percent more than Lee's live ballast, he assured me that the chainplates were amply strong.

Since two of the U-bolts had broken during the voyage south from Newport, I decided to examine the entire system. I began by taking off the 3 starboard shrouds, unscrewing the tie rods, and removing the U-bolts and aluminum blocks. I found that the balsa core deck was deformed, the balsa was soaked with sea water, and the aluminum blocks were severely corroded.

I immediately hired a prominent South African naval architect named Angelo Lavranos, and engaged an expert metal fabricator. One of the contestants in the BOC was Kanga Birtles who was a veteran boatbuilder in Australia. Kanga had a local friend who was a metallurgist. My friends Otto Kindlimann and Ken MacLachlan offered to coordinate everything.

On my second morning in Cape Town the seven of us had a meeting aboard SEBAGO. Angelo quickly designed a new chainplate structure, a more conventional arrangement without U-bolts. The metal fabricator agreed to build the chainplates, and the metallurgist found some special stainless steel (grade 316-L). We all agreed that the watersoaked core around the chainplate areas should be filled with solid fiberglass.

I started the repairs immediately. One of my helpers ground off a tapered oval area about 8"x 12" in the fiberglass at the top of the balsa core sandwich. Then we dug out the balsa down to the lower part of the sandwich. After everything was clean, dry, and well sanded, we laid up solid fiberglass in epoxy resin to the top of the deck. Meanwhile the new chainplates were made, one for each side. We quickly installed the chainplates, screwed down the tie rods, and connected the shrouds.

As soon as I arrived in Cape Town I had a mechanic check over the generator engine, which had been running poorly. The mechanic found that the head gasket was partially blown, which allowed a little water to enter the cylinders. The mechanic resurfaced the cylinder head block, ground the engine valves, replaced the head gasket, and soon had the engine running smoothly. He also repaired the alternator bracket.

Meanwhile Andy Mitchell, the local North sailmaker, replaced the broken full-length battens in my new mainsail with three-quarter length battens that began at the leech and went forward. The shorter battens—tapered fiberglass fishing poles—were held at the forward ends with special lashings. I had never seen battens used this way and had grave doubts about the scheme.

Although the battens didn't arrive until the last minute, I insisted on sea trials. We went out on a blustery day and found that when we eased the halyard for a reef, the forward ends of the battens (which stuck out an inch or two from the lashings) caught in the lower shrouds. I thought this arrangement was terrible, and when we got back to the dock I told Andy to come up with some-

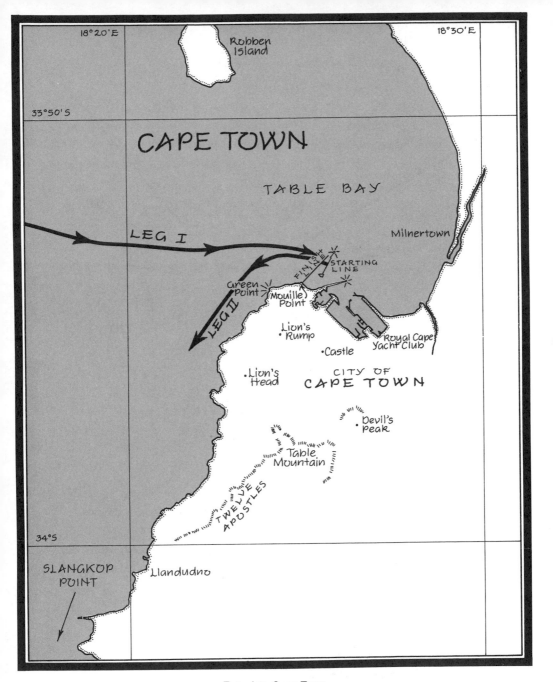

Entry into Cape Town.

thing better. He replaced the fishing poles with conventional short battens which scarcely supported the exaggerated roach of the new mainsails. Since the race was about to resume, the only thing I could do was to bend on the old mainsail.

While all this was going on, radio experts from a company called SMD tried to get the Japanese SSB radio to work properly. I

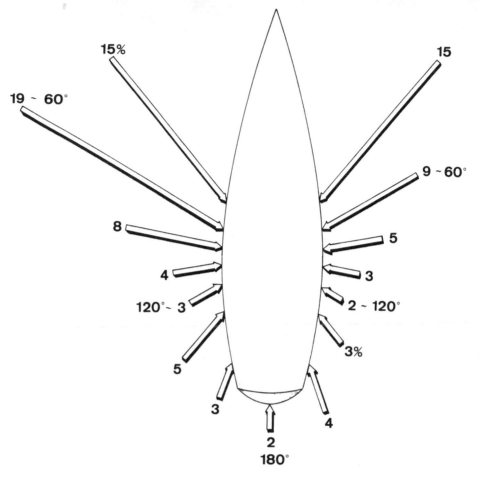

Wind angle relative to boat centerline. Percentage of observations for each wind angle. Leg 1, based on 412 observations.

True wind direction. Percentage of observations for each wind direction. Leg 1, based on 396 observations.

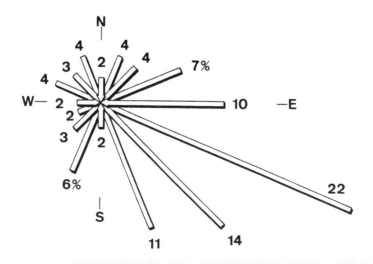

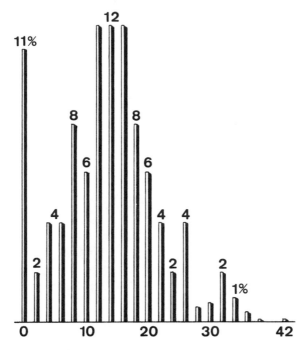

True wind speed vs. percentage of observations for each wind speed. Leg 1, based on 461 observations.

was told that the ground system needed enlarging, and that the coaxial cables between the radio and the antenna couplers were too small. I doubted all this, but told the experts to do what was necessary. The technicians took the Standard C satellite radio to their shop.

The day after I arrived in Cape Town we sent the two Alpha autopilots to California for repairs, and I bought a third. (They made it to South Africa just in time for the start.) Margaret and I and our helpers flushed out the freshwater tanks, cleaned the vessel generally, and bought provisions for the next leg. This took many trips to the supermarkets and the fruit and vegetable markets. The foodstuffs in Cape Town were excellent, there was a wide selection, and the prices were reasonable. I was advised to put aboard several cases of ultra high temperature (UHT) full cream milk, which keeps without refrigeration.

There were so many big and little jobs to do aboard SEBAGO that the 15 days in Cape Town rushed by in a blur that seemed more like 15 hours.

CHAPTER FOUR

Toward Australia

NOVEMBER 24, 1990. (SATURDAY). DAY 0.

<u>1655 GMT.</u> The start of the second leg was easy and relaxed, with a fluky wind from the SW. No one attacked the starting line because of the high penalty for crossing early (15 minutes for each second). There were dozens of spectator boats (mostly small) that were generally orderly except for a few whose captains were so busy talking that they never thought to look astern (a common fault). I heard lots of good wishes ("Godspeed, sailor.") from the people on the spectator boats. A few miles out I passed Robert Hooke on NIIHAU IV, whose mainsail and jib leeches were fluttering like ribbons in a wind.

Early this morning the radio people made another big effort (they've been at it for two weeks) to get the Standard C satellite radio going. Three technicians came at 0700 and worked like demons to install the set. Again it refused to get through to the U.S. (the radio people claimed the set had performed OK in their shop). About 1045, Bryan Jones, who was in charge and generally smiling and upbeat, began to look very worried.

Since I was scheduled to be towed to the starting line at 1220, at 1120 I told the technicians to yank out the cursed radio, the antenna, the big antenna cable, the laptop computer, and the printer. The satellite radio itself worked perfectly, but my signal could not get past the land station in England. Unfortunately the radio people were terribly in the way (just like in Newport) because Margaret and my helpers were loading stores and fresh food and doing other jobs while I was trying to lay out courses on the charts. The radio people meant well and certainly tried hard, but the satellite radio technology seemed to be one step ahead of the installers.

Just now we're approaching the Cape of Good Hope and Cape Agulhas. I am unsure whether we can weather the two capes, so I will have to sail carefully. We're going well except when a cross swell from the SW thumps into us and slows our speed. I have one reef in the mainsail, the forestaysail is up, and I have unrolled a little of the jib.

<u>1941.</u>   I crossed the 50-meter line south of the Cape of Good Hope light. It's already night and I'm worried about Bellows Rock, which breaks heavily. I'm excited to be at the southern tip of Africa, but these waters are hazardous. Heavy weather and lots of shipping. Margaret is only a few miles away in St. James.

<u>2110.</u>   Super sailor. Bah! Without checking, I thought I was at Good Hope when really I am only south of Haut Bay, about halfway to Good Hope! I immediately plotted a GPS position and checked the characteristic of the light on the headland near me when I didn't see the Agulhas light, which should have been visible in the distance. No wonder we have SW swells. I'm thoroughly rattled and blame it all on the rush before the start. Departure days are a real trial for singlehanders.

<u>2121.</u>   Just now while standing in the cockpit and watching the dark land rising up on my port hand I saw a strong green light. I was half asleep and thought it a funny place for a green light. Then the light moved, and I realized that it was on top of a mast. I've been studying the yacht through the binoculars, and I think it is Yukoh Tada on KODEN VIII.

I'm still shook up by my earlier navigation stupidity.

<u>2140.</u>   Tacked again at 50 meters depth. Sleepy, but there are ships around, and I must stay awake.

NOVEMBER 25, 1990. (SUNDAY). DAY 1.

<u>0027.</u>   Abeam of the Cape of Good Hope. Depth 96 meters.

<u>0250.</u>   A sudden wind at 0230 from S to SE put us aback. I am now on port tack heading south.

<u>0642.</u>   Driving too hard. Much easier and faster with a second reef and less jib. A westbound ship is nearby, but I'm too tired to call her up. Bright and sunny. Many birds, including a flock of gray and white birds that I will identify later. I must remember not to overload the autopilot. Cirrus clouds high in the sky.

<u>0925.</u>   A restless sleep. The sun was in my eyes, and wherever I moved, it seemed to follow me. Then I got a terrible cramp in my right thigh. The pain was numbing, and I thought I would be sick. However it passed. A lot of complaints! We are hurrying south at 8 knots. The mast is bent to leeward in the middle. I need to get out the wrenches and adjust the shrouds.

Table Mountain and the skyline of Cape Town.

1329.   As I walked to the weatherfax to try for the 1130Z chart, the yacht suddenly changed course. I looked out, and the tiller was hard over. I had just programmed the weatherfax antenna via the SSB tuner and was sure that RF interference from the radio had killed the autopilot. I was about to start changing the autopilot components when I heard the autopilot drive merrily working away. I looked in the lazarette and found that the 4 bolts that connect the autopilot to the rudder quadrant had come apart. I put lock washers on the bolts and tightened them. While hurrying forward to get some tools I saw a sail in the distance. Was it Yukoh Tada on KODEN VIII? Or Robin Davie on GLOBAL EXPOSURE?

1630.   When we sail close-hauled in strong winds (SE 25 knots) the size of the jib is critical. Fifteen rolls and we show 6.2 knots. Thirteen rolls, and the speed climbs to 7.2.

2200.   The autopilot linkage at the quadrant broke again. The weather was terrible, and since the autopilot wasn't working, the vessel was practically hove to. I was afraid to open the hatch to the lazarette because we were heeled to 40° (with the water ballast on the wrong side), and I feared we would be swamped. I pumped out the water ballast, which straightened up the yacht somewhat.

    Of the four bolts that hold the aluminum coupling together, two had sheared and the other two had worked loose. I dealt with three easily enough, but the fourth was a problem. I managed to drill it out with the Makita portable battery drill, but it was a tedious business at night. The drilling was hard going because of the location and angle, and it took all my energy to press against the drill. However the drill bit finally cut through. How I blessed that little piece of Japanese machinery.

By the time I finished, I was covered with grease. I replaced all the small fastenings with ¼"x20 stainless steel machine screws with nuts and large washers. And people ask me why I carry so many nuts and bolts on board!

I see a masthead light nearby. Someone in the BOC fleet. Time for a nap.

NOVEMBER 26, 1990. (MONDAY). DAY 2.

<u>1703.</u>   Wind SE 10 knots. I've exhausted myself and spent all day mounting the ICOM SSB radio above the chart table. To get proper space I had to move three other instruments. Wires are dangling everywhere, and the place looks like Thomas Edison's laboratory. More later.

<u>1716.</u>   Before I go to sleep I must write that I had an amusing chat with José Ugarte on BBV. José is always full of jokes. I told him that a friend in Cape Town had given me a bottle of wine—a nice cabernet sauvignon—that was so good that when I opened it, an angel flew out!

Don McIntyre on SPONSOR WANTED reported hundreds of tiny Portuguese men-of-war everywhere. "It's like an invasion," said Don.

"Maybe the Martians are taking over the world," I replied. "Here on SEBAGO I have a dozen purple blobs on the foredeck."

<u>2124.</u>   The wind is dying, and the yacht is rolling all over the place. One minute we're going 2 knots; the next minute 7. The radio talks of westerlies south of 40° (only 6 miles away). A good moment for a nap. I must rest and keep up my strength because there's lots of work ahead. I've got a few aches and pains and have been taking aspirins. Will I last until Sydney? Will I last until morning? More about the radio game later.

NOVEMBER 27, 1990. (TUESDAY). DAY 3.

<u>0603.</u>   Becalmed for 8 hours. Now 6 knots of wind from the SSW. I woke at 0300 (daylight), and did a few deck jobs while it was calm. I got the bow light working and tied 6 deck blocks to the lifelines to keep the blocks from banging. Then a quick breakfast. Now I must write about the radios.

I can hardly believe that after two weeks of fiddling, the Cape Town radio people (1) failed to commission the Standard C satellite radio (2) failed to get the big Japanese SSB radio working (3) failed to complete the weatherfax antenna installation. However there is no sense complaining about the past. I have to deal with the present and with what I have on board. The satellite radio is gone, and I have removed and stored away the defective SSB radio. I got out the spare SSB radio (an ICOM M-700) and the ICOM antenna tuner, which were packed away in layers of plastic bags in a locker. I screwed the ICOM radio to the shelf above the chart table and hooked up its power by soldering two wires.

1020.   Light wind from the SSE. Meanwhile there's much talk on the VHF radio. SPONSOR WANTED, BBV, CITY KIDS, GRINAKER, and SEBAGO are all together in a group. I learned that just before the start GRINAKER (on port tack) hit DURACELL (on starboard tack). Apparently both captains were below and the shore crews were steering. Bertie Reed admitted that the mishap was his responsibility and took GRINAKER back to the Royal Cape Yacht Club where her shore crew removed the bowsprit and fixed a chainplate and some rigging. Bertie was back at sea in two hours.

The collision knocked a hole in DURACELL's starboard side and her lifeline stanchions were damaged. Nevertheless Mike Plant kept going, and he plans repairs at sea. All credit to him.

I have just straightened up all the lines in the cockpit and must make a big effort to put each line in its bag when I am through adjusting it. There are 21 sail control lines that lead to 10 little storage bags, plus the mainsheet (#22) which goes to a small drum. Handling all these lines a dozen times a day is hard on the hands. I have been rubbing Vaseline on my fingers and palms and wearing gloves, but my hands are sore and swollen.

1058.   Good news! The ICOM SSB radio works well, at least at short range, according to José on BBV.

Early this morning I crawled back in the lazarette, removed the old SSB antenna tuner, and screwed the ICOM antenna tuner box in place. The end fitting on the coaxial cable that led forward to the radio was the wrong size, so I searched through the spare electrical gear and found an old coaxial plug of the right size. Then I took the plug to the rear compartment and opened up the wire to the stern light so I could steal a little electricity to heat my 12-volt soldering iron (since the coaxial plug required soldered connections). Finally I hooked up the red, green, yellow, and white control wires and screwed shut the waterproof antenna tuner box. It was tedious doing all this with the yacht hopping around, and

CONTESTANTS (21) AT THE START OF LEG 2

CAPTAIN	COUNTRY	SHIP NAME	DRAFT	RIG
CLASS 1 (eleven 60-footers)				
David Adams	Australia	*Innkeeper*	9'9"	sloop
Christophe Auguin	France	*Groupe Sceta*	12'0"	sloop
Isabelle Autissier	France	*Ecureuil-Poitou-Charentes*	9'8"	yawl
Kanga Birtles	Australia	*Jarkan*	10'2"	sloop
Nandor Fa	Hungary	*Alba Regia*	10'6"	sloop
Alain Gautier	France	*Generali Concorde*	12'6"	sloop
Philippe Jeantot	France	*Crédit Agricole IV*	12'7"	sloop
John Martin	South Africa	*Allied Bank*	13'1"	sloop
Mike Plant	U.S.A.	*Duracell*	11'6"	sloop
Bertie Reed	South Africa	*Grinaker*	11'3"	sloop
José Ugarte	Spain	*BBV Expo '92*	11'8"	sloop
CLASS 2 (six 50-footers)				
Jack Boye	U.S.A.	*Project City Kids*	9'0"	sloop
Yves Dupasquier	France	*Servant IV*	8'7"	sloop
Josh Hall	Great Britain	*Spirit of Ipswich*	9'0"	sloop
Don McIntyre	Australia	*Sponsor Wanted*	9'6"	sloop
Hal Roth	U.S.A.	*Sebago*	8'0"	cutter
Yukoh Tada	Japan	*Koden VIII*	6'6"	cutter
CORINTHIAN CLASS (four entries)				
Robin Davie	Great Britain	*Global Exposure*	7'0"	cutter
Robert Hooke	U.S.A.	*Niihau IV*	7'6"	cutter
Minoru Saito	Japan	*Shuten-dohji II*	7'1"	cutter
Paul Thackaberry	U.S.A.	*Volcano*	8'0"	cutter

after two hours I was trembling with fatigue. However the antenna is operational!

I collected my tools from the lazarette and went forward to the cabin where I had a big meal (at 0900) of beef stew, dinner rolls, and even a glass of Otto Kindlimann's wine (great stuff, but in the morning?). I still had to run the antenna through a two-way switch in the cabin so I could use the backstay antenna and ICOM antenna tuner on the weatherfax when it was time to receive a weather chart. I managed to juggle some coaxial end fittings, hooked up the switch, and the job was over. I still have to tidy up a bunch of drooping wires, but I can do this gradually over the next few weeks. I hope I am through with all this radio business.

These repairs at sea (autopilot quadrant, radios, antenna tuners) demand superhuman effort and are beyond all the normal sailing and living requirements. Fortunately the weather was light last night. I had a good sleep (plus naps today) and have recovered.

<u>1136.</u>   Minoru Saito on SHUTEN-DOHJI II started one day late.

<u>1317.</u>   Tacked to port. I changed from the genoa to the jib because we're being chased by some hard-looking stratus. Years ago Margaret and I learned on our first trip to Cape Horn that when we were pursued by low clouds with ragged, jagged bottoms (fracto-stratus) it was time to get the big sails down. Quickly!

<u>1548.</u>   A weak frontal system appears to be going eastward. In order to sit at peace at the chart table when the yacht is heeled, I finally put in two eyebolts and a safety line that clips around my waist. How nice it is to sit at the chart table (on the port tack) and be able to use two hands to write or hold the navigation instruments and not slide off the seat.

<u>1652.</u>   Tacked to starboard. Seas small, but lumpy. The 1630 Argos reports were impossible to understand because of static. Also no weather chart from the island of Reunion, which was a disappointment.

<u>1716.</u>   CITY KIDS reported a pod of whales very close. "One whale repeatedly jumped out of the water," said Jack Boye. Don McIntyre experienced strong currents last night and at one point he thought that both his GPS and log "had gone crook." Later Don spoke with Philippe Jeantot on CRÉDIT AGRICOLE, who found the same thing. Philippe stopped his vessel by bringing her head to wind, and his GPS showed 4.5 knots! Apparently this area has a lot of fickle SE winds, whales, and strange currents. One thing is sure: GPS technology is revolutionizing ocean voyaging.

NOVEMBER 28, 1990. (WEDNESDAY). DAY 4.

<u>0429.</u>   I have been hunting for the small VHF set. I can't imagine where it is. I've been through all the drawers, lockers, and usual hiding places. I had it a few days ago and took it out of its plastic case because it lacked a metal piece for watertightness. Now I've found the metal piece, but I can't find the radio. The absent-minded professor.

We're heeled 15–20° but are going along so well that I hesitate to change anything. The helm is neutral, we have a full load of water ballast to starboard, and the full main and full jib. We have been logging 8 to 8.5 knots for hours.

<u>0600.</u>   A new drama. I discovered that the cylinders of the diesel generator are full of water. This will mean severe restrictions on use of the radios, weatherfax, GPS, and lighting. (The solar panels work well, but the sunlight hours are limited in the Southern Ocean, and my four panels will probably only power the autopilot.) I managed to get the engine running (barely) by using the decompression levers, but the oil pressure warning horn sounded after 10 minutes. I started to change the oil but discovered only two liters on board. What an oversight! I have disconnected the exhaust hose and will put in a plug when not running the engine. Will these unplanned projects never cease?

A beautiful morning. Lots of black-browed albatrosses, white-chinned petrels, pintado petrels, and soft-plumaged petrels. How the last bird swoops and dives and plays in the air. I stood in the cockpit for hours watching.

<u>0929.</u>   Changing the engine oil was a terrible business. The problem is the useless little hand pumps that have practically no suction, and hose connections that fall apart. The engine oil was gray and watery. I hope the problem is water backing up in the exhaust hose (too low?) and not another blown head gasket. I used half a roll of paper towels to clean up the cabin sole, the engine, and me. I put in new oil to half level, but after a few minutes of running, the oil pressure warning light came on. I've disconnected the exhaust hose line to the transom and stuck in a wooden plug. I must think about the next step. I saved the old oil, which might be usable if I can come up with a way to filter out the water.

<u>1322.</u>   Wind from the SE and up and down in strength. I tacked south a few minutes ago. For lunch I ate the last of the beef stew that Fay MacLachlan made for me and opened the second bottle of Otto's fine wine. It's been hard to get Argos reports because of transmission problems. However I received the tail-end of a weatherfax map from Pretoria. I need to set an alarm clock so I don't miss the schedules. The signal from Reunion was too weak and only made gray dots on the weatherfax paper.

I wonder if the solar panels can run the autopilot all the way to Sydney if I shut off everything else? Of course I still have the Monitor wind vane steering gear which uses no electricity at all.

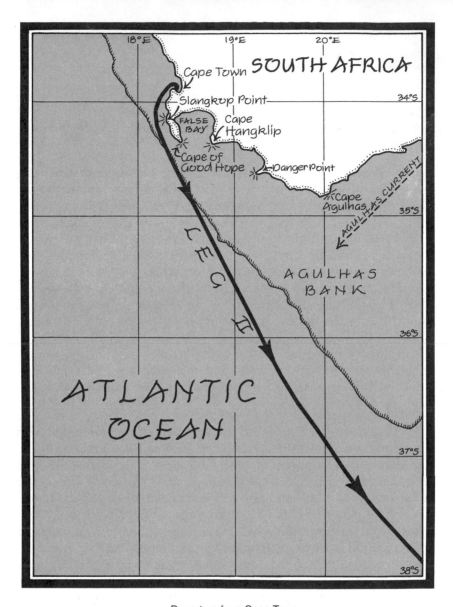

Departure from Cape Town.

<u>1817.</u>   Becalmed all afternoon, but a south wind came just as it was getting dark. I threw in one mainsail reef and have the jib reefed because it looks as if the wind will increase. I am worried about the engine, but we will see what we can do tomorrow. I moved the SSB mounting slightly and tidied up a few wires. I was pleased to get a legible weather chart from Pretoria. Washed the dishes and have the cabin in good order with all the tools put away and the clothes hung up. I even swept the cabin sole.

NOVEMBER 29, 1990. (THURSDAY). DAY 5.

<u>0343.</u>   It's already light (GMT), and the early morning sun is dead ahead. With 27° of westerly magnetic variation, the directions are beginning to get confused. Or maybe I am confused. Our heading is 145°M. (near SE), but our true course is 118°T., a little south of east (near ESE). I had a wonderful sleep from 2200 last night to 0300 this morning. The berth was comfortable and warm. No one was within miles, and I have unlimited sea room. Meanwhile the yacht clocked a steady 8 knots. I set the alarm clock and got up every hour to check things.

My main problem is power for the autopilot. The engine is doubtful because I'm short of new oil. Yesterday I put one liter of fresh oil in the engine and got a "low oil" warning signal after a few minutes of running. Options: (1) drain the one liter and put in the remaining liter of oil (2) add the remaining liter to the first liter which should give the engine ¾ of the full amount (but well above the low oil mark on the dipstick). I wonder how much risk there is if I run the engine at low RPMs with watery oil? In any case the batteries are fully charged, and I have some time to think about what to do. Perhaps one more oil change will purge the engine of salt water. Of course if the head gasket is blown, salt water will continue to run into the cylinders. I swear that an air-cooled generator with a hot exhaust is the way to go. Marine engines almost never wear out, but are consistently junked because of saltwater damage!

Now for some breakfast.

<u>0600.</u>   Wind SSW 16 knots. I roll the jib in and out as the wind comes and goes. We're heeling 20° to port but going 8.83 knots just now. One reef in the main. SEBAGO is surrounded by a flock of prions, a dozen pintado petrels, a few white-chinned petrels, and one or two black-browed albatrosses.

<u>1100.</u>   A badly chafed furling line on the jib. I think it's from the forward-most block being mounted too high. I must change the line before dark. A while ago the weather was light so I sorted out a pile of charts and tidied up a few more radio wires.

<u>1510.</u>   I have been dealing with the jib roller-furling line, which turned into a project. The lead to the roller drum was misaligned. I put a snatch block forward and fitted a new line (81 feet long), which I bent to the last 3 feet of the old line (coming from the drum) with a carrick bend whose ends I seized. The furling

lines are extremely important, and I must inspect them for chafe every day without fail.

2208.   A fair wind (NNW 14 knots) so I set the running rig. I'm glad I replaced the chafed jib furling line during daylight hours. This morning (which seems a long time ago) I tried to identify a prion that was around the yacht. Then I got involved in wiring and sailhandling. Perhaps tomorrow for the birds. I need to put up a lee cloth on the port pilot berth—a job I've been trying to do ever since Newport—because the yacht will soon be rolling merrily if the fair winds increase in strength.

Now that I'm heading SE in the Southern Ocean, I must not forget about Marion Island, a few days away. I remember Harry Harkimo being in sight of Marion in the 1986–87 BOC race and cursing the difference between the weather forecast being radioed from the island (which he could clearly see) and the wind that Harry was actually experiencing. ("The stupid idiots. Why don't they look out the window!")

NOVEMBER 30, 1990. (FRIDAY). DAY 6.

0444.   Here's the first of the Roaring Forties, and I'm a little nervous. The vessel is rocketing along at 10-12-14 knots. The autopilot is set to minimal current drain and can handle the steering loads, but can the solar panels supply the current? (I had planned to put on two additional solar panels before I left Newport, but ran out of time.)

I was aiming for 53° south. But suppose I don't have enough battery power and fail to get anything from the engine? I have changed course slightly to aim farther north, where I should have fair winds but not so strong.

0715.   I felt very blue and discouraged when I got up this morning at 0300Z (these GMT times are crazy). All the leaders have weather routing. Not only do I lack this, but it is a question whether I will have enough power to run my autopilot. However we are going along nicely, and—according to the battery meter— the solar panels have increased the battery power slightly. I have shut off everything electrical except the autopilot and the B&G sailing instruments.

A little while ago the wind increased to 30 knots. Things were flying around the cabin so I reefed the jib and put a second reef in the mainsail (much easier with the luff downhaul lines). It seemed very easy to crank the leech reefing pendant on the winch.

No wonder—when I finished I found that the wind had dropped to 19 knots!

I had a hearty breakfast of bacon, eggs, toast, and coffee, and feel a bit brighter, although I am going back to sleep for an hour. A little sun and a bit of blue sky. The 30-knot wind might have been the passage of a weak frontal system.

<u>0944.</u>   Barometer low, but the sky is a brilliant blue, and we're going nicely. I must decide on a target course. Several new birds.

<u>1123.</u>   Wind NE 30 knots. Third reef in the main and a big reduction in the size of the jib. Still going 8–9 knots. I have seldom seen a wind this strong blow out of a clear blue sky.

I am eating figs from Smyrna, and it makes me think of Turkey and Greece. How I miss Margaret. How I long to take her sailing in some pleasant places like Turkey and Greece and to retrace Ulysses' route.

<u>1716.</u>   Getting dark according to GMT, and I need the chart table light in order to see. A nice dinner, even if we are well heeled to starboard. The New Zealand "pouch" meals are in truth freeze-dried. I was a little disappointed when I found out yesterday, but I tried a lamb dish, and found it excellent. Tonight I had sweet and sour lamb, and it was good too. I cooked rice (which seemed to take forever), and the combination was tasty. Afterwards a good cup of coffee and shortbread cookies.

I have to think about the chafe problem at the forward spinnaker pole jaws. Already I can see a bit of frayed line. I wish Schaefer had made those special pole ends for me. I need to think about not running into Marion Island.

<u>2007.</u>   Checked over the autopilot and oiled various parts. All OK.

DECEMBER 1, 1990. (SATURDAY). DAY 7.

<u>0110.</u>   Eleven months of 1990 gone already. Time is like a train that runs faster and faster.

The sailing got lively about midnight when an east-going front passed. I pulled on my foul-weather gear, hurried outside, and rolled up most of the jib. Then the wind began to veer, and I gybed the mainsail in the dark. The cold rain felt good on my face. At the moment we have a SW wind and are jogging along at 6.5 knots under a triple-reefed mainsail.

<u>0200.</u>   Two reefs out of the main and the full jib poled out to starboard.

<u>0841.</u>   While gybing in the rain last night, I removed the temporary tie I use to hold the forward end of the spinnaker pole to the pulpit (while setting up the pole and lines) because I wanted to slip the jib sheet underneath the tie. Just then the pole escaped (as SEBAGO suddenly rolled) and the pole swung far out to starboard. I stupidly tried to catch it on the swing back, and the pole banged into my shoulder and arm. How dumb. The pole could have killed me! Now I have a big bruise on my right arm (I'm afraid to look). Will I ever learn? However I had a jolt of brandy and a nap under several blankets (to warm up) and I feel OK.

There's a continuing chafe problem between the jib sheet and the port spinnaker pole end fitting. This morning I winched the jib under the lee of the main so I could reach the clew. I tied on a temporary sheet and removed the chafed end from the port sheet. Even though I was wearing a safety harness, it was a bit risky standing on the lifelines while I leaned out and reached up. I need revolving pole-end fittings with rollers.

The running backstay control lines are chafed in several places, but these lines are only ¼" dia. and are easily replaced. I'm going to try to keep the lee running backstay out of the way of the mainsail by tying the unused backstay to the shrouds. Maybe I can eliminate the control lines altogether. At least it's something to try.

So far the solar panels are handling the autopilot OK. I miss the BBC and the chat hours with the other sailors.

<u>1300.</u>   This morning the WNW wind shifted to the NW, and SEBAGO began to run slightly by the lee. I decided to gybe the rig. I rolled up the jib, changed the spinnaker poles, the control lines, and was about to gybe the mainsail when I noticed a big squall approaching from the starboard quarter. The squall was a few minutes away, so I worked on a couple of minor deck jobs. When the squall came, the wind rose to 34 knots. Since one of the spinnaker poles was partially up, I dropped the forward end and tied it to the pulpit. At the time I noticed that the genoa on the forward roller-furling gear was loose and not properly rolled up. An upper fold of material had escaped and was flapping a little.

The rising wind was too much for the mainsail with one reef so I put in a second reef. By now the genoa definitely needed attention. However the mainsail reef was troublesome and took me 10 minutes or so. When I glanced up at the genoa again, I saw that it had unwound more and had begun to flog a little. Though the wind was strong, I thought I could easily unroll the sail a few turns and wind it up properly. However when I put one of the sheets on a winch, I couldn't do a thing because the sheets had wound up backwards into an impossible tangle at the clew of the sail. No matter what I did, I couldn't unsnarl the sheets; nor could I wind up the loose sail with the line on the furling drum.

In order to keep such a thing from happening, I always secured each genoa sheet to the pulpit with a short piece of light line to keep the sheet from fouling the jib or the jib furling gear (located a little farther aft). Then back in the cockpit I made a practice of pulling the slack from the unused sheets and belaying them to cleats on the sides of the coamings, one to port and the other to starboard. Somehow all four of these lines had come loose.

I'm not talking about the past tense but the present tense because the sail is out of control and flogging terribly *right now*. I simply don't know what to do and can scarcely write because of the shaking of the sail and the mast. How can a supposed expert get into such a mess? *How can I get the sail down?* Cut it away with a knife lashed to the boathook? How can I slide the sail luff down the extrusions when the sail is wrapped tightly at the bottom? With a winch? Maybe, but the wind is strong. I have tried everything.

DECEMBER 2, 1990. (SUNDAY). DAY 8.

0739.   Yesterday was the day of the ultimate adventure on the foredeck. Somehow the top part of the small genoa unwound, and as it did, the sheets coiled up backwards into a mass of knots and tangles. This sounds impossible, but it happened.

I tried everything: sheets in, sheets out; furling line in, furling line out. Meanwhile the top part of the sail began to flog viciously. At times I thought the mast was going to come down. The steering was hopeless because the sail pulled the yacht sideways.

I had to do something quickly. But what? Could I unwind the sheets by carrying the lines forward and passing them around and around the sail? With the sheets unwound, the entire sail would be free. I rushed forward with an armload of the cockpit end of the sheets. What I was attempting might have been possible in a calm or in a marina slip, but now there was 30–40 knots of wind, and just as I got forward with the sheets, a squall bore down on SEBAGO. The sail became an out-of-control monster. I grabbed my knife and cut the sheets, since passing them around and around was madness because I could have been swept overboard by the flailing sail and lines that whipped back and forth.

Suddenly the entire sail—all 800 sq. ft.—was free and unwound, but without sheets it was out of control. I let go the

Bashing to windward with reefed sails.

tack and the halyard and quickly pulled down the sail from the extrusion. Almost! Just when all of the sail except the head was down on deck, the sail whooshed from my hand and—held only by the head—raced up the extrusion. The entire sail streamed out from the mast like a flag of desperation. *Now what to do?* By accident I found that by sailing slightly different courses, the head of the sail would whoosh up and down the extrusions on the headstay. In the water one minute and then up to the top of the mast again. Finally on one down-whoosh, I managed to grab the sail and drag it on board. Just as I was groping for a tie, the wind filled the sail and swept all of it—except the head still in the extrusion—over the side. I still had a chance. I cut away the torn head at the bottom of the extrusion and began to pull the sail back on board (if only I could have reached a line to tie part of the sail to something on deck). I was making progress and almost had it when a gust of wind whisked the sail into the water, and it was gone. Irretrievably and finally gone.

All this time the yacht was still racing eastward. I let out a gasp as I looked far astern and saw the folds of my beautiful white Dacron sail in the water. Then it disappeared. The flapping, flogging, and terrible shaking had stopped. I sat on the foredeck and held my head. Had this been a bad dream?

With all this commotion the cockpit and decks were a shambles. Lines were everywhere, and some were trailing overboard. I began to tidy up the lines when the autopilot failed. I spent an hour replacing the control box and getting the autopilot working again. Then I resumed tidying up the sheets, halyards, and other lines by either coiling them or tucking them in their little stowage bags in the cockpit. Soon I had everything tidy except for one line that was over the side and stuck on something. I let go the other end of the line and tried to pull it past the unknown obstruction, but it didn't come. I began to hear a loud squeaking noise from the rudder, and when I tried to move the tiller by hand I could hardly turn it. No wonder the autopilot had burned out.

A line must have gotten around the rudder stock or between the hull and the rudder. It seemed to me that the turning action of the rudder back and forth would pulverize a ½" dia. Dacron line, so I attempted to force the rudder first one way, then the other. However the problem got worse and soon I had to use *a shoulder and both hands* to move the tiller which now makes terrible creaking noises.

1343.   It seems that the only thing to do is to return to South Africa. The Cape of Good Hope is 880 miles to the NW.

DECEMBER 3, 1990. (MONDAY). DAY 9.

0400.   I have set the full jib. The mainsail is still reefed, but the wind is dropping. The tiller is almost immovable. Pintado petrels, black-browed albatrosses, and prions show an intense and screaming interest in a discarded tea bag or a scrap of paper. It seems that when one bird looks at something, then all the other birds must take a look. A jealous society! I ate a big breakfast and then put the starboard running backstay shackle back together with a bolt after the shackle pin fell over the side.

1737.   This morning at 1000 at 41°14'S., 34°00'E., I finally got up my nerve, wrapped a life line around my chest, clamped the bread knife between my jaws, and jumped into the sea. Fortunately the ocean was calm with only a little swell. As expected, the culprit was a piece of line. However instead of being a series of twists and knots, a loop of line was jammed in a fore and aft direction along the top of the rudder and wedged between the hull and rudder for 12–15 inches. When the rudder moved, the jammed line rolled with it and made the rudder useless. Incredible! The chances of such an occurrence must have been one in a million. It took only a moment to cut away the line at each end of the jammed part. Then I climbed back on deck and moved the rudder to work out the short piece of line.

I decided to have a second look while I was at it so I jumped into the sea again to be sure the rudder was clear. I climbed up and down the steering vane at the stern. Easy down. Hard up. In fact, the second climb up was a bit dicey, and I barely made it. However I did, and a few minutes later we were underway and headed east. The cold water took my breath away, but the whole episode was over in a few minutes. What an experience for a lone sailor in the wilds of the Southern Ocean!

So far on this leg we've had problems with the SSB radio, the autopilot linkage, water in the generator, a flogging sail, and a line that jammed the rudder. Now we're back to regular sailing and normal shipboard life. I hope.

<u>1809.</u>   The Argos positions were a disappointment. I'm last, but now we're sailing well again, and I'm hopeful that we can work our way up in the fleet. Just now we're reaching along ESE, and I'm close to setting the running rig. We're involved with the western end of a high-pressure area. Winds NNE and a high barometer.

<u>1853.</u>   The sky is perfectly clear. The moon—almost full, but waning—is rising to port. Orion is closer to port and overhead, and I'm steering for Sirius. The Southern Cross is off to starboard. A busy day. I feel nervous, and just cranked a reef in the jib.

<u>2158.</u>   I'm fed up with the Cape Town radio operator, who failed to complete three calls—two local—and kept me waiting 65 minutes.

DECEMBER 4, 1990. (TUESDAY). DAY 10.

<u>0514.</u>   By chance I picked up a call between INNKEEPER and David Adam's router. David reported very strong northerly winds. His router said that the nearest significant weather is a high whose center is at 37°S. and 37°E. The next low is at 50°S. and 20°E. The first four yachts are all sailing at 11 knots except for GENERALI CONCORDE which is up to 13 knots. David sounded a little worried by the weather and the pace of the competition, which is clearly not for the faint of heart.

<u>0819.</u>   I repaired the stern light. Then, since the batteries are up, I telephoned Ken MacLachlan to thank him for his help when I was in Cape Town.

<u>1232.</u>   The news on the chat hour is that Nandor Fa on ALBA REGIA has withdrawn from the race because of steering problems. Nandor's left rudder is completely gone; his right rudder is still on the yacht but cannot be used. The Hungarian captain is in no danger, has plenty of food and water, and figures that it will take him about three weeks to sail to a South African port. Ham radio operator Alistair Campbell—who runs the Durban maritime net—suggested the anchorage at Marion Island as a place for repairs. Apparently Nandor—who is steering by adjusting his sails—is heading directly to South Africa. Imagine sailing in the Southern Ocean without a rudder!

<u>1241.</u>   I seem to have the runs and a little touch of fever. I have been resting and taking aspirins. Fortunately the weather is warm, the wind light, and the seas easy.

<u>1637.</u>   While working on deck I discovered cracks in the new fiberglass around the chainplates on the port side. The newly glassed area (solid) is an oval about 8x12 inches (with the long dimension fore-and-aft). The outboard half is cracked and raised about 1/32" above the rest of the deck. On the starboard side there is less cracking—only the tiniest beginning and not as long. The cracks show that the bashing in the strong SE winds the first few days strained the deck because the tie rods (which are inside the vessel and run from the chainplates to anchor points low down in the hull) were not tight enough. Today I cranked up on the tie rods with a 15" wrench. The port side (where the cracks are) was fairly tight. I took up ¾ to one turn. On the starboard side I took up about 2½ turns with ease. I want to tighten the rods as much as possible, but I'm terrified of stripping the threads, which would mean instant dismasting.

<u>1700.</u>   A little earlier I spoke with Colleen Johns—Sebago's media representative—in Rhode Island and told her about the jammed rudder. Our connection was poor, and I was glad I had made arrangements for her to record my little story. I made the call as short as possible to save power.

DECEMBER 5, 1990. (WEDNESDAY). DAY 11.

<u>0415.</u>   A good sleep in the lee settee berth. The distance to the Cape of Good Hope is 1,135 miles on a course of 295°T.

<u>0427.</u>   I have been examining the inside of the cabin in the chainplate areas and have found no leaks. From the angles on the

two bookcase ends it seems that the hull works athwartships a little, perhaps ⅛", or a bit more. The difficulty is that these sailing conditions are putting more loads on the rig than any Santa Cruz 50 has experienced.

I have the following problems:

#1. The cracks around the chainplates. If I were to get dismasted I'd be in a poor way.

#2. Electrical power. We are operating on solar power, which is adequate on bright days, and I have substantial battery capacity to bridge the dark and overcast intervals. Without power, of course, the autopilot is useless.

#3. Autopilot spares. I have only one control box in reserve. However the wind vane steering gear is in good order.

#4. My injured right shoulder. I am left-handed and can get along OK, but every time I raise my right arm I feel a twinge of pain. I probably just strained something.

The most worrying difficulty by far is the rigging problem I found yesterday.

Now let's look at the race. I am in last place, which is humiliating enough. The chances of me winning or even placing are negligible. Why continue? To complete another circumnavigation? If I get dismasted there's a good chance that I'll lose the yacht, which is certainly worth something. To retire with rigging and electrical problems is no black mark. One goal of the race was to win. Now that that is doubtful I should look toward something else. My gut feeling in all this is to write it off as an unsuccessful venture, to get Margaret on board, and to sail back to the U.S.

A squall from a passing front just knocked us over. Sailbags have been flying around, and everything in the galley storage chest got dumped.

0728.   At the moment, my enthusiasm for the race is gone. My usual upbeat spirits and the drive to win have simply been beaten out of me by all the technical problems. I don't mean to feel sorry for myself, but I'm discouraged. Very discouraged. Maybe after a little rest and a good meal I'll be in a more positive mood. I'm sure that other contestants in the race have problems too. If those ahead get becalmed, maybe I can catch up. Certainly I want to finish what I've started.

Since we're sailing well, I'm going to look into a new book for a few hours to get my mind on something else.

CHAPTER FIVE

Return to Cape Town

DECEMBER 5, 1990. (WEDNESDAY). DAY 11 (continued)

<u>0900.</u>   The cracks around the chainplates are much worse. I have no choice but to go back to Cape Town. My position is 42°16'S., 40°53'E. The course to the Cape of Good Hope is 294° + 35° of westerly variation or 329°—roughly NNW. The distance is 1,159 miles. The wind is west 30 knots. At the moment we're headed north with three reefs in the main, a small jib, and a full tank of water ballast to port.

<u>0930.</u>   I feel terrible when I think of all my supporters and the volunteers who helped me and wished me luck. However, I gave the project my best shot.

<u>1222.</u>   The autopilot quadrant engagement latch keeps unhooking and causes the yacht to gybe. After watching the latch for a time and seeing it unhook, I think the disconnect arrangement is too light. I finally put two small C-clamps on the part of the quadrant that is hopping around. Surprisingly, the autopilot is not working too hard. In fact, everything is quiet and peaceful inside the lazarette.

<u>1515.</u>   A weather chart from Pretoria shows an approaching high. Since we're heading north we should meet it halfway up on the easterly side, which should give us S and SSE winds. I have worked out that the small birds around the yacht are blue petrels which are similar to prions but have a steadier flight and glide more when they fly.

<u>2131.</u>   We're going well on an extremely rough sea. We sometimes shoot up to 8.5 knots even though we're flying storm canvas. I'm sure I would have been bashed to bits by now if it weren't for the center galley island to lean against and the three vertical aluminum poles to grab when I'm walking around. I feel quite relaxed about my decision to return to Cape Town.

<u>2141.</u>   How amazing it is that the world of the Southern Ocean exists. A lonely, beautiful, isolated world of birds and water and wind and ice. Of tumultuous storms. Of whales and sea leopards and dainty birds. Of huge seas and frigid gales with smoking winds.

<u>2155.</u>   There's a definite southerly component to the gale. I have headed up to 340°.

DECEMBER 6, 1990. (THURSDAY). DAY 12.

<u>0143.</u>   Going surprisingly well. Wind on the port beam. Seas large, but less than yesterday, when the sea and swell must have been 20 feet; today only 14 feet or so. The current continues to set us eastward.

<u>0400.</u>   Gray and gloomy. The low stratus looks like the background for a painting of the Devil. The seas are less than yesterday, but large enough to cause some crashing as we cross them; meanwhile I nervously watch the port chainplates. No leaks and no groaning of the deck, which is encouraging after the heavy winds and big seas of yesterday.

It's 1,021 miles to the Cape of Good Hope. I reported my situation to Alistair (ZS5MU) and told him that I was returning to South Africa. Alistair urged me to try for Port Elizabeth (on the east coast) instead of going all the way around the southern tip of Africa to Cape Town.

<u>1328.</u>   I had a talk with Nandor Fa on ALBA REGIA. Nandor's broken rudder stocks were made of stainless steel. One is gone completely. The second snapped but was kept from being lost "by a bolt that I put through." He talked about carbon fiber rudder stocks for future rudders. The report that he has withdrawn from the race was wrong. Nandor definitely plans to continue and has new rudders and an ace mechanic coming from Hungary to meet him in Port Elizabeth. Nandor also talked of "catching up to the others." Isn't the optimism of sailors wonderful?

<u>1340.</u>   After some hard looking at the "blue petrels" I have decided they are really broad-billed prions. The blue petrel has a horizontal white band aft of the black band across the tail. The white band is not found on the prions. The bird books speak of large flocks of prions, which may be so, but I have learned that individual prions make solo flights around ships as well (a solitary bird is flying around as I write). Also I have identified Antarctic

terns which are unmistakable grayish-white birds with large red-orange bills, black head caps, and flaring tail feathers.

<u>1437.</u>   The crack around the port chainplate is growing and is larger than it was two days ago. Yesterday the rig got a big work-out, especially on the port side. There is some creaking in the area. Do I dare tighten the tie rods more? Don't touch anything!

DECEMBER 7, 1990. (FRIDAY). DAY 13.

<u>0244.</u>   The weather is almost calm. However by nursing the yacht along we are doing 3–4 knots.
    A whale as long as the yacht was 2 or 3 boatlengths away when I looked out a little while ago. A rounded dorsal fin. After 10 minutes or so the creature dived, and I saw the usual flukes come out of the sea and then slowly disappear. There was a second whale nearby. Ed Blair, my whale-watching friend, should have been here.

<u>0251.</u>   The Cape of Good Hope bears 284° true. Distance 932 miles.

<u>0307.</u>   According to a field guide, the creatures I saw earlier were sperm whales.

<u>0501.</u>   Switched from the starboard water tank to the port tank. The birds I saw earlier were sooty albatrosses. Large birds with dark heads and a different flying pattern than the white-chinned petrels. Quite unlike the Antarctic giant petrel.

<u>0840.</u>   I called Cape Town and spoke with Ken MacLachlan, who has kindly offered his home and Fay's car. Unfortunately Ken and Fay are leaving for business in Europe next Thursday so I may not see them. I estimated my arrival in Cape Town in 5 to 9 days.

<u>1452.</u>   Discovered that I have used up all the weatherfax paper. I must buy some in Cape Town.

<u>1503.</u>   Much warmer. I am wearing just thermal underwear for the first time in two weeks.

<u>2107.</u>   I spoke with Robin Davie and Don McIntyre, both of whom are awed by the difficulties of sailing complex yachts in the Southern Ocean. "I'm just trying to get there," said Don. "Forget the race. Forget everything except survival." He reported that Jack Boye broke a headstay and has had a diesel leak. Oil is all over his cabin from a defective engine fitting. Rather gloomy accounts. Both men seemed chastened and subdued. Robin Davie suggested

that I go to Perth—on the west coast of Australia—for repairs. A good idea, but too late now.

DECEMBER 8, 1990. (SATURDAY). DAY 14.

<u>0413.</u>   Nasty outside. I'm trying to ease the vessel as much as possible. I hope the autopilot link to the quadrant behaves itself.

<u>0619.</u>   More rolls in the jib. Surprising how 2 or 3 rolls affect the drive of the vessel. We dropped from 7.5 to 6.75 knots.

<u>1200.</u>   It's 778 miles to the Cape of Good Hope.

<u>1931.</u>   Going well after a rough, bumpy day. I am into *Adventures of a Red Sea Smuggler* by Henry de Monfreid. I have read this book many times and like to follow de Monfreid's tracks on a Red Sea chart. It's a good yarn for a sailor, especially if you have slugged up the Red Sea against the prevailing NNW winds. A fantastic story and certainly a triumph of the human spirit.

DECEMBER 9, 1990. (SUNDAY). DAY 15.

<u>0154.</u>   More creaking from the port chainplates.

<u>0400.</u>   A heavy bank of clouds in the SW. Wind up to 26 knots for a while. I scared myself to death by measuring the distance to the Cape of Good Hope and coming out with 1,400 miles. I thought I had set my dividers for 100 miles, but they were adjusted for 50.

<u>0428.</u>   Since turning back for Cape Town at 0900 on December 5th, I have sailed 434 miles, 38% of the 1,136-mile distance. However, the weather is better now, and I have sharpened up my course. I will have to watch out for big ships.

<u>0627.</u>   My position is 37°25'S., 32°12'E. I had a talk with Nandor Fa on ALBA REGIA (which means "white castle" in Latin). Nandor is still pushing toward Cape Elizabeth where he hopes to fit new rudders. I wish I had his enthusiasm.

<u>1505.</u>   At last I put up a lee cloth on the port pilot berth so I won't fall out when I am asleep or the boat rolls.

<u>2315.</u>   I cracked my head on the cockpit dodger while rushing out on deck and almost knocked myself out. Maybe I banged some sense into myself.

DECEMBER 10, 1990. (MONDAY). DAY 16.

<u>0332.</u>   The Cape of Good Hope is 584 miles.

<u>0921.</u>   Sunny, with a bright blue sea and a brilliant sky. I replaced the port spinnaker foreguy line because of chafe. A lot of measuring from a great hank of 10-mm. line.

<u>1235.</u>   According to the experts there's an eastward-moving high-pressure area (1024 mb.) south of Cape Town at 43°S. 19°E. A cold front runs from 27°S. 0°E. and 30°S. 08°E. into a low of 1012 mb. at 35°S. 05°E. My wind should drop off, and then go to the SE.

<u>1528.</u>   Fewer birds as we creep northward, and the weather warms up. Fifty strokes of the big bilge pump to clear the bilge. Where does the water come from? My guess is the rear watertight compartment. The seals around the tiller head and the entrance hatch may be leaking.

<u>1530.</u>   My spirits are very low. It seems terrible to return to a port once you've left it. However the deck cracks are getting worse.

<u>1600.</u>   I just pulled off the remains of a big squid that got underneath a snatch block along the port rail. A terrible smell.

<u>1856.</u>   Wind dead aft. Changed course 20° to port.

<u>1910.</u>   The differences in the sailing conditions south of 40° are amazing. It's much colder, sometimes down to freezing, depending on the wind direction. Often 20–40 knots of wind. And the wind seems more dense or powerful somehow, with a whine that seems unique to the Southern Ocean.

<u>2145.</u>   How I dislike changing the headsail when I gybe the rig at night. Actually it's not the sail that's the problem, but the taking down of one spinnaker pole (and its four control lines), and putting up the opposite pole (and its four lines). I try to do the job faster each time to get it over with.

DECEMBER 11, 1990. (TUESDAY). DAY 17.

<u>0151.</u>   I stopped writing "from Cape Town toward Sydney" and am writing "toward Cape Town" as my logbook destination.

<u>0700.</u>   Wind east 28–31 knots. Two reefs in the main and a little of the headsail.

<u>1657.</u>   We've been going 7–8 knots all day. We're heeled to port about 20°, and with the double-reefed mainsail and partial jib (poled out) are a little overpowered.

<u>1830.</u>   We were hard-pressed and surrounded with gray, gloomy-looking fracto-stratus clouds, so I have put in the third reef. I think a front is passing. More comfortable now.

DECEMBER 12, 1990. (WEDNESDAY). DAY 18.

<u>0326.</u>   We're hard on the wind on the port tack, and a banging metallic sound is coming from the port shrouds. The sound is almost like someone thumping on the tie rods with a rubber mallet or knocking on the outside of the hull. A hollow, clanging sound that scares me.

<u>1000.</u>   How amazing it is that when tacking toward a goal, one tack is always fast and easy while the other is slow and troublesome. Can there be a mystery current or an unknown tidal stream at work? A banana-shaped hull or a warped rig?

<u>1200.</u>   Cape Point—the tip of Good Hope—bears 316°M. and is 228 miles.

<u>1300.</u>   At 1130 I spoke with Alistair Campbell who said I would be met by a towboat 10 miles from Cape Town.

The news from the fleet is that SPIRIT OF IPSWICH suffered a severe knockdown and damage. Josh Hall dislocated one of his knees. He managed to get the knee back together, but the experience was horrendous. ALLIED BANK's autopilots are giving out, and John Martin may have to steer by hand. VOLCANO is at 58°S.

SEBAGO's winds are predicted to come from the NW, just the direction we want to go. I have worked out the tacks carefully, and both the northerly and westerly tacks seem about the same. There is a big low at 45°S. 5°W. and a cold front with 8 isobar lines (each marking a 4-millibar difference) in only 5° of longitude.

<u>1412.</u>   Amazing how we go along at 7.5 knots on a smooth sea with the full jib and 2 reefs in the mainsail.

<u>1726.</u>   I see a ship 7–8 miles off the starboard bow. I must keep a careful watch.

<u>1817.</u>   An oil rig to starboard and two supply launches zipping around. A very large crude oil tanker (VLCC) ahead to starboard.

<u>2139.</u>   Position 35°00'S., 21°49'E.

DECEMBER 13, 1990. (THURSDAY). DAY 19.

<u>0431.</u>   Cape Point is 149 miles on a bearing of 313°T. A long night playing dodge 'em with enormous oil rigs. At least they're brightly lit. The hovering work boats are a menace and seem to have a love-hate relationship with sailing vessels. The night reminded me of sailing past Egyptian oil rigs in the Red Sea.

A beautiful dawn with high marbled clouds. Just now we have bright sunshine. I was up most of the night, though early on I had two 45-minute naps. As soon as I plot my position I will sleep a little.

<u>0447.</u>   It's 60 miles to shore from the 0431 fix. Depth 98 meters. Nothing in sight except an oil rig dead astern.

<u>0739.</u>   We're 60 miles east and a little south of Cape Agulhas and are in the SW quadrant of a high that's moving eastward. At the moment we're jogging along at 3–4 knots headed a little west of north while the wind comes from a little north of west. A good time to take a nap.

<u>0948.</u>   It's so easy to tack and forget to change the water in the ballast tanks.

<u>1200.</u>   News from Alistair: Robin Davie tore his mainsail but has bent on another. Yukoh Tada was knocked down three times. NIIHAU IV is on the wrong side of a low and has strong headwinds.

<u>1505.</u>   It's incredible how one can get used to anything. Now I tack to windward in weather of 24–30 knots without even thinking. I am really weary of this long journey back to Cape Town. I still have 158 miles to go. If only the wind would veer to the SW or S.

<u>1738.</u>   Now 33 miles SE of Cape Agulhas. I have almost stopped the yacht because of (1) headwinds—WNW 23 knots, (2) the danger of a lee shore if the wind moves around, and (3) heavy shipping traffic closer inshore. Although the sea is rough and upset, our motion is wonderfully smooth and easy.

DECEMBER 14, 1990. (FRIDAY). DAY 20.

<u>0015.</u>   The Cape Agulhas light is 24 miles west of us.

<u>0403.</u>   Very rough and a lot of hammering. Another drawer latch broke because of ridiculous little fastenings. I wish carpenters had

to go to sea. I just changed clothes because I got chilled wearing rubber-type oilskins. The problem is that one perspires and the clothing gets damp and cold.

I feel quite good after four hours of sleep in four one-hour naps last night. I am waiting for the wind to back to the north. Meanwhile we plod along. This passage seems endless. I read *Most Secret* by Nevil Shute once again. An excellent novel with real people—very ordinary and unspectacular types—but so believable.

<u>0440.</u>   Tacked to port (by wearing around in big seas) and saw at once why we have been going so poorly: the big westerly swell simply overpowers our progress to weather. We are now steering north magnetic (335°T.) and are near Cape Agulhas, the southern tip of Africa (like Cabo Froward in South America).

<u>0645.</u>   Tacked ¾ of a mile off a beach about 5 miles south of Cape Agulhas, whose tall candlestick lighthouse was silhouetted against the morning sun. Rough, relentless, eastbound seas. We bash onward.

<u>0949.</u>   I've been watching cape gannets out fishing. Large, ungainly, comical birds with a long stretched-out profile and wings quite far aft. A white body with a black tail. White wings with black tips. A yellowish crown and a thick, dark bill. Often four or five birds fly together in a loose formation. When these powerful fliers see fish, they peel off and go straight down from a height of 50 or 100 feet in spectacular vertical dives. Wow!

Yesterday when I wanted to go west, the wind was west. Today I want to go NW and—you guessed it. At least I am learning about the headlands of the South African coast. Agulhas, Quoin, Danger, Hangklip. It's just before 1000, and we've been sailing hard since midnight.

<u>1400.</u>   It's 50 miles to Cape Point. This offshore tack is terrible. I can only surmise that a surface current and the swell are heading us. The onshore tack is a knot or more faster. I will stay on this tack until 1600.

<u>1744.</u>   I was sound asleep and a million miles away when something woke me. I rushed outside. We were hove-to with the jib backed. The wind was down. A ship was nearby. A big green unladen ship with a lot of brownish bottom showing. Where was I? In the Mediterranean? Yes, that's it. The Med! Wake up, Roth! I let the jib sheet go on the port side and cranked in the starboard. But with the water ballast backed, we leaned over a lot. The sheet

coming out of the self-tailer caught in the turns on the winch, and I got a nasty override on the winch drum. Damn that ship! Go away. Where was I going? What was my destination? The course? Oh yes, the GPS. I rushed below and plotted where we were. The chart showed the tip of Africa. Things began to come back. Wake up! I was trying to get to Cape Town. I worked out a new course, went up and set the autopilot (which was almost on course), shook out a reef, changed the water ballast, and put on the water for coffee. We were off again. The damned ship was gone.

1943.   The distance to Cape Point is 28 miles on a bearing of 324°. Hangklip is 15 miles ahead and a little to starboard. I can see it silhouetted against the lights and buildings of the outlying settlements.

2336.   Still 15 miles SE of Cape Point in very light wind. I have tacked twice and am on the offshore tack and sailing as carefully as I can to keep from being set down on the dangers around Cape Point. I have asked Cape Town radio to tell the NSRI (National Sea Rescue Institute) that the 0600 tow date is off. I am to call Howard Godfrey when I'm closer.

DECEMBER 15, 1990. (SATURDAY). DAY 21.

0200.   We're barely able to stem the east-going current (tidal stream as well?). I don't dare head north until more wind comes up. At 2257 we were ten miles SSE of Bellows Rock, just south of Cape Point.

0409.   We're becalmed off the Cape of Good Hope—almost the southern tip of Africa—which bears 014°M. We're only 40 miles from Cape Town, but I can't go north until the wind strengthens. The east-setting current is against us, and the swell knocks the wind from the sails.
    This scene is unreal. I'm in a round-the-world race and becalmed off one of the world's great landmarks while trying to sail in the opposite direction. Am I asleep and dreaming? Am I really sailing or am I in a fantasy world? No novelist could think up such a setting. How can anyone keep his value sense in such a situation?

0413.   An eastbound ship to starboard.

0528.   The east-setting Southern Ocean current and the north-setting Benguela Current come together here. However their meeting ground is not a simple black and white line, but a lazy battleground where 1000 micro-currents push one way and then another. We go 100 yards north and come to a stop. Then we're set south 200 yards. Now we slowly pirouette left and stop. Then a turn to the right.

0627.   Ten miles SSE of Cape Point. A dozen cape gannets are circling us and plunge-diving for fish.

0754.   Trifling puffs of wind at last. The gray clouds have given way to bright sunshine, and with 7 knots of wind from the WNW, a smooth sea, and full sail, we are slowly creeping northward. Seals in little groups of two or three are sleeping on the surface with a flipper or two showing. I saw four such groups, and tried shouting to wake them up. All I got in return was the lazy shake of a flipper.

1400.   The sail along the 30-mile coast between Cape Point and Cape Town has been lovely. Not much wind, but we have kept going 2–3 miles offshore since 0800. I've been looking at green mountains, beaches, high cliffs, and an occasional group of houses. Just now we're opposite the Twelve Apostles, a series of steep ridges that climb from the sea to the clouds and terminate at Cape Town's Table Mountain, more than 1000 meters high.

1510.   We're under tow and about to enter the dock area of Cape Town. The weather's bright and sunny, and we're in the midst of a sailing regatta. Everybody is waving, but I feel like a failure.

CHAPTER SIX

Five Frantic Days

Some hours earlier, while sailing along the coast, I had used the VHF radio to telephone my friend Otto Kindlimann. Now as the launch towed me to the Royal Cape Yacht Club I suddenly saw Otto's giant figure hurrying down the dock to take SEBAGO's lines. Otto was a Swiss who had emigrated to South Africa years before and was a salesman for textile machinery. He was also a sailing nut and like many others I think he was a secret participant in the BOC race. Otto worked with me for five days and was helpful beyond belief. Without his smiling face, his enthusiasm, his immense strength, and his charging work ethic to urge people on ("Faster! Faster!"), I'd still be in Cape Town.

After SEBAGO was tied up, I spent a few minutes with reporters and photographers from the Cape Town newspapers and television stations. Then Otto took me out for a meal, during which I fell asleep—exhausted from the 21-day voyage and the strain of entering a big port. I slept the clock around, ate a big breakfast, and began to come to life.

My spirits and my enthusiasm for sailing had revived. Already I had begun to think about continuing in the race, and when I telephoned Margaret (who was back in the U.S.), she spoke out strongly for me to repair the boat and to go on.

"You're not a quitter," she said. "You may be a little behind, but maybe you can catch up. If you don't go on, you'll hate yourself. Life's full of challenges. Some things work. Some don't. You must never give up.

"I've been talking with Ed Boden. Both Ed and I think you should see about repairs and then get going as soon as possible. It's not just a race to win, but to complete. You know the race slogan: 'Anyone who finishes is a winner.' Ed thinks that if you pull out, you'll regret it for the rest of your life. And don't forget the thousands of schoolchildren who are following you. What will they think if you stop now?"

The date was Monday, December 17th. Everyone was shopping for Christmas gifts, and all of South Africa was about to close for the holidays. Many businesses were already shut, and a general slow-down had begun. There was a big sailing regatta and social scene at the yacht club. Getting any work done in Cape Town lay some-where between doubtful and impossible.

Nevertheless Otto and I started in. The cracks in the decks were our biggest problem. The tie rods had not been tensioned enough, which meant that the decks took too much of the shroud tension load. The new solid glass layup in the decks solved the deck compression and leaking problems, but the shroud loads had simply begun to tear out these small areas of solid glass.

During the 1986–87 BOC race I had met Eric Bongers, an experienced builder of custom yachts. Eric looked at the deck problem and suggested laying large fiberglass pads over the exist-ing decks and solid layup. "You need to spread the load over a big-ger area," he said. "Fortunately this repair is fairly easy. In a couple of days you should be back in the race."

Otto and I removed the chainplates, ground off the decks, and laid up 12" x 18" rectangular pads of fiberglass about 5⁄16" thick in epoxy resin. As soon as this was finished we drilled the pads for the chainplates and hooked up the shrouds and the tie rods. Mean-while, Angelo Lavranos, the naval architect, had calculated the correct tension for the tie rods. A metallurgist friend borrowed a torque wrench to tension the rods, and we tightened them *eleven to twelve turns more* than when I had started out on November 24th.

Meanwhile the engine mechanic pulled off the cylinder head, replaced the head gasket, ran the engine for a check, and, alas, again found water in the cylinders. The mechanic's boss now pulled on a pair of overalls and discovered that the metal of the cylinder block was soft and had allowed a tiny channel to develop *under* the head gasket. By rights Yanmar should have replaced the engine, but the engine was Japanese, had been sold to an Ameri-can in California, and was found defective in South Africa. There was no time to sort this out, so we called a company called Metal-stitchers, which repaired the channel. The mechanic quickly put everything back together, and the engine seemed to be OK.* I had now spent more money repairing the engine than it had cost when new.

---

*The engine has run perfectly ever since.

While these jobs were going on, we had another chance to work on the new mainsail with the batten problem. The battens previously fitted in Cape Town were unsatisfactory. There were no others, and there was no time to order anything different. Yet it was imperative that I have a spare mainsail because the old small mainsail was aging quickly in the winds of the Southern Ocean.

Since proper full-length battens and hardware were not available, we would have to use conventional short battens, the only thing we could get. But with short battens we would have to trim the sail drastically. This meant an expensive, agonizing decision to slice off much of the beautiful curved leech of the sail whose extra area we wanted in the light weather regions of the race. It was like amputating a leg, but there was no choice since it was madness to go off again without a proper backup sail. Andy Mitchell, the North sailmaker, said there was no time and that he was about to go on holiday. Otto and I had to convince a very reluctant man to undertake a job that seemed criminal, but had to be done.

Otto thought the water in the engine might have come from the exhaust hose being too close to the waterline, so he installed an extra high loop in the system. Meanwhile I was out shopping with Sue Scholtz—a winsome young woman connected with the race committee—who took me to the supermarkets and specialty shops so I could leave Cape Town well stocked. I had help from a dozen other people who did big and little jobs.

It was the Friday before Christmas. The whole country was closing down. Though sailors consider it bad luck to leave on a Friday, I had no choice. It was time to go. I kissed Sue good-bye and fondly shook Otto's big hand. I was all set for a second try at the Southern Ocean.

CHAPTER SEVEN

Second Try

DECEMBER 21, 1990. (FRIDAY). DAY 0.

__1600.__   After 5 days of frantic repairs in Cape Town, SEBAGO and I are off again for Sydney. It may be idiocy to continue in the race, but I'm going to try to catch up.

__1630.__   A man on the launch that towed me out kindly offered to hoist the mainsail. Unfortunately he cranked the halyard winch like a madman and ripped out the tack of the sail. I have a tack line to the Cunningham cringle above the damaged area to hold the sail in position and will start repairs as soon as possible. Once again the autopilot linkage to the rudder quadrant is giving trouble.

The summer sky is clear, and the wind is trifling. My views of Cape Town and Table Mountain are glorious. Just now I'm looking at Sea Point—a few miles off our port bow—a lovely upscale residential area along the ocean where Sue Scholtz and I shopped yesterday. Today I'm in another world.

__1830.__   The wind has died completely. The light on Slangkop Point bears 196°M.

__2350.__   Thick fog and no wind. A bit worrying in a well-traveled shipping lane. I can hardly believe it, but according to a GPS position we are 6½ miles off Cape Town and still 30 miles from Cape Point. Lights and ships in fog are deceptive and their shapes and sizes blur in and out.

DECEMBER 22, 1990. (SATURDAY). DAY 1.

__0637.__   A trace of wind from the west. I have been sewing away on the mainsail. I fitted two 1" wide nylon tapes about 17" long around the tack ring and am now sewing the tapes to the sail. The four ends of the two tapes overlap the sail about 8" so I have 32" of sewing for each of three rows or roughly 128" or about 10½ feet of stitching to do.

<u>1002.</u>   Wind NW 6 knots. During the calm we got set north and a little west, right back to Cape Town. I am still sewing on the mainsail tack. After trying various schemes I have settled on a pair of Vice-Grip pliers and a glove on my left (strong) hand. The work is slow and tedious because each stitch has to be forced through many layers of heavy material. I have taken down the main and we are running under the genoa.

<u>1322.</u>   I finished the mainsail repair. There is still a rip in the shelf foot, which I never use anyway. The tack ring seems good and strong now. I am quite sleepy but need to get around the Cape of Good Hope, just coming in sight. My turning point is 6 miles away according to the GPS.

<u>1550.</u>   Quite warm. Sunny. Blue sky. Summer! Wind west 14 knots. Changed the #2 reefing pendant, which was chafed, and cranked up the full mainsail. Rolled up the genoa snugly and poled out the jib. Unfortunately I lost one of the big doublehanded winch handles over the side. Only my second such loss in 25 years, but regrettable nevertheless. I'm too sleepy to work out the weather from Alistair Campbell on the ham network. More later.

<u>1956.</u>   For dinner I had the end of a stew I made yesterday from fresh Cape Town beef. The stew needed more onions, perhaps a pepper, a few mushrooms, and certainly more adequate seasoning. Maybe I should have put in a clove of garlic. I need a cook book. Or Margaret.

<u>2000.</u>   I have headed more to the south because the wind has backed to the WNW (13 knots). I am mourning the loss of my doublehanded winch handle. Somehow it wasn't clicked into the winch, and zip, it slipped over the side and was gone.

<u>2004.</u>   Alistair reported two cold fronts: one east and south; the second well south of my position. I am trying to arrange a chat hour with Nandor Fa. All the sewing today was hard on my hands, even with the glove and pliers.

DECEMBER 23, 1990. (SUNDAY). DAY 2.

<u>0503.</u>   Wind SW 22 knots. A weak front came through at 0330. Since the wind has veered I've headed more to the east. The sleep I

had last night was wonderful. I was exhausted by the departure and all the sail sewing.

The decks and cabin sole look terrible. The South African workmen certainly don't worry about the trails they leave behind. The fiberglass man and the engine mechanics were the messiest workmen I have ever known. Maybe I can paint the decks in Sydney. I have been trying a little acetone on a rag to wipe the oil from the cabin sole.

We're sailing well, but it's a long way to Sydney.

<u>0848.</u>   Fix, fix, fix all morning long. I greased and tightened the autopilot drive pivot point (which should be renewed). I drilled an anti-siphon hole in the top of the new gooseneck arrangement for the engine exhaust (which I hope will keep out water). I caulked the two new antenna cables that go through the after watertight compartment bulkhead.

<u>1124.</u>   A good two-hour sleep.

<u>1136.</u>   News from the fleet which is well south into the Roaring Forties and Screaming Fifties. Lots of gales and storm force winds: Isabelle has been dismasted. SPONSOR WANTED was knocked down three times. Kanga was washed over the side, but he had his harness on and got back on board.

<u>1416.</u>   We're going a little slower but are not as pressed. The motion and comfort level are better. My right shoulder is improving.

<u>1843.</u>   It's become very nasty. Wind west 28–31 knots. Big ugly seas. I have rolled up the jib and put in a third reef. We're going along at 7 knots. Astern I see low rolls of heavy clouds that look full of mischief. Yet it's calm and quiet in the cabin.

DECEMBER 24, 1990. (MONDAY). DAY 3.

<u>0107.</u>   Seas way down. Awakened by noise from the jib. Light rain. I can't imagine all these sailhandling procedures without the autopilot. Please keep working!

<u>0816.</u>   Wind after 5 hours of calms. A big breakfast of bacon, eggs, toast, and coffee. Cereal and tea earlier. A gloomy morning. Finished reading *People of the Deer* by Farley Mowat. A penetrating look at an Eskimo tribe wiped out by the white man. Well done and sympathetic. Many parallels with the Indians of Tierra del Fuego.

<u>1139.</u>   BBV's Argos device was washed overboard.

<u>1553.</u>   Heading south into the Roaring Forties on Christmas Eve seems a lugubrious prospect. Worse yet is beating into a SE wind to get to the zone of westerlies.

<u>1816.</u>   Going well with two reefs in the main, half a dozen rolls in the jib, and a full load of water ballast to port. I saw the wind coming and reefed the main in time. Ha! 19–22 knots of wind across the deck. Beautiful gray clouds at sunset.

<u>2320.</u>   Very black out. A pity the wind is from the south. Should I tack?

CHRISTMAS. (TUESDAY). DAY 4.

<u>0258.</u>   Just getting light. Tacked to starboard. Sea fairly flat. Low massed clouds and gusty winds. No fear of ships here.

<u>0900.</u>   The Queen's message on the BBC. Pleasant and reassuring. I am beginning to feel like a British subject. Why doesn't the U.S. President say something upbeat on Christmas?

<u>1041.</u>   Beautiful out. Sunny, blue sky, puffy cumulus clouds, warm. Very pleasant. If only the wind were from another direction.

<u>1510.</u>   I have been troubled with a slight skin irritation and spent a long time searching for the first-aid supplies and medicines. I finally discovered bandages and trauma supplies in two boxes at the bottom of the forward starboard settee locker. The medicines were packed with the trauma supplies and are listed on an old tabulation, full of crossed-out items. Very unsatisfactory.

The boxes were inside plastic bags that had become torn and were stowed in an area that occasionally gets a shot of bilge water when the yacht is heeled over. Everything was damp or wet and some of the medicine labels had come off or were smeared. In Sydney I must go through everything with a doctor and make a new up-to-date list. *It's important that each item be labeled what it is for.* A bunch of drug names mean nothing to a tired sailor far out at sea. I have moved the medical supplies to a drier, more convenient place.

<u>1914.</u>   The barometer is climbing, and the wind is dying. I have hung up the little folding Christmas tree that Margaret and I used aboard WHISPER for many years. The tree is made of green and red paper with silver trimming. I made myself a Christmas drink of

rum, sugar, hot water, lemon, cinnamon, and nutmeg. Some holiday music is on the radio, and I have opened several small gifts
from Margaret and friends in Cape Town. I miss Margaret and my
friends a lot.

DECEMBER 26, 1990. (WEDNESDAY). DAY 5.

<u>0516.</u>   Becalmed all night. I could have made a little distance,
but a persistent swell from the ESE kept stopping the vessel. With
more than 5,000 miles to go, it is not worth tacking back and forth
at one knot. Since the yacht was stopped, I checked the gear on
the foredeck and found that the slider on one of the spinnaker pole
end fittings was stuck. I oiled the fitting and put a new pull cord
on the latch. I also whipped several lines and tidied up the anchor
warp. Busy, busy! Then I went below to the navigation area and
moved the SSB radio and the GPS receiver a little to make them
easier to see and use. A job for a calm moment. I will move the
VHF radio another day.
     The sea is delightful outside. More like the Gulf of Maine on
a summer day. Three or four black-browed albatrosses and a storm
petrel are nearby. Now for some breakfast. I am absolutely slept
out and feel rested and full of energy.

<u>1031.</u>   The sky is full of delicate swirls of cirrus 6 or 7 miles
up. A low is coming. I discovered that if I give a yank on the second reef pendant when the first reef pendant is partially hove
down, the folds of the mainsail lie better and neater and the
chances of chafe are less.

<u>1139.</u>   I hunted up the Australian charts and put them in order.
So far I am following the same route that I sailed in 1986.

<u>1542.</u>   The joys of help from others! In Cape Town I asked a
man to fill three one-liter kerosene bottles from a 20-liter jug. Can
you believe that he lost the top to the jug, didn't tell me, and put
away an open jug? Or that a supposed radio expert lost the screws
to a terminal block and just plastered it on with silicon sealant?
And, oh yes, forgot to tighten the screws holding the electrical
connections? Or that an expensive electronics man left the bottom of an antenna tuner open to the salt environment? Or that
someone adjusting the autopilot compass forgot to tighten the
screws? What else is there that I don't know about?

<u>1654.</u>   Wind NE 9–15 knots. If I use a little water ballast in
light winds it's possible to straighten up the yacht so the mast is

vertical. However this slows us slightly, and it feels strange not to heel a little to leeward.

1730.   After a warning from Alistair for strong NW winds, I am watching the barometer carefully. Yesterday there was a lot of cirrus. Today the sky is clear.

1908.   Mars, reddish as always, is north of Aldebaran and is just ahead to port and high in the sky at "ten o'clock high" as the aviators would say. The Southern Cross is just to starboard at "two o'clock high."

I was sitting at the chart table when I heard a loud hissing sound. Was a jet flying overhead? Was it a whale? A sea monster? A nuclear submarine? I rushed outside. Nothing. The hissing stopped. A mystery.

DECEMBER 27, 1990. (THURSDAY). DAY 6.

0313.   Sea calm and a NE wind of 6 knots. I'm half scared to death by reports of an imminent 40-knot gale. No signs so far. In the meantime we're sailing SE at 4 knots. I had a good sleep and did many little jobs including repairs to the terminal block for the autopilot in the lazarette. I was going to attach a cleat to the outside of each cockpit coaming, but the job would be easier with two people, one inside and one outside.

0556.   It's only 0600, and already I've done a whole day's work. I've been trying to pad the outer end of the spinnaker poles to prevent chafe. I am still moving electronic gear around the navigation area to make the place neater and more efficient. My present problem is to lengthen the coaxial cable for the VHF radio antenna. Meanwhile I'm watching out for the big wind from the NW.

1338.   I am on the 1020 mb. isobar of the high shown on the morning weather chart from Pretoria. There are three lows coming from the west with centers at about 55°S. If I can pick up the westerly flow to the north I should have fair winds.

2353.   Wind 3 knots. Sea smooth. Barometer down a little. Lots of stars. Our track in the midnight sea is a glowing streak of white liquid fire. What sort of amazing chemicals are in the ocean?

I finished *A Short Walk in the Hindu Kush* by Eric Newby. An entertaining travel book by a clever writer. Lots of appealing dialogue by native drivers and porters in Afghanistan. Good writing, humor, and careful historical research.

DECEMBER 28, 1990. (FRIDAY). DAY 7.

<u>0410.</u>   A groggy sleep and a headache this morning. How wonderful to have the genoa on roller-furling gear. So easy to use and so easy on the sail and the crew. Some bad chafe on the starboard foreguy line where it makes more than a 90° turn through the foredeck block. I turned the line end-for-end. Maybe I can move the block a little aft and find a block with a wider sheave.

<u>0458.</u>   I feel better after a hearty breakfast of vegetarian pilaf—a freeze-dried meal from New Zealand. Quite good with a piece of bread submerged in the hot steaming soup. I didn't eat much yesterday, and I was hungry.

<u>0504.</u>   A little trouble with my rear end—a rash. The ship captain's medical book doesn't say anything about such things, and although there are 30–40 ointments, pills, syrups, and injections in the medical supplies, nothing in my portable pharmacy seems appropriate. I have been applying Neosporin ointment several times a day. With all my complaints I'm beginning to feel like a hypochondriac.

<u>0510.</u>   I don't understand this easterly wind, even though it's light. South of a high, the wind should be west.

<u>0818.</u>   Each day I try to do one job to improve the yacht. This morning I mounted a halyard bag in the cockpit to take the starboard coachroof control lines. This makes a total of 10 bags, and now each line or set of lines has a home. In all we have 22 control lines in the cockpit.

Just now with 11 knots of a reaching breeze we have 1,400 sq. ft. of sail set. I have begun *The Magician of Lublin* by Isaac Bashevis Singer. What a brilliant writer! No wonder he won the Nobel Prize.

<u>1557.</u>   Cooler—90% cloud cover. Barometer dropping. Did I mention that at noon I did a little touch-up varnishing in the cockpit? At 1500 I got a call through to Mr. Jeff Whitehead of WQBE, Parkersburg, West Virginia and talked to local schoolchildren about the Indian Ocean, repairs in Cape Town, albatrosses, keeping up my spirits, the West Virginia flag, and the mileage to Sydney. My call was part of the Student Ocean Challenge program. I am to make a call every week and have set up one at the same time next Friday at 1500 with Cape Town radio on Channel 2221. What a coincidence that my father was born in Parkersburg in 1902.

<u>2057.</u>   How far south shall I go as I head eastward?

DECEMBER 29, 1990. (SATURDAY). DAY 8.

<u>0609.</u>   I don't understand how we can have bright sunshine, a high barometer (1009 mb.), and NE winds. We need a second reef.

<u>0646.</u>   The birds are back again. Half a dozen broad-billed prions are darting around, and a sooty albatross is looking us over.

<u>0903.</u>   The weather is definitely colder. I am now wearing Musto layers 1 and 2 (longjohns plus light quilted foul-weather gear). I have cold feet and am about to put on heavier stockings. At 43°S. I'm beginning to see all the familiar things: super clear air (that you can breathe in great lungfuls), skies of the most delicate blue, lots of bird life, and strong winds. The barometer has been dropping for the past 24 hours. I presume a front is on the way.

<u>1033.</u>   The new weather chart shows us on the western flank of a high that has been harassing us with NE winds (22 knots just now) for days. The sea is beginning to get rough although the swells and waves are not over two meters.

<u>1523.</u>   A 24-hour run of 190 miles. The sky is covered with clouds except for an open patch ahead with the most delicate shade of turquoise.

<u>1632.</u>   A big wash and clean underwear. I am beginning to think that my rear-end problem (ugh!) is a fungus. I have begun treating it with a special cream. So far so good. I just got dressed (always oilskins now) and took a couple more rolls in the jib. We are going along at 8 knots. I had a look at the autopilot drive components which seem OK.

I've been watching a young albatross flying around the yacht. It seems incredible that such a stumpy body can be capable of such splendid flight, but, like a bumblebee, the albatross is a superb flier.

I enjoyed the book by Isaac Bashevis Singer a lot. A real story-teller who hides nothing but comes out as a moralist in spite of himself.

I keep thinking of my friends in Annapolis, Newport, and on Mt. Desert Island in Maine.

<u>2004.</u>   I had a brief talk with Nandor Fa at noon, but the radio propagation was poor, and I could understand only half of the conversation.

2330.   Little wind. Rolling heavily in swells from the north and NE. Gybed the main and shook out third reef. A cold rain is pelting down. I'm waiting for the wind to fill in so I can see which spinnaker pole to set.

DECEMBER 30, 1990. (SUNDAY). DAY 9.

0514.   Low clouds and fog. Damp and clammy. We're rolling heavily in a leftover swell. I am surprised at the light wind.
      What's beyond the threshold of my vision? Icebergs? Ships? Fishing vessels? Whales?

0742.   I don't understand this light wind. More chafe at the foredeck block for the foreguy. I have moved the block to the yacht centerline and snapped it to the midstay base for a trial. The route of the foreguy is a problem because of conflicts with anchors, lifelines, and spinnaker poles.

1332.   I have been pumping the bilge 25–30 strokes daily with the big Edson pump ever since Cape Town. Where is the water coming from? Yesterday I closed the 2″ dia. through-hull valve for the water ballast tanks, and today I shut the engine water intake valve. I must look further. A bit worrisome.

1817.   I have taken down the port spinnaker pole, headed up slightly, and picked up about one knot, although it puts us slightly off course. I am flying 1,400 sq. ft. of sail, which makes me nervous with the barometer at 998 mb. At the first sign of more wind I will furl the genoa.
      I moved the VHF radio on the shelf above the chart table. At last the electronic equipment is more usable and easier to read. I am still hunting for the leak that requires all the bilge pumping. I had the floorboards up to check the various bilge lines, three of which I labeled.

DECEMBER 31, 1990. (MONDAY). DAY 10.

0316.   A baffling combination of low barometer and light NE winds. I seem to be failing as a weather forecaster.

0649.   I filled the port water ballast tank.

0807.   I think a weather front may be passing, although the barometer is still dropping. I am eating salami and honey, a strange combination. I oiled all the latches on the winch handles.

1104.   Wind NE 31 knots. We were going along nicely with three reefs and 7–8 rolls in the jib. The autopilot was laboring so I decided to take two more rolls in the jib. When I did, the furling line broke at the furling drum. The sail unrolled immediately, and I suddenly had a flapping monster. To save the jib I let go the halyard and clawed down the sail. In so much wind the only thing I could do was to let the sail go into the water. I spent the next hour pulling the sail—soaking wet, but collapsed and docile—back on board. I used the staysail halyard and the sheets on the sail plus various ties and short lines. I finally shoved the sail into the forward watertight compartment. What an effort!

I hoisted the new storm jib, which is a nifty little sail, nicely made and very strong. Now we're somewhat underpowered, but with the barometer plunging who knows what's coming? I think we're on the east side of a low.

1415.   The needle of the barometer is almost horizontal and reads 980 mb. The storm jib is just right for this 40-knot NE wind. I suppose the next step is to take down the mainsail. However I'm in no hurry to go outside. I have closed both storm doors and have run off another 20° to 150°M.

1725.   Heavy rain until an hour ago. Then the sky began to clear in the west and a milky-yellow sun appeared beneath a low band of smooth clouds. The sun soon set, and the western sky turned a lurid pink, a color that would have scared God. Now the sky is clearing somewhat and the wind is less. Some large seas are running, up to 5 or 6 meters. I need to pole out the jib, but it is stowed in the forward watertight compartment. Do I dare use the genoa?

2134.   I couldn't face climbing into my heavy oilskins again, so I took a chance and managed to shake out the third reef while dressed in the light quilted set of Musto foul-weather gear that I wear all the time. This was foolish, but for once I got away with it and didn't get soaked. The sky is partially clear, and the moonlight is incredibly bright. It's been a hard day.

JANUARY 1, 1991. (TUESDAY). DAY 11.

0303.   A little sun. Very rough seas. There's no possibility of replacing the jib furling line and bending on a headsail until the conditions improve. I'm having trouble with the wind directions on the weather charts and the wind directions on my compass,

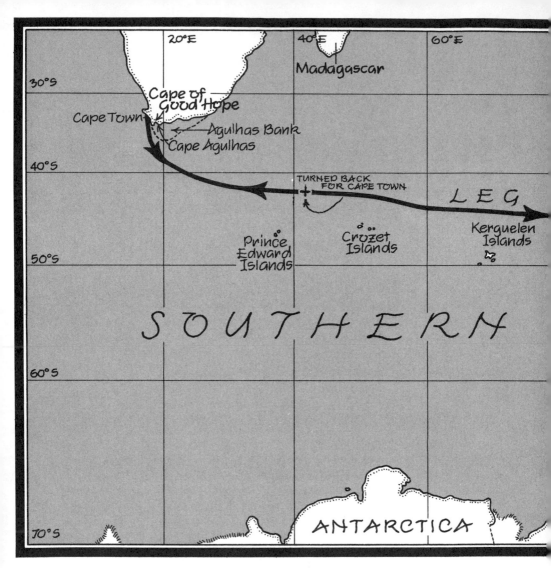

The Southern Ocean from Africa to Tasmania.

because the local variation is 40°W. A north wind (true) is almost NE (magnetic).

0633.   I put a new furling line on the roller-furling gear. The system needs to be improved because you must take half a dozen pieces of hardware apart on the foredeck, tie a single overhand knot in the end of the furling line, and then jam it into a tiny space. It's all very well in a marina slip but most unseamanlike and dangerous at sea. Nevertheless I got it all back together without losing anything and bent on the jib.

1147.   Wind NW 18 knots. A lot of work on deck. I needed three or four more turns of the furling line on the genoa furling

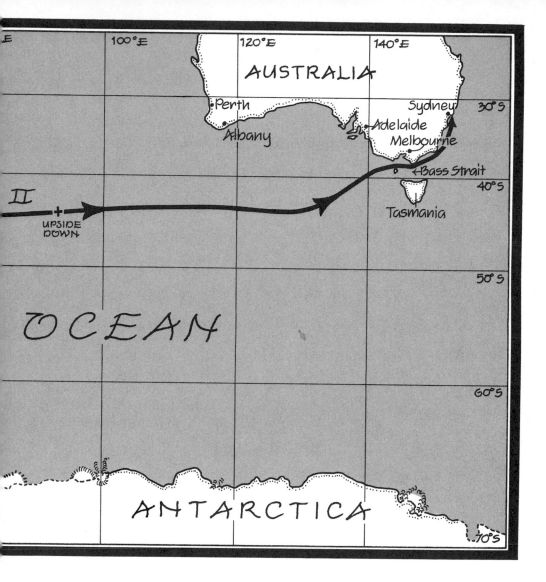

drum, but to do it meant an hour of threading and stringing line. If the furling line could be disconnected at the drum, the job would be easy.

While I was taking down the storm jib I happened to look astern and saw a big squall coming. I immediately furled the jib, and wham, we were hit by a blast from the west. Now the air has cleared, and I hope the wind will be steady for a while.

Alistair and the ham operators on the Durban maritime net spoke to a Danish yacht that was knocked down three times and rolled over once. The vessel has a leak and reported winds of 50–60 knots on the back of the low that's coming this way. The Danish yacht's position is 38°11'S., 30°45'E.

I've done so much winch cranking this morning that my shoulders feel as if they're coming off.

<u>1615.</u>   I made another attempt to straighten out the genoa furling line. Frustrating because of some terribly kinky line and the inability to disconnect the line at the furling drum.

<u>1724.</u>   The wind suddenly increased, and we were way overpowered. I pulled down the second reef, which got us under control. The downhaul lines that I tied to the three luff reefing cringles and the headboard are wonderful for getting the sail down when it's plastered against the rigging in strong following winds. Only ¼" dia. lines, but just right because the force can be applied where it's needed.
     Much colder. Alistair warned me about strong SW winds that are coming. I am all set to put in the third reef or to drop the mainsail altogether.

<u>1800.</u>   My nerves are shot because of too much weather intelligence. I put in the third reef, and we're going along at 7 and 8 knots (9.6 just now). Beautiful outside. Clear and cold. The Southern Cross is high in the sky to starboard, and a full moon is rising from the sea to port. I keep looking around for ships (none), land (none), and icebergs (none).

<u>2307.</u>   The dreamers who talk about the Southern Ocean should be here now. We're racing along with small sails (three reefs and a scrap of poled-out jib) and often have the end of the main boom in the water. The safest place to be is below in a bunk protected by a stout lee cloth and with pillows right and left. Back to the womb. We speed up to 10–11 knots for 5–6 seconds and then drop to 7–8 knots. It's a nervous kind of sailing.

JANUARY 2, 1991. (WEDNESDAY). DAY 12.

<u>0504.</u>   A series of heavy squalls from the SW at 0300. I started to furl the jib, but the wind (41 knots true) was strong enough to push the after headstay close to the forward stay. As the jib revolved it picked up the clew of the genoa and jammed the jib furling gear, Fortunately the sail was half furled. I changed course to run off before the squall, and we raced along at 12–15 knots for a few minutes. I feared the worst, but the autopilot and yacht handled everything very well. After the squall passed I went forward

and immediately saw the problem and the solution. I unwound the jib, rolled it up, and then partially unrolled and rolled the genoa to wind up the clew. I then set the poled-out jib. A contributing factor to the furling gear foul-up was easing the sheet too much. I should ease it a little and roll up a little of the sail, etc. However in strong winds anything can happen.

<u>0513.</u>   Hooray, we just crossed 50° east.

<u>0633.</u>   A large ground swell. About 5–6 meters with a 12-second period. The weather is much colder, and I have put on additional heavy long underwear.

According to the Durban maritime net the Danish couple abandoned their yacht SCOOP about 220 miles SE of Port Elizabeth. The vessel was a Beneteau 40, which sank after being knocked down three times and rolled over. A tug is on the way from Port Elizabeth in response to a Mayday call. Also a plane is flying out. Bad luck for SCOOP and her crew.

<u>1800.</u>   A passing rain shower. A long sleep. Finished reading *Cooper's Creek* by Alan Moorehead. A historical romp through early Australian exploration. With expert commentary. Not great, but good.

Still 4,112 miles to go to King Island at the west end of Bass Strait. Our run at noon was 209 miles. Can I keep my sanity for another month?

JANUARY 3, 1991. (THURSDAY). DAY 13.

<u>0131.</u>   At 2230 the motion of the yacht suddenly changed. I awoke at once, dressed quickly, and went outside. The yacht was jogging along at 2 knots or so with the jib backed against the starboard spinnaker pole. We were in long, gentle seas and riding slowly up and down. The wind was 22 knots from the WNW. The moment was strangely peaceful.

The autopilot was dead. I changed the drive unit in about 10 minutes. No problems except greasing the pin that connected the end of the drive shaft to the quadrant. I switched on the unit, and we got underway. I have shut off the yaw control on the autopilot to reduce wear and tear on the device.

I now have one set of autopilot spares and a little over 4,000 miles to go to King Island (or about 4,500 miles to Sydney). I just had breakfast (it gets light about 0030–0100 GMT). Maybe I'll go back to sleep.

<u>0451.</u>   We're about 180 miles north of the Îles Crozet, four small South Indian Ocean islands that belong to France. The westerly magnetic variation here is 43°, so to sail east our heading is 133°M.

<u>0647.</u>   The Danish couple on the 40-foot Beneteau was rescued yesterday by the tug from Port Elizabeth. A report says the vessel was swamped by a 25-meter wave.

<u>0846.</u>   I gybed the running rig, which takes about half an hour of huffing and puffing. The word yesterday was SW winds, but the barometer is high and climbing. The wind has backed to the north. We have a bit too much sail up and may need a second reef. I keep looking around for ships, yachts, fishing boats, liferafts, wreckage, tree trunks—anything, but there is nothing.

<u>1008.</u>   More wind. I put a second reef in the mainsail and rolled up the jib 8 turns. While I was cranking the reef in the main I noticed that the load on the reefing line bends the heavy padeye to which the turning block is attached. Horrors! The reefing hardware is grossly overloaded. Yet I've been using the same system for years. I must deal with this in Sydney.

<u>1015.</u>   The barometer is still rising (1019 mb.), and we're in bright sunshine. All the signs of a big high-pressure area. I'm falling asleep.

<u>1550.</u>   I have been eating scraps all day and suddenly got hungry for real food. I heated a can of meat and vegetables and ate it together with three slices of bread and a cup of tea. Plus two aspirins and a slug of brandy.

I am slightly worried about the amount of food on board. I don't have any more pouch meals and none of the #10 cans of freeze-dried beef stew and chicken stew that I normally carry. Maybe I should start fishing.

The barometer has gone from 980 to 1020 mb. in two days.

<u>1928.</u>   A waning moon. Clear sky. Orion to port. The Southern Cross to starboard. Now 45° of westerly variation. Our true wind is NW 22–26 knots.

<u>1936.</u>   The wind is moaning in the rigging. We're tearing along and sometimes surf up to 11–12 knots for a few seconds. On the 1020 isobar the weather map shows 25 knots of wind, which is about what we have.

<u>1948.</u>   I so well remember shooting the stars in the Southern Cross (Rigil Kentaurus, Hadar, Crux, Gacrux) when Margaret and I

sailed WHISPER around the world and made the run from French Polynesia to the Indian Ocean north of Australia through Torres Strait.

JANUARY 4, 1991. (FRIDAY). DAY 14.

0041.   Just light. Looks like a front coming from the west. The yacht is yawing a lot. I keep thinking that a better running scheme might be to take the mainsail down entirely and run under the eased genoa with no pole at all. Then as the wind strength varies, simply roll the sail in or out. Reefing and unreefing the main plus all the other cranking is wearing me out. And all the yawing makes for both a poor course and a lot of discomfort below. Probably a better scheme is to take an airplane.

0714.   A good breakfast of bacon and eggs, toast and coffee. The weather is mild and pleasant. The radio yammers on about Iraq and Saddam Hussein and the U.S.-U.N. force. I am reading in Nevil Shute and also the plays of Graham Greene. We are averaging about 160 miles per day, which suggests that we will arrive in Sydney on January 31st.

1226.   My radio contacts with South Africa are beginning to fade out. The news from the fleet is that GENERALI CONCORDE made a one-day run of 323 miles. Unfortunately Alain Gautier had a nasty mishap when his big mainsail accidentally gybed, and the mainsheet slammed him against the winches and lifelines on the starboard side, hurting his back, one hand, and giving him a hip wound that would not stop bleeding. Alain lay helpless in the cockpit for 30 minutes and spent the rest of the day in his berth. "I could only stand up for about three minutes and then I collapsed," he said.

　　　Alain is lucky to be alive.

　　　Aboard ECUREUIL, near Tasmania, Isabelle lost her mast when the yacht fell into a big trough between two waves. The French captain was hand steering in 35 knots of wind when the mast broke at the first spreader. Isabelle is setting up a jury rig. ALLIED BANK passed within five boatlengths of a large chunk of ice.

　　　I notice that the conversations on the chat hour are subdued. Not many jokes these days.

1526.   I made a call to radio station WQBE in West Virginia to update the schoolchildren on my voyage. I spoke of the distances from Cape Town to Sydney, about the obscure islands to the south, sperm whales, and a little about my daily routine. I forgot to mention the clipper ship route, which I'll talk about next week.

<u>1629.</u>   The B&G speedometer is reading only about half of what it should. I took out the impeller, which was covered with tiny white barnacles. I scraped them off, and re-inserted the impeller. However there was no difference in the reading. It's incredible that barnacles can collect on a rapidly spinning wheel.

<u>1738.</u>   I entered the calibration value (4.78) in the B&G unit, and the speed readout suddenly changed to its normal reading. Mystifying. I guess I will never understand computers.

JANUARY 5, 1991. (SATURDAY). DAY 15.

<u>0217.</u>   Lovely rays from the early morning sun. I'm still mystified why the speed log readings suddenly decreased by half. In any case the meter now seems to be working OK.

<u>0616.</u>   Wind NNE 29 knots. I have put in the third reef because the main boom was in the water and making a 10-foot roostertail. The weather is surprisingly warm, and we appear to be on the south end of a big high-pressure area. I keep looking out for icebergs but no sign of anything.
   I discovered a little book with Margaret's signature in it. From 1947. I wish I had known her then.

<u>0641.</u>   I requested Davina (ZS1GC) to send a fax to Pete Dunning to ask Margaret to bring a spare motor and wiring diagram for the autopilot to Sydney. Twenty years ago when I sailed I had no autopilot and no radio. Fax for the masses hadn't been invented. How times change.

<u>0659.</u>   Yesterday I logged 227 miles between two noon GPS positions. I think we're going better today and hope to break my record of 240 miles.

<u>0921.</u>   Since the wind is up to 33 knots from the NNE, I put the mainsail down entirely. We're running along nicely under the jib with two rolls. How nice it is with only one sail, no spinnaker pole, and no mass of lines. We're still going along at 8-9-10 knots.
   I'm starved. Time to slice the green mold from the bread, to make toast, a cup of tea, and to boil a couple of eggs. The eggs from Cape Town are the best I've ever eaten.

<u>1210.</u>   204 miles at noon.

1356.   Running under just a headsail is extremely satisfactory so far. Plenty of speed. The yacht is much, much safer to handle (no poles; fewer lines), and to gybe I only need to change the course and then the sheets. We roll more, but I can live with that. We're at 44°S., about 300 miles north of the Kerguelen Islands.

1423.   A lot of big waves outside, and one thumps into us hard two or three times an hour. Fortunately our speed tends to pull us away. The front is upon us. Gray, overcast, and cold. Perth is 2,454 miles on a true bearing of 072° or ENE.

2335.   The wind shift came through as the weather front passed going east. I simply changed the jib sheet and the running backstay. The cockpit lines keep getting washed over the side when a wave sweeps the vessel. I need more cleats on the cockpit coamings. Miserable out. Fog and light rain. Iceberg weather. Dawn is just breaking, which seems crazy at midnight (GMT).

JANUARY 6, 1991. (SUNDAY). DAY 16.

0324.   Wind from the south. Cold, wet, clammy, foggy. I've been watching two sooty albatrosses—unmistakable in their dark gray suits.

1128.   About 50% cumulus cloud cover with the sun ducking in and out. It's bitterly cold. I now have the jib poled out to starboard and the main up with one reef.

1422.   Success with a white sauce over tuna, my first ever. Delicious, and what a difference in taste! Devina, on the Durban ham net, gave me a few tips.

JANUARY 7, 1991. (MONDAY). DAY 17.

0334.   At 0030 we were slatting away with a light following wind, so I dropped the mainsail (which was hard to get down because the top slides were binding). I rolled up the jib and tried running with the full genoa. Unlike the other day, however—when I ran successfully with the jib alone in strong winds—the genoa arrangement was a failure because the swell kept knocking the wind from the sail. So I rolled up the genoa, hoisted the mainsail, and poled out the jib. Back to convention.

A pretty morning. Cumulus clouds and a weak sun. I had a good sleep and just finished an orange, bacon and eggs, toast, and coffee. I continue to worry about my food supply. Normally I carry extra pouch meals and an oversupply of freeze-dried food, but these things are gone.

The radio is full of speculation about Saddam Hussein and the prospect of a war with Iraq. I am reading a curious little book called *A Short History of the World* by H. G. Wells. Quite good. A remarkable synopsis of the world's significant events. How, I wonder, did Wells decide what to include and what to leave out?

<u>0853.</u>   I hoped to install the latches for the main companionway doors (a job left over from Newport), but I discovered several broken parts. I found three turning blocks for the mainsail reefing pendants, but the existing (and bent) padeyes are in the way. In addition, I need to work out an alternate lead to the mast winch in case the reefing winch is unusable for any reason. These jobs will have to wait until Sydney. I poked epoxy into half a dozen holes in the hull layup in the lazarette where copper grounding strips had once been fastened. And finally, I did a little patch varnishing on the cockpit dodger trim strip.

<u>0937.</u>   Amazing to sail hour after hour, day after day, week after week and never see another ship or trace of a human being. All this fuss over tiny Kuwait when this enormous wilderness of water exists south of the continents. Of course oil hasn't been found here yet.

<u>2117.</u>   One of the cameras jammed so I changed the film to another.

<u>2331.</u>   It looks a bit squally to windward so I put in a second reef. I can't get used to the dawn—an orange smear in the east—coming at midnight when we operate on GMT.

JANUARY 8, 1991. (TUESDAY). DAY 18.

<u>0320.</u>   It's now 3,486 miles to Sydney.

<u>0408.</u>   We're reaching along nicely with the full jib and the mainsail with one reef. There's a bit of chafe where the foot of the jib touches the bow pulpit, so I raised the sail a little. The poor jib is looking almost as sad as the main, but with more than 13,000 miles I guess such wear is expected. A bit of blue bottom paint doesn't help its appearance.

<u>0513.</u>   SEBAGO will not steer properly on a reach if there's too much mainsail area. With 16–17 knots of true wind she wants to round up, no matter how much you ease the mainsheet.

<u>0839.</u>   A squally, rainy morning with unsettled wind. I have poled out the jib to port again. I just took an inventory of food and found more than I reckoned. The port water tank is about 60 percent full.

<u>0849.</u>   So far the weather charts from Melbourne are poor. I can't make out the lines of longitude, but at least we're getting something. The charts should gradually improve.

JANUARY 9, 1991. (WEDNESDAY). DAY 19.

<u>0042.</u>   We have been sailing at more than 8 knots all night with 2 reefs in the mainsail and 4–5 rolls in the jib. This solo sailing is madness. There's no one to talk to. I simply eat, sleep, sail, fix things, listen to the radio, and read a little. In the meantime I wear out the yacht and my life for no real purpose. Also there's a chance of running into something or falling over the side. It's absolute madness.

Yet—and I pause to look out at the sea—I'm attracted to solo sailing because such an enterprise—like rock climbing high in the Alps—is among the most difficult of challenges. At one time or another I'm forced to use all my abilities, all my energy, and all my resources. Plus I get some feeling of pleasure and satisfaction at completing a good passage.

<u>0246.</u>   Breakfast and a slightly better weather map from Australia. Many of the lines on the little map are fragmentary or nonexistent, but I have drawn in some of the lines that are missing and have worked out the latitude and longitude. I think we should get SW winds.

<u>0250.</u>   I heard a good interview on the BBC with Phillip Knightley, who has done a new book on war correspondents and their problems. From the Boer War right up to the Gulf Crisis.

<u>0352.</u>   I am now speaking with Art (VK6ART) and Roy (VK6BO) in Perth. I took a few photographs from the bow with an old Nikon FM. The automatic Nikon appears to be dead (that makes two). Maybe I can get the cameras repaired in Sydney.

<u>0904.</u>   Heavy swirls of fog, although the sun is trying hard to come out. My feet are blocks of ice. The 0815 weather chart is quite good. We're on the bottom (south side) of a giant high, so we should have fair winds. I can't find the chart of Tasmania.

<u>1154.</u>   I finally found the Tasmanian chart folded inside another chart. The fog continues because a warm wind from the north is blowing across a cold sea.

<u>1356.</u>   No floating trees, whales, ships, or old oil drums in these waters. Gray and raw. Getting dark already. I had a tasty meal of corn with chopped up pork (from a can) with a white sauce. I am learning that a white sauce can do great things to dull ingredients. The big news on the radio is the talk between the U.S. and Iraq. Will there be war?

<u>1719.</u>   Hard pressed. Put in the third reef. Still going along at 8 knots.

<u>1800.</u>   More rolls in the jib; I have run off slightly to the SSE.

<u>1822.</u>   Wind now 31 knots.

JANUARY 10, 1991. (THURSDAY). DAY 20.

<u>0227.</u>   Way overpowered. I took down the mainsail, which was easier than I had anticipated. I then dropped the port spinnaker pole to the pulpit and put the jib to starboard. Very large seas breaking here and there. Strictly safety harness weather. We had been going 9.5, 9.8, 9.6 knots. Now we're going 8 and 7.9. Overcast this morning, but not so foggy. The magnetic variation is beginning to decrease.

A lot of rolling last night. I started out in the starboard (leeward) bunk (no lee cloth), but had to move to the port pilot berth which has a stout lee cloth. With pillows and blankets the berth is very comfortable. Too rough for cooking today. I am munching cheese and crackers.

<u>0822.</u>   The only thing I can do is to shelter in the port pilot berth and stay quiet. I'm reading about the wreck of the PRO PATRIA (1933) by James Norman Hall, a rather dreamy reflection of Pitcairn Island and the BOUNTY mutiny.

<u>1008.</u>   I was in the cockpit and stepping below to the cabin when a big pair of hands suddenly thrust themselves out at me. I shouted with surprise and then realized that the hands were two

gloves drying on hooks that had swung out in front of me as the boat rolled. What a fright! What a lot of laughing!

<u>1134.</u>   The barometer is plunging. The wind is 32 knots from the north, and I have shut both halves of the companionway storm door.

<u>1341.</u>   I don't like the look of the seas. The barometer is still falling. The safest place is in my bunk.

<u>1738.</u>   I can't recall a rougher night.

<u>1911.</u>   Normally I can walk around below. When it's rough I go from handhold to handhold. Today I have been holding on with both hands and wedging my body against a bulkhead, the chart table, or the galley counter. I've opened the top half of the companionway door and can see that the wind has veered a little to the west. The clouds are gone. The stars are bright, and I have been admiring the thin white slice of the new moon.

<u>2218.</u>   Just getting light. I would like to unhook the port jib sheet from the end of the port spinnaker pole, which is resting on the pulpit. However it's not necessary just now, and I don't care to go up on the foredeck because the seas are enormous. I've headed a little more north (course 110°M.) to take the WNW seas more astern. The past 12 hours have been nasty.

CHAPTER EIGHT

Upside Down

JANUARY 11, 1991. (FRIDAY). DAY 21.

<u>0137.</u>　　The wind is only 36 knots, but the sea conditions are simply terrible. Water is flying all over the place. Every time a wave breaks on board, the cockpit gets filled. Fortunately the water quickly runs out via the four 3″ dia. cockpit drains.

We're running nicely before the wind at 10 to 12 knots with no mainsail and only about ⅓ of the jib. However I'm worried that if we ever get broadside to the waves or have to stop, we could get rolled over. The barometer has started to rise, and this time is the worst of all.

<u>1056.</u>　　Position 43°42′S., 92°25′E.* A lot has happened since my 0137 entry. The wind increased, and the seas grew larger—real Cape Horn graybeards. The autopilot couldn't keep up with the steering and quit. Since the barometer had stabilized at 1001 mb., I thought the depression would hurry toward the east, the wind would ease, and I could see about repairing the autopilot.

I began to steer by hand about 0215 and got along OK except that the wind blew harder and harder and was soon up to a steady 46 to 48 knots. The seas built up accordingly, and I had all I could do to steer. I lost control several times when waves broke over the yacht. Soon I was soaked, but coping marginally. At times the only way I could hold the tiller was to take a couple of turns with the tail of one of the ¾″ dia. running backstay lines leading from a winch.

I was in a heavy westerly storm with big seas (say 30–35 feet). This isn't as bad as it sounds because the waves were long and fairly regular and measured 600 or 700 feet—12 to 14 boatlengths—between crests. The yacht climbed smoothly up and

*We were in the SE Indian Ocean about 4,000 miles south of Calcutta, India. The nearest land was an uninhabited speck named Ile St. Paul which was 730 miles to the WNW. Perth, Australia lay 1,200 miles to the ENE.

down as these irregularly formed mountains of water passed to the east every 10 or 11 seconds. My problem was caused by the swells (say 15–20 feet) that came from a slightly different direction and were left over from an old storm (or from a distant storm). When a sea and a swell got mixed up, there was suddenly a very steep and high wave (say 50 feet). The waves got out of sequence, and the distance between the waves became less. And when the height of a wave (50 feet) gets to be ¹⁄₇th of its length (350 feet) the wave will break every time.

While I steered I could occasionally hear a wave boom and crash in the distance. Sometimes one broke closer—a wave that was steep and shaped like a tooth on a huge gear wheel. These gigantic, isolated breaking waves looked like solitary mountain peaks or maybe one of the Egyptian pyramids. All of a sudden one of them would rear up out of the sea. An instant later I was looking at a cascading waterfall with hundreds of tons of upset water turning over and over. The power and noise of the tumbling water were incredible.

When a wave broke and the water fell over on itself, it trapped air here and there. The dark sea became a light greenish-blue or turquoise for about 45 seconds or maybe a minute while the upset water bubbled and seethed and frothed. Gradually the sea calmed down, the air escaped, and the water became its usual dark blue.

I knew that if one of these steep waves broke underneath us we would be in big trouble. Already we had rolled heavily and put the masthead in the sea three times. SEBAGO had 8,000 pounds of lead in her ballast keel, however, and she quickly rolled upright.

We were sailing fast. The steering was heavy, and I madly pushed and pulled on the tiller—first one way, then another. This was one of the times when a singlehander has to forget everything except to keep her going. . . . Nothing else was important but to steer. . . . I felt that if I could pull out a few reserves of energy and hand steer for three or four hours we might get clear of the breaking seas.

Suddenly there was a great roar and crash. The next thing I knew I was in the sea and could feel water running underneath my heavy oilskins and into my boots. Then my head broke the surface. I never thought I would see SEBAGO's blue keel while at sea, but there it was alongside me. Jesus, she was upside down. What a moment!

Then the boat rolled, and the mast appeared and lay flat on the surface. I was tied to the yacht and scrambled aboard across the port lifelines, which were level with the sea. The boathook whizzed by my head and disappeared. A winch handle rattled loosely in the cockpit next to me. I distinctly recall thinking about the righting moment of the yacht. The line "I wonder if the naval architect did his sums correctly" went through my head.

All forward motion had stopped, and we lay dead in the water. After a few seconds—who knows how long it was?—the boat rolled upright. As she came up I heard things crashing and banging below. Water poured off the mast and headsail. I glanced at the rig, which looked OK except that the masthead light fixture was broken and dangling by its electric wires. The B&G masthead unit was either damaged or gone because the true windspeed dial on the cockpit instrument read zero.

The first thing I did was to sit down. I took off my boots, emptied them of water, squeezed out my stockings and boot liners, and then put everything back on. Just like crossing a stream in the mountains.

We had been running at high speed (up to 12 knots) with part of the jib. When the vessel came up, the sail was backed and filled with wind and we were hove-to. There was still plenty of wind blowing and too much load on the sail, so I wound up most of it. This made us slightly more comfortable.

Would we get hit by another such wave?

I went below to pump out the yacht and found an appalling mess. During the rush in Cape Town, several of the floorboards had not been screwed down properly and came out when the yacht rolled. The icebox (which I used for general food stowage) was upside down. Bottles and dishes were rolling everywhere. All the fastenings (16 boxes of nuts and bolts, screws, washers, clevis pins, etc.) had erupted from a locker and spilled. When the yacht was upside down, the chart table lid had opened and dumped all of the navigation instruments, dividers, choice spare parts, and so on. The contents of one bookcase got upset.

All these things—especially the nuts and bolts—were rolling around on the cabin sole and making an incredible amount of noise. Much of the stuff has fallen into the bilge where the floorboards were missing. (The hardware is clattering away as I write.) Although the companionway door was shut during the capsize, there was a lot of water below that had come through the forward ventilator and by way of the mast via the halyard slots.

The Edson hand pump was a godsend—a gallon a stroke, and it never got clogged although the bilge was loaded with bolts, paperback book covers, ballpoint pens, matchsticks, scratch pads, broken glass, sponges—debris of every sort. I blessed my friend Willie Keen of Edson, who had helped me install the pump.

After I pumped out, I went on deck and set the Monitor wind vane, which I hope will steer the yacht while I deal with the wreckage below. Much of the electrical system is wet, and I have no idea whether I can get the autopilot working again.

The bevel gears of the Monitor vane were out of alignment so I had to climb down on the vane frame at the stern to deal with them. There was a lot of water flying around, but since I was already soaked it made no difference. I soon got the vane gear working, and off we went under good control (with the tiny sail). We've been going for some hours on a reasonable course at 7 knots, which shows how much wind there is. I'm glad that I have a non-electric steering system on board.

I began to get cold from my wet clothes so I stripped down and wiped myself hard with a dry towel. Some dry long underwear felt marvelous and warm. Then I put on a thick sweater, spare oilskins, and dry stockings. While I was steering I got knocked around by the tiller, and I have a few bruises on my chest and legs.

Meanwhile I have begun to clean up below. Most things are wet, and many of the drawers have water in them. It will take days—weeks—to dry out everything.

I'm exhausted, and my nerves are shot. In my mind's eye I still have the incredible image of the yacht stopped dead with her mast in the water. I am climbing into the swamped cockpit and wondering if she will come up. The size of those breaking seas was remarkable. Nothing afloat on earth can withstand such power.

1613.   Picked up the mess in the cabin for a few hours. We're going almost directly downwind at 7.6 knots. With no mainsail up, however, we're rolling a lot. I ate part of a can of lamb curry for supper. Now to rest.

2220.   A good sleep. I feel a bit brighter. I have made a lot of progress with the confusion below, but there's a long way to go. The cursed fastenings are everywhere. The sea is still quite rough, and the prediction is for two more lows. The problem is the close spacing of the isobars.

JANUARY 12, 1991. (SATURDAY). DAY 22.

0238.   Wind SW 28 knots. Better weather, but a big sea is still running. I have put up the triple reefed mainsail and poled out the jib to starboard. I am so used to looking at the B&G true windspeed dial that I am going to have to learn to observe windspeed again by looking at the sea.

<u>0300.</u>   Bad news. A squall (there have been squalls all morning) hit us just as I was taking down the port spinnaker pole. I was at the mast unhooking the pole when the yacht suddenly heeled. The pole slipped from my hands and fell over the lifelines into the water. I managed to grab the forward end of the pole as it was going overboard, but I couldn't hold it, and the pole slipped away. I am so angry with myself that I could scream! However, that won't bring back the pole, which I saw floating away on a distant wave. Henceforth I'll always keep one of the sheets or guys tied to a pole so there will be no possibility of losing it.

<u>1654.</u>   Wind west 17 knots. A good two-hour nap. A lot of work today. I installed a new autopilot control box and a drive unit. More mopping up below. I'm still collecting nuts and bolts. I found two pencils inside the cockpit bilge pump. Much of the bedding is soaked, and water got into most of the drawers, which seems inconceivable and shows how much water must have been flying around.

Outside the day is pleasant and warm, and the extreme swell is going down. I will never forget the tremendous breaking seas that I saw yesterday. They were hundreds of feet across the front and were more like waterfalls than ocean waves.

The alarm clock doesn't work anymore after its smash yesterday. Perhaps I can use the B&G countdown alarm. During the day I put a larger air blade on the Monitor vane, which made a big improvement. I lucked out on the bevel gear setting in the vane mechanism—it's working OK. The little piece of chain in the linkage between the vane and the tiller makes it easy to adjust the helm.

When I woke up, I rushed into the cockpit. The mainsail needed a second reef, but I waited a moment because after a deep sleep I have learned to evaluate things for a few minutes before doing anything.

<u>1915.</u>   A squall the vane couldn't handle. I had to hurry into the cockpit to help out. I am watching the weather charts, which show two deep lows coming this way. Meanwhile the barometer is high (1022 mb.), and we're going along nicely.

JANUARY 13, 1991. (SUNDAY). DAY 23.

<u>0158.</u>   The enormous swell is gone. At last I can sit comfortably and write. I gybed the rig after figuring out an idiot-proof

scheme for changing the spinnaker pole from one side to the other. I keep it tied to the ship in two places. The Monitor vane is steering nicely.

All sorts of things are missing below. The butter dish, the sugar pot, the paper clip box. My ruined alarm clock is a big loss. So far I haven't overslept, but it could be a danger near land. I'm hungry, so off to the galley.

0432.   I heard on the BBC that Alec Rose died. After his 1967–68 voyage around the world, 500,000 people turned out to welcome him home. "It was the high point of my life," he said later. In the U.S. you'd find two bill collectors, a guy trying to sell you something, and a customs man wailing for overtime. Or have I become too cynical?

0500.   I tightened the bottom bolts on the steering vane mounting, a job I must remember to do daily. This part of the Monitor definitely needs improving. Why not drill a small hole through the hex head part of the bolts and tie each bolt to the frame with twisted safety wire in aircraft fashion?*

0525.   Amazing. A little while ago we rolled a little and I heard a strange rattle. I pulled up a piece of the galley floor and not only found the sugar shaker, butter crock, and a saucepan lid, but 200 nuts and bolts.

0933.   It's warm and sunny so I'm trying to dry the cushions and the wet bedding. I'm gradually taking off layers of clothing.

1157.   I opened the camera drawer and found two inches of saltwater in the bottom. Everything was corroded and ruined. The handheld VHF radio, three cameras, four lenses, an exposure meter, and a tape recorder are nothing but junk. There's no sense complaining. An accident. End of story.

1228.   Although GMT is only a little past noon, the sun is already setting. This seems crazy.

1326.   I began to shake out a reef, but we're going along so nicely I will wait. I wonder if any water got into the radar antenna when we were upside down?

2337.   Raw and nasty outside. Low, gray stratus. Hard to get the vane to steer.

*This modification and others were adopted by Monitor. I also passed along four design improvements to Schaefer regarding the prototype headsail furling gears that I carried. This shows the benefits to manufacturers from putting their equipment in such races.

JANUARY 14, 1991. (MONDAY). DAY 24.

<u>0115.</u>   Sorted out a mass of fastenings, garbage, and ruined odds and ends (tape recorder, lens pouches) that I tossed in the wastebasket after the capsize. It's a pity the camera drawer got flooded. The problem is what to do with the wet bedding and wet foam cushions.

<u>0435.</u>   We're nearing Australia. Only 896 miles from Perth and 1,872 miles to King Island. The yacht is rolling heavily. I filled half the port water ballast tank to keep us more upright.

<u>0503.</u>   A very rough sea. The wind has gone more aft so I pumped out the water ballast tank. The radar set doesn't work. I suppose saltwater leaked into the antenna.

<u>0648.</u>   Lots of dreams. I was in a funny situation (a sexy woman named Lulu Flame), and I woke up roaring with laughter.

<u>1012.</u>   I've been looking at the masthead with the binoculars, and see that the lighting fixture is gone as well as the wind anemometer and the wind direction pointer. The VHF antenna is bent about 30°.

<u>1410.</u>   A strong north wind (33 knots) as the SW end of a high moves east. A big difference overhead—from 90 percent cloud cover to a clear sky. Orion is high to port, and the Southern Cross is high to starboard. I can't believe this wind will last. I am falling asleep.

<u>1851.</u>   Still more wind—35 knots from the north. Three reefs in the main and the tiniest scrap of poled-out jib. We're right on course. This weather reminds me of the sailing before I arrived in Cape Town. A clear sky, a whistling wind, and a high barometer. Then I was trying to go to windward; now, fortunately, the wind is aft of the beam. How the wind does whistle!

The Monitor vane is working well. No electric power demands and no motors or control boxes to burn out.

<u>2245.</u>   A good sleep. I'm warm and relaxed. How wonderful it is to be rested. The wind is a little less but still over 30 knots. The port jib sheet looks pretty sad where it has been hard against the spinnaker pole jaws. Every few hours I move the sheet slightly in or out to keep the line from chafing. What I need at the end of the pole is a nicely rounded sheave.

I am talking to ham radio operators in Perth, who pass along the weather forecast each morning. Pleasant fellows who live for their radios and schedules. An occasional wave sweeps the cockpit and sometimes washes the lines out of their stowage bags along the cockpit coamings.

I keep finding things in the cabin. A few nuts and bolts have been falling out of a bundle of wires above the galley work area. Yesterday I used the long mechanical finger (a super tool) to fish two ruined hand calculators out of the bilge, plus more nuts and bolts, Scotch tape, plastic lids, and ballpoint pens.

JANUARY 15, 1991. (TUESDAY). DAY 25.

<u>0406.</u>   My birthday today. Greetings from many people via the Perth ham network.

<u>0513.</u>   To deal with the chafed jib sheet, I let go the windward sheet (the sail was poled out) and cranked in the leeward sheet as much as possible. Then by standing on the top leeward life line I was just able to reach the clew, untie the line, end-for-end the sheet, and re-tie the line to the clew of the sail. In order to reach the clew I had to unroll the entire sail, which speeded up the yacht. Water was flying everywhere, the vessel was heeled way to leeward, and I had all I could do to hang on with one hand while I dealt with the sheet with the other hand. (Careful, don't slip.)

Once I had the sheet reeved and led back to the cockpit I was able to cut away the chafed part and put a whipping on the end of the line at my leisure. All of this would have made a good video sequence if a photographer had been on board.

<u>0719.</u>   I discovered that my alarm clock stopped working at 0521 on January 11th, the exact time of the capsize.

I spoke with Mark Schrader, the race director, in Sydney and learned that Yukoh Tada is very dissatisfied with his vessel because she has a corkscrew capsizing tendency ("death roll"). Jack Boye flew out an expert mechanic from Newport to work on CITY KIDS whose mast and rig are a shambles. Isabelle Autissier is getting a new mast. NIIHAU IV (Robert Hooke) was struck by a fishing boat a little south of Sydney and was severely holed above the waterline. Robert arrived in Sydney by automobile.

I told Mark about my capsize. In general it was encouraging to speak with him because he was very upbeat and pleased that I am still in the race. He wished me a happy birthday.

I just had a big breakfast and ate the last of the bacon. According to the weather forecast a big front is close behind me. The usual gale warnings. Time for a nap.

<u>1500.</u>   Tightened the wind vane mounting bolts. Then I sorted out the flashlights and batteries, heaved out three useless flashlights, and all batteries that didn't measure 1.5 volts. The French divers' flashlight that I keep in the cockpit was full of water and hopelessly corroded in spite of a well-lubricated O-ring. I still have a dozen flashlights on board, the best of which are the little Duracell lights which keep working because the design holds the batteries tightly, and they have a good switch arrangement.

<u>1510.</u>   The radio is full of talk about the Gulf Crisis. The weather front that was supposed to pass this morning still has not come.

<u>1906.</u>   The automatic magnetic variation control in the GPS suddenly began to work again. The software went dead when I crossed the Equator. Since then I have been dealing with true courses, and adding and subtracting magnetic variation by hand.

JANUARY 16, 1991. (WEDNESDAY). DAY 26.

<u>0033.</u>   Wonderful! Happiness is a moderating wind and easier seas. Light rain and thin stratus.

<u>0444.</u>   Dense fog. At last I got a weatherfax copy whose numbers I can read.

<u>0648.</u>   Still quite foggy. However the weather is warmer, the wind has dropped to 15 knots from the NNW, and I am stalking the decks in my blue thermal underwear. One pair of bottoms and three tops are just right. I just shook out the second reef and am about to take out the first.

<u>1142.</u>   Light rain and wind from the SSE at 22 knots. On deck for several hours. Gybed, a second reef, put the spinnaker pole away, adjusted the wind vane, tidied up the cockpit lines, and fumed at the headwind, which I think is the passage of a weak front. Dark, gloomy stratus.

<u>1340.</u>   The course is not ideal, but we have some room to maneuver.

<u>2208.</u>   Headwinds and 1,352 miles to King Island. A high-pressure area—that neither the weather chart nor the forecast men-

tioned—has caught up with us. I need 7 days of fair or reaching winds (at 193 miles per day) to make King Island.

JANUARY 17, 1991. (THURSDAY). DAY 27.

0153.   Another two hours on deck. The SE wind was increasing, so I put in a third reef. However the wind then eased a little and the vessel didn't have enough drive. I shook out the third reef, and we're sailing better. I'm concerned about getting too far north before I reach King Island. We're now 7°—420 miles—from the Australian mainland.

0340.   The BBC has almost non-stop news about the start of the war in Iraq and the bombing of Baghdad. The announcers are all very excited.

0350.   The 0210 weather chart shows two highs with a front between them (I have trouble understanding this). I am on the north side of this complex system. A low is approaching from the SW. Just now the SE wind is not steady, and I need to adjust the course often.

When I get a fair wind I will head south a little to give me maneuvering room for Bass Strait. I don't want to get pressed along the south Australian coast.

0552.   I just fished another cupful of nuts and bolts from the bilge. And speaking of the bilge, I have been pumping 50 strokes a day with the big Edson pump. Is it possible that the bilge pickup line from the water ballast tank pump (an alternate way of pumping the bilge) could be letting water *into* the yacht?

1134.   I installed a new Primus burner on the cooking stove and tightened the wind vane mounting bolts.

1216.   We're on a new chart (#4709) which is always a pleasant sign of progress. Our course has been poor—only 073°M. We should be 25° higher. I am hoping for NW winds as the high passes to the east, and we get on its south side. Black Pyramid, our way-point for Bass Strait, is 1,284 miles.

1252.   Night already—at noon! Our course is terrible—060° to 070°M. Rain showers all around. The wind is almost easterly. Tropical cyclone Alison is at 22°S. 84°E. and moving this way. That's all I need.

JANUARY 18, 1991. (FRIDAY). DAY 28.

<u>0316.</u>   Becalmed for 13 hours. The sun is out—warm and bright—and I have the yacht open to dry her out. Blankets and wet sheets on the lifelines and a mass of wet clothes in the cockpit. I moved the sails (a good job for a weightlifter) from the forward cabin so I could properly replace the wooden floors which got loose during the capsize. I then screwed down the main floor piece and put the sails back. Meanwhile I had breakfast and have been listening to news of the Gulf War.

<u>0759.</u>   Sailing nicely on a calm sea. Gybing the running rig and switching the spinnaker pole from one side to the other takes 25 minutes. The weather is much warmer. I still have the hatches open, and wet and damp clothing drying in the cockpit. I folded up the storm jib.

<u>0823.</u>   I've got the autopilot working and have disconnected the wind vane. I've found that if the water blade of the steering gear is left in the water when the gear is not in use, the bevel gears soon manage to slip past one another. With the blade in the water it's impossible (and dangerous—you could clip off a finger) to align the gears because of the force of the water on the blade. To adjust the gears, it's best to take the blade out of the water. Then there's no pressure on the gears, and it's easy to align them.

<u>2215.</u>   A front is passing headed eastward. Outside it's all gray, with rain and gusty winds.

JANUARY 19, 1991. (SATURDAY). DAY 29.

<u>0302.</u>   We ran under just the double-reefed mainsail from 2200 to 0200. Much heavy rolling. As soon as it got light (at 0200), I maneuvered the spinnaker pole from port to starboard—past the baby stay, the midstay, and the two headstays. With all the rolling, swinging the 21-foot pole around the foredeck is a dangerous business—even in daylight.

<u>0621.</u>   A good breakfast of curried hake and boiled eggs. I have been reading Francis Chichester's autobiography *The Lonely Sea and the Sky* which is quite good. His 1930-era flying experiences in Australia and New Zealand make Chichester a real pioneer flier. His little Gipsy Moth plane weighed only 880 pounds, had open cockpits, no brakes, a tiny four-cylinder engine, and carried

60 gallons of gasoline. Chichester had incredible problems with floats when he turned Gipsy Moth into a seaplane. The floats were made of several different aluminum alloys which reacted electrically with seawater (a galvanic couple) and caused terrible leaks.

Chichester's celestial navigation scheme of aiming to one side of a target and then when abeam of the target turning 90° toward it was remarkable. What courage it must have taken to have made that turn over the wilds of the ocean!

<u>0802.</u>   Colder and overcast with low stratus. My radio is filled with news of the Gulf War. What will Iraq do with its missiles? How will Israel respond?

<u>1118.</u>   Will I be able to get to Sydney soon enough to prepare for the next leg before the start on February 3rd? I need to buy stores, deal with the leak, sails, winches, etc. I would like to rest for a few days, but I suppose I'll be busier than ever.

<u>1146.</u>   I've been making a list of boat jobs to do in Sydney. If the weather cooperates, I think I can cross off three or four during the next few days. Today I improved the latch on the navigator's seat and sorted out all the fastenings.

<u>1853.</u>   An unsteady wind from the south. I switched between the running rig and the fore-and-aft rig several times (by leaving the pole up and handling all the lines from the cockpit) and finally settled for the running rig and the autopilot, which is excellent in such conditions. I must wear gloves whenever possible. Once again my hands are in poor shape from line handling.

<u>2214.</u>   Cooler and an overcast sky. Yesterday's strong SW wind has become a light breeze from the south. There's still a big SW swell, and we are rolling all over the place. I presume the swell will die out. I cleaned the electrical contacts on the bow light, which is now working and put more bedding compound around the wires.

JANUARY 20, 1991. (SUNDAY). DAY 30.

<u>0043.</u>   Overcast. Chilly. Less swell, but a lot of rolling. Busy repairing latches for the companionway door.

<u>0123.</u>   Rolled up the jib. Slatting terribly. No wind. Westerly swell. Yesterday (I forgot to note it) we passed what appeared to be an orange oil drum. It seemed to be plastic, tied up neatly with black cord. Something from the space program? Or a liferaft?

<u>0340.</u>   Still becalmed. I've sailed too far north again. According to the Argos report at 2017 yesterday, I had 1,486 miles to go to Sydney.

<u>0729.</u>   We must be on the western side of the high. I changed from the starboard running rig to close-hauled with the port fore-and-aft rig because the wind has gone from SW 5 knots to NE 8.

<u>0957.</u>   The funniest thing on the radio today was a discussion of vegetarian dogfood. By dog owners who were so serious about their pets' diets that it was hilarious.

Since the capsize I have been plagued by matchsticks. An entire large box of wooden matches got dumped. Many were washed into the bilge and wound up jamming the valves of the small bilge pump. I must have fished out 50 or 60 matchsticks so far.

<u>1038.</u>   A few albatrosses are circling around, but the white-chinned petrels have vanished. I am now seeing tiny white-bellied storm petrels which swoop and twist and dart a foot or two above the water (wings raised, feet trailing and sometimes pattering on the water) as they feed on tiny particles.

<u>1122.</u>   Approaching noon, but the sun has just set and it's getting dark. The day has been beautiful—pink sunset light on scattered cumulus. I don't know how much water is left in the starboard tank, but I will draw from it until it's empty because the port tank is about half full. I have been working on the companionway door latches. Tomorrow I will have been at sea for one month.

<u>1530.</u>   Second reef. A half tank of water ballast to port. Pitch black outside. Failed to get the vane to steer and am on autopilot.

I suppose the essence of adventure is a little danger. If you didn't scare yourself to death once in a while, life would have no zest.

<u>1828.</u>   A bang in the night? I didn't hear a thing, but there must have been a loud noise because the wind vane water blade has broken off and is trailing in the sea on its safety line. We must have struck something hard and unyielding. The heavy stainless steel shaft latch bracket (the part that allows the main shaft to be unlocked and to pivot back and upward so the water blade can be lifted from the water) is all twisted and broken. Fortunately the autopilot (number 3, my last spare) is steering well. Can I repair the vane gear? Do I have the spare parts?

<u>1857.</u>   Squall; 3–4 rolls in the jib.

<u>2320.</u>   Busy with repairs to the vane gear. I have all the components in the cabin and have straightened the sides of the hinge pivots on the main shaft. I found a suitable ⅜″ dia. pin, and figured out how to install the spring that holds the latch arm in position. I have the water blade ready to be installed, but it will be hard to reach down to fit the bolts.

A dark and gloomy morning with light drizzle. The sea is absolutely flat. We're going well with three rolls in the jib, two reefs in the mainsail, and a tank of water ballast to port.

JANUARY 21, 1991. (MONDAY). DAY 31.

<u>0154.</u>   Hove-to for two hours trying to repair the vane gear. I clipped my safety harness to the backstay, climbed over the aft pulpit, and partially sat on the vane mounts. (The birds probably wondered what the crazy man was doing now.) It took only a few minutes to put on the water blade, but the latch mechanism doesn't fit at all.

The spare latch doesn't mate to the solid block of stainless steel at the bottom of the upper main shaft. The book of directions says that each latch is custom assembled. I tried every dodge, artifice, and scheme that I could think of—including half an hour of hand filing. I finally gave up because I kept dipping my feet in the sea and they turned to blocks of ice. I must think what to try next.

<u>0211.</u>   Eight rolls in jib. Wind NE 18. I am falling asleep.

<u>0714.</u>   A good sleep, and my feet finally got warm. I am feeling a bit stupid because of my inability to repair the wind vane. I have no assurance that the autopilot will last to Sydney. I *must* repair the vane in the next couple of days before I get near land.

<u>1000.</u>   Good news. The vane gear is working! I put a large hose clamp around the two parts of the water blade pivot to hold them together. I got a little wet installing the clamp and almost didn't try it, but it is working. At least so far. I am tremendously heartened. The bevel gears have slipped one cog, but I will deal with that later.

<u>1052.</u>   We always have a dozen white-bellied storm-petrels flitting around the yacht. Dear little fellows that Margaret would love.

With all the overcast days, the solar panel output has been low, so I fired up the engine. It hasn't been run since the capsize, but it started at once. The charging voltage was 14.9, much too high. I turned an adjustment screw (all the way) on the voltage regulator to lower the voltage to 14.25–14.35, which was still too high since the batteries were only partially charged. The regulator probably got wet when all the water was flying around in the cabin.

<u>1530.</u>   How can there be easterly winds day after day?

<u>1751.</u>   Impossible to sleep because of the pounding. Will this night ever end?

JANUARY 22, 1991. (TUESDAY). DAY 32.

<u>0207.</u>   It's 737 miles to Black Pyramid at the south entrance to Bass Strait. The vane is steering OK as we hammer along to the NE with 26 knots of wind from the east.

<u>0253.</u>   The new weather map does not look good. We're in the boundary area between the south side of a large, weak low (with three centers) over SW Australia, and the north side of an enormous high to our south. The high is long and skinny and measures about 400 miles from north to south. From east to west the high is several thousand miles long. All this suggests SE winds. Meanwhile we bang along at 055°.

<u>0759.</u>   The wind has backed a trifle to the south. Brighter out, and a few glimmers of blue sky. Barometer 1011 mb.

<u>0902.</u>   SE winds 26–30 knots. We're bashing along on 070°M.

<u>1229.</u>   The roughest night of my sailing career. (Half the time we're airborne as I write.) I put on my oilskins to deal with a noisy halyard and then sat under the cockpit shelter. In spite of the rough sea the sunset was lovely. The sky cleared a little. Pinkish clouds that got lighter and lighter and suddenly turned to gray. Two white-headed petrels flew alongside. Overhead a new moon shone down.

The sailing is so rough that I have had to immobilize the cooking stove by turning it upside down in its gimbals. I feel a little sick, which is something.

<u>2204.</u>   Course 060°M. Wind 36 knots from the ESE—the third day of easterly winds. The main is double-reefed, and I have rolled up the jib entirely. I was out looking at things and am not sure that another reef would help. The sailing conditions are ghastly. We keep falling off waves with sickening crunches. It's a wonder the mast is still standing.

Weather charts seem to be of doubtful help for a vessel in the Southern Ocean. By and large a small ship has to take things as they come. The weather systems move at two or three times the speed of a yacht and we're overtaken, whether we go E, SE, or NE. I suppose if I had a weather routing service and it was successful I would see things differently.

At the moment we're jogging along at 5.2 knots on the starboard tack with a full ballast tank to windward while I wait for this cursed storm to blow itself out. I am warm, well rested, and am eating a little cold cereal with the excellent whole milk from Cape Town.

I am still thinking about Chichester's autobiography and his pioneer flying. He certainly had a zest for life. To think of crossing the Tasman Sea in a tiny open-cockpit plane and using a sextant en route seems phenomenal. Chichester also had the greatest trouble on his cross-country flights when he stopped for fuel, repairs, and sleep. Newspaper reporters and others bothered him so mercilessly that, though exhausted, he couldn't wait to get up in the air again. The stops were more troublesome than the flying.

JANUARY 23, 1991. (WEDNESDAY). DAY 33.

<u>0048.</u>   A severe gale. The wind has been blowing long enough so that the seas have built up to substantial size. I know the wind is strong when it blows streaks of foam from the water. The cloud cover is low but not thick, and I can see shafts of sunlight from time to time. The barometer has been steady (1010–1012 mb.) for almost two days, which I take as a bad sign because no change seems indicated.

Just now I made some adjustments to the steering vane and had to crawl to the back of the cockpit. A little earlier I managed to fire up the stove, cook some rice, and heat a can of chicken and vegetables. I ate my dinner with half a piece of bread and a small glass of Otto's red wine. It was all delicious, and I could almost feel the energy flowing into my veins as I ate.

After reading Chichester's autobiography I wonder if my sailing ventures would be easier in an airplane. A small plane with floats. A magic carpet that could be landed anywhere. Say in the remote parts of New Zealand's Queen Charlotte islands. At least in an airplane if you flew into a gale you could climb above it or go around it.

I wonder what the conditions will be in Bass Strait?

Clearing skies after a storm. I hurry to make more sail.

<u>0312.</u>   Wind SE 47 knots. Third reef. I got dressed, snapped on my safety line, and went forward. When I let the halyard go, I thought the sail would explode into ribbons, but I carried on with the reefing procedure with no problems. I put an extra lashing on the clew (around the boom). The seas have white streaks, and the wind is really whistling. I was a little nervous and apprehensive about going forward, but once into the routine of reefing, it was easy. Outside—with the noise of the wind—I couldn't hear the pounding and hammering of the vessel at all.

<u>0319.</u>   Practically all the public weather forecasts from shore stations have been of no use to me. The only thing the weather broadcasts do is to make me enraged because the information is either (1) wrong, unclear, and vague or (2) too late. A report describing the weather at point X is not a forecast. Maybe I'm getting cynical, but the subjunctive, smokescreen, maybe, doubtful, uncertain, perhaps language of meteorologists is about as indefinite as that of economists.

0354. Wind less. Riding fairly well with third reef. The blade of the wind vane gear is fluttering like the wings of a butterfly. I'm surprised it hasn't broken off.

0721. Gray and dark out. According to Sydney radio, the low-pressure area to the NW will move south, which should bring southerly winds. There's a large sea running. Not as big as when we got rolled, but the waves are certainly significant.

1258. Less wind (32 knots from the SE), but up and down. I unrolled a tiny bit of the jib. The vane is steering marginally. We logged 113 miles at noon.

1427. Not a good night. The wind continues to go up and down in strength and is gusty and turbulent. At one stage the vessel hove herself to. I rushed up into the cockpit (stupidly without putting on my heavy oilskins) and got soaked.

2126. It took 45 strokes of the Edson pump to clear the bilge. The engine runs perfectly, but the Quad-cycle voltage regulator only charges at 28 amps (instead of 95) at 13.5 volts. The standby regulator charges at 16 volts plus (which will ruin the batteries) at 75 amps. At the moment our power demands are just the B&G instruments and an occasional use of the GPS.

Seas and wind (SE 24 knots) down. Gray, dark, and raining (drizzle). My spirits are as somber as the weather, and I feel as lethargic as a snail. I must make some breakfast.

JANUARY 24, 1991. (THURSDAY). DAY 34.

0138. The cursed SE wind continues but is not so strong (22 knots). The seas are a little less, or maybe I have become so used to the spray, waves breaking over the vessel, and banging, that—like a nervous affliction—I no longer notice the annoyance.

0152. The scoundrels! After the gale I've been in for three days (with no prediction), the cursed weathermen now say there's going to be a gale and speak of very rough seas and E to SE winds up to 40 knots! Once again (and again and again) the weather people *report an existing weather condition instead of predicting it.*

0639. Hooray, hooray! At last a wind shift to the south (22 knots) and a dramatic improvement in the sea conditions. There's still a large sea running, but the big waves are down in size. The weather prediction was perfect—only 3 days late.

I'm right on target for Black Pyramid, which is less than 500 miles away. The vane is steering well. I accidentally looked into a mirror and scared myself ("Who's that?"). I immediately shaved and got cleaned up a little.

The white-bellied storm petrels that were with us for a week are gone. No albatrosses either. The only birds around the yacht are white-headed petrels. I read *Dangerous Trade*, a novel about a British submarine in World War II by Gilbert Hackforth-Jones. Nicely written, with good character development. When I finished I couldn't help but wonder how Nevil Shute would have handled the story. I think Shute would have written the novel in the first person and developed the captain—the principal character—a good deal more.

1108.   I went on deck to shake out a reef and found the entire wind vane gear flopping around because one of the two bottom frame bolts had come out again. I put in a new bolt, but the job took half an hour of hanging down over the transom. With the waves that were running, the water often came up to my elbows. The job was pleasant, somehow, because the water was so clean. Incredibly clean.

I then shook out the third reef, unwound most of the jib, and engaged the autopilot because rain squalls were on all sides (it looked like the passage of a front.) Meanwhile two curious white-headed petrels flew back and forth only a boatlength away. The great storm seems over, and I am headed for Bass Strait. Storms are terrible, but there's always a time when they ease off and dissipate. Like a person's temper.

1655.   I have changed my target from Black Pyramid to Cape Wickham at the north end of King Island. The approach from our current position is better, the distance is shorter, and there's a powerful light on Cape Wickham. I have been reading the sailing instructions for Sydney and getting set for my arrival.

2338.   After an hour of trying I finally contacted Sydney radio and got through to the schoolchildren in West Virginia with my weekly report.

JANUARY 25, 1991. (FRIDAY). DAY 35.

0146.   A gusty west wind of 30 knots. Third reef in the main and many rolls in the jib. When the yacht is pressed from astern it's remarkable how immediate the relief is when I pull down a piece of the mainsail. The leech reefing pendant doesn't have to be pulled tight; it's just the reduction in sail area exposed to the strong wind. The motion eases, and the steering becomes easier at once.

I have been cleaning the icebox, which was a mess from some old spilled milk. The food stocks are way down, and at mealtimes I have to work hard to come up with something substantial and appealing.

0243. We're logging 8.43 knots in continuing squalls and light rain. A few patches of blue and an occasional glimpse of the sun.

0329. The bilge was completely filled again, and I needed 50 strokes of the big pump to get rid of the water. Where is it coming from? I am going to close off the aft watertight compartment and see what happens.

According to the Argos position at 2000 yesterday I had 986 miles to go to Sydney. I couldn't raise the Perth radio hams so my report was relayed by VKZDM (Edgar) near Sydney.

0412. I fished another dozen big nuts and bolts from the bilge as well as a miniature cassette tape (ruined) and part of a pencil sharpener (all rusty). I put a wooden plug in the drain line from the lazarette to see if that isolates the leak to the bilge. Just now we speeded up to 10 knots with two tiny sails. I am going to try to sleep a little extra in case I have to stay awake along the Australian coast.

0937. The mainsheet winch stopped working. I took it apart and found the pawls stuck and the main bearings completely jammed with salt. I cleaned off the worst of the salt and oiled the pawls. All 12 winches will need a thorough overhaul in Sydney. I also oiled one of the line jammers on the top of the cockpit dodger. I am unsure how to lubricate the jammers or what to use. In any case all I have is light machine oil.

I just gybed the running rig. Certainly changing the long pole from one side of the deck to the other with the yacht rolling in big seas is knocking at death's door. I'll be glad to get another pole in Sydney so there'll be one for each side. I've thought a lot about how to secure the poles so I won't lose one over the side again. The obvious way is to leave both the foreguy and the afterguy permanently tied to the pole. Not so neat, but both lines will then serve as safety lines.

1015. Wind WNW 28 knots. Big seas. While I had the winch apart, we surfed at high speed on three or four consecutive waves, each of which broke ahead of us. The scene would have made a good photograph, but of course I had no camera in my hands. I still haven't decided which side of King Island to pass. It depends on daylight and the weather.

For lunch I cooked noodles and flavored them with sharp cheese. Delicious, but I must be careful not to overcook the pasta. The only birds today were white-headed petrels and one young wandering albatross.

<u>1101.</u>   Low, heavy clouds with ragged bottoms. I can see the moon dimly shining above, so the cloud cover can't be too thick. I have been thinking more about King Island. The Cape Wickham approach seems the more sensible route because (1) it has good lights if I arrive at night (2) fewer dangers (3) a wider fairway.

<u>1628.</u>   A noon-to-noon run of 189 miles. More squalls and rain. Where does all this wind (NW 30 knots) come from? The low is supposed to be moving SE, but it seems that we're sailing at the speed of the low. Hence the barometer stays the same.

I am reading *Catalina*, a novel by Somerset Maugham. I like the first part in which a crippled girl miraculously recovers the use of her paralyzed right leg after three tries before a church group. By the third try, everyone (including the reader) is desperately hoping for the miracle. Unfortunately the characters then become unreal.

<u>1634.</u>   According to the GPS, Cape Wickham is 217 miles on 070°M. Our position is 40°17′S., 139°18′E.

JANUARY 26, 1991. (SATURDAY). DAY 36.

<u>0109.</u>   The hose clamp that I put on the wind vane gear shaft to hold the latch parts together has come off. Perhaps I can stop in the lee of King Island and put on two clamps to hold the latch.

<u>0255.</u>   The 0210 weather map shows a hard-looking low approaching. I hope it holds off until we get past Gabo Island at the SE corner of Australia. We just crossed north of 40°S. and it's much warmer. We even have sun.

I dried out the stern light, cleaned the bulb contacts, and rubbed Vaseline around the edge seal. I will deal with the bow light (not working again) when the seas ease off. I spoke with Margaret in Sydney and was surprised to learn that she brought the components for a telex system. Apparently she didn't receive my message not to buy anything because we have no radio suitable for such an installation.

<u>0307.</u>   Still extremely rough. The wind remains strong. Now 131 miles to Gabo Island.

<u>0646.</u>   Less wind and smaller seas. Third reef out. With more mainsail the motion is definitely easier. I have been looking for the leak over the starboard pilot berth. The bedding, pillows, and cushion are soaked. The leak is just forward of the chainplates and may be from the bolts holding one of the spinnaker pole supports.
    The starboard water tank is empty.

<u>0857.</u>   I see some curious thin black matter in the drinking water from the port tank. The bits could be leaf fragments, black plastic, blobs of poisonous amoebas, or God knows what. I am drinking the water and I'm still alive so it must be OK. This sort of warped logic reminds me of Conor O'Brien's voyage around the world in 1923 when he wrote (in *Across Three Oceans*): "The supply has to be good or the natives would die of it."

<u>1019.</u>   A rain shower with a lovely rainbow just before sunset. The rainbow was a complete half-oval with a partially-developed second rainbow. While I was looking at the rainbows, a diving petrel rushed past the yacht. The bird was unmistakable because of its rapid flight and whirring wings—the bird that flies underwater.

<u>1253.</u>   A run of 195 miles at noon. I was working at the chart table when suddenly a spotlight shined in the window. I jumped up and rushed outside. It was the moon! I just talked with VK6ART (Art) who has spoken to me daily for the past month.

<u>1509.</u>   Moonlight and stars between squalls. The Southern Cross is overhead to starboard. Orion is overhead to port. I gybed the running rig. The wind is supposed to go SW. Sleepy. We're rolling heavily in a swell which never stops. King Island is 37 miles ahead.

<u>1649.</u>   Gybed and gybed back again and changed course slightly. I picked up the loom of the Cape Wickham light and identified it. Light rain and lots of sail drill. One of the running backstays caught on an upper batten pocket. Always in the middle of the night. The bow running light has a lot of water in it in spite of gaskets and bedding compound. Terrible rolling.

<u>1814.</u>   The Cape Wickham light bears 100°. This line plotted on the chart goes right through the GPS position. No sign of other vessels.

<u>2316.</u>   We're near King Island and are passing tens of thousands of small dark birds (sitting on the water or flying low) which I

haven't been able to identify. The birds are like miniature white-chinned petrels, but very dark brown. Could they be noddies? I have never seen such a mass of identical birds. There could be a million or more.

A big breakfast. The yacht is sailing well although the wind has been unsteady. We have the same lumpy swell (maybe a little less) here in Bass Strait that we had out in the ocean. I've been looking at a pilot chart of the SE Australian coast and am astonished at the strength of the various storms. Fortunately our wind is only 22 knots from the SW.

JANUARY 27, 1991. (SUNDAY). DAY 37.

<u>0055.</u>   Going well in the lee of King Island. One squall after another—like soldiers marching in a parade. The sky overhead—when clear—is a lovely deep blue with lots of cirrus from a big low that's coming. I am back to using a hand-bearing compass to take bearings of lights and points on land. Much plotting on large-scale charts.

<u>0107.</u>   I can just make out mountains on the NW corner of Tasmania.

<u>0340.</u>   I'm cooking up a real storm of corned beef, rice, tomato paste, onions, part of a bouillon cube, and mushrooms. How will it taste?

<u>0534.</u>   A good dinner of solid food which I needed. Busy sweeping the cabin sole which is partially dry for the first time in weeks. The hull leak continues. I checked the lazarette and found only a little water (I had the drain hose plugged) so the leak is not aft. I have shut off the through-hull for the water ballast tanks to see what happens. According to the Argos report for 1930 yesterday, we had 529 miles to go to Sydney.

<u>1145.</u>   We're a little south of the Curtis Group of islets. I have been watching three mountain peaks (one 1,100 feet high) rising from the strait. The key navigational mark here is the powerful light on Deal Island in the Kent Group. I can just see the light which bears 070°M.

<u>1501.</u>   The light on Hogan Island is supposed to be Fl.(2)6 sec. according to my 1986 chart. However I get Fl.(3)12 sec. Can the characteristic have been changed? I should have a new light list on board, but I forgot to buy one.

<u>1518.</u>   The wind has shifted to the NW. We're approaching the Deal Island light. Why am I so nervous? Because it's the middle of the night, and we're south of Judgement Rocks . . .

JANUARY 28, 1991. (MONDAY). DAY 38.

<u>0127.</u>   Frustrations! The wind went light so I shook out two reefs, which disclosed a badly frayed #2 reefing pendant. I hunted up a spare line, sewed the ends together, and pulled the lines through the boom. Like a fool I forgot to fasten the bitter end, which came through the boom with the rest of the line. I then spent an hour fishing a messenger line (I finally used another one of the reefing pendants). While all this was going on, the other end of the pendant slipped through the leech reefing grommet of the sail. I had to drop and hoist the sail twice to reeve the pendant. I am so frustrated I could scream. Meanwhile we're sailing well on a rainy day. The sea is down. We're 102 miles from Gabo Island. I need to eat and sleep. I have noticed a lot of mast bend—more than I want.

<u>0503.</u>   Need to gybe. A gorgeous sunny afternoon. I have one portlight and the galley hatch open. The warm air is drying out everything. For the first time since Cape Town I have taken off my thermal underwear and put on a T-shirt and trousers. How nice to have pockets. We're about 75 miles from Gabo Island and 305 miles from Sydney. I want to eat something, have a nap, and then work on a *USA Today* newspaper story.

<u>0537.</u>   This warm weather is such a shock after the Southern Ocean. If this fair wind (SSW 17 knots) lasts, I'll be in Sydney in two days.

<u>1300.</u>   The wind has gone around to the north. One reef in the main.

<u>1350.</u>   Passed a coasting vessel—presumably bound for Tasmania— stopped in the sea. Thunderstorms and rain showers are on all sides. Every few minutes we get a white flash (like a searchlight) followed by fierce rumbles of thunder.

<u>1400.</u>   A navigational light—group Fl.(2)10 sec.—bears 325°. Probably Pt. Hicks on the south coast.

<u>1614.</u>   Rain showers. I saw a moonbow, my first ever. From one horizon to the zenith in the darkness of night.

<u>1852.</u>   An enormous cumulonimbus cloud behind us is climbing up and up and is streaked with forked lightning in the dim light of dawn. There's certainly a lot of dramatic weather as we approach the SE coast of Australia. Eating a breakfast of eggs, toast (last of butter), and tea.

<u>2016.</u>   A very heavy squall (40 knots and a tropical downpour) just as we reached the slim pencil lighthouse of Gabo Island. The squall swept toward the NE and was over us for about 15 minutes. Fortunately I had rolled up the jib and ran at 9 knots under the mainsail with one reef. The fresh water was refreshing and certainly washed SEBAGO and my oilskins. Now I'm only a mile or two from the coast and am looking at low dome-shaped mountains and great masses of sand along the shore to port as we sail northward. Only 230 miles to go. How wonderful to be sailing in smooth water!

Seeing Gabo Island reminds me to be careful. Desmond Hampton was wrecked on Gabo in the 1982–83 race, and Jacques de Roux fell overboard and was lost near here in the 1986–87 race.

<u>2032.</u>   Abeam of Cape Howe. Miles of sand dunes along the shore.

JANUARY 29, 1991. (TUESDAY). DAY 39.

<u>0137.</u>   Running well with a fresh breeze (SW 25 knots) on a flat sea, SEBAGO's best point of sailing.

<u>0350.</u>   A turbulent wind of 32 knots from the south. I should switch the spinnaker pole from one side to the other, but we're logging almost 8 knots under the double-reefed mainsail alone. It's tricky to gybe in such winds. I am falling asleep.

<u>0545.</u>   Wind less strong and veering toward the SE. Gybed the pole and put out the jib to starboard. A wave broke on board north of Montague Island and soaked all my clothes that were drying in the cockpit. A little water splashed down the open galley hatch.

We passed a south-going yacht motoring into 22 knots of wind and head seas. A coasting ship out a few miles was also southbound. I would like to take a nap, but I can't risk it now.

<u>0921.</u>   Getting dark. So far we have had a good run through Bass Strait to Gabo Island and up to Bateman Bay (just passed). The seas are small, but choppy and rough. I am sleepy. However I must stay awake because of the shipping traffic.

<u>1009.</u>   Brush Island light ahead. The full moon just appeared from behind a great zeppelin-shaped cloud. The wind has been dropping little by little. At 0300 it was in the south and has veered (anti-clockwise in this hemisphere) until it's almost easterly. This morning the Australian coastline was a weather shore. Now it's a lee shore.

I reeved a longer line (65 feet) in one of the four-part Schaefer tackles I use to control the main boom when gybing, especially in strong winds. Together with the main sheet, I use two tackles: one to port and one to starboard, and take up on one and ease the other as the boom swings across. I find the tackles simple, powerful, and positive, and they won't break the boom like rigid vangs.

<u>1030.</u>   I shook out the first reef in the mainsail an hour ago. We kept going at 7.5 knots, but little by little the wind and our speed have decreased.

<u>2059.</u>   Becalmed all night. I put up the big genoa, but there was still a lot of slatting. I had several naps and feel quite rested. It's surprising how much brighter I am after sleeping for 45 minutes.

I am fed up with the radio. All Sydney radio can say half the time is "Standby. Standby," as if the person at sea has nothing to do but to wait around. I could do without radios entirely, as I did for the first 20 years of my sailing life.

<u>2155.</u>   The autopilot is steering very poorly. It's almost as if there is a magnetic anomaly. There's a strange swell from the south and probably a strong tidal surge from Jervis Bay. I think a combination of sea conditions is giving the autopilot a hard time.

JANUARY 30, 1991. (WEDNESDAY). DAY 40.

<u>0233.</u>   More sail drill. Pole down, and the fore-and-aft rig set on the starboard tack. Smooth water. No swell. When we passed Jervis Bay and Perpendicular Point, the sea was all upset with whitecaps, swell, and wavelets. There must be a strong local current or tidal action.

I have the U.S flag, the Australian flag, and the racing pennant ready to put up. I have been folding blankets, hanging up clothes, putting away tools, cooking things, and sweeping up the cabin sole.

The water that I pump from the port freshwater tank continues to have bits of foreign matter that look like tiny pieces of lettuce leaves. Only dark brownish-green. Smooth and slippery, with an almost oily feeling. I can get rid of the stuff with a tea strainer, but I wonder what it is.

<u>0546.</u>   The wind has veered to the NE, which means tacking along the coast. Hard work with the sheets. I have brought the doublehanded winch handle to the cockpit from the mast. The double handle definitely makes tacking easier, although it's still heavy work.

The coast is beautiful. Green and hilly with long whitish-yellow sand beaches. Lovely rolling uplands. It's too bad that I won't have time to travel around a little. We're 57 miles from Sydney. According to the weather chart we should have SW winds.

<u>0817.</u>   Bashing into headwinds at the end of a passage is no good at all. I am seeing a ship about every two hours. This morning I was just climbing into the cockpit with a dish of spaghetti and tomato sauce when a fishing boat steamed close astern of us. Everybody waved. The leaf fragments or algae (or whatever they are) in the freshwater tank are getting worse.

<u>1231.</u>   A poor night. Wind NNW 20 knots. Close-hauled and hammering into short head seas. The bow is light out again. A ship passes about every two hours.

<u>1753.</u>   The pounding was enough to break the filament in the bulb in the bow navigation light. I have identified the light (Macquarie) on South Head at the entrance to Sydney Harbour. Behind me I can see the faintest glimmer of dawn in the east.

<u>1806.</u>   Macquarie light is 18 miles on 323°M.

<u>1922.</u>   The wind has shifted to the west, the seas are easing off, and the Sydney headlands are beginning to show through the misty dawn. The early sun has brushed a metallic yellow over everything. It's been a tough passage. Now the end is near. We're under full sail and headed for the finish line.

CHAPTER NINE

Interval in Sydney

It was a bright and sunny Wednesday morning when I crossed the finish line in Sydney. The timekeeper on the committee boat fired a shotgun in the air, and suddenly the long passage from Cape Town was over.

A minute later someone on a towboat threw me a line, and a BOC launch came alongside with a dozen people waving and shouting. The whole gang came aboard, including Margaret, race director Mark Schrader, a television cameraman, and Chris Iacono, the Sebago representative for Australia. Chris was a cheerful, hard-driving Australian who ran a marine supply company and was an administrative whiz. I had told him earlier on the radio that SEBAGO was leaking between two and three gallons an hour and needed to be hauled out at once because my pumping arm was wearing out.

"I've made all the arrangements," said Chris. "You'll be out of the water at the Royal Yacht Squadron in a few hours."

I was also met by my friend Ian Hansen, who had sailed out to Sydney Heads in his beautifully restored 45-foot Alan Payne sloop KARALEE, which had been built in 1952. The yacht was a marvel of varnish, gorgeous woodwork, and shiny paint. Ian was both a first-class shipwright and a splendid marine artist. It was wonderful to see him.

I was thrilled to be with Margaret and my friends, and we talked non-stop while we pulled down the mainsail and leisurely folded and tied it to the top of the boom. A photographer with the big black video camera on his shoulder followed every move. Meanwhile the towboat whisked us along a busy five-mile stretch of Sydney Harbour. We slipped past police launches, big high-sided ferryboats, towering cargo ships, tugs pulling barges with tippy-looking cranes, gray navy ships, yachts, windsurfers—every sort of craft.

To our right and left the hills above the smooth water were chockablock with apartments, houses, and office blocks. Enor-

mous hotels and glass-fronted skyscrapers rose above the down-
town section. We passed the Sydney opera house (whose design
made me think of giant flower petals). Then we swung underneath
the noisy Sydney Harbour bridge (buses, trucks, cars bumper-to-
bumper, a siren in the distance) and turned into Darling Harbour
where a press conference was scheduled. Everything was rush,
hurry, quick!

It was the end of January, and the Australian summer heat
was scorching. There were throngs of people everywhere, and the
uniform of the country was shorts and T-shirts. I could feel the
heat, but I couldn't quite believe it because I was so used to wearing layers and layers of heavy clothes which now seemed ridiculous. The isolated world of the Southern Ocean was light years
away in geography, climate, and spirit. I had so looked forward to
arriving, but for a moment I felt like heading back out to sea
where things were not so noisy or so demanding. The harness of
civilization seemed a little too tight.

We tied up in Darling Harbour for an hour while I talked to
people from the newspapers and television stations and answered
questions from a small crowd that had collected. Because of my
return to Cape Town for repairs I was the last of the 21 competitors to arrive in Sydney. In all I had taken 67 days, a number that
made me wince. John Martin in his 60-foot million-dollar-marvel
ALLIED BANK had been first. He had taken only 26 days and had
been in Australia for almost six weeks. I was flattered that John
had come down to see me arrive. He clasped my hand long and
slowly while he congratulated me on my passage. We both knew
that although one tried hard to be first, the main thing was to
arrive. . . .

The start of the next leg was less than four days away, and
SEBAGO needed a lot of work. The towboat gave us a pluck across
Sydney Harbour to Kirribilli where we were to be hauled out. The
Royal Yacht Squadron was hidden in a lovely bay with flower-
decked houses that came down to the water. A hundred yachts
and small boats lay on moorings on the limpid, turquoise-colored
water. The weather was warm and sunny, and the wind barely ruf-
fled the water. After the Southern Ocean I felt that I could have
happily stayed there for a month while I swam and rested and read
books and took long walks with Margaret and my friends. I had to
shake my head hard to wake up from my dream.

Three other BOC yachts were at the Royal Yacht Squadron.
The two Japanese boats were out of the water and surrounded by
scaffolding. CITY KIDS from New York was at a dock, and we rafted

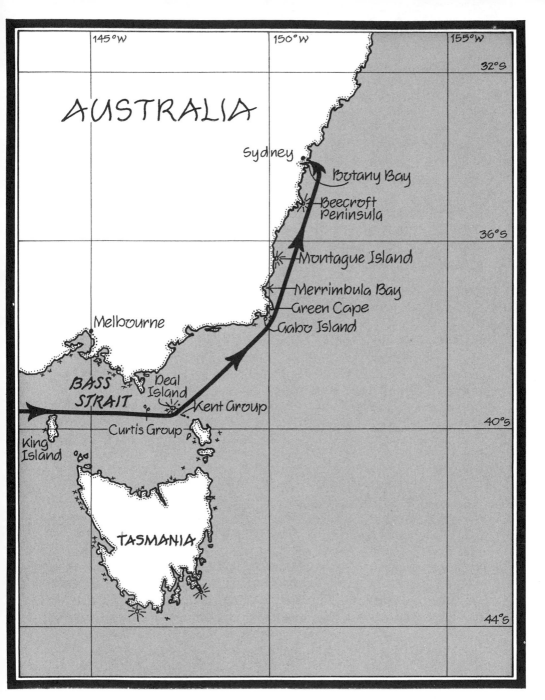

Bass Strait to Sydney.

up alongside her. Her captain, Jack Boye, had had a rough and stormy trip from Cape Town. He had lost his headsail halyards and had broken the spreaders and a lot of the standing rigging that supported the mast. Jack was fed up with the special B&R rig and wanted to put in a conventional mast, but there wasn't enough time. In desperation, he asked Steve Pettengill, the ace mechanic who had built the water ballast tanks in SEBAGO, to fly out from Newport and take charge of the repairs.

Margaret had rented a little car and she drove me to Ian Hansen's house, where I collapsed in bed after a meal and a talk with Ian and Kayelene, my friends from the 1986–87 race. Josh Hall from SPIRIT OF IPSWICH and his wife were also staying with the Hansens, so the house was a real sailing center. Josh had severely injured one knee during a knockdown on the trip from Cape Town and had undergone an operation when he arrived in Sydney. He was clomping around the house with a big knee brace.

I learned that Robert Hook's NIIHAU IV had collided with a fishing boat near Sydney. An enormous hole (4 ft.x7 ft.) had been knocked in the topsides, and it was only through luck that the yacht hadn't sunk. NIIHAU was undergoing extensive repairs in a small port south of Sydney. The yacht was also getting a new mast because of storm damage. Alain Gautier was still recovering from the violent accidental gybe that had thrown him across GENERALI CONCORDE's cockpit, hurled him into a bank of winches, and left him bleeding and unconscious. John Martin's helpers were fitting a new bow pulpit (her fourth) to ALLIED BANK after the pulpit was completely destroyed when a furling gear system let go. A gang of fiberglass workers was trying to strengthen the forward part of GROUPE SCETA's cored fiberglass hull. David Adams on INN-KEEPER was plagued by a broken gooseneck and by cracks in his aluminum deck through which water poured into the cabin below. On ECUREUIL, Isabelle Autissier was helping a group of riggers fit a new spar after her mast had buckled near the NE coast of Tasmania. And so on through the fleet. The report seemed more like a list of war damage after the Battle of the Southern Ocean. And the war was only half over because there were 6,000 more miles to go.

The next morning SEBAGO was out of the water. We saw at once that the leak was where the hull and the after end of the keel met. During the capsize the athwartships joint between the back of the keel and the hull had been strained. I got an expert fiberglass workman named Andrew to begin grinding into the problem. I not only wanted to repair the leak but to strengthen the whole area.

My friend Ian Hansen came down to give me a hand. Gil Forrester, an engineer I had met during the 1986–87 BOC race, also appeared. Gil began to overhaul the 12 two-speed winches. Meanwhile Ian went up the mast to see about the masthead instruments, the bent VHF antenna, and the missing lights. Colin Bull, another friend from the earlier BOC race, went shopping for parts.

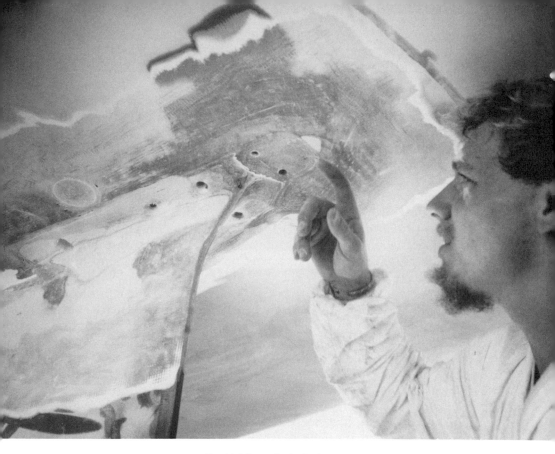

Keel joint repairs in Sydney.

Chris Iacono and I pulled off the jib, genoa, and mainsail and took them to a sailmaker. We opened up the water tanks, decided that the black leaf-like bits were algae, and flushed out the tanks with a special chemical. Chris' daughter Nadia cleaned the interior lockers and drawers. Greg, one of Chris' sons, began to sand and paint the bottom. Margaret and I hustled around trying to coordinate all these things.

Since there wasn't time to send the Alpha autopilots back and forth to California we hired an electrician, who opened up the control boxes and drive units. The repairman found that the solder in the brush holders had melted in the motors of the drive units, and that we needed new circuit boards for the control boxes. We telephoned Silicon Valley and asked that the parts be put on the next airplane.

Next to us at the Royal Yacht Squadron was Yukoh Tada's KODEN VIII which had been knocked down a number of times during the trip from Cape Town. I had heard earlier that her captain complained that his boat had a violent corkscrew motion. Yukoh had designed KODEN and blamed himself for her shortcomings. He sat around gritting his teeth. Other captains in the race were more practical, went aboard, and discovered that KODEN's forepeak was filled with wet sails, anchors, spare winches, extra food, and all sorts of heavy gear that might well have caused the trouble in a yacht that weighed only 11,000 pounds. Yukoh was advised to dry out everything and get rid of the extra weight forward. In addition, Yukoh's helpers were removing an experimental daggerboard forward of the keel. In spite of all this, Yukoh was extremely dejected.

Minoru Saito, the other Japanese entrant, had a swarm of helpers working on SHUTEN-DOHJI II. Minoru's main problem had been sail damage, and he had long discussions with sailmakers while they pulled sails up and down and threw Japanese and English words at one another.

The personalities of the two Japanese captains were completely different. Minoru, 56, was a retired oil company executive who had taken up ocean racing to replace an earlier hobby of mountain climbing. He was always smiling, stoically accepted bad weather and technical problems, and appeared to be having a wonderful time. Perhaps an earlier heart attack had taught him to enjoy life one day at a time.

Yukoh Tada, on the other hand, was much more flamboyant and high-strung. He had been a cab driver in Tokyo, dabbled in abstract art, played the jazz saxophone, and was deep into Zen Buddhism. Although he was always pleasant, I felt that this Kerouac-type character was tiptoeing on the edge of a volcano. Yukoh, who was sailing in his second BOC race, was determined to win and be famous in Japan. Minoru merely wanted to finish in one piece for his own satisfaction.

Everyone was hard at work on SEBAGO when Andrew—covered in dust—came bounding up the ladder to the cockpit. "I've found the cause of the leak," he said excitedly. All work stopped, and everyone gathered around the keel. Eight ½" dia. stainless steel bolts—which fastened a complex T-shaped fiberglass part between the back of the keel and the hull—had not been bedded when the hull was built. In addition the bolts had *rolled* threads instead of *cut* threads, which meant that the unthreaded shank portions of the bolts were a smaller diameter than the threaded parts. The hull leak came from water going through a few thin layers of ruptured glass and then working upward along the unthreaded parts of the bolts. Andrew and I immediately replaced the defective bolts, liberally bedded them with the best quality sealant, and tightened the nuts. Now at last we could put down the inside floorboards in the cabin and begin to make some order in my little floating home.

The next morning a tall, slim, silver-haired man walked by

the yacht while we were looking over the hull repairs. Ian Hansen introduced me to Alan Payne, one of Australia's best-known naval architects. We asked Alan about adding fiberglass to the hull aft of the keel to cover the bolt heads. He looked the problem over and suggested that a long streamlined fillet of carefully laid-up fiberglass would cover the bolt heads, strengthen the joint, and actually improve the water flow over the area. Alan took a piece of chalk, marked out his recommendations, and the fiberglass man started to work.

Hans Bernwall, the manufacturer of the Monitor vane gear, had flown in from San Francisco to service his steering systems on various BOC yachts. Hans listened to my woes, changed the breakaway latch gear, and began making various adjustments. The electrician replaced several corroded wires that led to the voltage regulator from the generator. Margaret had brought new spinnaker pole end fittings from the U.S. All we needed to complete a new pole was a piece of 100 mm. dia. aluminum irrigation pipe 6.4 meters long. Although we tried everywhere we finally had to go to a yacht spar shop that supplied an over-diameter piece that required adapters for the end fittings.

I took my whole crew to the prize-giving dinner on the evening of February 1st. Afterwards I had a long talk with Yukoh Tada, whose yacht was in the water and ready to start. "I am not prepared just yet," he said. "In a few more days perhaps." Instead of the laughing, nodding, Yukoh I had known in Newport, I was speaking to a tired old man. The skin on his face was like parchment, and his eyes no longer sparkled.

Three days had passed in a blur. The next leg of the race was to begin in 24 hours. Although we'd done wonders on SEBAGO, the yacht wasn't ready because the hull repairs were still underway, the autopilot parts hadn't arrived, and the sails were only half repaired. I would have to start a few days late.

On Sunday, February 3rd, we declared a partial holiday and all went out to watch the restart of the race. At 1300 a cannon boomed on a warship, and the fleet of 18 (NIIHAU IV and KODEN VIII were also to start later) was soon streaking east and then south past Sydney Heads, pursued by a pack of spectator boats that gradually dropped behind. John Martin on ALLIED BANK and the French contingent were sailing very fast. My heart felt heavy not to be with the others heading out to sea.

On Monday, Gil Forrester and Ian Hansen finished overhauling the winches. The two men then repaired the companionway door latches and put in stronger padeyes to take the blocks for the reefing pendants. Chris Iacono appeared with the new spinnaker pole. The sailmaker heaved three sailbags on board. Margaret and I (and Nadia and Colin Bull) went shopping for food stores. (It was a long way to Cape Horn.) Colin Bull's wife—who was a doctor—sorted out my medical supplies, dealt with the labels ("What's it for?"), and wrote a few prescriptions to replace outdated medicines. The electrician tried hard to hook up the new telex equipment, but the single sideband radio did not have the correct circuitry so we abandoned the telex project. The yacht was rapidly going back together.

By Tuesday, February 5th, Andrew had finished the hull-keel repair. There was ¾" of fiberglass (set in epoxy) over the bolts. The whole area was nicely faired and looked better (and we knew it would be much stronger) than when the yacht was built. Andrew did a marvelous job, and the hull-keel joint was as smooth as a dolphin's back.

The following morning SEBAGO was lowered into the water. We spent most of the day bending on the sails and putting food stores aboard. Late that afternoon we slipped out for a little sail to try everything and to let Colin, Gil, Ian, Chris, and Nadia—who had so generously helped me—steer a little. Although the breeze was light, SEBAGO glided along like a feather. We were ready to go.

The start in Sydney. Five yachts hurry eastward toward the Tasman Sea.

CHAPTER TEN

The Tasman Sea
and Cook Strait

FEBRUARY 7, 1991. (THURSDAY). DAY 0.

<u>0900 local time.</u>   SEBAGO and I slipped away from Sydney Heads an hour ago for the start of the third leg of the BOC race. A jovial gang in the Iacono family yacht towed us to the starting line to see us off. I saw Chris, Irma, Nadia, and Richard Iacono, Gil and Susana Forrester, Ian Hansen, Mark and Michele Schrader, Steve Wilkins (the electrician), his wife Irene, and of course Margaret. There was practically no wind (north 3 knots) so while shouts of "Watch out for whales" and "Be careful of Cape Horn" drifted across the water, I put up a red, white, and blue asymmetrical spinnaker and slowly crept offshore.

<u>1035.</u>   While below I heard a bang and looked out to find the spinnaker tack way up in the air. The fancy tack strap broke because of incredibly bad sewing by the sailmaker. I tied down the tack with a short piece of line.

<u>1200.</u>   Wind NNE 11 knots. I've been trying various sail combinations and have finally settled on the full genoa and the mainsail with one reef. It's warm and pleasant, the seas are easy, and I'm falling asleep. All my clothes and bedding have been washed and dried. Irma—Chris' wife—even ironed everything. I've been spoiled rotten—and I love it! Because of all the improvements and repairs to the yacht, I feel very confident. We're headed for Cook Strait between North and South Islands in New Zealand.

<u>1630.</u>   Very hot, and the sun is punishing. Difficult to get the vane to steer within 10–15°. More like 20°. I didn't have enough turns of the furling line on the genoa drum so I rove three additional turns, a tedious job. All kinds of nice food aboard.

FEBRUARY 7, 1991. (THURSDAY). DAY 1.

<u>0750 GMT.</u>   The first order of business is to put the ship on Greenwich meridian time (GMT). This is complicated because GMT is 11 hours earlier than local Australian time. Yesterday—Thursday morning—we left at 0800 local time, or 2100 GMT on Wednesday night, February 6th. This means that daylight comes about 1900 GMT. As I sail eastward, with the clock on GMT, daylight will come one hour earlier for each 15° of longitude, so by the time I reach the Atlantic, sunrise will be at 0600 or 0700.

I have a lot of trouble with this, and I'm forever subtracting hours when I should be adding. Nevertheless I'm convinced that for a long west-to-east voyage (or vice-versa), a ship should run on GMT—at least in the navigation and radio departments.

The 8-day stop in Sydney was mostly hard work. Margaret and the Australians were wonderful. People somehow get caught up in my sailing enterprises and help me again and again. It's not a question of pay or money, but the pleasure of helping as anonymous volunteers and being part of a project. A kind of self-gratification. On some level these people identify with me or with what I'm trying to do. I've been sailing to distant corners of the world for a quarter of a century, and people always appear and always want to help. I guess at some level every man or woman wants to sail around the world in his own vessel or climb a high mountain by himself. He dreams of these things. This quest has got to be a basic unquenched drive in people. I know it's there.

<u>0828.</u>   Wind NNE 6. Seas light. The new inside compass that Chris Iacono installed is marvelous. The compass is one of those upside-down gimbaled jobs that is screwed to the overhead ceiling. I just glance up from the chart table or one of the settee berths and I can see our heading.

<u>0922.</u>   Hard-looking low clouds to port. A lovely sunset.

<u>1002.</u>   I left my alarm clock in Sydney.

<u>1116.</u>   The night sky is clear, and the Clouds of Magellan are dazzling. Hundreds of stars. I'm surprised that I can still see the loom of the lights of Sydney, which is 70 miles to the east.

<u>1724.</u>   Light rain. Wind stopped by a large cloud.

<u>2021.</u>   We're surrounded by low rain clouds and have been becalmed for three hours. The wind is 5 knots from the SE. My bunk is filled with an incredible assortment of plastic boxes, food gifts, hats, a video camera, books, and pillows. No room for me at

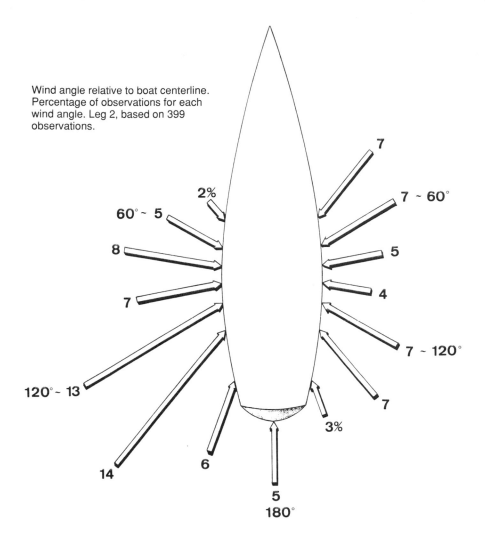

Wind angle relative to boat centerline. Percentage of observations for each wind angle. Leg 2, based on 399 observations.

2%

60° ~ 5

8

7

120° ~ 13

14

6

5
180°

7

7 ~ 60°

5

4

7 ~ 120°

7

3%

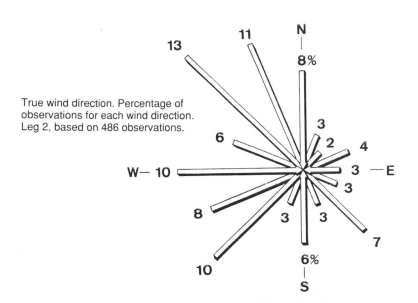

True wind direction. Percentage of observations for each wind direction. Leg 2, based on 486 observations.

13

11

N
8%

3

6

2

4

W— 10

3 —E

3

8

3

3

7

10

6%
S

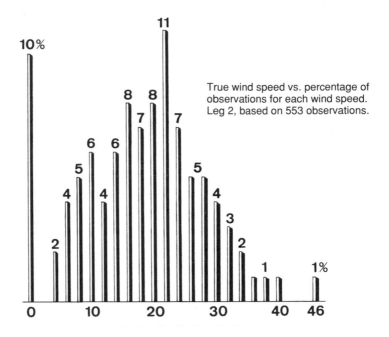

True wind speed vs. percentage of observations for each wind speed. Leg 2, based on 553 observations.

gifts, hats, a video camera, books, and pillows. No room for me at all. I'm trying to stow the stuff.

<u>2123.</u>   Cloud banks on all sides, some very dark, others streaked with sunlight. There's no point putting up more sail till the weather settles down a little.

<u>2339.</u>   The sky's clearing, and the wind's going back to the ENE (10 knots). I have tacked several times but will stay on port because of the swell. Steak and tea and aspirins for breakfast. Uruguay seems a million miles away. The radio is yelping about a heavy gale to the south. I wonder what it will do to the fleet?

FEBRUARY 8, 1991. (FRIDAY). DAY 2.

<u>0401.</u>   A beautiful summer day. Fleecy clouds and a deep blue sea. Unfortunately the wind (ENE 8 knots) is blowing from where I want to go, and I can't sail too close to the wind because of a lumpy swell. We're headed for Puysegur point at the SW corner of New Zealand's South Island.

<u>0817.</u>   I heard on the chat hour that CRÉDIT AGRICOLE got knocked down yesterday and had her keel in the air. Philippe's mainsail was ripped and his gooseneck and wind generators were broken. "Much damage to many things," said Philippe.

Kanga Birtles on JARKAN discovered that by accident he had left his seaboots ashore in Sydney. So far Kanga has been working in bare feet, but he's worried about cold feet in the south.

<u>0820.</u>   I got the electric bilge pump working after cleaning out the hoses and filter, a dirty job. Then I wiped and oiled all the big tools. I miss my alarm clock, an item I need for naps and radio schedules.

<u>1357.</u>   Wind NE 20 knots. Low clouds and light rain. One reef plus a few rolls in the jib. I tuned in to the special weather forecast for the BOC fleet. Once again, instead of reading the forecast at dictation speed, the operator read the forecast at normal talking speed, which is impossible to copy. I'm afraid I lost my temper. "What good is all this carefully collected information if the end user can't get it?" I told him. "Please read the forecast *slowly* and use GMT for all times. Half are in GMT and half are in local time which makes the forecast hopeless."

<u>1413.</u>   My sailing speed in the Tasman Sea has been wretched so far, but the winds have been light and contrary.

<u>1949.</u>   Puysegur Point on the SW corner of South Island is 726 miles on 126°M. Cook Strait is 821 miles on 094°M. Cook Strait looks impossible with these winds, so I am heading for Puysegur.

<u>2133.</u>   Cereal, eggs, and pastrami for breakfast. The fried pastrami was good but spicy. I must keep eating the fresh meat before my little block of ice in the chest is gone. Colin Bull sent along some nice pastries, which are going fast. I cut a few new 60" ties from ⅜" line, and put them on the lifelines for general use.

<u>2137.</u>   After sailing SEBAGO 17,000 miles with water ballast and her present rig, I would change her as follows:
    (1) Cut 5–6 feet from the mast and get rid of the heavy, overbuilt structure at the masthead.
    (2) Junk the genoa, second headstay, and furling gear. These two changes would save 150 pounds (or more) aloft and make a big performance difference. As a practical matter I find that I use the genoa very little. The two headstays divide the forward rig load and are troublesome to keep evenly tensioned. Also the windage and movement of the furled genoa are considerations. The jib is an all-around sail and extremely important. The windier it gets, the more I roll up the sail. The big genoa can be replaced with an asymmetrical spinnaker (in a sock) hoisted off the wind. I no longer use the forestaysail at all because I can carry more sail with water ballast. In other words, the yacht is more powerful.

<u>2156.</u>   If I read the weather maps correctly I should soon have NW winds from the big low in Bass Strait.

<u>2201.</u>   I must study the directions for the video camera I bought in Sydney. Also I must work on an article for the *USA Today* newspaper.

<u>2223.</u>   I've taken alarm clocks for granted for so long that without one I'm lost. The GPS has a timing device, but it's too complicated. I have an alarm on my wrist watch, but the alarm is so feeble that I don't hear it. Grumble, grumble!

FEBRUARY 9, 1991. (SATURDAY). DAY 3.

<u>0102.</u>   According to the Pilot chart for February we'll have fewer gales if we go east via Cook Strait. The five-degree squares for the foot of South Island show 5, 9, 8, and 8 (percent of observations with winds of 34 knots or more). For Cook Strait the squares show 4, 2, 2, and 1. The averages are 7.5 vs. 2.25. Of course who has ever found an average wind? Since everyone else in the race has gone directly south around the bottom of New Zealand, maybe we'll find better winds in Cook Strait. We're so far back that I've got to try something different. Even if it is a little riskier.

<u>0335.</u>   A ghastly weather report for points farther south. The wind has veered, so I am on 090°M. with 768 miles to the Strait. The news is that SERVANT IV hit a whale this morning. Minor damage to her port bow. NIIHAU is supposed to start today. Three messages for SEBAGO : (1) Margaret found the alarm clock. (2) The *USA Today* story is due. (3) A technical expert has more information on the telex (already junked).

<u>0710.</u>   Only half a kilo of butter and 1½ loaves of bread. Can there be more elsewhere? I just fried a piece of steak, which I had with a cup of tea, two stalks of celery, and a plum.

<u>0813.</u>   Philippe's knockdown was in 65 knots. Damage to one furling gear, the wind chargers, the mainsail, and the boom. Much talk about colliding ocean wave systems during the chat hour. Discussion between José and Philippe about how hard to push and when to ease off. "It's a fine line between disaster and winning the race." The report about GENERALI CONCORDE hitting a whale was false; nevertheless SPONSOR WANTED (now renamed BUTTERCUP), BBV, and SERVANT IV have struck whales.

<u>0902.</u>   I've been looking through Harrison's bird book to identify a pair of terns. I found nothing, but I happened to see a painting of a black-billed gull, a small whitish-gray bird with a black bill

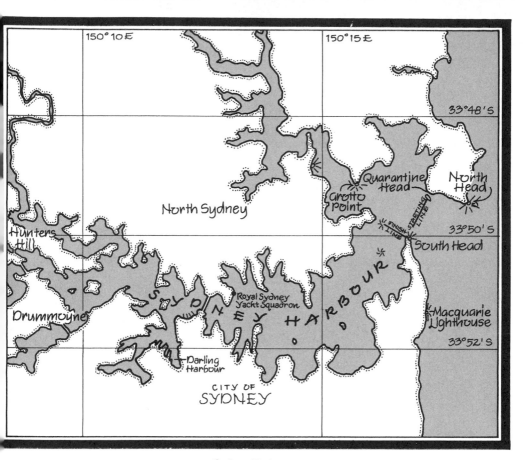

Sydney Harbour.

and a dark ring around the eye. A strange sort of gull that looks more like a tern.

<u>1203.</u>   A day's run of 171 miles. Cape Farewell is 711 miles on 089°M. The wind is almost gone, only 4–5 knots from the NE. When I pumped out the ballast tanks I noticed water in the leeward tank. Not a lot, but I suspect that a little salt water is leaking past the crossfeed valve.

<u>2057.</u>   Becalmed since 1600. Busy cleaning the galley and emptying the icebox of water. Ice all melted.

<u>2158.</u>   A little wind (5 knots) from the NE. Overcast with low stratus. Very hot (I am wearing an old short-sleeved shirt and pajama bottoms.) The weather forecast—enough to scare a listener to death—predicts awesome gales, but so far nothing here at all. I checked the engine bilge tray which was clean. No water and only a trace of oil.

Today I must deal with the story for *USA Today*. It's an effort to write at sea while heeled to 20° and bouncing along. I must also study the video camera manual. In the rush at Sydney I forgot to give Margaret the broken snatch blocks and the cameras that need repairs.

I have begun an enthralling novel called *The Boat* by Lothar-Günther Buchheim. The writing is extremely good.

<u>2350.</u>   Yesterday I had a plan to get rid of the genoa, furling gear, and all of its weight and windage. Today I have the genoa up, and it's pulling mightily. So much for my big schemes.

FEBRUARY 10, 1991. (SUNDAY). DAY 4.

<u>0442.</u>   A long low line of dark clouds to the SW. Looks menacing.

<u>0600.</u>   I finished *The Boat*. First-rate stuff. A grim subject superbly handled by both a submarine veteran and a careful observer of men. The Germans never properly countered the development of short wavelength radar, which allowed British aircraft to detect and bomb submarines when they surfaced.

<u>0859.</u>   Becalmed. Warm rain showers. We're south of a low to the north, and north of a low to the south. The dividing isobars are 1010 mb., which is what our barometer reads.

<u>1755.</u>   Eight knots of wind from the SE for two hours, but now it's calm again. More rain. Glimmers of bluish light on a few low clouds as dawn comes. So far the passage between Sydney and New Zealand has been more like crossing the doldrums than a stormy sea.

<u>1935.</u>   More rain and gray skies, plus 18 knots of wind from the SSE. We're right on course (090°M.) with one reef in the mainsail and three rolls in the jib. The water ballast is a blessing in this narrow boat.

<u>1939.</u>   My mind is still on the German submarine novel that I finished yesterday. Why did men do it? To have been an engine room mechanic or a torpedo man was the worst job on earth. Yet the men were all volunteers. The book jacket is a painting—certainly exaggerated—of a submarine going through a mine field with nasty-looking mines anchored at all levels on all sides. I wonder how modern nuclear-powered submarines deal with mines laid at sea?

<u>2116.</u>   I sharpened three knives, got two flashlights working, and made four sail ties. Lashed the kerosene jugs in the lazarette, tied up five fenders, and sorted out a pile of lines.

FEBRUARY 11, 1991. (MONDAY). DAY 5.

<u>0405.</u>   Horrors! The GPS is acting up. I'm writing down the ship's position every few hours to keep a record of latitude and longitude. Just now I see that an erroneous position has vanished. These problems may be connected with the GPS satellites, which are not supposed to be fully operational yet. Our waypoint #1, five miles north of Cook Strait's Cape Farewell, is 507 miles on a bearing of 085°M.

<u>0600.</u>   I found a 2″ flying fish on deck. Incredible. A tiny minnow in the wrong sea.

<u>0749.</u>   Wind south, 16 knots. Misty and rainy. At last we're flying. All afternoon (local time) SEBAGO has been hurrying along at 8 to 8.5 knots. We've been a bit overcanvassed the last hour, so I took four rolls in the jib. Same speed, but we're less pressed.

I can't seem to sleep. The weather is cooler so I got out my blue Musto jacket, which was repaired (the left arm came adrift) by Irma Iacono in Sydney. I found another rip on the right cuff so I stitched it up with black thread. I'd never make a tailor, but the jacket's serviceable.

<u>1150.</u>   The news is that Robert Hooke and NIIHAU IV started from Sydney yesterday. NIIHAU's hull has been repaired, and the yacht has a new mast. Robin Davie and I have been trying to call Robert to encourage him a little.

<u>1547.</u>   Heavy warm rain. Amazing how a strange noise alerts a sailor (a mother listening to her child). I heard an unusual clatter and went on deck. Sure enough. The port running backstay control line was whipping around because a small turning block had come adrift.

<u>1830.</u>   I radioed my *USA Today* story to the U.S. at 1700 via Sydney radio and answered questions relating to it and other stories for half an hour. What a strain to give instant answers to a non-sailor in terms that are simple and exciting (I hope).

<u>2109.</u>   I've noticed that in plugging to windward, I'm better off with a smaller mainsail and more headsail (which is easier to adjust in area). We go at the same speed, but with less heel.

<u>2215.</u>   The other BOC sailors and I agree that the public marine weather broadcasts are largely useless. They seem designed by meteorologists to confuse people. The reports are incredibly dreary, much too long, full of hazy words, and of little practical help. Plus

they're read too fast with local and GMT times all mixed up. The best forecasts, of course, are private ones directed to a client vessel. The few that I've heard (by accident) are always extremely short, clear, and to the point, just what the public broadcasts are not.

A forecast should be twenty words and answer four questions:
1. Which way will the wind blow?
2. How strong will it be?
3. When will this happen?
4. Are calms or heavy weather ahead?
("At 1400Z your wind will switch to 310° and blow at 13 knots. No gales or calms are in sight.")

<u>2330.</u>   I'm only at 39°S. I must get through Cook Strait and south to 50°–58°S. where the mileage between the degrees of longitude is less so that I can get east more quickly. I've been studying the Sony video camera manual and have been trying out the camera and the editing-playback feature. Amazing that you can shoot, rewind, and see what you've done.

FEBRUARY 12, 1991. (TUESDAY). DAY 6.

<u>0027.</u>   Cape Farewell is 370 miles on 087°M. Finished reading *To Have or Have Not*. Vintage Hemingway. Quite short and not as good as I remembered. A few good parts though. The 1937 prices and wages seem incredible. A meal with a bottle of beer cost 25¢. Yet thinking about the era I can recall the 1939 Cleveland World Exposition (I was 12 years old) where a steaming plate of Chin's chow mein was 18¢ and included a big glass of milk.

<u>0301.</u>   A wonderful sleep. I finally feel rested after the rigors of Sydney. Cleaned out the icebox and fed some over-ripe luncheon meat to the white-chinned petrels.

<u>0427.</u>   The shape of the mainsail is terrible. The sail looks as if the two upper battens are missing (they're not). The weather has cleared, and we have sun and a gorgeous sky. Occasional patches of fog, and once in a while a big swell from the SW rolls past. The new weather map shows a big high sliding up behind us.

<u>0702.</u>   The sailing has been lovely, some of the most pleasant of the entire trip. SEBAGO is going 7–8 knots, rolling slightly in a sea a bit forward of the beam. We're headed east; the 12-knot wind is SSE so the apparent wind allows the sheets to be eased just a touch. The sea is a series of grayish swells, easy and smooth, and

we gently rise up and down, like the chest of a sleeping child. Overhead, lines of heavy low clouds are on all sides. A burst of sun glimmers through a chink in the clouds, and I see a patch of blue for a minute or two, then the door to the sky closes.

I wonder how I am doing in comparison with the other competitors, who are far to the south and flying along? I am quite far east, but my weather since Sydney has been light and variable. What about Yukoh Tada, who is still in Sydney? What sort of weather will I have east of South Island? Still 323 miles to go to Cape Farewell.

Philippe Jeantot, aboard CRÉDIT AGRICOLE at 59°S., reported warm weather and light winds. Philippe was in shirtsleeves, and wearing shoes instead of sea boots.

1400.   A run of 166 miles at noon, but we've been becalmed since 1300. Since all we were doing was slatting and ruining the sails, I have wound up the jib. I am going to sleep.

1900.   Wind SSE 6 knots. Full sail and heading east.

2038.   A rainy day again with little clumps of clouds scattered in the sky. I hear various New Zealand fishermen on the radio and a lot of Japanese so I must sharpen up my watchkeeping. The BBC had a good jazz program built around Thelonius Monk's tune "Round Midnight" with Miles Davis, Steve Lacey, and Sonny Rollins.

2313.   Robin Davie passed on the message that Minoru Saito on SHUTEN-DOHJI II was knocked down near the SW tip of New Zealand and damaged his #2 jib. Minoru also lost his topping lift, masthead instruments, and his liferaft, apparently because the hydrostatic release got wet. VOLCANO stopped at Bluff, at the southern tip of South Island, for 7 hours while Paul Thackaberry filled his diesel tank (mysteriously empty) and bought a few supplies. Jack Boye got hit on the head by his main boom. No damage to the boom, but Jack says that he keeps hallucinating about ice cream.

2330.   I shackled two more of the small running backstay recovery line blocks to the rail and re-routed and shortened the port line, which is very subject to chafe. Wind south 8 knots. I will keep working SE until we get to 40°S. for a better shot at Cook Strait.

I seem to be hungry all the time and just ate a second breakfast. I found a second loaf of bread (rainbow-colored from mold) and heaved it over the side. A pity that I couldn't salvage even one slice. The Australian supermarket eggs have paper-thin shells and are abysmal. Already I have had a bad egg (ugh!) and now crack each one into a cup before using. I should have dealt directly with a farmer who liked his chickens.

FEBRUARY 13, 1991. (WEDNESDAY). DAY 7.

<u>0005.</u>   A beautiful day but again almost no wind. Lots of sun and cirrus. Not a chance of moving with the running rig in wind this light.

<u>0258.</u>   Almost no wind. I've headed a bit south to keep the fore-and-aft rig working.

<u>0616.</u>   I've been sitting in the cockpit while we glide eastward toward the west coast of New Zealand, and our biggest sails billow out with an 8-knot wind from the south. The sky seems enormous with swirls of cirrus 5 miles high, little puffs of billowy altocumulus in the middle heights, long streaks of flat stratus touching the far horizons, and a rain shower miles away. An artist could spend a month painting the tiny shapes, and mixing a hundred shades of blue and gray.
   A solitary dolphin is following us, puffing and splashing off the port quarter. A few white-chinned petrels are nearby, hoping for bread scraps. The setting is a huge sky, a quiet ocean, and a tiny sailboat. It's all so peaceful and lovely.

<u>0707.</u>   Something different for dinner: a delicious cheese and leek soup. Excellent.

<u>1519.</u>   Amazing that we can make 4.5 knots in 5 knots of wind. With the wind just forward of the beam we increase the apparent wind so I have changed course a little (125°M.) to use what little wind there is. No sign of a fishing fleet.

<u>2237.</u>   Wind west 8 knots. I put up the new spinnaker pole to port to hold out the jib.

FEBRUARY 14, 1991. (THURSDAY). DAY 8.

<u>0052.</u>   SSW wind (6 knots) still fluky. Gybed the rig again. I am leaving the foreguy and afterguy tied to the ends of the poles so there's no chance of losing a pole. The new pole end with the roller seems excellent.

CONTESTANTS (21) AT THE START OF LEG 3

CAPTAIN	COUNTRY	SHIP NAME	DESIGNER
CLASS 1 (eleven 60-footers)			
David Adams	Australia	*Innkeeper*	Kell Steinman
Christophe Auguin	France	*Groupe Sceta*	Groupe Finot
Isabelle Autissier	France	*Ecureuil-Poitou-Charentes*	Harlé & Mortain
Kanga Birtles	Australia	*Jarkan*	John King
Nandor Fa	Hungary	*Alba Regia*	Nandor Fa
Alain Gautier	France	*Generali Concorde*	Finot & Conq
Philippe Jeantot	France	*Crédit Agricole IV*	Marc Lombard
John Martin	South Africa	*Allied Bank*	Angelo Lavranos
Mike Plant	U.S.A.	*Duracell*	Rodger Martin
Bertie Reed	South Africa	*Grinaker*	Rodger Martin
José Ugarte	Spain	*BBV Expo '92*	Bouvet & Petit
CLASS 2 (six 50-footers)			
Jack Boye	U.S.A.	*Project City Kids*	John Cherubini
Yves Dupasquier	France	*Servant IV*	Jean Beret
Josh Hall	Great Britain	*Spirit of Ipswich*	Rodger Martin
Don McIntyre	Australia	*Buttercup* (renamed)	Adams & Radford
Hal Roth	U.S.A.	*Sebago*	Bill Lee
Yukoh Tada	Japan	*Koden VIII*	Yukoh Tada
CORINTHIAN CLASS (four entries)			
Robin Davie	Great Britain	*Global Exposure*	Bergstrom & Ridder
Robert Hooke	U.S.A.	*Niihau IV*	Ron Holland
Minoru Saito	Japan	*Shuten-dohji II*	Adams & Radford
Paul Thackaberry	U.S.A.	*Volcano*	Paul Thackaberry

<u>0727.</u>   Wind north 5 knots. I trimmed and filed smooth the ends of all the cotter pins on the rigging turnbuckles. The jagged ends of cotter pins are a nasty hazard for sails and ankles. In case I get becalmed or in trouble in Cook Strait I have my main anchor all set to go. While I was flaking down the nylon line on the foredeck, four dolphins came alongside. They swam in formation and even breathed in unison.

<u>0932.</u>   Wind north 10 knots. This is the sort of sailing I like: a quiet sea, a light steady wind, and a clear sky so I can see the stars—my friends—twinkling up there. It's so pleasant standing in

the cockpit. I love such nights. So peaceful. No stress. No problems. Just perfection.

I'm nervous about going far south in the Southern Ocean after getting rolled in the Indian Ocean. I was lucky to have gotten back on board.

<u>1210.</u>   A run of 105 miles at noon. Loom of fishing boat lights to the south.

<u>1314.</u>   Changed to the running rig with a NW wind of 15 knots. I hate to deal with the pole at night, but the deck light makes the job easier. I think the scheme of having two control lines permanently rove is going to work OK. At least the pole can't escape.

<u>1840.</u>   Running rig down.

<u>1940.</u>   Running rig up.

<u>2331.</u>   The usual navigator's blues. No sign of land, which I work out to be 17 miles away. The depth—140 meters—tallies. No fishing boats or big vessels.

<u>2355.</u>   Flat water. Going well in 18 knots of west wind. We're yawing up to 18° to port, probably because of a cross-setting tidal stream. A couple of cape gannets (all white with dark-brown wing tips and tail; top of head yellow) are circling around us. Big, goofy-looking birds. Dr. Seuss would love them.

FEBRUARY 15, 1991. (FRIDAY). DAY 9.

<u>0002.</u>   Water 104 meters deep. Distance to waypoint 1 (five miles north of Cape Farewell) is 6.3 miles. We've come 1,100 miles in 8½ days (only 129 miles per day), but the winds have been light, and we were becalmed for 16 hours. Certainly an easy crossing of the stormy Tasman Sea. I'm well rested for the strait.

<u>0038.</u>   Land to starboard. Hazy and misty. Whitecaps and 22 knots of wind from the west. One reef in the main and 3 rolls in the jib. A hot sun.

<u>0049.</u>   Stephens Island, my main guidepost for Cook Strait, is 58 miles on 084°M.

<u>0131.</u>   We're tearing along in smooth green water, a sort of olive drab color. I keep taking down sail (second reef; six rolls in the jib), and we're still going 8.5 knots. The yacht is yawing a lot, so I have increased the yaw correction on the autopilot. (This yaw

phenomenon may be usual, and only noticed in relation to land.) No sign of traffic, but I must stay up and be alert. It's very hot, and I'm in shirt sleeves.

<u>0301.</u>   The tidal stream is contrary and is pushing us all over the place. The seas are short. It's 39 miles to Stephens Island.

<u>0418.</u>   The strait is surprisingly rough. I seem to recall a smoother passage in 1987. I opened the valve to the starboard freshwater tank and closed the valve to the port tank. I want to draw equal amounts from each tank.

<u>0422.</u>   Wind up to 26 knots. Small seas but steep, rough, and breaking now and then. I'm sleepy, but will have to stay up today and tonight.

I read a pleasant, upbeat little book by Paul Gallico called *The Hurricane Story*, a boy's book about the British fighter plane of World War II. In one place Gallico tells about a man who was frightened by something, and the author wonders whether the person would be at his best if the same thing happened again. Would he be cautious and timid and not do his utmost? "He may be the bravest chap in the world," says Gallico, "but when he comes face to face with his opponent once more, he will be remembering that those fists once knocked him loose from his senses and can do it again. Thus he will be that much more cautious and . . . be that much further away from turning the tables."

Will this apply to me in the next big storm in the Southern Ocean? I certainly have no desire to meet another sea like the one that rolled us.

<u>0437.</u>   Lots of gannets out fishing. It seems a pity not to stop in New Zealand to sail some of these waters. There is the most appealing sound on the easternmost tip of South Island. Queen Charlotte Sound (I know another one in British Columbia) has all sorts of likely anchorages, walks ashore, hills to climb, and places to visit. Margaret and I need a new WHISPER and an end to this ocean racing madness.

<u>0510.</u>   More wind. Up to 32 knots. Boom in the water two or three times, cockpit filled, and a bucket of water below, some on the electrical panel. I put on oilskins and quickly pulled down the third reef. The yacht responded at once. Before the reef we were doing a steady 9–10 knots, but the steering was uncertain in these short seas.

<u>0604.</u>   Wind WNW 24–28 knots. I'll be glad to get behind Stephens Island (where I make a big course change) for protection

from these wretched seas. I reckon another hour or so. I could gybe now, but it will be wiser to do it near the light. Perhaps the wind will ease off at sunset, which should be about that time.

<u>0827.</u>   Passed Stephens Island. Just dark. Blowing hard (NW 30) and the boat is rolling heavily in short seas. Had a tough time with the poles and lines, but OK now. Thank heavens for the two tackles on the main boom. The next problem is to find The Brothers light. Behind us I can see an enormous black cloud above Stephens Island. The wind—whistling as it comes—is pouring down from the huge cloud like air from a gigantic punctured balloon.

The Tasman Sea and New Zealand.

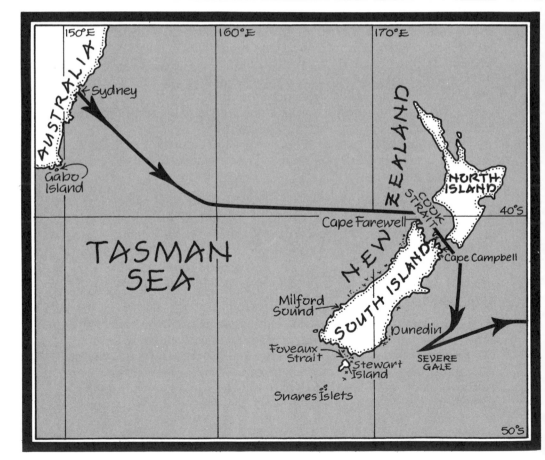

The poles on the foredeck almost got me this time. I'm certainly glad that I wore my harness. I have turned on the masthead navigation light.

<u>0911.</u>   The Brothers light is 26 miles SE. Wind (NW 31) dead aft, but we must stay on this course because of rocks. The sea is much easier because we're in the lee of South Island since we turned at the Stephens Island light.

<u>1005.</u>   It's been blowing hard (NW 34). I think a front went through. The big black clouds have moved ahead of us, and the wind is dropping as I write. The Brothers light is ahead.

<u>1253.</u>   One ship, one tug and barge, and one small vessel, all headed west. With luck this course should clear New Zealand. The wind is light in the lee of The Brothers light, but I suspect it will increase. The weatherfax just printed two New Zealand weather charts that don't show the actual wind conditions at all.

It's hard to stay awake.

<u>1400.</u>   We're near Cape Terawhiti and the big city of Wellington. An anchored ship is along the coast to port. The wind is dying, and I had to scramble to make enough sail to keep control near two fishing boats. Much fast unreefing and pole handling.

<u>1430.</u>   A small ferry or excursion boat just dashed past looking very festive with a lot of colored lights. I was worried about being run down so I turned on my powerful deck running lights. Everybody waved, so SEBAGO must have been seen, although I must have been hardly visible in the cockpit.

<u>1600.</u>   Wind south 15 knots. Set a course a little south of east for the open Pacific. Water ballast to starboard. Nothing in sight ahead. The next land will be Cape Horn. Goodnight all!

CHAPTER ELEVEN

Gales and Ice

FEBRUARY 16, 1991. (SATURDAY). DAY 10.

<u>0154.</u>   From the eastern entrance of Cook Strait that we just left (Cape Campbell at 41°44'S.), the straight or rhumb line distance to Cape Horn (at 56°S.) is 4,723 miles.

A great circle route (which dips to 66°54'S.) is 4,160 miles or 563 miles shorter, but at what cost in storms and ice? We'd sail a shorter distance, but it's impossible because of destructive pack ice. A modified great circle route to 60°S. is 4,244 miles or 479 miles less. This latitude would certainly put us in iceberg territory. A more modified route down to 56°, the latitude of Cape Horn, is 4,391 miles or 332 miles less. This ought to be possible. First, however, we must sail south for 840 miles (14° of latitude). If we shape a course roughly SE, we'll gradually drop into the higher southern latitudes. And hopefully into winds from westerly quadrants.

<u>0230.</u>   Wind east 14 knots. We're on the port tack on a heading of 150°M. or 171°T. since the magnetic variation here is 21°E. One reef in the main and 5 rolls in the jib. I must not forget about the Chatham Islands, 400 miles to the ESE.

<u>0415.</u>   I finished *One Two Buckle My Shoe* by Agatha Christie, the first Christie that I've ever read. I found the writing excellent and the characters well drawn, but the plot is too complex and unbelievable for my taste. Since Agatha Christie is one of the all-time best-selling authors, this shows how little I know about the taste of mystery fans.

<u>0538.</u>   I'm still recovering from the strains of yesterday. Handling these big boats in restricted waters and turbulent weather is not for the faint of heart. Yet it's all so challenging and exciting.

The wind (ENE 17 knots) is up a little. While I was tucking in the second reef I saw two signs that we're approaching the Southern Ocean. We passed a patch of floating kelp, and I saw the first albatross since Sydney.

The Class 1 fleet positions on February 13th:
1. GENERALI CONCORDE. 4,148 miles to go to Uruguay.
2. GROUPE SCETA. 73 miles behind first.
3. ALLIED BANK. 132 miles behind first.
4. INNKEEPER. 142 miles behind first.

All were at 59° to 60°S. and sailing at 9.1 to 10.2 knots. It's surprising how close together the leaders are. ALLIED BANK and the two high-powered French yachts keep changing positions. All have reported ice.

<u>0558.</u>   We're 80 miles SE of Wellington.

<u>1307.</u>   A couple of aspirins and a long nap have done wonders for me. Very black outside. We're going well considering that we're stuck in a high pressure area (1017 mb.). Our progress has been all south, so I have headed a little more east, which puts us hard on the wind. The new inside compass is a big help. No shipping traffic around here. It's difficult to believe that the rhumb line course to Cape Horn is 75°M. while the great circle route is 124°M. The easterly variation is now 22°.

<u>1328.</u>   Margaret bought me a nifty little pocket calculator (Citizen) that's both attractive (black trim) and uses a sensible battery (one AA penlight instead of a special hard-to-find battery). I like to think I'm good at arithmetic, but I almost always discover a mistake or two when I check the carried-forward daily mileage for a couple of weeks.

<u>1748.</u>   Wind gusty and from the east at 22 knots. Gray and overcast.

<u>2236.</u>   A ghastly meal. I tried boiling some eggs, but they're terrible. I finally heaved them over the side. I then made some hot cereal, and had an orange and a muffin (one left).

<u>2344.</u>   Third reef in the mainsail as the ENE wind continues to increase. I guess we're back to the birds and storms of the south. The new weather chart shows the bottoms of two lows angling toward us from the W and NNW.

The mainsail sets OK with 1, 2, or 3 reefs, but looks like a bag when used un-reefed (unlikely at this latitude.) There are black-browed, sooty, and wandering albatrosses circling us as well as white-chinned and soft-plumaged petrels. The sea is quite flat for this amount of wind.

I'm still reeling from the eggs I tried to eat. I'm keeping my distance from eggs for a few days.

FEBRUARY 17, 1991. (SUNDAY). DAY 11.

<u>0156.</u>   I've never seen so many albatrosses. I have eight flying around the yacht plus the usual white-chinned petrels.

I just spoke with Robin Davie, who is at the back of the main fleet. He said the 60-footers are deep into the ice country, and everyone is talking about icebergs and growlers. Nandor Fa has seen 15 icebergs; David Adams (at 62°12'S.) counted 30 in 24 hours. David said that INNKEEPER had struck a few small bits of ice "but nothing serious." GENERALI CONCORDE, while sailing at 7 knots, hit a small growler, which made two dents in the aluminum hull just above the waterline on the starboard side and broke one of the secondary rudders at the transom.

It seems to me that this sort of Russian roulette is stupid. It's neither a calculated risk nor a gamble, but simply a game of chicken and follow the leader.

I heard that KODEN pulled out of the competition. This leaves 20 yachts in the race.*

<u>0234.</u>   Wind ENE 25 knots. We're going SE at 7.1 knots in heavy rain. I feel much better after eating some steaming rice with a small can of meat and vegetables. Wholesome and filling.

<u>0611.</u>   SEBAGO is hopping around, and it's hard to write. We're headed for Norman Island in the Bounty group, 191 miles to the SE. The Bounty Islets—337 miles SE of New Zealand's South Island—consist of 5 tiny dots of land and 3 sunken rocks according to my chart. I don't know if the islets are inhabited or not. They're at 47°45'S., and a little west of the International Dateline (180°). I'll wager that not many people have ever heard of the Bounty Islets.

<u>0634.</u>   Three reefs in the main, 16 rolls in the jib, and we're still logging 6.1 knots. The wind is 27–31 knots and has veered to the NE. Very gray out, and the seas are beginning to rise. I've closed the storm doors. I had hoped for a weather chart at 0300, but without an alarm clock, appointments are difficult. I'm using my wristwatch, but apparently I didn't hear the alarm because of the noise of the wind and water.

<u>1516.</u>   The song of the gale is a cross between a shriek and a wail. The latest weather chart puts us on the SE quadrant of the

*I learned later that Yukoh Tada, disturbed over the performance of his yacht KODEN VIII and perhaps other things, committed suicide in Sydney. Yukoh's death was a tragedy and upset everyone. I was particularly shaken, remembering the several hours I'd spent with him in Sydney before I sailed. Yukoh had always seemed a pleasant, happy-go-lucky fellow, but I guess that was only on the surface. What a pity!

storm. However the low is moving a little north, and we're heading south which should increase our distance from the center. (A big high-pressure area is behind and south of the low, and we will be on the wrong side of the high, but that's a couple of days away.)

<u>1830.</u>   Wind now 33 knots true, from the east. I have eased off from 150° to 170°M.

<u>1850.</u>   I reckon the wind should swing to the SE (the wind I have found so often in this race). We could then head NE and E as the wind backs to the S. What a learning process! Weather advisor, where are you?

<u>1918.</u>   More wind, and we're heeling way over in spite of the water ballast on the high side.

<u>2104.</u>   Wind ESE 37 knots. A real screamer. I dressed and went out for a look. Rolled up all of the jib except a little triangle to keep us from rounding up. Tidied up a few lines. Seas 15–20 feet. Some water in the leeward water ballast tank so I pumped it out and topped up the windward tank. Intermittent rain, but a bit brighter in the sky. Can this be the center of the low passing east?

<u>2213.</u>   Eased off another 10 degrees to 190°M. or 215°T. There is really no choice. When the wind backs to SE, I'll go on the other tack. I'll have to wear the yacht around and think how to handle the water ballast. Sometimes the wind eases for a few moments— is the gale over?—but then it comes back with fury. Going to the toilet is an adventure with this motion, but somehow one survives.

I eat a little. An orange. Crackers and cheese. Sips of water. A small carton of fruit juice. I'm glad that I put an extra lashing on the clew of the mainsail. This storm certainly interferes with getting on toward Cape Horn. In fact we're going south and a little west, away from Cape Horn at the moment. I have begun reading *Dr. Zhivago* and just got involved with all the Russian characters when this cursed storm caught us. Humbug!

<u>2324.</u>   Wind SE 42 knots. Dry and snug inside; tons of water on the deck outside. I dream of an easy summer sail to Newfoundland with Margaret and our Maine friends, Jim and Dorothy Carey.

We're heeled 45°, and the spinnaker poles—lashed with four or five ties each—beat a merry tattoo on the deck. We're heading SW, which should accelerate our distance from this horrid storm.

<u>2335.</u>   Yesterday I finished a little paperback titled *The Greatest Race in the World* by J.R.L. Anderson. The book is about the

1964 singlehanded trans-Atlantic race from England to the U.S. Pleasant and subdued, with a nice emphasis on the contestants as ordinary people. Not supermen at all. Eric Tabarly won, and for the first time I felt I got to know him a bit.

2350.   I used the electric bilge pump to clear the bilge, which was full—God knows from where. Probably the water is leaking in via the halyard exit slots in the mast. Thank heavens for the pump, and Ian and Gil who repaired it in Sydney. The sky seems brighter. I wonder if we couldn't head NE just as well as SW? I'll wait another hour and then go on deck to survey things.

FEBRUARY 18, 1991. (MONDAY). DAY 12.

0200.   Raining. Wind SE 38–44 knots. The storm shrieks on. What's so frustrating is to be sailing away from my goal. I dressed and went out to look at the yacht and the seas and tried a few photographs. (Can you believe I have no exposure meter?) We're over at 30–40° most of the time but going along quite well. What's so tiring is the scream of the wind and the thump of the waves.

0338.   The barometer has gone up one millibar (to 998), the wind is a little less, and there may be hope. The seas are more developed, however, and a big one laid us over a few minutes ago. My problem is how to reverse course and to deal with the water ballast. I'll open the valves to transfer the water from port to starboard, which will heel us severely—and then turn away through the wind from say 220° to 270° to 360° to 060° as I gybe the mainsail. This should put the SE wind a little forward of the starboard beam and take us NE.

0600.   Sleet rattling on the coachroof.

0700.   The past two hours have not been nice. I reversed course without trouble, but the 29-knot wind went back up to 39 knots and is extremely turbulent. I increased the jib area a little, but had to roll it up again. While I was in the cockpit a snow squall suddenly swept on board and pushed the wind to 50 knots for a few minutes. The gusts felt like a cold knife against my face and snapped off the wooden air blade on the wind vane gear. It was good to get below out of the wind.

It's colder, and I've pulled on some longjohns. I opened some vegetarian food (mixed vegetables I thought, glancing at a luscious photograph on the can), but it turned out to be a wheat gluten and nut mixture that looked exactly like dogfood and tasted ghastly. I must hunt through the food stores for pouch meals and freeze-dried packets. I'm still searching for the cucumbers, cauliflower, cabbages, tomatoes, and grapefruit. I must look further. Also I cannot find the chocolate bars. I bought half a dozen large bars that must be somewhere in the cabin.

More sleet is rattling on the coachroof.

<u>0724.</u>   Sunset, but no sun. I see a bit of pink in some distant clouds and a little clearing. Plus several squall lines. According to the weather chart we'll be on the east side of the approaching high, which should mean SW winds.

<u>1210.</u>   Otago Harbour on the SE coast of New Zealand's South Island is only 200 miles to the WNW.

<u>1919.</u>   This storm was the first time in my sailing career that I've ever had to run off. I sailed in the wrong direction (under the triple-reefed mainsail) for 10 hours. There was no other choice in such seas. Now the wind is less (ESE 25 knots), but the direction is poor. Cape Horn seems a million miles away.

<u>2056.</u>   A message from Robin Davie with news of the fleet. John Martin struck some ice, and ALLIED BANK's hull has been damaged. Apparently there's delamination in the forward part of the hull. John has his sails down and is heading north.

Nandor Fa, at 63°S., aboard ALBA REGIA, had to sail north for 20 miles to detour around a huge ice field.

I think these 60-foot yacht captains are crazy to be going so far south. Look at the trouble they're in. I hope ALLIED BANK is not too badly damaged, so that John can make his way to safety. It's the end of the race for him.

<u>2308.</u>   I seem far away from all the high drama going on with the main fleet. It's depressing to sail back and forth and get nowhere. I've opened a bottle of wine to have half a cup to cheer myself a little. After a big hunt I found some heavy stockings and the chocolate.

FEBRUARY 19, 1991. (TUESDAY). DAY 13.

<u>0012.</u>   Nothing to do but to mark time and wait for a wind shift. I have cleaned out several drawers. Pasternak's *Dr. Zhivago* is great stuff. Really a set of dozens of short sketches of Russian life from 1910–1920 and the troubles of the revolution. A hundred or more characters with the usual unpronounceable names of six or eight syllables. Certainly the Russians are smart, clever, and

have an abiding love for the countryside. Politically hopeless. Each of the hundred or more chapters could be the start of the book. I wonder if a similar book could be written of Gorbachev's Russia?

<u>1050.</u>   A big bang and then a rumbling noise. The furling line for the jib had parted. I dressed quickly, clamped a small flashlight between my teeth, switched on the deck light, and hurried forward. The line chafed through either at the block aft of the furling drum or at one of the forward stanchion blocks.

I quickly rove the broken line from the cockpit forward through various blocks (large enough to pass a knot) and unwound two turns from the furling drum at the stem. This gave me enough line to get aft of the forward lead block. Then I tied both parts together with a carrick bend and secured the ends with racking seizings. Back in the cockpit I cranked in the furling line. I'll have a look for the cause of the chafe in the morning—7 hours from now—when it's light.

Fortunately the east wind had dropped to 18 knots. Even so, half a dozen waves sluiced over me. My Musto oilskins are excellent. I need a little tailoring adjustment at the front of the neck. Otherwise very good protection. If I interpret the 0945 weather chart correctly, we should get easterly winds, then northerly winds.

<u>1542.</u>   East wind up to 22 knots, down to 10, and back up to 16.

<u>2324.</u>   I rolled up the jib and rove a new 100-foot furling line. The only thing I could do was to tie the new line to the old line about one meter aft of the drum. When the weather is calm and the sail is unwound, I will disassemble the furling gear so I can lead the end of the new line inside the drum. I might be able to do this in a light following wind. However I'm terrified of losing the parts overboard.

With regard to the chafe, I suspect the forward block, which I have lashed in a different position. I must inspect this line daily because it is constantly moving. If this line breaks in a gale, the sail will be destroyed.

<u>2346.</u>   So far I have been bashing into easterly winds for four days and four hours, or *100 hours in all* (this sounds like a song title). Where, oh where, are those great westerly winds?

FEBRUARY 20, 1991. (WEDNESDAY). DAY 14.

<u>0426.</u>   Wind SSE 14 knots. Still trying to improve the lead of the jib furling line where it leaves the drum, but the lead is diffi-

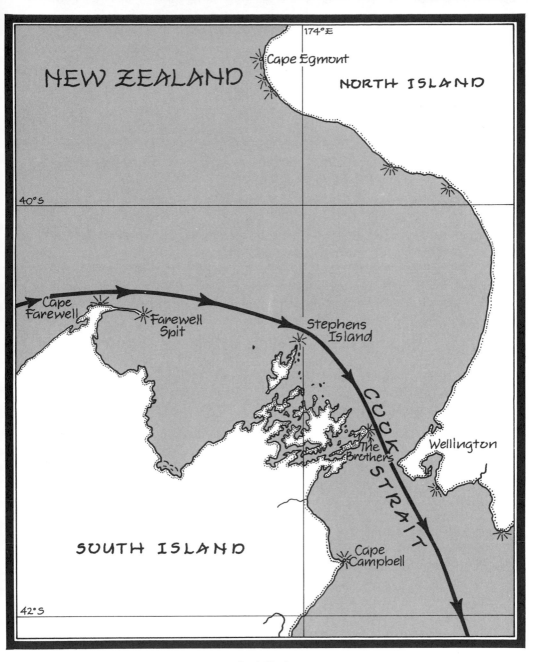

Cook Strait.

cult because of the pulpit and port spinnaker pole. I discovered that the inside lip of the top of the furling drum has a sharp edge which needs to be rounded.

Many albatrosses soaring about, no doubt from Chatham Island, 155 miles to the ENE.

<u>0504.</u>   Rain showers, and it's quite warm. I'm taking off my

heavy clothes. Neither voltage regulator for the big alternator is working properly.

<u>0609.</u>   It's fascinating to look at the figures on the GPS. We're only 1½ miles from the International Dateline. As we sail east, I'm watching to see if the instrument will jump from east longitude to west and start downward from 180°.

<u>0620.</u>   Hooray! We're in west longitude, and the numbers are falling. Only 113° of longitude to Cape Horn. Since I'm keeping GMT on the ship, all I have to do is to change from east longitude to west longitude and not change the date.

I've been watching a dozen young wandering albatrosses circling us. The birds are completely dark brown on top. White faces. Wings white underneath with a black border along the trailing edges. Very pretty and quite striking.

<u>0743.</u>   Wind up and down. Jib in and out. My shoulders ache. As usual, the boat goes faster with less sail. The water ballast is marvelous. When the weather eases off, I must put the anchor below. I'm going to try a different lead (via the midstay deck fitting) for the jib furling lead.

<u>0750.</u>   I heard on the chat hour that Robert Hooke (NIIHAU IV) has returned to Sydney and withdrawn from the race. Apparently there were problems with his new mast. I'm sorry that Robert is out after all his efforts to continue. That leaves Isabelle and 18 men in the race.

Eight of the eleven 60-footers are south of 60°. GENERALI CONCORDE, CRÉDIT AGRICOLE, and ALBA REGIA are within a few miles of 65°S. (where one degree of longitude is only 25.4 miles). All report "dozens of enormous blocks of ice."

Alain Gautier—whose English is quite good and who talks a lot on the radio—says that he has been sailing in fog near icebergs (he stopped counting when he got to 40) and among growlers floating just awash. "Such sailing is a little mad," he said, "but it makes the difference."

Philippe Jeantot on CRÉDIT radioed that his mainsail split. Then the gooseneck holding the forward end of the main boom broke. Later his vessel struck a growler.

"The impact broke the block of ice in two," said Philippe, "and a piece of the ice passed underneath the hull. The ice made a terrifying noise, and got jammed between the twin rudders. I was unable to steer for two hours until the ice finally broke away. When I went up on the foredeck to check things, I found that the forward-most stem piece of the hull, about 18 inches long and made in foam for this eventuality, was torn off as far as the waterline."

<u>0816.</u>   John Martin is abandoning ALLIED BANK because of severe hull and keel damage after striking ice. John says that the keel seems to be loose, and he can feel the core of the hull flexing away from the inside skin. Bertie Reed is to pick up John. Unfortunately John is caught in the NE corner of a low and has winds of 65 knots, according to the reports.

It's night time, the radio propagation is good, and the inter-ship channel on 4 megs is coming through quite well. A few minutes ago I heard John speaking with Robin Davie. Just now (0821 GMT), I can hear John and Bertie discussing their relative locations, and talking over plans for transferring John to GRINAKER. Their talk is confident and understated, although John sounds nervous.

Bertie is 25 miles from ALLIED BANK. Their position is 120 miles south and 1,929 miles west of Cape Horn, far out in the Southern Ocean, in one of the most isolated places on earth.

When a sailor gives his position in degrees and minutes, it's normal. When you hear him reading off degrees, minutes, and *seconds*, you know he's got a problem. Three times now in the two BOC races that I've been in, I've heard degrees, minutes, and *seconds* read off, and each time it's meant big trouble.

At this point there are 19 of us still in the race. Seventeen of us have our radios carefully tuned and are listening to John and Bertie, hoping that John can get from ALLIED BANK to GRINAKER. The tension on the airwaves is almost palpable because each of us is well aware that John will have only one chance.

Certainly it's a tricky business to find a tiny yacht in a huge ocean. And even trickier to pick up a man from another vessel. All the contestants have the necessary sailing skills, but in poor weather the chances for disaster increase enormously. And once you find the other vessel you don't dare go too close when a big sea is running, because if the rigs ever touch, both masts would come down.

It's a time of testing and measuring for John and Bertie, a time for plucky sailing, a time for prayers and hope, and a time for a little luck.

I learned much later that the wind was 35 knots when John struck the ice. ALLIED BANK was reaching along at 11 knots. "Earlier I had spotted a three-mile iceberg on radar and had given it a berth of about five miles to avoid any chance of

A big westerly swell in the Southern Ocean and the everpresent albatross.

hitting a growler," said John. "Ironically, the ice that ALLIED BANK hit was five miles ahead of the main berg. The boat came off a wave and crashed into a growler that was about 20 ft. long with no more than one foot of ice showing out of the water. I saw it as it passed by the starboard quarter."

John rushed below and found that the forward part of the keelson, the hull's central longitudinal stiffener—which had been laminated from 12 layers of composite carbon and Kevlar cloth—had sheared in two. "The keelson had cracked clean through, and the hull was moving so much that a sailbag was trapped in the gap," he said.

John immediately took down the sails and turned the boat north toward warmer waters. Then he began to shore up the damaged area with a cut-down spinnaker pole, using sailbags as padding. "I was fortunate because the weather had calmed down," said John. "It was the best piece of repair work I have ever done. I was really pleased and confident enough to continue on toward Cape Horn. But the next day the hurricane hit us. It was blowing 65 knots, and the boat was twisting so much you could hear the two skins tearing away from the central core."

John called Cape Town for help. His message was quickly relayed to Bertie Reed on GRINAKER, which was 40 miles west of ALLIED BANK. Bertie called John, who was sailing at nine knots under bare poles. Five hours later—shortly after daybreak—Bertie had ALLIED BANK in sight, having used his satellite navigation system and radar to find the crippled vessel.

John had packed food, water, and thermal clothing in a kit bag, and had put on a wet suit. He then opened the yacht's seacocks and hatches to make sure she'd sink.

"It was still blowing 35 knots with big seas running, so I decided to launch my liferaft and wait for Bertie to sweep past and pick me up," said John. Unfortunately, the line that attached the raft to ALLIED BANK broke, and suddenly John— who was in the liferaft—began to blow downwind rapidly. "I was at least half a mile from the yacht before Bertie realized the raft was not tethered," said John. "Fortunately for me, Bertie followed the raft and picked me up on his second attempt."

"I didn't realize that John was in his liferaft until I had circled ALLIED BANK," Bertie said later. "By that time, the rope holding the raft had broken, and John had been blown downwind. I lost sight of the raft several times."

When John—wet, dangerously chilled, and miserable— finally climbed aboard GRINAKER, he turned to the captain.

"Thanks," said John.

"It's a pleasure," said Bertie.

CHAPTER TWELVE

Eastward, Ever Eastward

FEBRUARY 20, 1991. (WEDNESDAY). DAY 14. (continued)

<u>1254.</u>   144 miles at noon. We're 118 miles SW of Chatham Island. A chill wind from the south sent me to the clothing locker again. Going well but a little bumpy. Pitch black outside except that every whitecap—and there are hundreds—is a necklace of glistening pearls.

My life seems so calm and easy after the drama of the ALLIED BANK rescue last night. Hurricanes, collisions with ice, liferafts— it was all too much.

<u>1513.</u>   There's an incredible amount of interest in the ALLIED BANK-GRINAKER rescue. The hams are all in orbit, and Sydney radio is busy repeating rumors, none based on reality.

<u>1944.</u>   Big blue seas and rough. Cumulonimbus clouds towering astern. I've a headache from all the excitement of last night.

<u>2329.</u>   Wind SSW 28–32 knots. We're running with a double-reefed mainsail and a tiny bit of jib. The autopilot is steering perfectly while we fly along at 8.5 knots. Tons of water cascade over the deck. I need to wear the chart table seatbelt while writing this. I'm making a big effort to cook a pan of ramen noodles, but the motion of the stove is pretty lively. I just read the list of ingredients, which include MSG, salt, and sodium—all on the forbidden list.

I finished *Dr. Zhivago*, an epic that gives the sweep and breadth of an enormous, complex country and at the same time tells a fine love story. It teaches one to grab at love and cherish it at the moment, not at some indefinite time in the future.

I'm into Alan Moorehead's *A Late Education*, a book that I like a lot and have read many times.

FEBRUARY 21, 1991. (THURSDAY). DAY 15.

<u>0020.</u>   Heavy squalls, but we rush onward. The bottoms of all the stratus are jagged, dark, and full of wind.

<u>0426.</u>   How can it be so rough? Every other wave washes over us, and the waves fill the cockpit again and again. More rain and squalls although there's blue sky and sun at intervals.

<u>0536.</u>   A terrible sea. The vessel was quite out of control so I pulled on my oilskins, went 30° more off the wind, and (carefully using my safety harness) put in the third reef. I got the main halyard around three or four upper mast steps, but I eased the halyard and let the rolling of the vessel swing the line clear. (This makes me feel so clever! The fox in action! Life's tiny victories!)

The third reef made a big difference in the motion; suddenly SEBAGO was docile and under control. The wind is still 26–34 knots from the south, but less turbulent. There's a nasty sea running; yet 6 or 8 young wandering albatrosses circle just above the waves. I have both storm doors closed because 2 or 3 times every hour a wave breaks on board with a great crash and fills the cockpit.

<u>0550.</u>   I was horrified to find drops of water in my good pilot berth on the port side. The portlight above it hadn't been closed tightly all the way from Sydney.

<u>1220.</u>   A run of 197 miles at noon. Clear sky; stars; lots of water flying around. Wind south 30 knots.

<u>1907.</u>   Big seas. Autopilot steering perfectly. Can I keep this all together for another 4,000 miles?

<u>2029.</u>   The wind has veered (SSW 33–38 knots), and I need the running rig. However it's too rough and stormy to set the starboard spinnaker pole.

<u>2045.</u>   Robin Davie passed along the word that the 60-foot fleet has been caught on the wrong side of a huge low. The boats are into 60-knot headwinds and are being forced farther south. DURACELL has been hit very hard. Farther west, BUTTERCUP was rolled 360° and has much broken gear and a very shaken captain. No word from GRINAKER. The contacts with Robin (who is 1,179 miles east of me) are heartening.

<u>2135.</u>   Wind up and down, 33–38 knots. It eased to 28–30 so I let out two rolls of the jib. This jumped our speed to 9.5 knots, but

waves began to hammer us. I again rolled up the two turns, our speed dropped to 7.8 knots, and the ride has become less violent.

I've discovered a sensational improvement for my oilskins. After I'm all dressed, I take a piece of ⅜" dia. line about 4 ft. long, pull it snugly around my neck, and tie a square knot in front of me. The tie holds the oilskins firmly around my neck, keeps the hood in position, and I stay much drier. I'm going to sew the middle of the tie to the lower part of the back of the collar so the line's always handy.

FEBRUARY 22, 1991. (FRIDAY). DAY 16.

<u>0238.</u>   Wind south 38 knots. Barometer 1005 mb. Bright sun and cumulus clouds. We roar onward while it blows hard outside. No luck getting the Argos positions because they're read too fast on a noisy frequency. I'm enjoying Alan Moorehead's book *A Late Education*. It and *Eclipse* (also by Moorehead) are two of my favorites.

<u>0355.</u>   By chance I tuned in to "The Seven Seas Program" on the BBC which told of the trials of ALLIED BANK. "All the yachts carry radar," said the announcer, "and pass along ice sightings to their fellow competitors." The program reported that Alain Gautier, the leader, is currently becalmed.

<u>0449.</u>   A poor contact with SPIRIT OF IPSWICH. Josh said that JARKAN, DURACELL, BBV, and INNKEEPER all have 65-knot headwinds.

<u>1211.</u>   A run of 175 miles at noon. The straight-line distance to Cape Horn is 3,948 miles at 073°M. The great circle route is 3,595 miles at 115°M.

<u>1304.</u>   We're getting a hard beating from the sea, so I've eased off 10° to the north. The wind has veered a little toward the east.

<u>1329.</u>   Wind up to 41 knots in the squalls. Increasing the jib area by a tiny fraction has picked up our speed to 8.3 knots. Still very rough. I walk around like a robot, wedging my feet and going from handhold to handhold. I'm terrified of breaking a bone. The only safe place is the port pilot berth where I'm headed. A while ago I discovered a little package of nine slices of rye bread made with sunflower seeds. I made toast with two slices. Delicious. I wish I'd bought a dozen packages.

The engine generator voltage regulator dials go from 12.60 to

14.50 volts after 15 minutes of running. I wish I understood more about batteries and regulators.

<u>1443.</u>   In spite of squalls, the wind is dropping a little.

<u>1953.</u>   Wind south 27 knots. Gusty and turbulent. A rough and confused sea, but the height of the waves is less. I think we'll see an improvement in a few hours. I'm anxious to deal with a deck leak and to reeve the jib furling line to the inside of the drum up forward.

The battery charging system has broken down. The battery meter shows 150 amps on the downside (from 400). Yet when I charge with the Quad regulator the charging rate is only 36 amps (instead of 95 or 100). After 10 minutes the voltage climbs to 14.50 (the forbidden limit) and I shut off the engine. I've done this four times. I reckon I'm charging at the rate of 36 amps, but in ⅙th of an hour I'm gaining only 6 amps, which is trifling.

FEBRUARY 23, 1991. (SATURDAY). DAY 17.

<u>0313.</u>   A good nap and a big breakfast of eggs cooked with cheese and onions, toast, and a cup of tea followed by a cup of coffee. Wind south 22 knots. Surprisingly warm. The sea is extremely rough, and I creep from one handhold to the next. I've unrolled some of the jib, and we've picked up three quarters of a knot. I'd like to inspect the jib furling line up forward, but every third wave breaks over us, and with these rough seas I might get launched over the bow. I reckon if the line hasn't chafed through by now it must be OK.

We're 1,111 miles behind GLOBAL EXPOSURE and have picked up 68 miles on her.

<u>0334.</u>   I've been thinking how to deal with the forward end of the jib furling line which has been so troublesome. My best idea so far is to thread an eyebolt into the furling drum axle. Then I can simply tie the end of the furling line to the head of the eyebolt. This will allow the furling line to be changed without taking the whole lower drum unit apart.

<u>0400.</u>   After studying the weather charts I'm heading farther south. I'm afraid we'll be stuck on the north side of an approaching high.

<u>1211.</u>   198 miles at noon. The radio is full of news of the Gulf War and the land campaign.

<u>1949.</u>   I try hard to analyze the weather charts carefully, but the winds that come are often different from what I predict. At the moment the wind is SE 12 knots. I ran off for a few minutes while I unreefed the mainsail.

<u>2056.</u>   Tacked south to get below the center of the high. My true course is SSW, away from Cape Horn. I pulled another wooden matchstick from the cockpit bilge pump, a souvenir of the rollover in the Indian Ocean.

FEBRUARY 24, 1991. (SUNDAY). DAY 18.

<u>0104.</u>   Drat! Despite my efforts with the weather charts and a position I thought excellent, I'm stuck in the middle of a high (barometer 1018 mb.). I thought the high was north of me and heading ENE. I might just as well continue south. Meanwhile I may have solved the problem of the lead of the furling gear line by moving a few blocks.

I tried to pep up some packaged onion soup with a fresh chopped onion, brandy, and Worcestershire sauce, but the taste was terrible. The powerful additives must have worked against one another. How does one know in advance? There's a good recipe for onion soup in *After 50,000 Miles*. However my copy has disappeared.

<u>0338.</u>   Since there's practically no wind, I've been busy with deck jobs. I re-bedded a leaking bolt on the starboard aft spinnaker pole hold-down fitting. Then I moved the anchor and warp from the foredeck to below in the cabin (next to the generator). The anchor seemed surprisingly heavy. Am I getting weak?

I think most of the water that gets inside the mast and runs below into the bilge comes from waves that slop aboard and pour into several lower halyard exit slots and a number of rivet holes.

<u>0740.</u>   An excellent radio signal from Ron (ZL4MK) in New Zealand. Ron passes on the Argos reports and weather.

<u>1200.</u>   Becalmed since 0600. Only 70 miles in the last 24 hours.

<u>1312.</u>   Wind NE 8 knots. Barometer 1020 mb. With NE winds we're in the western sector of the high.

<u>2126.</u>   Josh Hall reported a leak in the after watertight compartment of SPIRIT OF IPSWICH. Initially he used a bucket to get rid of the water, but eventually set up an electric pump in the main

cabin. Josh connected the bilge hose from the leaking compartment to the inlet side of the pump and used a piece of flexible hose to lead the outflow overboard. Water was soon flowing nicely so Josh turned to other things. A while later he came in from a job on deck and was horrified to find that the outlet hose had come off and saltwater was pouring into a quarter berth. "My bed!" he shrieked.

2349.   Wind NNE 11 knots, and we're sailing well. The barometer's up to 1022 mb. I found some chafe at the exit sheave of the #2 reefing pendant on the main boom. The problem is that each succeeding pendant bears on the earlier reefing point's sheave. Hard to describe. I must watch these lines. I jammed some thin plastic sheeting (held with duct tape) in the loose radar mast mounting at the transom.

I'm dreaming a lot when I sleep. My friend in California—Bob Van Blaricom—was with me in a sailing dream. How real and vivid these dreams are.

The sea is calm. I keep looking around for ships, yachts, people in liferafts, fish, whales, dolphins, icebergs—anything.

I feel wretched because I've done so poorly in the race. Leg 1 was a disaster because of broken chainplates, failed autopilots, and a dumb tactical decision of failing to get enough easting in the North Atlantic.

On Leg 2 I wasted two days with a jammed rudder. Then I really got behind because of returning to Cape Town to deal with the improperly installed chainplates. Later the rollover caused all sorts of damage which took time to repair in Sydney.

So far on Leg 3 we've been sailing well, but the Tasman crossing was mostly in calms and light winds. Since New Zealand we've had incredibly adverse winds and now calms. However, this all sounds like a series of excuses which I hate. I want results, not excuses. We must do better. Just now I'm trying to get south of 50°S. (we're at 46°30'S.) where I hope to find westerly winds.

FEBRUARY 25, 1991. (MONDAY). DAY 19.

0311.   I opened the battery compartment and checked the four six-volt Prevailer batteries. Each measured 6.72 volts. No corrosion at all around the terminals. Everything looked new.

Wind north 8-9 knots and gradually veering. We're logging 6–7 knots on a calm sea. The radio is filled with news of the Kuwait land invasion.

<u>1339.</u>   A run of 156 miles at noon. I must get away from this poky high-pressure area.

<u>1912.</u>   Sunny and warm with all sorts of distant cloud banks, mostly altocumulus.

<u>2150.</u>   I switched on the radio and heard Kanga reporting from 62°S.: "In the middle of the night a huge wave knocked us down, and the mast got shoved to 45 degrees below the horizontal. The ceiling suddenly became the floor where I was dumped and tried to hang on. Meanwhile the contents of the fridge and all the loose gear in the cabin poured down on me. The water temperature is one degree above freezing, I'm thousands of miles from home, and the boat's uninsured. I'm heading north."

<u>2348.</u>   A good wind from the NNW (15 knots) which we can just hold with the fore-and-aft rig. The polar weather charts have become hopeless. New Zealand transmits an Australian chart that's probably faxed to Wellington. The quality is terrible, and the charts are useless.

I found a bag of rice that was stored in one of the settee lockers that gets an occasional slosh of bilge water. The rice—which came in a skimpy plastic bag—was put in a second thin plastic bag, but water seeped through both bags. A pity. The rice smells awful. I have been trying to dry it both on the stove and in the sun. The bag of rice should have been slipped inside a glass jar with a good lid and stored in a dry place.

I'm falling asleep.

FEBRUARY 26, 1991. (TUESDAY). DAY 20.

<u>0145.</u>   At last we have a reasonable wind (NW 20 knots) and are hurrying SE. I heaved the mildewed rice over the side.

<u>0259.</u>   I had just put in the second reef when the wind dropped. Apparently blocked by the heavy clouds astern. Second reef out.

<u>0315.</u>   In spite of continuing messages to WOM from half the people in the fleet, the announcer reads the Argos position reports faster than ever. It's impossible to write them down.

<u>0506.</u>   All sorts of dramatic clouds at sunset (GMT). Great banks of heavy fracto-stratus floating low in the sky. One bank has an abrupt triangular end with a rough uneven texture that looks like a slice of angel food cake. I have been expecting an abrupt wind change, but it appears to have settled in the west.

First 19 knots; now we're down to 12 true (7 apparent), and we're banging and slatting in the swell.

More trouble with the jib furling line. I moved the lead block (aft of the drum) forward along the port rail, but the line kept bearing against the sharp edge of the bottom of the upper plate of the drum. Now I've moved the block to a strop through the mooring cleat, which is immediately aft of the furling drum. I must watch this closely.

0655. Wind north (16 knots). Sea smooth. A layer of altocumulus with the moon shining weakly through the clouds. I've changed course to head more south. Still under the influence of high pressure (1020 mb.).

1152. Refreshed after a wonderful sleep. More vivid dreams. I met Joan Miller, the wife of a photographer friend. I haven't seen her for 30 years and knew her only slightly. Amazing that she would be somewhere in my brain. The things buried in the human mind are incredible. Like the 90 percent of the iceberg that's below the surface of the sea.

Do I dream so much because I secretly want to get away from the Southern Ocean? After so much trouble to outfit the yacht and to compete in this great undertaking? I suppose a psychiatrist would have a good time with all this. Nevertheless I feel quite stable and in control of things.

1846. Sailing well. Wind 17–20 knots (NNW). The apparent wind is on the beam. Two reefs in the main and the full jib. Logging 8.5 knots.

I heard that the midstay deck fitting broke on INNKEEPER and that David Adams is throwing out water with a bucket.

2315. A steady 9.2 knots. Earlier this morning I lengthened the strop of the jib furling line block aft of the drum. My *bête noire*.

FEBRUARY 27, 1991. (WEDNESDAY). DAY 21.

0107. We must be in the outer regions of a big high (1014 mb.) because for once we're in the southern quadrant and have a fair wind. The sun is out, and it's quite hot in the lee corner of the cockpit shelter. The only clouds are a few cirrus swirls way up high.

0138. Wind NNW 27 knots. Seas beginning to build up. Two or three times an hour a wave slams on board with a big crash.

Ill-fated *Allied Bank* in Newport before the race. With her draft of 13'1" and her over-all length of 60 feet, she seems a gigantic vessel for one person to manage. We eventually learned that instead of lead ballast, this yacht's ballast was made up of spent uranium which is heavier than lead and apparently is free from radioactivity. Note the twin rudders whose stocks are made of carbon fiber with blades of high-density foam.

<u>0300.</u>   More wind. Third reef in the mainsail.

<u>0404.</u>   Oilskins on again to tighten the leech lines on the main-sail and to ease the mainsheet. The barometer's plunging.

<u>0544.</u>   A good meal of rice, beef, and onions followed by a cup of tea. Who knows what the night will bring?

<u>1110.</u>   Wind NNW 31 knots. Things are gradually getting out of control. I cranked in most of the jib. (What a wonderful arrange-ment with the double winch handle and the furling gear.) We slowed down from 8.5 to 6.5 knots. Maybe I overdid it, but let's try it for a while . . . The moon is shining weakly through scud-ding clouds. The seas have grown to 15 feet or so. I wish the wind would veer to the west or WNW so we could run with it. Earlier tonight I heard Nandor Fa talking of snow and sleet and intense cold.

I am into Eric Newby's book *The Last Grain Race* which I have read before. The owner of Newby's ship (and others) was a Finn named Gustav Erikson whose tight-fisted management was legendary. Item: Because drinking water cost a little more in Ire-land, the ship bought all its fresh water for the round trip between Ireland and Australia in Australia where it cost only $5 a ton.

<u>1123.</u>   It took 98 strokes on the small cockpit pump to clear the bilge. The view astern is eerie with the moon and thin, rapidly moving clouds which look like mysterious fog or smoke.

<u>1210.</u>   A 200-mile run at noon.

<u>1832.</u>   Very heavy going. Wind north 46–48 knots. The sea is swept by hurricane gusts that throw great sheets of white spray high in the air. Often the spray rattles on deck and sounds like cinders hurled against a window pane.

It's cold and nasty, and I've put on a second thermal underwear top. The barometer has dropped from 1014 to 1003 mb. in the last 18 hours, and I've headed ESE to run off a little before the storm. Only the triple-reefed mainsail is up, but it's too much sail. I hesitate to take down the main entirely because the job is so troublesome. A full tank of water ballast to port helps keep us upright.

I was on deck a while ago tightening the leech of the mainsail when suddenly there were a dozen dolphins alongside. I've never seen dolphins in a severe storm before, but there they were— swimming at high speed, and twisting, turning, cavorting, jumping. Friends in the sea.

A front must be passing because of the low clouds and rain.

<u>2122.</u>   A poor radio contact with Robin on 16 megs. The 60-foot leaders go around Cape Horn today. Discouraging to think that I have more than 3,000 miles to go. The motion is pretty lively, and I can hardly write. Should I take down the mainsail?

The wind is blowing so much spray that the sea seems covered with smoke or mist, almost like steam or a white gas. A piece of chain under the forward cabin sole is making a lot of noise, but the sailbags are piled on the floor, and there's no chance of dealing with the chain now.

FEBRUARY 28, 1991. (THURSDAY). DAY 22.

<u>0005.</u>   I took down the mainsail an hour before midnight. The wind was 45 knots, and it was raining heavily. Seas were breaking all over the place. We were clearly overpowered, and it was the only thing to do. I was apprehensive and nervous about going forward, but once at the mast the job went quickly.

As soon as the sail was down, the motion and heel were easier. Yet we still show 6–7 knots. We're rolling heavily as ballasted vessels always do without their mainsails. I hope we can get through this storm without any trouble—47 knots of true wind in the Southern Ocean is a hard breeze.

<u>0150.</u>   No change. Nothing to do but to stay in the port pilot berth with the big lee cloth where I can pad myself with pillows and read or sleep. Still raining hard.

<u>0634.</u>   A dramatic change in the weather. The wind dropped to 30 knots (NW) so I put up the triple-reefed mainsail. The halyard was fouled on two mast steps, but I got it clear and the sail up. We needed the running rig so I put up the port pole. Then I shook out the third reef. A lot of deck work. The sky is bathed in a peculiar yellowish light. The motion of the yacht is a hundredfold better with the mainsail set.

<u>1226.</u>   A run of 158 miles at noon. We're at 50°39'S., 149°16'W. A clear midnight sky with stars and a full moon that seems like a searchlight. Still a big swell. There's practically no wind (west 8 knots). From one extreme to the other.

<u>1833.</u>   Clear and sunny. The sky is very blue and patterned with swirls of cirrus. The batteries are gradually going down. I must reduce my use of electricity.

The news from the Gulf is that Saddam Hussein and Iraq have collapsed in a war that lasted only 100 hours. What a farce after Hussein's big talk! Another pathetic megalomaniac.

I'm at the end of *The Last Grain Race*. As in his book on the Hindu Kush, Newby is wonderfully clever at writing dialogue, this time of Finnish and Swedish sailors trying to speak English.

The news from the race is that Alain Gautier is past Cape Horn. My immediate goals are to get the engine charging system working and to sail east of 140°W. so I can move to the Cape Horn chart.

<u>2201.</u>   I've been looking at the Quad regulator and cleaning up salt water damage. Two fuses were not making contact, and the strip connector between the two main components had some corrosion. I cleaned the fuses, terminals, replaced the strip connector, and checked the continuity of everything with a multimeter. When the voltage drops below 12.85, I'll fire up the engine and see what happens.

The sea's a little smoother, but we're only going 5 knots before a wind of 11 knots. Robin told me that while surfing on a big wave his Monitor vane shaft got bent. We spent a long time discussing repairs.

MARCH 1, 1991. (FRIDAY). DAY 23.

<u>0243.</u>   Light winds from the west. Only 6 knots over the deck at the moment. I am wildly keen to catch up with the fleet, but

there's absolutely nothing I can do. I have been sorting fastenings and labeled the 11 boxes stored under the navigator's seat. After the rollover and spillage of all the hardware I put a good latch on the seat.

0438.   An easy day with light winds and a smooth sea—some difference from yesterday. The sun is just setting, and the sea is suffused with a yellowish light. Earlier I saw an Antarctic skua on his solitary, lonely way. Dark, with broad, stubby wings with white patches at the wing tips. I have had a good rest today and eaten lots to make up for yesterday. My only complaint is cold feet. I'm going to change my stockings.

I'm trying to write a one-page fund-raising letter. A difficult letter because it needs to be brief, to the point, dynamic, and appealing.

Yesterday on the BBC I heard a French restaurant owner talking about French bread. He was so sincere, so enthusiastic, and so devoted to his subject that I couldn't help but smile. Nothing else in the world had any importance except those loaves of bread.

0738.   A pleasant talk with ZL4MK (Ron) in New Zealand. Tonight the full moon is almost overhead and shining through a thin film of cirrus, which show a NW wind up high. A ghostly ring around the moon. The wind on deck is light and trifling. Time for a nap before something happens.

1322.   Heavy dew. Water running over everything. The outer edge of the ring around the moon is the color of rusty iron. Wind SW 9 knots. I haven't put out the starboard pole because with a little course change we can use the fore-and-aft rig on starboard, which is faster. I'm always choosing between a direct slow course and a faster off-course route.

1700.   A line of squalls to the south. To the east are immense backlighted cumulonimbus edged with pure white from the rising sun. The south wind seems 20 degrees colder. Where are my gloves? I am putting half a tank of water ballast to starboard. I cranked up the generator (with 12.65 volts in the batteries), but the regulator output is only 38 amps (instead of 100).

1852.   Funny how you get to know a vessel. As soon as I saw the beam wind from the south this morning I said to myself: two reefs. During breakfast we labored under one reef. Now with two, SEBAGO is much happier, and we're going faster.

I need to telephone Margaret about fund-raising and to ask her to bring a few critical parts to Uruguay.

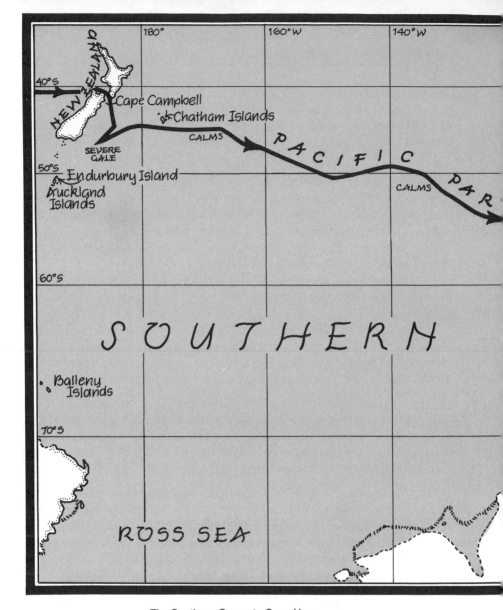

The Southern Ocean to Cape Horn.

<u>1921.</u>   Wind SSE 19–22 knots. Twelve rolls in the jib. Squalls ahead and to windward. A white-headed petrel and a soft-plumaged petrel are flying alongside.

<u>2004.</u>   A beautiful sailing day with a cold wind from the south. Every wave is topped by a whitecap. My feet are cold, and I must put on more clothing. Brrrrr.

<u>2231.</u>   Down to three reefs again. Where, oh where, are those

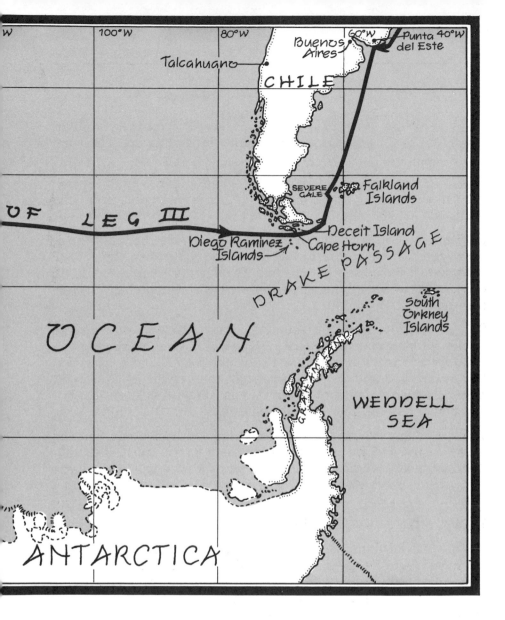

fair, following winds? We seem to be in another big high. Clear, cumulus clouds, and a barometer of 1017 mb. I'm discouraged by all the strong winds from ahead and each side instead of from aft. Already we're pressed with three reefs so I'll have to reduce the jib still further.

2248.   More rolls in the jib. The vessel responds quickly to two or three rolls. Too much and I was down to 5.7 knots. A turn or two out, and we speeded up to 7.52 knots.

MARCH 2, 1991. (SATURDAY). DAY 24.

<u>0004.</u>   Wind south 29–33 knots. Eased off 5° on the autopilot. We're going 6.77 knots under the main with three reefs. The wind has an eerie wail to it.

<u>0141.</u>   I reckon we're in the NE quadrant of a high. Somewhere, sometime, somehow we must get strong winds from the west, NW, or SW.

<u>0318.</u>   Once again the WOM announcer read the Argos positions too fast. As communicators to the BOC fleet the AT&T operators are a failure. Yet if I had the announcers in a room and could talk to them I'm sure I could deal with the problem in five minutes.

<u>0656.</u>   A foul night outside. At times great seas sweep right over us. I continue to adjust the jib area. A scrap of the clew is good for an extra knot. If we get much above 7.5 knots, however, the beam wind and the big seas begin to overwhelm us. I don't think the loss of control has anything to do with boat design, but is a function of the hairy sailing conditions.

<u>1256.</u>   Noon-to-noon, 166 miles. Wind south 21 knots. The big wind is gone and the seas are much less. I let out most of the jib. A bright moon overhead. I slammed one of the storm doors on my left forefinger, which hurts a lot. The batteries are gradually going down.

<u>1320.</u>   We're almost on the Cape Horn chart.

<u>1646.</u>   Cold, damp, nasty, and a rough sea. Stormy-looking stratus everywhere, although there are holes in the clouds with bits of blue showing through. I must work on the generator problem. I found some spare leather gloves but they're much too small. How did I ever get a size fit for a young girl? No chance for a swap out here. I tried WOM and Portishead (England) last night for a call to Margaret, but no luck.

<u>1918.</u>   Wind south 30 knots. Barometer 1020 mb. We're in the NE quadrant of a high. S and SE winds from high-pressure areas have plagued us ever since Newport. The wind bears about 150°M. and we're steering 65–70°M. In true directions we're heading a little south of east with a southerly wind. I will try to head south when possible.

    Although the yacht is hopping around a lot I managed to cook a good breakfast (wearing oilskins of course). I fried a little bacon and the remnant from some canned ham and then cooked two eggs on top (flipped over halfway along). Preceded by half a grape-fruit. Plus a cup of tea and then a cup of filter coffee.

The beauty of SEBAGO's interior design is the central galley island (with its two deep sinks), which is so handy to lean against or grab. By now I'd be a battered wreck without the center island to keep me from being thrown across the cabin.

When the weather moderates I must work on the charging system. I'm going to replace the Quad Cycle components with spares. If that fails I'll try a conventional regulator.

I finished reading *The Sea Wolf* by Jack London. Curiously overdrawn characters and a somewhat far-fetched yarn. Wolf Larsen and the man telling the story were well drawn, but London's superman characterization is too extreme for my taste. No one can be *that* good and *that* strong.

I am trying Michener's opus on South Africa. It seems long with a lot of side stories.

<u>2120.</u>   News from Robin Davie: BUTTERCUP was knocked down. SPIRIT OF IPSWICH reports a broken main boom after a mixup with an enormous sea. A big wave tore off GROUP SCETA's Argos transmitter. Paul Thackaberry gybed his mainsail in heavy going, but the sail and boom accidentally gybed back, and Paul got slammed in the face. A black eye, cuts, butterfly bandages, and a lot of swelling. The fleet's getting bashed.

CHAPTER THIRTEEN

Cape Horn
Where Are You?

MARCH 3, 1991. (SUNDAY). DAY 25.

<u>0027 GMT.</u>   (1427 local time). Our longitude is 139°58′W. We're finally across 140°W. and on the Cape Horn chart. Now I can see the tip of South America.

<u>0445.</u>   Just getting dark. The sea seems a little less rough. It's cold, and my feet are blocks of ice. I take off my shoes and wrap my feet in a doubled blanket when possible.

<u>0508.</u>   When I run the generator the battery voltage goes from 12.65 to 14.50 in less than two minutes. As soon as the weather moderates I must work on the regulator problem.

<u>1043.</u>   Wind SSE from 20 to 28 knots. Weak moonlight through low clouds. I am getting under the blankets to get warm.

<u>1210.</u>   A 177 mile-run at noon.

<u>1702.</u>   Wind and sea down. Cloudy and cold. Barometer 1023 mb. and climbing.

<u>1940.</u>   I've improved the winch handle locking device that keeps a handle in the winch by simply putting a washer at the bottom of the pivot. Easy enough after half an hour of fiddling. I wonder why Lewmar, the manufacturer, doesn't do it?

Six big squalls are dotted around us like Indians circling a wagon train in an old Western movie. A beautiful day, but crisp and cold. About 60 percent cloud cover. The most delicate blue far to the south. The blue is the same shade I used to see in the winter over the White Mountains along the California-Nevada border 35 years ago.

While reefing and unreefing the jib I noticed that the furling line was in trouble again. I shortened the strop that holds the lead block above the forward mooring cleat about two inches. I'm convinced the only way to make certain of proper alignment of the furling line to the furling drum under all conditions is to build in a metal lead arm as part of the furling drum as Hood (U.S.) and Goïot (France) do.

<u>2123.</u>   I spoke with Robin, who said that many of the 60-footers were rounding Cape Horn today. He said that Josh was trying to splint his broken main boom with a spinnaker pole and pieces of wood.

<u>2213.</u>   Squalls all morning. Headsail in and out like a yo-yo. The roller–furling sail with the foam luff pad, the big winch, and the two-handed winch handle combine to make sail changing quick, safe, and simple.

MARCH 4, 1991. (MONDAY). DAY 26.

<u>0048.</u>   Wind SE 16. Sea going down. Cold and chilly. A gray world. I needed a metal file for something and found a lot of rust so I cleaned and oiled all the files, which haven't been touched for ages. I heaved three worn ones over the side. We lost four slot screwdrivers in Sydney so I must find a hardware store in Uruguay.

The wind hangs in the SE, which is so discouraging. If it goes to the east I will tack south. We must get into the westerly airflow before I run out of food and patience. I am reading *The Covenant* by Michener. He is too windy and wordy for me—more a popular historian than a novelist. Otto Kindlimann gave me the book and urged me to read it, so I am plowing along.

<u>1000.</u>   Becalmed since 0600. Now 11 knots of breeze from the SSE.

<u>1330.</u>   Dawn is a yellowish knife blade on the horizon. A dozen tiny puffs of cloud float on the distant yellow. We head south, hunting for the elusive western airstream.

<u>1721.</u>   What can I do to get fair winds? I am so discouraged. A calm sea, cumulus clouds, nice blue sky, and frustration. I have thrown the race away because of cursed radio problems and lack of weather information.

<u>2024.</u>   Wind SE 3 knots, and the barometer is still climbing. 1024 mb! The weather—except for no wind—is beautiful. The air is crisp, and the sky and sea are deep blue. A little swell from the SW. Overhead are swirls of cirrus, brush strokes of ice crystals up toward heaven. The cirrus swirls seem out of focus and smudged, as if after having been formed they were smeared by wind, like

smoke from a chimney. There are a few patches of cumulus low down, but most of the sky is clear. The sun is bright and friendly.

Not much luck with the alternator problem so far. While tacking up a loose copper grounding strip for the radio I noticed that the generator fuel filter was half full of water and sediment, so I drained it and made the usual mess. To bleed the fuel system of air I followed the Yanmar instructions. They don't even mention purging the line to the fuel injection pump, which of course was full of air. I cranked the engine—as the book said—until the cylinders were full of salt water because the exhaust valves were held open by the decompression levers and cooling water ran back into the engine. I stopped and recalled something from my mechanical past. Oh yes. Shut off the intake water and open the drain line from the exhaust manifold. Voilà! Water poured out. I then bled the injection pump, and fuel flowed to the injectors, which I bled in turn. The engine started instantly. So much for the nifty directions.

I have been sitting in the cockpit stitching a rip in one of my gloves. Very pleasant in the sun. I wish Margaret was here. No sign of other vessels, people, trash, whales, birds, or anything. Earlier I berated myself for the lack of weather information, but I did try hard to get the Standard C and telex operational. Receiving weather routing from a mainland station is not only ruinously expensive, but tricky technologically. I believe that outside weather routing schemes should be banned in these races.

MARCH 5, 1991. (TUESDAY). DAY 27.

<u>0122.</u>   Still almost becalmed on a Southern Ocean that's like the Gulf of Maine in June. I wired a solid-state Silver Bullet voltage regulator to the big alternator. This regulator is supposed to be defective, but we'll see when the voltage is down. Today, however, the solar cells are working hard and the voltage is up. Very calm and tranquil, and I feel quite relaxed. Robin passed the news that IPSWICH, CITY KIDS, and BUTTERCUP are near Cape Horn and are encountering 50- to 60-knot fair winds along with huge seas. VOLCANO has an easterly gale and is down to 59°S.

<u>0345.</u>   A lovely sunset. A thousand worlds within a thousand worlds. I watched for the green flash but didn't see it. Just pinks and reds slowly tumbling into grays and blues.

<u>1403.</u>   Dawn. Some hard-looking stratus a couple of miles to starboard. A miserable run at noon—only 61 miles. What can I say?

<u>1709.</u>   We've done 9.2 miles in five hours. The sea and sky look more like the doldrums.

<u>2330.</u>   I spent several hours trying to change the starboard spinnaker pole outer end fitting for a new Schaefer fitting with a built-in sheave. A similar fitting works well on the port pole. I managed to unscrew three of the four mounting fastenings and drilled and chiseled out the fourth machine screw. In spite of a lot of pounding and prying, however, I couldn't loosen the old fitting, a job that I'll have to do on shore. The battery drill with cobalt drill bits is a miraculous tool.

MARCH 6, 1991. (WEDNESDAY). DAY 28.

<u>0036.</u>   I clamped the video camera to the shelf above the chart table and took some footage of me cooking bacon and eggs and making coffee. It's wonderful to be able to crank back the film and look in the camera finder to see what you've shot. I spoke with Robin this morning. Jack Boye is around Cape Horn. Don McIntyre went around in the moonlight last night "chirruping like a five-year-old schoolboy." Josh plans to anchor in the lee of one of the Cape Horn islands to repair his boom "perhaps with the assistance of the Chilean navy."

<u>0301.</u>   I finally got a call through to Margaret. We spoke for 56 minutes ($278.87). The main thing was a solicitation letter to a prominent editor I know, a discussion of other prospects, a brief shopping list, Margaret's travel plans, and a report on my lack of progress. Margaret will leave New York on March 15th and fly to Montevideo on Pan Am. She will stay in the apartment of Mito van Peborgh, an old friend from our Argentine sailing days.

<u>1034.</u>   Sea very smooth. Wind north 4–5 knots. I can see a piece of the moon and clouds up perhaps 2,000 feet that are moving from the NW. I'm wearing ordinary shoes on deck. Pole up, pole down, lines in and out. First one side; then the other. It's surprising how well I can see in the weak moonlight. By now of course I have the positions of all the lines well worked out. In a perfect world I could use two additional jammers on each side of the cockpit coamings to hold the foreguys and afterguys instead of cleats.

<u>1123.</u>   The radio is full of news of the Gulf War winding down. The burning oil wells in Kuwait will apparently take years to con-

trol. The famous oil well firefighter Red Adair is preparing to go to Kuwait. His company—which has five employees—is turning away 4,000 job applications per day, apparently from people "who want a little excitement in their lives." Maybe these people should try an ocean sailing race.

A good dinner tonight. I made a cream sauce with a little cheese, added a can of tuna (packed in brine, not oil), and finally some cooked spaghetti. A nice steaming pot.

1205.   Only 64 miles at noon. Barometer 1027 mb. Except for a few puffs from the north we've been becalmed for 48 hours.

1614.   I heard a noise of air or a snort and saw a large black fin. A whale ahead and to port, 30–35 feet long. I've been looking through The College of the Atlantic's whale book, but I can't identify the creature.

1754.   Spectacular black and white dolphins alongside. Jumping and diving and leaping. Since the weather was light, I rushed up to the bow with the video camera. Beautiful creatures.

1830.   We're finally across 130°W. I've noticed that during cold weather I crave candy and sweet things. Years ago when I interviewed the late William Colby, the Sierra Club mentor, he told me that during summer outings, when a camping group climbed from Yosemite Valley to the higher, colder meadows at 10,000 feet, the sugar consumption rose hugely. I still have five packets of freeze-dried dessert (Apple DeLight, etc.) which I find sweet (a bit cloying even) but quite satisfying.

2310.   Wind gone. Genoa furled.

MARCH 7, 1991. (THURSDAY). DAY 29.

0150.   At last a little wind (NE 7 knots), and we're underway.

0221.   A small bird has been flitting around the cockpit. Either a prion or a blue petrel. I need to see it again to check its tail. A blue petrel has a white horizontal band. The prion's is black.

I spoke with Robin Davie this morning. He said that a Chilean naval vessel gave SPIRIT OF IPSWICH a tow to a bay near Cape Horn. Josh anchored, repaired his boom, had a hot shower on the Chilean ship, and got going the following morning (today?). Robin reported strong SW winds and heavy squalls. He has repaired his

Monitor vane shaft (straightened it partially after an impact with something unknown). Robin left out one roller bearing pin to accommodate the bent shaft. Clever.

<u>0412.</u>   Stratus with ragged bottoms (a danger sign) ahead and to port. The wind was NE 13 knots and rising so I put in one reef and started to pump water ballast when the wind dropped to 7 knots.

I have been hunting for rice, hoping for a second bag.

<u>0440.</u>   The sky is covered with low clouds. The sun has set underneath, a thin line of red and gold in the west. Barometer 1023 mb.

I am plugging along in Michener's book on South Africa and not enjoying it. It's a kind of endless soap opera with a hundred or more characters.

<u>0634.</u>   I replaced a pricking needle in one of the stove burners.

<u>1210.</u>   We've made 109 miles at noon. Not good, but better than days of 61 and 64 miles. The barometer has dropped 6 mb. in 6 hours.

<u>1557.</u>   Wind NE 13–15 knots. More hard-looking clouds.

<u>1710.</u>   Our course is terrible with the NE wind. The calms and contrary winds since New Zealand are beyond belief. I should be near Cape Horn by now. I'm worried about my food stores and fresh water. Fortunately there are a few provisions in the ditch bag for the liferaft.

<u>1949.</u>   I spoke with Minoru last night. He said "my mainsail is broken," and that he was proceeding under storm jib. He was using his wind vane because his autopilot is out of order. He reported SW winds of 25–40 knots, sometimes 40–50 knots. I like Minoru because he is always so cheerful.

<u>2122.</u>   Robin told of heavy going and various knockdowns. He broke three plywood wind vane blades last night, blew out his staysail, and lost his dividers. VOLCANO nipped around Cape Horn at 0820 in 25–35 knots.

SPIRIT OF IPSWICH tried Le Maire Strait between Tierra del Fuego and Isla de los Estados, but halfway through got NNW headwinds up to 40 knots. Josh was set to within one mile of Isla de los Estados (6–7 knots of tidal stream) when he decided to get out. He turned 180°, retraced his course, and sailed around the island, leaving it to port as he headed east and north.

<u>2339.</u>   The barometer has dropped 17 mb. in 24 hours. Wind NE 12 knots. Formless low clouds (almost fog), drizzle, and cold. I

am now wearing a Patagonia hood and gloves in the cabin. My feet are cold, and I just got out some dry boot liners. I finally retrieved the loose chain in the forward cabin and stuffed it in a sailbag.

The bird yesterday was not a blue petrel but a solitary, curious broad-billed prion (because of the horizontal black band on its tail).

MARCH 8, 1991. (FRIDAY). DAY 30.

<u>0019.</u>   Surrounded by low clouds and mist. I expect the NE wind to be replaced by a blast from the west.

<u>0035.</u>   We're at 53°S., and I am thinking about tacking to the north. We're sailing at 105°M. (137° true). My desired course is 063°M. (095° true). So we're 42° off course. If we tack through 90° we'll be on 015°M. (047° true), which will be 48° off course. So the present course is better. Additionally we're gaining something from heading south, great circle-wise. Big banks of heavy, low, dark clouds to port.

<u>0305.</u>   I believe a weather front is passing, and the wind will shift to the SW. A cold drizzle and a falling barometer.

<u>0428.</u>   Becalmed.

<u>1216.</u>   Only 116 miles at noon. I'm discouraged. A few puffs from the SW, then nothing. Our average for 30 days is only 138.7 miles per day. No strong SW, W, or NW winds at all.

<u>1556.</u>   Becalmed for 9 of the last 11 hours. Finally 10 knots of wind from the SSW. Rain showers all around. The stratus is a bit higher today, and I see a smudge or two of blue. A few shafts of sunlight here and there so the day is more cheerful. With all the rolling we chafed a few small holes in the mainsail at the second panel above the foot where the reefed sail rubs on the bolt for the vang strap. I wiped off the sail with acetone and slapped on sticky-back Dacron patches. This tape is remarkable stuff.

<u>1835.</u>   It takes me 30 minutes to gybe the running rig:
     (1) Roll up the headsail and let the pole go forward and down on the pulpit.
     (2) Go forward, tie the pole end loosely to the pulpit, unhook the sheet, untie the topping lift, and put the pole away.
     (3) Back to the cockpit, pull the slack from the old pole lines, deal with the running backstays, change course, and gybe the mainsail.

(4) Ease the new pole lines in the cockpit, walk forward and lift and rig the new pole, not forgetting the security line around the pulpit at the forward end of the pole.

(5) Back to the cockpit to take up on the topping lift.

(6) Forward to the bow pulpit to untie the pole security line.

(7) Back to the cockpit to raise the outer pole end, release the furled jib, crank in the sheet, and adjust the foreguy and afterguy.

(8) Tidy up the lines in the cockpit.

1954.   Replaced the chafed #2 reefing pendant. I have been tying running bowlines around the boom to secure the ends of the pendants. However I find that I can simply tie bowlines through the mainsheet block bales (underneath the boom) closest to the pendant. This way the bowline won't get jammed in the reefing cringle on the leech, a cause of chafe.

Lots of sleep, and I feel good. A nagging worry about food and water. (What we need are reasonable winds for 10 days or so.)

MARCH 9, 1991. (SATURDAY). DAY 31.

0038.   Wind west 15 knots. Barometer 1000 mb. Going nicely. The batteries are down, and I'm working on the voltage regulators.

0307.   I was halfway through fitting the Quad Cycle spares when suddenly we were over on our ear with the mainsail backed and the jib flapping. A 30-knot squall from the south caught us with full sail up and the autopilot trimmed for a west wind. I tried to horse the yacht around, but the backed mainsail made steering impossible. I rolled up the jib and then eased the starboard boom tackle to relieve the pressure on the mainsail. We got back on course, and I put two reefs in the mainsail. I then dropped the port spinnaker pole, tied it down, dealt with the running backstays, and then tidied up the lines. A busy hour—or was it two?

The sunsets at this latitude (53°S.) are gorgeous. Tonight the western sky was full of billowing clouds etched against a turquoise background. As the sun disappeared there was an orange glow, then a soft pink, and finally a quiet blue that shaded into gray and darkness.

The batteries are still going down, so I have stopped radio transmissions. For a while the Quad Cycle worked at a lower charging rate. I will change another circuit board. The device seems impossibly complicated.

0404.   I keep looking for icebergs. The sky is almost clear. Orion is overhead to port, and the Southern Cross is to starboard. I have been reading in the engine manual about the alternator (with a built-in regulator) that charges the generator starting battery. If the Quad Cycle spare does not work I am thinking of running the output line from the small alternator to the main batteries.

<u>0415.</u>   Boatspeed 8.79 knots, right on course. A degree of longitude at this latitude is 36 miles.

<u>0917.</u>   The air has a real bite to it.

<u>1205.</u>   Better—170 miles at noon.

<u>1600.</u>   Colder with a wind from the south (18 knots). I have put on a thick expedition-weight longjohn top, which makes three plus my jacket. I noticed the difference right away. I am also wearing gloves when I sleep. I wear boots with liners all the time. Gloomy and dark out. We won't get much from the solar panels today.

<u>1752.</u>   No luck with the Quad Cycle regulator. I replaced two circuit boards and checked the continuity of many wires and connections. I checked all 6 fuses and their holders. I found a blown 7½–amp fuse (ah-hah!) and thought I had found the problem, but when I replaced the fuse the performance was the same. The ammeter shows a charging rate of 46 amps, and the voltage climbs from 12.75 to 14.5 in 2–3 minutes (when I shut off the engine so I don't charge above 14.5 volts). I'd like to describe the symptoms to Rick Proctor, the man in Seattle who makes the unit, but—ironically—I don't have the power to call him.

MARCH 10, 1991. (SUNDAY). DAY 32.

<u>0434.</u>   Wind SSW 17 knots. Since the batteries are down and the weather seems settled (famous last words) I hooked up the wind vane steering gear. I have two reefs in the main and most of the jib poled out to starboard. The vessel is rolling a lot, and I have been commuting between the galley and the cockpit to adjust the vane. I can do the adjustment in the dark if I remember "starboard starboard top" which means that when on the starboard tack and I want to go to starboard, I pull the top (upper) adjustment line.

A hearty dinner of vegetables and sausages (from a can) cooked with rice. Only one portion of rice left. A tragedy when the bag of rice got wet.

The upside-down compass on the ceiling of the cabin is marvelous—especially when I'm using the vane gear. At night I shine a light up from the chart table, the galley, or a bunk. The autopilot has steered such straight courses for 32 days that I've taken them for granted.

<u>0939.</u>   Wind west 26 knots. We were running by the lee so I rolled up the jib and took the pole down. Gybed the mainsail to starboard. Surprising speed with just the double-reefed mainsail. Changed the steering vane weather helm bias by moving the tiller line chain a few links. A clever innovation.

Rolling heavily. Sky clear. Lots of stars. Sliver of moon enough to illuminate everything with a weak light. Cold, and I need plenty of clothing. Especially gloves.

<u>1150.</u>   Great shaking of the mainsail. Up quickly, dressed, and outside to find that a big squall had just passed. Sailing nicely. Excitement over.

<u>1204.</u>   Day's run—194 miles at noon. A few glimmers of a bluish dawn.

<u>1745.</u>   Lots of action. I've been on deck for two hours (we just surfed to 11 knots and are doing 9.7 at the moment). Tired and hungry. At the moment it's snowing. During the night we ran with just the double-reefed mainsail. This morning I set the port pole and a little of the jib. Water was flying all over the place, and I had to be cautious on the foredeck.

The wind increased to 31 knots from the west so I put in the third reef. With this wind it's easier to control the total sail area by using the deeply reefed mainsail and adjusting the jib area, which I can do from the cockpit. The wind vane is working OK, but we swing a lot. Not the steady course of the autopilot. It was hard to crank in the reefing pendant for the third reef, and I had to stop for breath many times.

Now to eat, have a little wash, and to put on some clean longjohns. Still snowing. The cockpit seats are all white.

<u>2043.</u>   Running hard with two small sails. Occasionally out of control in big seas, but the vane has recovered each time and is steering well. Some blue sky and sun (good for the solar panels). A few of the big seas have made me nervous, especially when we cascade down the front of one into the trough (Valley of Death?). However the bow sections seem buoyant enough, and we always come up—or have so far. (Maybe I should be writing with water-proof ink.)

The starboard water tank is empty so I have switched to the port tank, which I used for one week in the Tasman, a period that seems ages ago (one month). The wind and water are cold enough so that I really need gloves. I have gloves hanging all around the cabin, drying out.

I feel blue that I'm so far behind in the race. I've certainly tried hard. If only the keel repairs had been completed so I could have left with the others from Sydney. Then to have had no real wind for a whole week in the Southern Ocean is mind-boggling.

<u>2055.</u>   Every 10 minutes or so a big wave pushes us off course. Fortunately these seas are nothing like the monsters in the Indian Ocean that turned us over.

MARCH 11, 1991. (MONDAY). DAY 33.

<u>0050.</u>   Cape Horn is 1,576 miles on 064°M. The vane gear is steering nicely, although we're swinging a good deal. I suppose the autopilot would have its hands full in these seas as well. I made a powerful spaghetti sauce (over macaroni). Tasty and filling.

<u>0544.</u>   The length of this voyage in the Southern Ocean is beginning to get to me, and I miss talking with the other competitors on the radio. I suppose man is a social animal on some level. Now we're making excellent time, but we need these runs consistently to do well in the race. If we can keep going at this rate for another week we should be at Cape Horn. Once around Isla de los Estados, and headed north, life will be easier, safer, and different.

Certainly these winds and ocean conditions are perilous for a small vessel. Yet we run along hour after hour while great seas thunder outside. It's incredible that man has fashioned a contrivance that can use the winds so well.

I finished Michener's novel *The Covenant* on South Africa. On balance I declare it a good job. A lot of history and a lot of pages (almost 1,100).

<u>1110.</u>   A lot of heavy sleeping. I miss the alarm clock.

<u>1239.</u>   A good run—212 miles at noon. Wind west 25 knots.

<u>1344.</u>   Dark, gray, and raining lightly. A good day to go to the movies. We continue to roll heavily. A light breakfast. Then I washed a little and put on clean (and heavier) thermal underwear. The Patagonia clothing is nicely made, and the fabrics are thick, smooth, and of high quality. Even so I'm wearing one short-sleeved undershirt and two long-sleeved undershirts under my quilted Musto oilskins.

<u>1822.</u>   A couple of hours on deck. The vane kept steering 090° instead of 060°. I finally took down the running rig and with the apparent wind a hair abaft the beam, tried the fore-and-aft rig. We sailed OK and rolled much less, but the vane swung the course from 030° to 075°. I hooked up the autopilot, which steers a much better course. While walking down the port deck I noticed that a special cir-clip had come out of the new jib sheet block. I put in a cotter pin. So far I'm not impressed with the new Ronstan blocks because the aluminum sheaves are already corroded and have been at sea only one month. It may be an unfair criticism, but much of the Australian food and marine equipment is beautifully packaged but once beyond the fancy wrappings, the quality is average to poor.

<u>1910.</u>   I must be losing my marbles. I could not spell exquisite. I tried equisite, ehsquisit, etc . . .
    Gloves are hanging up all over the cabin. Leather gloves are not really suitable because they're too hard to dry (after rinsing in fresh water). What I need are some of those giant yellow plastic gardener's gloves Margaret and I used on WHISPER. The plastic gloves handle 90% of the grasping jobs, and can be wiped dry and easily slipped on and off. For warmth, a pair of polypropylene gloves can be worn inside them. For the other 10%, the gloves can be pulled off and the undergloves or bare hands used.

<u>1948.</u>   A few minutes ago I wrote WHISPER, and suddenly all the memories of 19 years of voyages in her came flooding back. So many places. So many friends.

<u>2227.</u>   Going well. Wind (NW 25 knots) backing a little. Apparent wind abeam. Half a tank of water ballast to port. A good sleep. I am reading *The Glass Menagerie* by Tennessee Williams. A play about losers and wailers during the Depression. Rather far-out stage directions that call for a slide show while the play goes on, the slides amplifying the lines of the actors.

MARCH 12, 1991. (TUESDAY). DAY 34.

<u>0040.</u>   The fore-and-aft reaching rig is so easy and powerful, and we often slip up to 9.2 knots without any strain or effort. And almost no chafe possibilities. Thinking of chafe, I must deal with the rubbing of the lee running backstay on the upper spreader. I can tape the spreader, sew a short piece of hose over the line at the critical place, or move the line slightly aft by

moving the lee running backstay control line block. I'll do all three things in Uruguay.

I finished *The Glass Menagerie*. Good, but too short. I wanted more meat and potatoes. The scene between the shy girl and the former high school hero was excellent, but I craved for more. I see that Helen Hayes played the lead in New York. Wouldn't it have been something to have seen her in the role in 1946?

Still 1,400 miles to go to Cape Horn. Will this long passage ever end? I miss the old Zenith radio. How nice it was to turn the dial and to listen to the world. Self-contained batteries. I have a tiny Sony set on board, but the dialing is complicated. How can I rig an aerial? Maybe I can tap into the two-position switch between the SSB and weatherfax antenna.

0243.   Nasty out. Wind NW 28–30 knots. A wave from the north slammed into us with a mighty thump. No place for the faint of heart. I rolled up more of the jib, which has cut our speed to 7.9 knots.

In order to save electricity I have everything off except the autopilot and one light. I got out the Sony radio, which shows some damage from salt water. I put in new batteries, found an aerial plug in the electrical box and have tapped into the SSB antenna. Presto! I am listening to the BBC (15,250 kHz) and various South American stations. I must start concentrating on Spanish.

0920.   Barometer 995 mb. Radio Japan, Radio Moscow, plus music from the tiny Sony radio. All from four AA batteries.

0934.   We've been averaging 8.6 knots since noon yesterday.

1422.   I slept through the noon hour and had to calculate backwards to get the 12 o'clock position. We've gone 198 miles in the last 24 hours. Wind NW 24–29 knots. Weather gray, cloudy, and gloomy with light drizzle. I'm wearing enough clothes to start a haberdashery.

1444.   How nice to have classical music in the cabin. Radio Moscow has pleasant music programs, plus the news (which is mild these days). Last night I had a stomachache, probably from eating cold food yesterday. I have been sipping a cup of steaming herb tea, which seems to help. Now for a hot breakfast.

I am running out of many things. The rice and hot cereal are almost finished. The fresh fruit (except for oranges and one apple) is long gone. We have half a tank of fresh water. If things get critical I can stop in the Falklands. However I don't want to stop. I want to go! I must get to Uruguay as soon as possible.

<u>1610.</u>   Wind less and backing to the north. Breakfast of an orange, hot cereal, two toasted crackers with butter and jam, and a cup of tea. Drizzle outside. We're heeled 20° to starboard. Since we're a little south of our course I headed up slightly. While I was eating breakfast I heard a record of Edith Piaf singing old popular French songs. I practically wept with sentiment and nostalgia.

<u>1743.</u>   More sail up because the wind is down to 22 knots from the NNW. The sea is less rough, but the cold drizzle continues. I noticed a little water in the lee water ballast tank. I pumped it out and filled half the windward tank. This water must leak through the 3″ dia. crossover valve. Perhaps a bit of foreign matter is in the seals.
     I heated a can marked "steak and onions," which I ate with crackers. No sign of any steak. Maybe some fragments. In any case it was tasty and filling. I am no longer so fussy. I am pumping about 20 gallons a day from the bilge. I suspect the water comes down inside the mast.

<u>1835.</u>   Wind less. 14 knots from NNW. Full jib. Raining hard. I have been sorting through the Cape Horn charts.

<u>2200.</u>   The wind has suddenly collapsed, and we're in dense fog. The seas continue to ease, and the barometer is down to 990 mb. Busy cooking something hot and nourishing while I dart out to look for icebergs.

<u>2245.</u>   Dense fog with the dimmest orb of the sun glimmering astern. The wind (NNW 11 knots) is a little abaft the port beam. I hesitate to set up the running rig because as the wind increases and we speed up, the apparent wind will move forward. Except for the cold this situation reminds me of the Gulf of Maine or the Bering Sea north of the Aleutians. However we're 1,200 miles west of Cape Horn, and I feel exposed.

MARCH 13, 1991. (WEDNESDAY). DAY 35.

<u>0011.</u>   Wind west 16 knots. We're steering 060°M. plus 32° of easterly variation, or 092°T. While putting up the port spinnaker pole for the running rig, I noticed the starboard jib sheet was partially chafed through where it bears on the pole end fitting. I unwound the jib to port and sheeted it in tightly so I could reach the clew. By standing on the life lines (careful) I was just able to untie the slack starboard sheet, re-tie it past the chafe, and cut off the damaged part. I must replace the sheets, which are getting shorter and shorter.

Two reefs in the main and the full jib. We're going along OK but are underpowered. The problem is the low barometer. The last time this situation occurred, a squall brought a great blast from the SW. My gut feeling is to leave things as they are and wait a bit.

<u>0027.</u>   The fog comes and goes. It's not high in a vertical dimension because I can often see blue sky. At sea level, however, the fog is thick. I feel helpless and half expect an iceberg to appear suddenly. If the radar set were working and I had electricity I would look through the eye of the radar.

<u>0401.</u>   Wind NW 25–31 knots. It's so easy to write "third reef" and so hard to crank the winch. I'm wringing wet from perspiration and just had something to eat to replenish some of the energy I used up. The wind is back, and we have the same rig and wind as yesterday. When I put in the third reef I always run a lashing through the clew and around the boom and aft to a strong point in case the pendant gives way when the conditions are severe. It's dangerous putting these lashings on because I must stand on the coachroof at the end of the boom with both hands up to deal with the line. I always wear a safety harness for this job.

The hell with it. I'm going to bed.

<u>1103.</u>   Unable to get water in the ballast tanks because we're heeled way over.

<u>1204.</u>   A run of 162 miles at noon. Wind NNE 29 knots. Barometer 984. I managed to prime the water ballast pump by going downwind for a minute or two. Once we rolled a little, the pump picked up its prime. Simple solutions are the most elusive.

It's just getting light on a miserable-looking world. Blue-gray, raining, and a foul wind. Nevertheless the water ballast makes a big difference. I'm glad I put in the third reef earlier. The jib is almost entirely rolled up. In spite of all my clothes, three blankets, and gloves, I was cold last night. The trouble is gaps in the blankets or *gaposis* (a new disease). I just unwrapped my secret weapon, an eiderdown sleeping bag.

<u>1532.</u>   Nasty outside with big seas and cold rain that makes my arthritic fingers ache. Waves keep breaking over the yacht. A big one slammed against the weather portlights hard enough so that seawater squirted around the edges (and past the seals) like water through a sieve. I hope the dogs on the portlights hold. I used a sponge to mop up. Of course if I told this to the portlight manufacturer, I'd be accused of gross exaggeration.

The wind is rapidly veering (now NNW 31 knots), and I have

eased off on the course to take the waves more on the port quarter. The seas look upset and unpleasant, but nothing like the waves that rolled us in the Indian Ocean.

I slipped into the sleeping bag for a nap. The eiderdown bag was lovely and warm, with no leaks of cold air. Every 10 or 15 minutes a wave crashes into the side of SEBAGO. Sometimes the wind drops to 25 knots. Water from the portlights is dripping everywhere.

Shall I cook the last of the rice and have a big meal? Or shall I split it and have two smaller meals?

1800.   Seas less. Squalls astern and a very pale blue sky. Can the foul weather be over? I hope I don't have to gybe, since I spent the last hour setting the port pole. The nifty experimental spinnaker pole end that Schaefer made is all beat up and full of jagged edges where the soft aluminum has hit the pulpit or other hard things. The next model should be made of stainless steel welded plates with a micarta sheave.

2242.   Wind west 28 knots. Only the triple-reefed mainsail and a little of the jib. The autopilot is doing a good job. Cape Horn is 1,010 miles on 067°M.

2255.   By the amount of daylight I judge it to be late afternoon. We're at 94°W. longitude which is six hours earlier than GMT, so the local time is about 1700.

MARCH 14, 1991. (THURSDAY). DAY 36.

0045.   Running hard in big seas. An afternoon of sun and blue sky with some cloud cover. Very cold.

0457.   Going well. Lots of stars.

1118.   Just getting light. An easy night of reading and sleeping in the warm down bag. The safest place by far in the yacht. I get up every hour to look around. Cold and crisp. Wind down to 22 knots from the west so I have been letting out more of the jib—all but three rolls. Our course is a little low (060°) but the wind is too far aft to go higher without gybing, which I will do later. Now for breakfast.

1328.   A 192 mile-run at noon. Wind west 24 knots. Position 54°07'S., 95°05'W. 907 miles to Cape Horn. Going well on a rough sea. Dawn was about 45 minutes ago. Blue sky overhead. A long, low, thick cloud bank is south of us, aimed east and west. The edge of the bank has a rough texture and looks like a loaf of bread that's been cut with a dull knife.

It's a miracle I can cook a nice breakfast (onions, canned meat, eggs, tea, coffee, and warmed crackers) with such violent motion.

1502.   We're steering 062°M. but need 069°M. or 7° more. However that would put the wind dead aft. Best to wait for a change in wind or for the angle to increase so we can gybe suitably. We're making good 7.2–8.3 knots.

Last night I dreamed that someone stole my billfold. The dream was so real that when I woke up I immediately began to plan how to get a new driver's license and credit cards. It took me a few minutes before I realized that out here no one can steal anything.

1924.   Sunny and clear. By far the nicest day of the 36-day passage so far. I have been working out courses and distances after Cape Horn. My plan is to leave Isla de los Estados close to port. Then almost straight north, depending on the wind.

We're about 875 miles from Cape Horn. To the Isla de los Estados waypoint is 146 miles farther. Then 1,248 miles to Uruguay. Or a total of 2,269 miles divided by a 170-mile per day average = 13.3 days or March 26th. Something like that. Do I have food and water for two weeks? Once north of 50°S. I'll feel easier about setting big sails.

I've been troubled with cold feet. I finally changed my stockings, boot liners, and massaged my toes and the balls of my feet. The sleeping bag is good, but it takes several hours for my feet to warm up.

2149.   I shaved and combed my hair, and I'm cleaning up the cabin. Took a couple of photographs. Stockings and boot liners out in the sun to dry. Spirits up. Yacht rolling heavily with the wind aft. More sail set.

MARCH 15, 1991. (FRIDAY). DAY 37.

0045.   Sun just setting in the west. Wind NW 13 knots. Full sail.

0148.   Software problems with the GPS. A new symbol appeared on the screen, and the instruction book says nothing. I have spent the last hour trying to unscramble "ASF is applied to the L/L mode." The book does not define ASF. I haven't the faintest idea what to do.

<u>0738.</u>   Going better. Drizzle outside and inky dark.

<u>0937.</u>   I'm completely baffled by the hours of darkness and GMT. The divergence appears to be increasing as we travel east, just the opposite of what I'd expect.

<u>1027.</u>   Getting light with a dim dawn in the east. Stars overhead and clouds around the horizon. A mild night, which shows that all the weather in the Southern Ocean is not bad. The swell continues relentlessly, however, and I must be careful to keep my feet well apart and to wedge myself in places with my feet and butt if I use my hands for something.

<u>1207.</u>   166 miles at noon. Wind west 13 knots. Cape Horn is 741 miles on 071°M.
      Vivid dreams about chasing pickpockets.
      My confusion about the time may have to do with the very long dawns and dusks at this latitude. Although I caught glimmers of light at 1027, only now (at 1215) do I see pinkish clouds near the sun in the east.

<u>1438.</u>   Another small hole in the mainsail from the vang yoke (or perhaps the starboard vang tackle). I slapped on a sticky-back tape patch.
      After a while you get so used to the ground swell that you tend to ignore it. However, when I eased the starboard boom tackle to bring the boom inboard to deal with the sail repair, the main boom swung back and forth with great gear-breaking crashes. When I finished with the sail repair and eased the boom again (carefully taking up on the starboard tackle and easing the port tackle) I looked at the swell. A period of about 10 seconds, but not consistent. I judge the swell height to be roughly 20 feet (the length of the spinnaker pole). This is not as extreme as it appears because of the period of 10 seconds. In other words, long rollers that rise up and down gradually.
      Beautiful outside. About 90% cloud cover of rather formless altocumulus. A weak filtered sun.

<u>1542.</u>   I opened a can of vegetable protein and heated it with tomato paste and water. Meanwhile I cooked one cup of macaroni. Very good. The tomato paste flavors the neutral vegetable protein. I'm learning.
      A great Mozart program on BBC. Some lovely piano and opera excerpts. The clarinet concerto was splendid.

<u>1642.</u>   The weather continues mild. I can hardly believe we have full working sail up on a flat sea (except for the swell). Many

gray petrels, a few white-chinned petrels, some white-headed petrels, and an occasional juvenile wandering albatross.

1748.   Oh joy! I was transferring food stores from forward to the galley, and I found a small bag of rice! Happiness is a 500-gram bag of brown rice. Wonderful! There's a bank of some heavy-looking solid clouds working up from the SW that I must watch.

1908.   The wind is almost dead aft, which I hate. I re-tied the #2 reefing pendant on a boom bale farther forward. By the time the race is over I will have the running rigging perfected. I looked in the race instructions and see that Uruguay radio broadcasts the Argos positions at 1800Z. I got in on the last of the transmission. I have tuned the ICOM to 10 new frequencies, so I will be all set tomorrow.

2027.   Cape Horn is 680 miles on 072°M.

MARCH 16, 1991. (SATURDAY). DAY 38.

0023.   I was sitting reading after a good dinner when I realized the motion of the vessel was different. I looked out. The sun was gone, the sails were backed, and a blustery wind of 22 knots had drifted in from the south. Now two hours later we have 3 reefs in the main, half a tank of water ballast to starboard, and 7 rolls in the jib. The temperature has dropped 20 degrees.

The weather can certainly change in a hurry in these waters. We have been sliding along on a close reach at 7.5 knots. As I write, however, the wind is falling away. And so it goes.

0119.   Wind up and down during this long hour of dusk. Third reef out. Then a few minutes later 3 more rolls in the jib. We must keep her going.

Dinner was a big success with brown rice, vegetable protein, and tomato paste. This evening I added nuts and raisins. I like white rice better, but I'm very glad to have the brown.

0142.   The Southern Cross is overhead to starboard, a great beacon of stars in the night sky.

0611.   Wind south 13 knots. Seas down. Full jib and mainsail. Black and cold out, although it seemed lighter in the east after my eyes got used to the night. I shook out the reefs, which stopped a lot of creaking and groaning around the clew of the reefed sail where the Dacron was bunched and compressed. The best system of reefing a mainsail has got to be a roller reefing boom of some kind or a wind-up system at the luff. Slab reefing is too much work.

1025.   Dawn is a handful of blue ribbons low in the east. My nose is dripping, and I've pulled my wool cap down over my ears. Thick gloves feel good.

1200.   A run of 170 miles at noon. Cape Horn is 570 miles on 073°M. The sun is up on the eastern horizon.

1355.   I reversed the port jib sheet and shortened and whipped the end. Wind south 13–18 knots. I've headed a little more south to get to 56° in case we get a southerly gale. With the westerly swell we need the wind at about 120° apparent to set up the running rig. I have put on a Patagonia skiing hat to keep my ears warm. Elastic around the ears and snug enough not to fall off.

1731.   Going well with the running rig to starboard. I moved the foreguy to a block on the stem, where it's clear of the pulpit and lifelines. A big improvement, and I can use the same block for both the port and starboard foreguys.

Week after week I go on, and there's nary a sign of a human in this vast watery plain of the Southern Ocean. Why go to space for a new world? Why pay millions of dollars for rockets to shoot people and life support systems high above the earth? Move down here with a slow-moving ship or a raft society of some kind and do space-type experiments. Here there's a smog-free atmosphere, and with a solar panel or wind generator farm there could be enough electricity to run the stations and convert salt water to fresh. Hydroponic vegetables, beans, and sprouts could be grown. I know there's krill in the Southern Ocean, and certainly other things yet to be discovered. There could be a whole human society down here. Scientists or social outcasts or both. One of the appeals of space is for orbiting signal stations; perhaps this could be done from antennas on a series of moored barges or buoys spaced around the Southern Ocean. I know it sounds crazy, but so did Sputnik before 1957.

I'm reading a book called *A Song For Nagasaki* by Paul Glynn, a Catholic priest who lives in Sydney. So far the story is good, but the writing is so cliché-ridden that it's an effort to continue. Why don't amateur writers get a professional to look over their material?

<u>2249.</u>   We're doing 8.3 knots in a gradually increasing wind (SW 19–22 knots). One reef in the main. I need to watch that we don't get overpowered. My feet are perpetually cold unless I wrap them in several folds of a blanket. We're 57 miles from the latitude of Cape Horn.

MARCH 17, 1991. (SUNDAY). DAY 39.

<u>0037.</u>   Just getting dark. Some hard-looking clouds to windward so I put in a second reef. We've dropped from 8.6 to 7.5 knots, and I'm watching the wind. I'm getting nervous as we approach Cape Horn (473 miles). We must hurry, but we need to sail with care.

<u>0603.</u>   Little by little we're closing in on the tip of South America, but the voyage goes so slowly. Utter blackness outside. Will I see any ships near Cape Horn?

A Song For Nagasaki is about a Japanese doctor who was in Nagasaki when it was atom-bombed by the U.S. in 1945.

<u>1155.</u>   Sun low in the east. Small puffy clouds floating above a bank of lead-like stratus piled on the eastern horizon. Pink over dark gray.

<u>1228.</u>   A run of 187 miles at noon. There's definitely a north-setting current here. I'm trying to work a little to the south, but we're barely making the Cape Horn waypoint.

I notice that every time we roll, the lower shroud on each side tightens with a slight jerk and then loosens, tightens and then loosens. This must have happened 10,000 times or more, and can't be right. I've wrapped a piece of ⅜" dia. shock cord tightly around the lower, middle, and upper shrouds about 6 feet above the deck to stop this jerking.

<u>1528.</u>   Less wind and full sail. On and on we glide, like a bird in the air, a glider beneath a cloud, a sunbeam on a wall.

<u>1622.</u>   My two-burner kerosene primus stove has worked well ever since Newport. I use about one liter of kerosene a week, which I take from six one-liter bottles that I keep stored in the galley. I just filled four of the bottles from a kerosene jug in the lazarette. So far I've only replaced a few minor parts in the burners. I have enough kerosene on board to run the stove for two years. It's necessary to pre-heat each burner with alcohol before using, but a gallon of alcohol lasts at least two months.

The autopilot continues to work valiantly, although the electric motor has a ghastly strangled sound.

This morning for breakfast I cooked some rice, opened a can of tuna in brine (which I drained), and made a cream sauce (which never seemed to thicken enough). When the rice was done (25 minutes), I added the rice and tuna to the cream sauce, which I then stirred and heated. Powerful.

1635.   It's 349 miles to Cape Horn. The wind has dropped to 12 knots.

1841.   While gybing the mainsail I noticed that the snapshackle at the bottom of the starboard boom tackle—which pulls the boom both down and forward—was broken. Schaefer makes the pin with a 90° hard shoulder where the diameter is reduced for the inside spring, and the pin breaks there every time.

Just as I eased the tackle to replace the broken snapshackle with a screw-pin shackle, the yacht rolled on a big swell. The boom crashed from side to side, and I dropped the shackle pin over the side. I finally put a lashing between the tackle and the rail, but in the hurry, three lines got left underneath the tackle instead of on top where they belong.

The weather has been warm and mild all day. Imagine full sail this close to Cape Horn. I have been wearing ordinary sailing shoes on deck. Time for a nap.

2155.   I reeved a new starboard foreguy line, 80 feet long.

2217.   Very little wind (WSW 11 knots) for running. Some swell and banging and slatting. A few rain showers around, and half a rainbow to port.

MARCH 18, 1991. (MONDAY). DAY 40.

0215.   Wind WSW 11 knots. Light wind almost dead astern. Only 19 miles to 56°S. Barometer dropping.

0448.   Gybed again. This time in the middle of the night with a flashlight clamped between my teeth. The sea was calm so I started out in my lightweight blue oilskins. A cool drizzle turned to cold hard rain, so I went below, stripped off the blue, and put on my heavy red oilskins to finish the job. The rain was refreshing and washed off everything. The shower has moved eastward and left a sky full of stars.

<u>1204.</u>   A run of 154 miles at noon. Wind WSW 15 knots. A frustrating 24 hours with light winds almost dead astern. I've gybed four times. During the last gybe I remembered to oil the latches on the inboard ends of the spinnaker poles. Low, dark, heavy rolls of clouds around the horizon. I had reasonable naps during the night and feel quite good. We're 12 miles north of Cape Horn and about 220 miles west. Come on wind. Blow a little!

<u>1445.</u>   Wind still light and fickle. The sky is covered with low stratus. Dark and gloomy in the south. Shafts of sun and light gray and white in the north. At noon the nearest land was 90 miles north.

It's exciting to approach Cape Horn. The yacht has sailed well on this leg, and I find no fault with my sailing. It's just that the winds have been abysmal. Or am I making excuses?

<u>1822.</u>   A smooth sea and a rain shower during which the wind veered to the SSW. Both the clouds and the water are gray.

<u>2107.</u>   Wind south 15 knots. Again we're making no southing so I headed south another 5°. A definite north-setting current. How wonderful to have a GPS satellite device. Land is 60 miles to the north.

<u>2202.</u>   Barometer 993 mb. Except for a little heel, our ride is smooth and effortless.

<u>2255.</u>   More wind. One reef. Three-quarters of a tank of water ballast to windward (starboard) makes a big difference in heel and speed (9.2 knots now and then). Although we've headed 6° or more south from our course, we've only picked up one additional mile (to 55°58'S.) in two hours. I presume the north-setting current will ease, and the east-setting current will take precedence as we get close to land.

<u>2352.</u>   Wind south 18–22 knots. A second reef plus 8 rolls in the jib. Even with a south wind, the sea is smooth.

MARCH 19, 1991. (TUESDAY). DAY 41.

<u>0116.</u>   I spoke too soon. The ocean is beginning to get rough.

<u>0513.</u>   Cape Horn is 070° and 91 miles. The depth is 147 meters.

<u>0803.</u>   Cold and black outside. I need lots of clothes. Especially over my neck and hands. Wind less, and more aft so I let out much of the jib, and we've picked up speed. I reckon we're 15 miles south of Islas Ildefonso and about 35 miles NNW of Islas Diego Ramirez. I've been looking around outside, but it's too dark to see anything.

<u>0959.</u>   I was dealing with the starboard spinnaker pole and hauling on the topping lift when I looked aft. A great black cloud—barely visible in the dim light—was bearing down on SE-BAGO. I left up a scrap of sail and went below while the squall pushed us up to 7-8-9-10 before dropping to 7.5 knots.

<u>1040.</u>   Land Ho! Something is sticking out of the sea far off the port bow. A distant island or mountain. Just visible between dark clouds. Big flakes of snow are swirling around the cockpit. A couple of squalls passed to starboard. Very dark, almost blue-black in the dawn light. As the squalls hissed to the east, their jagged bottoms were etched against a white background on either side. Dramatic stuff.

<u>1205.</u>   189 miles at noon. Many islands ahead to port. Everything is gray and dark. A gloomy ocean heaving up and down, low brooding clouds, cliffs and low rounded mountains, distant snow fields.

I forgot to mention that I'm finally on chart #4200, the southern part of South America (Rio de la Plata to Cabo de Hornos). I just got out a pair of dry gloves.

<u>1350.</u>   I have the logbook in the cockpit where I'm trying to write. A snow squall comes, and suddenly everything is white. Then a few minutes later the air is clear, and I look ahead to port. I can see snow fields on the distant slopes of the mountains on Isla Hoste and Tierra del Fuego. As I look from my left to my right and use a forefinger to trace the downward profile of the land toward the south, I stop at the last piece of land, a dark triangular promontory. It's Cape Horn.

CHAPTER FOURTEEN

A Minuet with a Gale

MARCH 19, 1991. (TUESDAY). DAY 41 (continued)

<u>1400.</u>   Squall after squall. One minute the wind is 30 knots, and we're half over on our side. Fifteen minutes later the wind has collapsed, and we're upright and barely moving. Then a frosty blast from the SW.

<u>1430.</u>   Heavy snow. Santa Claus weather. For a time thick flakes of snow reduced visibility to two boatlengths. Then suddenly the weather cleared on the port bow, and I could see Cape Horn, 24 miles away.

<u>1510.</u>   Snowing again.

<u>1819.</u>   A busy couple of hours. I'm pooped. I gradually made more sail as we got close to land. The weather improved. I took a few still photographs and some video footage near Cape Horn. Then a squall appeared over the land and the sea. In a few minutes the weather changed completely. I could see a mass of whitecaps coming so I cranked seven turns in the jib. I put one reef in the main and kept right on going and put in a second. The sun disappeared, and suddenly it was quite cold. As soon as we pass a few rocky islets we can head for the waypoint east of Isla de los Estados which is 140 miles to the NE.

During the last few days the magnetic variation has changed from 33°E. to 15°E.

<u>1854.</u>   I have been out looking at Cape Horn and thinking that each of my three trips past this great black headland was a chapter heading in the story of my life. Will I ever see this place again?

<u>2022.</u>   A ship is about two miles astern of us and coming this way. Except for the ferries at Wellington when we went through Cook Strait, this is the first ship I've seen since Sydney. But what kind of a ship? Fishermen? The vessel is too big. Pirates? Too remote. Oceanographic research? Chilean navy?

I went below to cook something, and suddenly I heard an out-board motor and shouting. I turned off the stove and went outside. An inflatable from the ship with two ratings and a Chilean sub-lieutenant was alongside. The officer came aboard and said that his people had been watching for me. The ship was the ATF GAL-VARINO, a Chilean navy twin-screw patrol vessel about 40 meters long. The officer was a young man named Gaston Droguett. He asked if I was OK and whether I needed anything. I said no, and we chatted for a few minutes. Gaston learned English in England where he lived for a year with his father, who was the Chilean naval attaché. I was very touched by the visit. Such kindnesses make me feel very humble.

After Gaston left I called up the captain of the GALVARINO to thank him for his attentions. "Did he know my friend Admiral Eduardo Allen?" "Oh yes, but he's in the house now." I thought back to my first rounding of Cape Horn with Margaret and real-ized it was in 1974, 17 years earlier. Admiral Allen would have retired a long time ago. The GALVARINO came near to pick up the inflatable. Everyone was on the side of the bridge waving. It was all too much! Now I must get back to business, and sail to Uruguay as fast as possible.

MARCH 20, 1991. (WEDNESDAY). DAY 42.

<u>0201.</u>   Last evening at 2230 the wind fell to 6 knots from the NW. Our course lay to the NE. The sea was calm except for little swirls of tidal action. I set the genoa and got it working by heading into the wind enough to get up speed and then bearing off on course. This system works to perfection. A few times we got up to 8 knots.

It seemed risky to leave up 1400 sq. ft. of sails and go to sleep near Cape Horn. However I was extremely tired after all the excitement. I laid out my heavy oilskins alongside the berth and turned in. I had a wonderful sleep for 90 minutes and got up at 0100. The wind had risen to 16 knots, and heavier puffs were com-ing down from the mountains far off to port. I furled the genoa, put in 2 reefs, filled the port ballast tank, and let out a little of the jib. We're now going 7.4 knots just a little off course.

<u>0801.</u>   More blessed sleep and I feel warm and rested. A bit groggy perhaps. The sleeping bag is excellent. We're in the lee of Tierra del Fuego, which shields us from the Southern Ocean swell. The sea is easy and smooth. Pitch black outside. Too bad we've got a headwind.

Reaching across big seas from the north as we head westward with two reefs in the mainsail.

<u>0842.</u>   The faintest streak of dawn in the east. We need wind from the west or south.

<u>1044.</u>   The view off to port is incredible. I've been watching a lurid pink from the dawn brushing its way over the tops of snow squalls and the distant mountains of Isla de los Estados. Too bad my cameras are full of salt water.

We must get north or NE. Where are all those SE winds that have haunted this trip? I bore off for a minute or two to tie down the port spinnaker pole, which was loose and making a terrible noise.

<u>1156.</u>   Sailing well against the wind. I've been looking at the jagged skyline of Isla de los Estados. I wonder whether Margaret and I will ever make a trip to this remote island? Margaret would like the penguins. I like the notion of spending a month anchored in the deep bays with a well-stored vessel and an oil stove. We could hike all over the island.

<u>1203.</u>   The waypoint for Punta del Este shows 1,257 miles on 006°M. How long will it take? If I average 180 miles a day, we're looking at a week. Lunch of brown rice with half a can of Australian Irish stew. Ghastly stuff colored the most sickening shade of pink. Ugh! However I was desperately hungry, and in a pinch one is not too fussy.

<u>1243.</u>   Put 7 rolls in the jib. Wind north 19 knots. Speed 7.3. Heating a can of pineapple for dessert. Nice to warm my fingers over the fire.

<u>1517.</u>   Wind 11–20 knots from the north. I tacked because we gain a 10° advantage. Where are all the westerlies that are shown on the pilot charts? Quite cold. A weak white sun. Isla de los Estados is dim in the distance off to port. Many storm petrels flying around. Now and then we pass great clumps of brownish kelp in the water. Some of the stalks are 2″ in diameter and must be 60 feet long. All twisted and knotted together.

<u>1709.</u>   We're passing through the great meeting ground of the waters of the Pacific and the Atlantic. I've been watching hundreds—thousands—of small waves (4–5 feet high) striking one another and sometimes making little explosions of water and spray. These tidal waves were against us and slowed us as we bounced up and down.

However a few minutes ago I tacked, and suddenly all this water movement was with us because the waves were coming from the west. Our speed increased 1.5 knots, and the banging and crashing stopped. We must get north and away from all this tidal action. It's snowing again.

<u>1730.</u>   We're 25 miles east of Isla de los Estados and still in a strong tidal stream.

<u>1937.</u>   Wind NNE 11 knots, but unsteady in direction and strength. Rain and sleet on a gray day. The sea is quite calm. My fingers are so stiff I can hardly write. Every time I get ready for a nap, the wind changes.

<u>2206.</u>   Awakened by the yacht slamming into seas. I went out and rolled up a few turns of the jib. Five minutes later we were down to five knots. I unwound the jib and shook out a reef, which pushed us back to 7 knots. Ten minutes later we started all over again, and so on. The main thing is to keep driving northward.

Everything is gray outside. The sea is dark gray paint. The clouds are light gray paint. A monochromatic world without color, life, or accents. The batteries are getting lower and lower. I keep hoping for some hot sun to dry out the yacht and blast the solar panels.

<u>2342.</u>   Two or three times a minute we bash into a small head sea with a terrific wallop. I've eased off 10 degrees.

MARCH 21, 1991. (THURSDAY).
FIRST DAY OF SPRING. DAY 43.

0126.   The NE wind is gone. We're becalmed. According to the pilot chart, the odds are for west or SW winds.

0258.   Wind south 25 knots. A second reef in the mainsail. I must work out a course to leave the Falklands to starboard.

1051.   Finally we're going well, with full sail, a fair wind, and presumably a fair current. The barometer up to 1004 mb. I hope this wind will last for a few days. The batteries are way down. The meter reads minus 243, the lowest I've seen. A nice sunrise to starboard. Many birds around us. For breakfast I fried my last egg together with a fresh sliced onion and some canned meat, plus a cup of steaming coffee.

1202.   Course to Uruguay: 009°M. Distance 1,134 miles. A disappointing run yesterday. However today looks good. We must keep up our hope and spirits.

1236.   Incredible. One day it's desperation reefs at 0200 in the snow. The next day I'm hanging out towels and wet gloves to dry in the sun. If you want surprises, just go sailing.
      An Argos report puts SHUTEN-DOHJI II at 38°43'S., 56°12'W. with 225 miles to go.

2120.   A dramatic improvement in the weather. Tonight I must look out for the unlighted islets along the NW coast of West Falkland Island.

2255.   Jason West Cay, the westernmost, is 55 miles NE. Since it bears 44°M. and we're steering 15°-20°M., I see no problem as long as the wind cooperates. I got out all the Rio de la Plata charts and decided on the best ones for Punta del Este. Tomorrow I will look at the sailing instructions and work out the details. Today the sailing has been grand. We're gradually pulling away from the cold and troubles of the Southern Ocean to easier seas. Once across 50°S. I will breathe easier.

2350.   Half a tank of water ballast to port. Close-hauled with full sail. Wind gradually backing through north. I'm watching out for Jason West Cay.

MARCH 22, 1991. (FRIDAY). DAY 44.

0012.   An astonishing sight to port. Along the western horizon is a series of about 20 indistinct white lights exactly like the loom of lights from a city or the lights from fishing boats—say a line of trawlers. However I don't think it's either of these, but the setting sun reflected underneath a line of low stratus to the west. The lights could have to do with the aurora australis of the southern hemisphere. I'm going out to look some more.

0027.   Jason West Cay bears 051°M and is 45 miles. Every bit of northing we get increases our safety angle. We changed course to 030° a while ago. How wonderful to have the GPS instead of taking star sights at night.

0042.   I have put the western coordinates of Jason West Cay (50°58'S., 61°28'W.) in the GPS as a waypoint which shows a bearing of 052°M at 42 miles.

0100.   The bright lights to the west are fishing boats after all, strung out from north to south. There are 20–30 vessels, and their lights illuminate the clouds. I climbed up on the main boom, but I cannot see the lights themselves, only a glow above each ship.

I'm extremely nervous tonight. I've just made a cup of tea to try to calm down. The problem in this little game is to get past Jason West Cay with the wind backing. We're sailing as close to the wind as possible, but we're gradually heading toward Jason.

0407.   A busy night. I had up full sail in 19 knots on the wind. Our course was getting poorer because the wind continued to back. Yesterday it went from S-SSW-W-NW- and now it is N., the direction I want to go. I tacked, rolled up the jib, bore off for the fishing fleet, and put in two reefs. I then let out some jib and sailed a little on the starboard tack. The course was poor and would have put me in the fishing fleet. I tacked again to port. Now with two reefs and a small jib I can sail better. I topped up the water ballast tank to port. Pulling down one reef and then a second is a puff and a drag. No wonder I'm hungry.

0435.   No sleep tonight. A good thing I had a nap earlier. Wind now 25 knots from the north. Will I ever get to Uruguay?

0614.   A pity to stop the ship. However we were 20 miles from Jason West Cay, which was becoming a lee shore. On our course of 050° the whole northern shore of the Falklands would have been a lee shore as well. There's no telling how strong this storm will become, so I tacked toward the Argentine mainland, 590 miles to the west. The jib is rolled up, and we're jogging along under the double-reefed mainsail at 2 knots or so. Water ballast to windward. Wind 28–30 knots from the north. What else can I do?

<u>1130.</u>   A frightful gale from the north is screeching outside—37 knots and a bad sea. I've headed more to the west to ease the motion and to keep from breaking things. What a pity to get this gale when I was going so well yesterday. If only the cursed gale was from the south instead of the north. This new delay ruins my hope of reaching Punta del Este in time for the prize-giving and the start for the next leg.

<u>1206.</u>   Wind north 39 knots. Barometer 989 mb. The weather is absolutely shocking, and there's a terrible sea running. I reckon the low is west of us. If it's moving east, the wind will veer from N to NW to W. We did 128 miles between noon positions in the last 24 hours.

<u>1509.</u>   A busy two hours. I put the third reef in the mainsail, but the wind was too strong for me to get the reef cranked down all the way. The vessel was rolling heavily, and the halyard got around the mast steps. After a struggle I got the halyard free, although I had to drop the sail and climb the mast for about 10 feet to reach the halyard.

The north wind has dropped from 46 to 32 knots, but the barometer has plunged to 981 mb. The sea conditions are abysmal, and squalls and sleet continue to blast us. Some difference from yesterday when we had sun, light seas, and a fair wind. I got soaked working at the mast and have just dried myself and put on three fresh thermal underwear tops. A bowl of hot noodles tasted good.

I've seen two fishing boats. We just passed the second which was anchored with a long nylon string on the bank—at a depth of 174 meters.

<u>2009.</u>   A violent snow and sleet squall passed over us, and the wind suddenly jumped to the NW. I shifted the water ballast and tried to tack, but we weren't going fast enough. I wore her around, and we began to sail much better. I let out more jib. The sky began to clear to the NW. Higher clouds—altocumulus, altostratus, and even a few bits of blue and streaks of sun.

I've been worried about the barometer, which is down to 976 mb., but it hasn't moved with the windshift. The sea is extremely rough, and I wonder if the barometer mechanism broke during one of the big bangs when we fell off a wave. Anyway, we're doing 7–8 knots with part of the jib and two reefs in the main. The mainsail isn't set just right, but I am too weary to go forward. I must have made 30 trips to the foredeck in the last 24 hours. I'm sipping some herb tea.

2221.   Now the clouds are at middle heights and of all shapes and sizes. Patches of altostratus mixed with altocumulus. Some are long thin sausages; others are puffs of cotton. I've been watching the setting sun which has filtered underneath the clouds. A few minutes ago all the delicate furrows and rolls were bathed in a yellow light. Then it became a weak pink that gradually reddened and finally turned to a fiery crimson. This was mixed with the bluish-gray of the clouds in the places hidden from the sun. A lovely scene.

MARCH 23, 1991. (SATURDAY). DAY 45.

0212.   More squalls. The new moon was setting when I got up to deal with four or five screamers from the west. I furled the jib entirely, let out the mainsheet, and eased off a bit on the course. We still flew along at 8 knots. The wind remains fresh so I have let her go under the mainsail alone. The barometer is finally rising. The sky is clear, and Orion is a gleaming beacon in the sky off to port. We're at 49°44′S., finally north of 50°S. Hooray!

1317.   Wind WNW 32 knots. Barometer 988 mb. At 1100 I dressed, bore off, and put in the third reef, a configuration that SEBAGO knows well. I also filled the port water ballast tank after heading downwind for a moment to prime the pump. I reckon we will be sailing like this for a while so I reefed the sail carefully and put a tie through the clew, around the boom, and to the outhaul fitting.

Now we're hurrying northward across large rolling seas from the west at 48°S. Where were these winds when I was becalmed at 48°S. in the Pacific? The sea is still extremely rough. I am sitting crosswise at the chart table with both feet propped against the galley counter as we crash along.

The sun is out, the sky is mostly cloudless, and the temperature is definitely warmer. The Falkland gale was particularly nasty, and I'm glad it's behind us. The pointer of the barometer is moving a little, but I still think the instrument is broken. Nevertheless I will write down its readings for a day or two. Some storm to break the barometer! I'm going to move to a lee berth, pad myself with pillows, and try to read. I am on *Wind and Strategy* by Stuart Walker, a meaty, complex volume on weather prediction for dinghy sailors.

1540.   The motion is simply terrible. So much water is flying around that I've closed both storm doors. I began to fear for the rig,

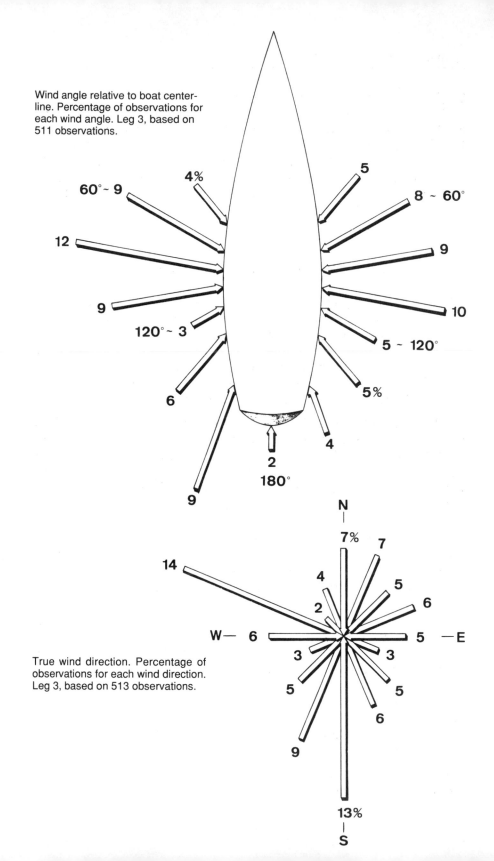

Wind angle relative to boat center-line. Percentage of observations for each wind angle. Leg 3, based on 511 observations.

4%

60° ~ 9

5

8 ~ 60°

12

9

9

10

120° ~ 3

5 ~ 120°

6

5%

4

2

180°

9

True wind direction. Percentage of observations for each wind direction. Leg 3, based on 513 observations.

N

7%

7

14

4

5

2

6

W— 6

5 —E

3

3

5

5

6

9

13%

S

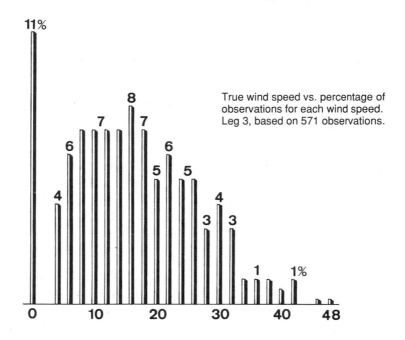

True wind speed vs. percentage of observations for each wind speed. Leg 3, based on 571 observations.

so I rolled up about half of the little part of the jib that was set. The speed dropped at once. Nevertheless we're still doing 7.5 knots in very large westerly seas with white breaking crests. (One just smashed into us with the force of a truck driving into a concrete wall.)

Margaret and I made this same run in 1974 in WHISPER. I have no recollection of the passage except that when we got to the latitude of Mar del Plata, the west wind suddenly stopped. I don't recall the wind being this strong. Maybe it will ease at sunset.

2156. Going well. I've done little except to lounge on the starboard settee berth reading. I am into the 1989 Royal Cruising Club Journal, which is delightful.

2210. Wind WNW 18–19 knots.

2250. Seas less, although a wave goes over the coachroof every 10 minutes or so. Full jib and on course (014°M). The western sky has clouded over with altostratus.

MARCH 24, 1991. (SUNDAY). DAY 46.

0003. Squall or front going through. Rain and lightning. The bottoms of the stratus clouds look all ripped and torn as the wind blasts down. Wind 24–26 knots. I rolled up most of the jib.

0030. An incredible scene in the west. A squall has moved on, and the wind remains WNW. The sky is clear except for a few high clouds. I can see Orion, half a new moon, and a hundred stars. Then just over the horizon are the looms of 20 fishing boats lighting up the sky like a string of luminous pearls.

<u>0511.</u>   The big wind is finished. Three reefs out, water ballast out, full jib. We're headed WNW to keep a thin wind (SSW 8 knots) on the beam. No chance of running with wind this light in the leftover slop from the storm. The barometer continues to rise. The pressure was down to 976 mb., which I have trouble believing. I was all set to take the barometer apart. I figured that the actuating chain had slipped a cog. Who has slipped a cog?

<u>0732.</u>   A busy night. Wind WNW 17 knots. The lights of the fishing boats below the horizon to the west make me think of footlights between an audience and the actors.

The GPS is wonderful. A position on demand, plus distance and bearing to the next waypoint. A navigator's dream. What a safety measure!

<u>1050.</u>   A good sleep. I dreamed that I was flying in a military jet. The usual improbable fantasy. We're sailing well, a steady 8.2 knots. This is the sort of weather that I expected in the South Atlantic. Not 976 mb. gales.

<u>1210.</u>   We did 191 miles at noon.

<u>1418.</u>   I've been trying to contact radio stations CWA and CWF in Uruguay. I have also called WOM, Cape Town Radio, and the hams in South Africa, on St. Helena, and in Uruguay. I wonder if my low batteries are hampering my signals? The voltage seems to be up. I will try tonight when the propagation may be better.

<u>2058.</u>   I finally got through to Newport via Portishead, England, and spoke to Pete Dunning on the race committee. The connection to Portishead was perfect, and the call to the U.S. clicked right through. I have a feeling that the problem in Uruguay is the lack of English-speaking operators.

<u>2122.</u>   Cloudless sky. The sun is just setting. Two fishing trawlers astern.

MARCH 25, 1991. (MONDAY). DAY 47.

<u>0039.</u>   Groggy from a hard sleep. The nightly row of fishing boats is gone.

<u>0215.</u>   Jib in and out for passing squall. The sky to windward looks clear. Bright moonlight.

<u>0532.</u>   Punta del Este is 506 miles on 019°M.

<u>0719.</u>   Quite fresh outside. WNW 17 knots. Going along at 9 knots, but hard pressed. I have been watching the loom of the lights of a fishing boat for over an hour, and we have still not come up on the vessel. The moon set a while ago, and it is very black outside.

I have been reading a gloomy article by Hugo du Plessis about hurricanes and the Caribbean. Du Plessis says: "Too many yachts, not enough protection, and the chances are that you'll be sunk by another yacht (or a mass of interlocked yachts) blown down on you." I'm afraid I agree.

<u>0805.</u>   A steady 8.6 knots with very little jib. We're hard pressed by wind pouring down from a band of thin clouds to windward. We're still not up to the fishing boats. They are beginning to seem like phantoms.

I've been reading more in Stuart Walker's book on weather systems. The author's style is difficult, and I am not very bright regarding theoretical weather discussions.

<u>0901.</u>   Desperately sleepy. Hard to stay awake. How I miss an alarm clock. The loom of fishing boat lights has turned out to be from at least 6 boats, and we have still not worked up to them. I have headed up slightly to leave them all to starboard. The first streaks of dawn are just breaking. I see another thin cloud to windward. Will it be full of wind too?

<u>1215.</u>   Hooray! A run of 237 miles in the right direction. And we finally passed the fishing boats. I had a nap for an hour, which has brought me back to life. I cooked a packet of dehydrated New Zealand green peas for 10 minutes and garnished them with a little butter. Delicious.

The barometer reads 1019 mb., which reflects a climb of 43 points in three days. Wind SW 21 knots. I'm about to pole out the jib to port. I spoke with Punta del Este and passed along our position.

<u>1631.</u>   The wind, surfing, and motion are all a little less. We are 10° shy of our course, but I don't fancy gybing if I can avoid it. I suspect that the wind will ease at sunset (SW 26–30 knots a while ago). I wonder what effect the high barometer will have on the wind. I'm still in a state of shock at the thought of the barometer moving from 976 to 1022 (current reading)—46 points in 3 days. Some pressure changes!

I'm still reading in the Royal Cruising Club book, *Roving Commissions* (1989). Delightful accounts and a high standard of writing.

<u>1957.</u>   Definitely warmer. I spoke with Margaret who is in Uruguay and busy eating steaks. She said that CRÉDIT AGRICOLE hit a big piece of ice in the Southern Ocean.

<u>2228.</u>   Gybing in 30 knots is a business. One pole down, lines away, other pole up, put on four lines, safety tie off, crank away. Haul in the mainsheet while easing one tackle, deal with running backstays, etc. I do it as fast as possible, but the drill takes an hour or so because there are always little problems. Today I noticed that a deck block for a running backstay control line had broken. The cursed little blocks are a nuisance. I fitted a larger block, but it took half an hour.

We've been running well most of the day. The wind has been veering slowly. With the barometer so high I don't know what's going to happen.

<u>2251.</u>   Fishing boat ahead. When I turned on the masthead light I found the voltage regulator switch on and a drain of 2½ amps! The defective regulator requires manual switching off, something else to remember.

<u>2340.</u>   We passed a small southbound coasting vessel (headed to the Falklands?). Excellent white lights fore and aft, plus a bright red light to port. Only two gallons of freshwater left.

MARCH 26, 1991. (TUESDAY). DAY 48.

<u>0243.</u>   It's 312 miles to Punta del Este. I am writing this by flashlight because something has happened to the lighting circuit. The rest of the electrical system is OK. I am making tests with the multimeter.

<u>0346.</u>   Light system working. I traced the problem to loose screws and corrosion in the main panel, which is too close to the companionway and saltwater.

<u>0438.</u>   Nice to have moonlight. I'm sleepy, but I'm up to look around and have a cup of hot chocolate.

<u>0907.</u>   A dumb dream about car salesmen who try to rip you off. How does my mind think of such subjects after 48 days at sea?

I figure we will pass about 25 miles off the Argentine coast. Can I keep her going? The wind is SSE 17 knots.

1204.   A good run of 207 miles at noon. Wind lighter and puffy as I thought it would be near Mar del Plata. Full sail. I tried the fore-and-aft reaching rig, but the puffs didn't last. Back to the starboard running rig. It's easy to do this from the cockpit by easing the pole forward and down and resting it on the pulpit. Then I crank in the opposite sheet. Or the reverse. We had a good run yesterday, but today will be different. No sense putting up a spinnaker because of the swell and the erratic, light wind (SE 10 knots).

1255.   The race has been a little disappointing because I haven't been able to spend any time away from the yacht at the various stops. Instead it's been fix, fix, fix as soon as I get in. And being so far behind has cut me off from radio communication with the other contestants. Part of the interest for me is the contact with the other competitors—knowing their problems, solutions, and observations. This voyage has really been singlehanding.

1706.   We're 35 miles off the Argentine coast. I put up the green spinnaker for an hour, but there wasn't enough wind to get much out of it. We're much better off with a poled-out headsail. It's easier to set and use, there are no terrible spinnaker wraps, and the poled-out sail will look after itself and can be reefed. It's a lot of work to put up a spinnaker, and I always feel smug when I get a spinnaker down in one piece. An asymmetrical spinnaker (without a pole and the wrap problem) is a completely different animal and much simpler to use.

I have taken off my long underwear and am wearing a shirt and trousers. It's warm and pleasant in the sun. No sign of ships or fishing boats. Still 208 miles to go. Many birds. Black-browed albatrosses, soft-plumaged petrels, white-chinned petrels, storm petrels, and I saw a pintado petrel, the first in a long time.

2301.   The ocean is very smooth. We're logging 6.3 knots in a light, unsteady wind.

MARCH 27, 1991. (WEDNESDAY). DAY 49.

0002.   Running rig set up.

0504.   Punta del Este bears 032°M and is 145 miles.

0530.   We're 22 miles off the Argentine coast. The Punta Médanos light (not seen) bears 305°M.

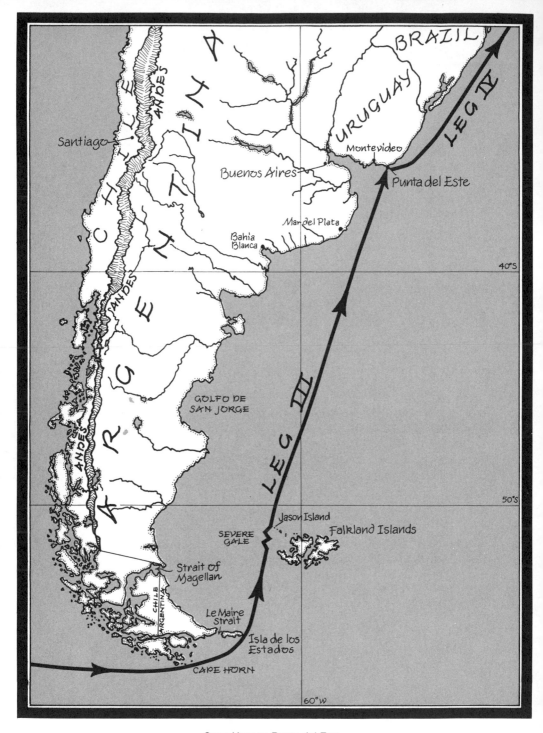

Cape Horn to Punta del Este.

<u>0553.</u>   Fishing boat 3 miles to port. The constellation of Scorpio (Antares) is high overhead to port.

0756.   A long night. I put the starboard pole away and set the genoa on the fore-and-aft rig. Unfortunately the wind fell away to nothing except for occasional puffs from the east. I've been nursing her along, but the progress is pathetic.

1210.   Only 118 miles at noon. Wind almost calm. Two fishing boats off to starboard. Odd-looking steel vessels with high bows, aft wheelhouses, and very rusty. We're in the coffee-colored waters of the Rio de la Plata. Still 120 miles to go, which will take days at this rate. Come on wind. Blow!

1855.   Becalmed since 1300. Barometer 1025 mb. I started on the work list. I removed the Walker log taffrail mount on the port quarter deck (obstructing a running backstay block). I bent on the new mainsail, which took two hours. There were 5 battens, all nicely labeled, but only 4 batten pockets. The material is stiff to handle, especially where there are multiple thicknesses.

2010.   Wind east 5 knots, and we glide along. I'm a little worried about the reefing arrangements for the new mainsail. I've only reeved the first and second pendants. What a pity this sail has been so butchered and cut down in area. And all because of North's stupidity in not following directions.

Just under 100 miles to the target. The weather is quite warm. I'm wearing khaki trousers, ordinary underwear, and an L. L. Bean shirt. The Southern Ocean seems light years away.

2245.   The entire mainsail and the genoa are up, a total of 1,400 sq.ft.—a lot of sail. The sea is perfectly smooth. Almost a full moon. Cirrus streaks up high, and the barometer is dropping slightly.

MARCH 28, 1991. (THURSDAY). DAY 50.

0016.   Much talk on the radio with Punta del Este and Newport. Of course! I'm the only one left sailing. I should get to Punta del Este today.

At the moment I am 81 miles away and heading 037°M. I have eased off a little to keep up speed. The main push is to get close to the target. Then to do a little tacking if necessary. Of course during the long leg the wind may shift favorably. The wind (ENE 6 knots) is up and down, and my speed varies between 4.5–6.5 knots.

I must have a little sleep. Outside the moonlight glistens on a perfectly smooth Rio de la Plata. I saw lots of birds today, particularly soft-plumaged petrels with wonderful shades of brown on their wings (and dim bars of white as well). I must remember to put up the U.S. flag, the Uruguayan courtesy flag, and the racing pennant.

<u>0717.</u>   Becalmed since 0200. Bright moon, low cumulus clouds scattered here and there, and a wind of 1–2 knots from the direction of the target. I have been trying to tack with the genoa, but the exercise is hopeless. I have been sorting out the reefing pendants for the mainsail.

<u>1100.</u>   Five knots of wind from the ENE.

<u>1220.</u>   Only 49 miles in the last 24 hours, with 71 miles to go. A big cargo ship 5 miles astern, probably bound for Buenos Aires.

<u>1609.</u>   Tacking back and forth toward the goal.

<u>2044.</u>   At last some wind, and we're going nicely. The decision is whether to harden up and go more slowly or to ease off a little, romp to the coast, and then tack east to the finish line.

<u>2054.</u>   We're close to Banco Inglés (off to port), a dangerous shoal a little north of the middle of the great estuary of the Rio de

la Plata (which measures 120 miles across at the mouth on a NE-SW line). The water depth is 8½ fathoms at the moment.

<u>2222.</u>   Close-hauled on the starboard tack. Lights on the Uruguayan shore are beginning to appear. I'm excited and trim the sails every five minutes.

MARCH 29, 1991. (FRIDAY). DAY 51.

<u>0242.</u>   Wind NNE 21 knots. Two ships ahead off the starboard bow about four miles away. We tacked to the east at 0215 and are going 8 knots. The lights along the Uruguayan coast are 6–10 miles to the north. Another 5 miles and we'll be on the large scale chart of Punta del Este.

<u>0410.</u>   Passed three anchored big ships, each blazing with lights and topped by a red flashing light.

<u>0715 GMT.</u>   (0315 local time.) Across the finish line. Boats alongside, everybody waving, a gang on board. A big hug and a kiss from Margaret. People pressing flowers into my hands. Powerful flashlights from many directions. Sails down and towline attached after 51 days and 7,603 miles. Some run!

My third rounding of Cape Horn was before a moderate NW wind while I savored the view of the great black promontory at the southern tip of South America.

CHAPTER FIFTEEN

Four Days in Lotus Land

SEBAGO and I finished the long Southern Ocean leg of the race a little after three o'clock in the morning. I reckoned the yacht would be towed into the small harbor at Punta del Este, tied up, and that everyone would go to bed. However I had forgotten that the Argentines and Uruguayans are night people, and that earlier the same evening the prizes for the third leg of the race had been awarded during a gala reception. There was still an air of festivity along the waterfront, and as SEBAGO entered the harbor the public relations people turned on powerful electric lights at the seawall berthing area. Fifty or sixty people applauded as we tied up.

In a few minutes we had SEBAGO's stern tied to a buoy and ran the bow in toward the seawall where we made fast. (The other 17 BOC yachts were tied similarly.) I climbed over the bow pulpit and jumped ashore. A lot of people crowded around. An official presented me with a bottle of champagne, the media people took photographs, and reporters asked a few questions. I could hardly believe all this activity at four o'clock in the morning.

Margaret introduced me to Fernando and Darreline Crispo, the SEBAGO representatives for Uruguay. I had been sailing hard all day and half the night, and I was hungry. Margaret and the Crispos took me to an all-night restaurant. While I ate I listened to the melodious hum of Spanish in the background and answered questions (in English) from Margaret and my new friends. It was nice to be among people.

Margaret was staying at the summer apartment of Mito and Josefine van Peborgh, our sailing friends from Argentina, and I soon fell into a comfortable bed. I slept until late, had a bath, put on clean clothes, and sat down to talk with Mito, Josefine, and Margaret, who spoiled me with a deluxe breakfast and lots of gossipy talk.

Punta del Este is located at the southeast tip of Uruguay and is a summer playground for wealthy Argentines and Brazilians who like the miles of white beaches and the clean air. The sun-drenched resort city is built at the end of a little peninsula which marks the division between the estuary of the Rio de la Plata (to the west) and the Atlantic (to the east). Margaret and I had last been there in 1975 during a sailing trip from Buenos Aires to Ilha de Santa Catarina in Brazil. Now, 16 years later, I saw dozens of new high-rise condominiums and nicely designed modern apartments. It was the end of March, and the high season was about over. The holiday population of 450,000 would shortly fall to 45,000.

Late in the morning Margaret and I walked down to the harbor. SEBAGO was in remarkably good order after her long voyage from Australia. Nevertheless I had the usual list of projects, a few crisis jobs, and had to shop for food since there was almost nothing to eat on board. Peter and Kay Brown, a cruising couple who were sailing around the world on their yacht TOROKINA II volunteered to help us for a few days. Peter began to overhaul the 12 winches, which was a big job. Margaret and Kay Brown did some cleaning and sorting in the cabin. Meanwhile I took a few stitches in several sails and wondered how to deal with SEBAGO's electrical problems. I needed a first-class electrician, but how was I to find such an expert in a foreign resort city that was closing down?

There was a knock on the hull, and Renato Piombi, a keen sailor I'd met in San Francisco many years earlier, climbed on board. I was astonished to learn that he was vacationing nearby.

"Do you need anything?" said Renato.

"Yes, I'm desperate for an electrician. Do you know how to repair voltage regulators?"

"I can fix a house doorbell and change light bulbs, but I stop there. However I know a marvelous unemployed computer expert from Montevideo named Julian who moonlights as a boat electrician. Unfortunately he charges U.S. prices, but he's your man. I will call him."

The rules of the race required a 48-hour layover at each stop. Because of my late start in Sydney, the calms in the Southern Ocean, and the Falkland gale that had delayed me, I was the last to arrive in Uruguay. The BOC fleet was to start the next day, but since the race committee wouldn't waive the 48-hour rule, I would not be allowed to go with the fleet, which was a big disappointment.

A little before noon the next day (March 30th) my crew and I took a long lunch hour. We climbed aboard the race committee launch and chugged out to see the start of the fourth leg of the race. Thousands of people lined the seawall and the beaches or watched from anchored launches and sailboats. The race northward was expected to be in light winds and easy seas, so the BOC captains were relaxed and lighthearted. The day was sunny and warm, a southwest wind barely wrinkled the water, and all 17 yachts had put up enormous light-weather sails.

At the stroke of noon the starting gun boomed from an Uruguayan naval ship. The yachts sailed south from Bahia de Maldonado west of the city, gybed around several wreck buoys off the south point of Punta del Este, and headed northeast into the Atlantic. As the yachts glided past one another there was a lot of friendly shouting between the captains. I saw many beautiful new sails, especially on Isabelle's ECUREUIL, which came very close to our anchored launch. Isabelle had the only two-masted yacht (a yawl) in the race, and her new Kevlar and Dacron sails were a credit to her French sailmaker. I was feeling glum and rather sorry for myself until Isabelle spotted me as she glided past and shouted in her musical voice: "Hurry, Hal, and catch us in a few days!" Isabelle was exuberant and full of life, and her words cheered me a lot.

The leader of the fleet so far was GENERALI CONCORDE. Alain Gautier was 21 hours ahead of second-place GROUPE SCETA, whose Christophe Auguin was wildly keen to overtake GENERALI. Christophe had had an enormous new special mainsail rushed to completion. The sail had six full-length battens and a colossal curved roach that pushed the leech of the sail far aft of the running backstay. GROUPE SCETA's normal sail was 1,450 sq. ft. The new sail was 15 sq. meters larger or 1,615 sq. ft., quite a piece of canvas for one person to fondle and handle and curse in a fresh breeze.

The three fastest 60-foot yachts in the race (the "aircraft carriers") were GROUPE SCETA, GENERALI CONCORDE, and CRÉDIT AGRICOLE IV. Their speed came (1) from their great sail-carrying ability which was possible because of deep draft, heavy ballast, and extreme beam. With a hull width of 18–19 feet, their water ballast was extremely effective. (2) To compliment these special hulls, the yachts had lofty, lightweight rigs (carbon fiber masts and Kevlar sails) with enormous sail plans. The masts were located forward with emphasis on the mainsail and only slightly overlapping headsails. (3) The builders had rigorously cut weight during construction to achieve the light displacements demanded by the architects. Finally (4) each vessel had professional shore-based weather routing.

The other seven 60-footers were sailed with energy and spirit, but were simply outclassed because they were a generation behind in design. In the 50-foot class, SERVANT IV was supreme, and she was often ahead of one or two of the slower 60-footers. SERVANT's design was striking. The French designers had taken daring chances and—except for South African Angelo Lavranos, who had designed ALLIED BANK—clearly outclassed the naval architects from other countries.

As the fleet headed out, BBV EXPO, the Spanish entry, turned and sailed back to the harbor. José Ugarte's mainsail had split near the head. José and his shore crew quickly made repairs, and the brightly-decorated Spanish racer soon started again. As the fleet sailed over the horizon, I felt forlorn and abandoned.

The next day Fernando Crispo drove up in his elegant antique Mercedes. He and Darreline took Margaret and me to the supermarket where we spent half the day buying food. Inflation was a big problem in Uruguay, and although the exchange rate with the U.S. dollar seemed favorable, the food was expensive because of high taxes. Fernando and Darreline were excited to be connected with the race, and Margaret and I had several pleasant meals with this delightful couple.

There had been much publicity about the race in both the local and Buenos Aires newspapers and television stations. Since I was the only sailor left, I was suddenly in the newspapers and involved with talk shows that were broadcast from SEBAGO's cockpit. My Spanish wasn't up to fast interviews, so the programs were conducted in both English and Spanish which seemed a little bizarre.

Early on Monday, Renato arrived with Julian, the electrician, and in a confusion of Spanish, English, and hastily-penciled diagrams I managed to show him what was wrong. Julian had never seen a Quad Cycle voltage regulator, but he understood conventional regulators perfectly, and in a few hours of rewiring and soldering and changing things around he had the alternator charging the batteries at the rate of 105 amps. In addition he replaced a blown transistor in a spare regulator and made improvements in the generator wiring. Except for the Quad Cycle regulator, everything in the electrical system was working.

Peter Brown almost had the winches overhauled, Margaret had painted the stove well in the galley, and Renato appeared with a new boat hook to replace the one lost in the Indian Ocean capsize. I spent a couple of hours up the mast inspecting the rigging and changing lines. Late in the afternoon Fernando took me shopping to replace a few lost tools.

The area around Punta del Este was lovely, and I wished I had had time to see a little of the country. The region had an aura of peacefulness about it, somehow a feeling of unhurriedness and the calmness of an earlier century. But I was caught up in the race. Everything was hurry, hurry, even more so for me because I was so far behind. Sightseeing would have to be another time.

On Tuesday morning I shook hands with a long line of people, and with six others aboard SEBAGO, including two television cameramen, I was towed outside the harbor. As I put up the mainsail, a south wind of 20 knots came up. SEBAGO heeled and began to sail fast. A little water was soon flying around. I was busy reefing the mainsail and running around the decks. My passengers—who had been so anxious to come along for a few minutes—began to look alarmed. Suddenly they wanted to go ashore. These tippy yachts were dangerous! Ocean racing? Go to sea? Never!

I sailed into the lee of Isla Gorriti, transferred my passengers to a launch, and tidied up the main halyard and jib sheets. Television cameras had been set up on the end of the Punta del Este seawall, and I had been asked to sail close for photographs. I flew by hard on the wind, heeled way over. The starting gun boomed, and everybody waved. I was off for the U. S.

CHAPTER SIXTEEN

Calms and Frigate Birds

APRIL 2, 1991. (TUESDAY). DAY 0.

<u>1608.</u>   As soon as SEBAGO and I rounded the two wreck buoys south of Punta del Este I was able to ease the sheets and change to the running rig. We headed out in the Atlantic, and I relaxed a bit. The Uruguayan coast is shoal for miles so I'm heading almost east until I get a little offing. So far each of the three stops has been crowded with work, crisis projects, and non-stop dealing with people. Everyone has been pleasant and helpful, but too much activity has been compressed into too short a time. The stops have been exhausting.

It's much better to be at sea where I can take a deep breath and not worry about giving the right answer to someone. There's a certain tranquillity and a relaxed frame of mind that a sailor gets into on these long trips. Going ashore and then leaving again seems to ruin my sense of peace and mindset. . . . I guess I must sound like a real loner.

<u>1715.</u>   Wind WSW 21 knots. I've been sitting in the cockpit looking at the skyline of Punta del Este. It's a pretty city, especially with the long white Atlantic beaches and the deep blue of the ocean in the foreground.

<u>1937.</u>   Along the Uruguayan coast. Depth 24 meters. Hard to get offshore. Once we get north of Cabo Polonio (30 miles on a bearing of 056°M.) the coast falls off a little to the west.

<u>2102.</u>   A Russian tanker changed course and came close for a cheery wave and a blast of her horn. I spoke with José Ugarte, who is almost becalmed at 30°15'S., 46°54'W.

<u>2327.</u>   We're at Cabo Polonio and should begin to get offshore. The wind is gradually veering, and I think we'll soon need the fore-and-aft rig. The bigger mainsail is certainly more powerful.

APRIL 3, 1991. (WEDNESDAY). DAY 1.

<u>0107.</u>   Low clouds gradually spreading from the south and blocking the moon. My stomach isn't right. It has nothing to do with sailing, but with an overly rich meal two days ago when I got violently ill. My friends in Uruguay seemed insulted if I didn't eat the mountains of food they put in front of me. In addition to my stomach, I smashed my right thumb during all the departure excitement. Grumble, grumble!

<u>0115.</u>   How pleasant to have a fair wind and to sail in balmy climates.

<u>0750.</u>   No wind since 0200. We're becalmed 27 miles offshore. Various ships going north and south. Margaret provisioned the vessel very well including some bottled water which is fortunate because the Uruguayan dock water has an earthy taste and is no good for tea or coffee. When I sleep I get up every 45 minutes to check for ships.

<u>1204.</u>   A little wind from the south. I suspect it will freshen so I have poled out the jib.

<u>1245</u>   "A nice cruise," says Philippe Jeantot. "The sea is calm, the breeze is light, and the moon is full."

<u>1620.</u>   I struggled through the radio transmission of a complicated letter to a French-Canadian schoolgirl who wrote me about ocean pollution.

<u>1900.</u>   Wind SSW 19 knots. We're reaching along in great style on a flat sea (8.8 knots just now). If we can keep going at this speed we should catch some of the fleet, I hope. I see a layer of altocumulus with the sun above. Soft-plumaged petrels, a few white-chinned petrels, and an occasional black-browed albatross that looks lost. I ate some macaroni and cheese, a bland dish that should suit my sore stomach.

<u>2008.</u>   Graham Greene has died in Switzerland at the age of 86. He was one of my favorite authors—gutsy, outspoken, and the hell with the opposition.

<u>2101.</u>   Many fishing boats and big ships. A fishing boat just crossed close in front of us so I am keeping a careful lookout.

<u>2118.</u>   I'm heading roughly NE toward a point in the sea (983 miles on 067°M.) which is 280 miles east of Cabo Frio (a promi-

nent headland 65 miles east of Rio de Janeiro). The advantages of staying offshore are: (1) less adverse current (2) less shipping traffic (3) steadier winds (4) a better line for the Fernando de Noronha waypoint at the bulge of Brazil.

<u>2342.</u>   Overcast with thin clouds. The stars are dim and hard to see. The sea is a little rough. Depth 65 meters.

<u>2346.</u>   Much talk about Graham Greene on the BBC. John Le Carré said that he "enjoyed" Greene's novels. I am not satisfied with "enjoyed." I want to be enlightened, excited, moved, thrilled, horrified, intrigued, insulted, mystified, or fascinated by a novel.

APRIL 4, 1991. (THURSDAY). DAY 2.

<u>0655.</u>   Wind SSW 21 knots. Barometer 1021 mb. A good night at 8 knots running hard with one reef in the big mainsail alone (no headsail poled out opposite). The steering seems no different, and the rig is simpler without a pole and the four control lines. I thought we were working offshore and would soon be seaward of traffic, yet I saw a fishing boat at 0400, and we just passed close to a southbound merchant ship. We're in a south-setting current of about ¼ knot.

<u>0920.</u>   First flying fish on deck. A tiny three-incher.

<u>1240.</u>   A run of 195 miles at noon. I poled out the jib to starboard. There's no doubt that the best running rig is an eased mainsail balanced with a poled-out headsail opposite. I wonder how the big mainsails and small jibs balance on the 60-footers going downwind.

<u>1737.</u>   More wind (SSW 23–25 knots), but we merely go faster (9.3 knots). Can this last? It's gorgeous out with a blue sea and blue sky. Some of the best sailing of the race.

<u>1955.</u>   A steady 9–10 knots and slightly out of control. An occasional large sea—about 25 feet high—rumbles up from the south. I put on a safety harness, went forward, and cranked a second reef in the mainsail. Even so we're still doing 8–9. If we can keep this up for a few days we'll catch the fleet. I had a powerful dinner of steak from Uruguay, a canned salad from England, and a delicious fresh pear from Argentina.

<u>2102.</u>   Every 15 minutes or so we get rolled 40–50° by a big wave. There must be a colossal storm in the south somewhere.

APRIL 5, 1991. (FRIDAY). DAY 3.

<u>0223.</u>   I heaved the six loaves of "long life" bread over the side. The loaves were incredibly dry, hard as concrete, and covered with enough yellow, green, and brown mold to start a penicillin factory. All the competitors bought the bread. I think someone played a vast joke on us.

<u>0831.</u>   First light in the east. Less wind, and the big seas from the south have eased off. During the night I kept getting rolled off the port settee berth and finally crawled into the port pilot berth with the big lee cloth.

<u>1032.</u>   Full main and poled-out jib. The genoa is not furled properly, which is worrisome. We need a longer furling line, and two or three additional turns on the drum. I would replace the line, but I am afraid of dropping the parts of the furling gear overboard.

<u>1040.</u>   While I was in Punta del Este I asked Bertie Reed about picking up John Martin after ALLIED BANK had struck the ice. "Once John was on board, the voyage changed," said Bertie. "When you're alone, you come to terms with the responsibilities of sailing the vessel, changing sails, cooking meals, and looking after yourself. With someone else on board the whole thing is different, and the peace of the voyage is broken. It was necessary to pick up John, of course, but my life only got back to normal after John was taken off by the Chilean navy."

<u>1232.</u>   192 miles at noon. Much talk on the chat hour about the ham radio operators, their compulsion to talk and not to listen, and their non-attention to Minoru on SHUTEN-DOHJI II , whose English demands careful attention. I discovered that everyone has discarded the loaves of "long life" bread.

<u>1400.</u>   Wind SSW 13 knots. I poled out the genoa to starboard and have unrolled the jib to port. Full mainsail. We're flying almost 2,000 sq. ft. of sail.

<u>1744.</u>   After all the terrible weather of the first three legs of the race, I can hardly believe the sunshine, blue sea, blue sky, flying fish, and fair winds. I feel sleepy and very lazy.

<u>2245.</u>   A delicious meal of rice and Uruguayan meatballs with sauce. I discovered a lettuce that had gone off because it was covered by a plastic bag of tomatoes. I must remember to take vegeta-

bles and fruit out of plastic bags and to store foodstuffs so that air can get around them.

2345.   Sailing nicely. I'm a bit nervous with the full mainsail up. However the sea is smooth, and we're reaching along at 8.4 knots with 20 knots of wind from the south. I'm ready to bear off and reef the main any time. The moon is down and the stars seem close: Venus to port and low; the Southern Cross off the starboard beam and high. No sign of shipping.

The Argos positions are incredibly difficult to receive. An Argentine telephone company is transmitting on top of WOM, and the WOM announcers steadily refuse to repeat everything twice. Instead they joke about the race and talk a lot. What I want is information, which means numbers. All else is irrelevant.

APRIL 6, 1991. (SATURDAY). DAY 4.

0631.   Sea calm. Wind dying. A little bit of moon. A very light breeze.

0900.   We're becalmed at 28°S. latitude.

1138.   Still no wind. After reading the instructions for the dead Quad Cycle voltage regulator which controls the alternator output, I inspected each of its 11 wires and 4 fuses. Then I fired up the engine, switched on the regulator, and presto—it worked! Perhaps the wiring changes to the standby regulator in Punta del Este corrected the Quad Cycle as well. Or the warm weather may have dried out a faulty connection somewhere. The waves that came aboard in the Southern Ocean certainly caused a lot of problems. Thank heavens for the Arco solar panels which have been running faultlessly for five years.

1210.   A day's run of 163 miles. The lack of wind is going to ruin our wonderful start.

1300.   It's impossible to receive the WOM Argos reports because the telephone company in Argentina uses the same frequencies, and plays recorded messages over and over.

1330.   A southbound ship two miles ahead crossing our track. I just varnished the trim strip around the cockpit dodger.

1400.   Again we're in the awkward steering zone between the fore-and-aft rig and the running rig. I have unrolled the jib behind the mainsail. I don't want to change course if I can help it. About 500 miles to go to the waypoint east of Cabo Frio.

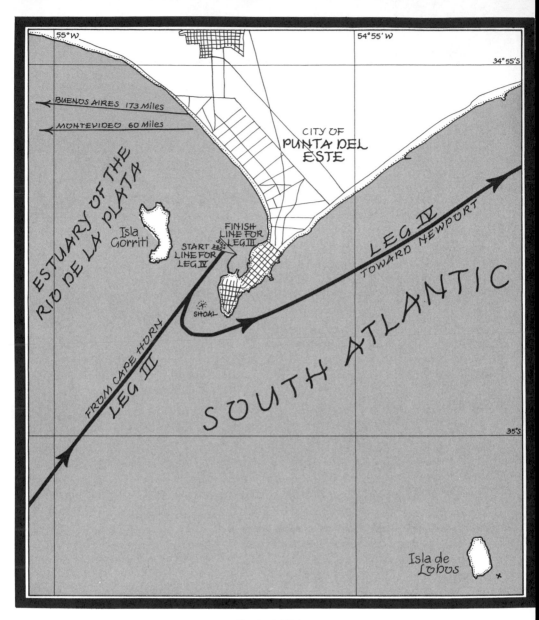

Punta del Este.

1439.   SSW wind 8 knots. We're making about 4 knots. If we could head up we could sail faster, but I must not sail higher than 073°, the course to the waypoint.

I've been sorting out the fruit and vegetable locker. I have a string bag of onions and a string bag of carrots drying in the sun. What I need are several open-mesh cloth bags to hold the fruit up in the air, not jammed together in a closed locker.

1537.   Wind 7–8 knots from the SSW. High cirrus and lower

cumulus. Swell from the SSW, which I hope is the forerunner of more wind. What I desperately need is weather information. If only I knew what the wind is doing 50 or 100 miles to the east. The overhead weather satellites and the ships in that zone know, but I have no way of getting the reports.

2004. The sea is a deep blue, the temperature is mild, and a few cumulus clouds float easily in a calm sky as we glide northward. How pleasant it is to sail between the latitudes of 20°–30°.

2213. The daily runs of the fleet are staggering. I did 163 miles today while GROUPE SCETA logged 249 and GENERALI CONCORDE recorded 244. However it's impossible to push harder because my wind is so light.

APRIL 7, 1991. (SUNDAY). DAY 5.

0206. Wind ESE 6 knots. We're going 5.5 knots. Sea smooth. Although the genoa is pulling nicely, I suspect we'll soon be stopped.

0343. No wind. A weak and waning moon. I've rolled up the genoa to keep it from slatting against the spreaders. The Quad Cycle regulator is controlling the alternator to perfection.

0547. We're going 5.5 knots with a trace of easterly wind.

0656. Wind almost calm. How can I catch the others when I have no weather information? I'm going to try the weatherfax again.

1208. 112 miles at noon. Minoru on SHUTEN-DOHJI II reports severe shoulder pains. His position is 23°22'S., 38°31'W. My wind is light, and to keep SEBAGO going takes real patience.

1313. I tuned in to Norfolk for weather charts, but the daytime radio propagation is poor. I will try tonight. At the moment the wind is 12 knots one minute and 4 knots a minute later. In the last hour I've gone from the cabin to the cockpit a dozen times to adjust the sails.

I got a distinct whiff of tropical land while on deck just now. An overpowering, pungent smell of earth, although I am 200 miles from the closest land. This makes no sense.

1645. Swell from the SE, but the wind is 12 knots from the ENE, the direction we're trying to go. Our course is 030°M. instead of 078°. We're about 50° off course. Cabo Frio is 191 miles on

035°M., so we'll be to leeward of Cabo Frio which is 280 miles west of the waypoint I had hoped to reach. My choice is either to tack and sail ESE on the port tack (away from our target) or to sail NNE toward the Brazilian coast. Come on wind! Shift to the south!

<u>1803.</u>   It's getting warmer all the time. Wind still ENE, but on the starboard tack (we're heading 025°M.) we sail better because the SSE-setting current is not such a problem. The swell from the SE continues. Nothing to do but to press on.

<u>1900.</u>   So far I have tried two small bottles of wine from Uruguay that Fernando Crispo gave me. Tasty and pleasant.

<u>2155.</u>   The Argos reports are disappointing. My last two days have been filled with calms and headwinds while the others have rocketed ahead.

<u>2330.</u>   I've been thinking about the race in general and how unfair it is for the smaller classes. The 27,500-mile sailing requirement, the qualifying voyage, and all the expensive safety and radio equipment for the two smaller classes are identical with the 60-foot class. Yet the prizes are geared to the big class, whose winner receives $100,000, a giant trophy, and 90 percent of the organizational publicity (which the sponsors want). The winner of Class 2 gets $30,000.

In my judgment, there should be a single 50-foot class for the race. Since the cost of a 50-footer is half that of a 60-footer, the financing and sponsorship would be easier. There are plenty of eager sailors; the problem is money.

Nigel Rowe of the BOC Group told me that he would like to have 50 entries in the race. A race with a single, less costly class would be infinitely easier to run and publicize (less confusion; more interest and excitement), and the man in the street could identify more with the race because the size of the vessels would be closer to ordinary racer-cruisers and non-professional, amateur sailing. It's possible to go cruising in a 50-footer with an 8-foot draft. A 60-footer with a 12-foot draft is ridiculous. A Sunday sailor can fathom sailing a 50-footer; a 60-footer with an 80-foot mast blows his mind.

APRIL 8, 1991. (MONDAY). DAY 6.

<u>0137.</u>   Wind 19 knots from the ENE. Second reef in main. A poor night hammering away into a head sea.

<u>0500.</u>   Two small oil tankers close to port.

0605. We're 121 miles from Cabo Frio on a course of 030°. Still bashing away to windward. It looks as if I'm going to finish up in Rio de Janeiro instead of at Cabo Frio.

1118. A wretched night. I grind my teeth when I think of the other BOC sailors rushing north with fair winds. The barometer has climbed a little, and the wind is down slightly. We're sailing away from the center of the low so perhaps our wind and seas will diminish.

A few times during the last 24 hours the wind has veered a little toward the north. I have promptly tacked to make easting, but then I make no northing. This sort of sailing is agony.

1210. A 114 mile-run at noon. Wind NE 18 knots.

1321. We're heading 095°M. or 075°T. Fair weather, and the sky is beautiful. It's quite warm, and butter is now easy to spread.

1538. Cabo Frio bears 015°M. and is 103 miles away.

1612. I have the latest times and frequencies of the Brazilian and Argentine weather stations, but in spite of their claims, they do not transmit weather charts. I can hear the U.S. Coast Guard station in Norfolk, Virginia. However I am out of range for my weatherfax machine to print a legible chart.

1718. Based on the distance to Cabo Frio, I work out that we're sailing at 5.6 knots over the ground. Our boatspeed is 6.4 knots which suggests 0.8 knot of adverse current. (I wish the speed over the ground readout on the GPS was better.) This means 17 hours to reach Cabo Frio or 1000 hours tomorrow. We're sailing as close to the wind as possible, and banging and crashing along.

Outside I see three layers of clouds. High up are cirrocumulus or a mackerel sky, which is lovely and pebbled. Lower down in the middle sky is a gauzelike stratus, a thin wispy veil. Still lower down, cumulus clouds are spotted here and there, several developed vertically into small towers of cumulonimbus. But what do they mean? What wind direction and strength will I have tomorrow? Should I sail east or north to find the best wind? Lots of questions.

1850. The wind and sea are down a little, and I have unwound more of the jib. I am reading *What They Don't Teach You at Harvard Business School* by Mark McCormick. A business executive's game plan for measuring people.

APRIL 9, 1991. (TUESDAY). DAY 7.

<u>0115.</u>   Ship off to port. Wind ENE 17 knots. Course 020°M. Close-hauled on the starboard tack. Cabo Frio is 41 miles and bears NNE.

<u>0204.</u>   I can plainly see the loom of the lights of Rio de Janeiro and Cabo Frio.

<u>0218.</u>   I have the lights of three vessels in sight.

<u>0409.</u>   A flashing 10-second light ahead a little to starboard. The Cabo Frio light, I presume, although my 1962 chart shows a 28-second characteristic.
     This is the fifth time I've sailed past this tropical cape. The first time was with Margaret in WHISPER in 1976 when we stopped at nearby Búzios and went up a little river to the Rio Yacht Club's out-station. We dropped a stern anchor (luckily just right) when we sailed into the dock and made it look so easy. Then twice southward (more offshore) on the way to Cape Town and twice north during the BOC races.

<u>0501.</u>   Wind ENE 14 knots. We need to get more offshore so I've tacked to the ESE. A ship to the south. I'm very sleepy.

<u>1157.</u>   I was on the offshore tack and fast asleep on the starboard settee berth when I heard an engine. I was out in the cockpit in a flash. A small yellow Brazilian fishing boat was about 100 yards away, chugging along while the crew worked on a heavy fishing line and floats. I tacked to the north, and at 7.3 knots we soon sped away. Several miles away was a similar vessel. Both were wooden, with high prows, lots of sheer, and 30 or 35 feet long. At least three crew.

<u>1215.</u>   A run of 102 miles at noon. We're 34 miles ESE of Cabo Frio. After plotting our position on chart 1331, I see that on this course we won't even make Cabo de São Tomé at 22°N.

<u>1231.</u>   An onshore mountain bears 315°M. Is it 2,657-foot São João? I hate being this close to shore. When I tacked at 1100 and went forward to deal with the running backstays, I noticed some crude oil splashed about here and there. I suddenly remembered all the offshore oil wells along this coast. Another hazard.

<u>1408.</u>   Phase One of this passage is over with Cabo Frio. The next point is Fernando de Noronha, the big island east of the bulge of Brazil. I have been sorting over the food and re-arranging the stores. Then I shaved and combed my hair. I feel quite rested.

The harbor of Punta del Este and a line of the 60-foot racing yachts.

1440.   The mountain mentioned above is clearly Cabo Frio.

1613.   Sailing can certainly be hard work. I am trying to go north as fast as possible, but the winds are hopeless. During the last hour I furled the jib (65 cranks) and set the genoa (170 cranks). The genoa did poorly so I furled it (170 cranks) and put out the jib (65 cranks).

1620.   Container ship to starboard. Fishing boat to port. Sea flat. Sailing well, but not fast.

1900.   Wind east 11 knots. We're in 24 fathoms about 18 miles offshore. Ships, fishing boats, oil rigs, tugs pulling barges, shoals— all sorts of hazards. Give me the safety of deep water any time. I hope I am up to this 24 hours a day. I have been eating adequately, but I need a nap. Ahead to seaward are many oil rigs. I'll need to tack near them to round Cabo de São Tomé. The GPS is wonderful for coastal navigation because it tells you exactly where you are.

1924.   Lots of boobies out fishing. Sleek brown heads and yellow bills. Young masked boobies, I think. Lovely clouds again today. All sorts of cirrus (fingerprint, swirls, cirrocumulus) and middle layer (altocumulus). The sky seems high and elevated somehow. We're gliding along the shallow offshore plain. I'm ready to tack and will head offshore as soon as we get to 10 fathoms.

2004.   In 19 fathoms. The water is very green. How fortunate I am to have detailed charts.

<u>2042.</u>   Tacked at 2039. We need to sail 28 miles on this tack to clear the shoals off Cabo de São Tomé. I think it's possible to sneak along the beach in 3½ fathoms and get past the shoal, but not at night, with an old chart, and alone.

<u>2144.</u>   Wind 7 knots from the east. At least five oil platforms are in sight, along with two lighthouses, two ships, and lights along the coast. To work my way NE along this coast is going to take patience.

I am absolutely crushed by the Argos reports. A few days ago I was 381 miles behind SERVANT IV; today I am 713 miles behind. Even with my late start it's discouraging. Here I am bumbling along this coast with its stupid winds, shipping traffic, and oil rigs when I should be 100 miles east and hurrying northward. I started out well, but the past three days have been wretched. However I must keep trying.

<u>2202.</u>   The Cabo de São Tomé light bears 050°. The light should flash every 12 seconds, but blinks erratically every 48 seconds.

APRIL 10, 1991. (WEDNESDAY). DAY 8.

<u>0351.</u>   Becalmed since midnight except for a few puffs from the ENE. Much sail drill, but little movement except for my nerves when an oil service launch motored past, and the captain blinded me with a colossal searchlight while he looked us over.

There are a dozen huge oil rig platforms in a north-south line about 30 miles offshore. On each platform—separated by a mile or two from the next—waste oil and gas are burned off, and the light from the burning gas then flares into the sky with an enormous flickering reddish-yellow light. This ghostly light is reflected from any low clouds, and the general impression is of a fiendish light from the bowels of the earth. Coupled with the eerie light is the smell of burning sulfur and oil. The general effect is truly the scene of hell itself (or what nuclear destruction might be like). All this can be seen 20–30 miles away. I find it unsettling.

The huge oil platforms require fleets of supply and service vessels that shuttle back and forth to the mainland. More urgent business is conducted by helicopters that buzz overhead. All the local fishing boats use the offshore platforms as navigation marks in the sea so there's plenty of traffic.

<u>0533.</u>   Wind ENE 3 knots. Almost stopped. A large southbound ship kept on a collision course with us until the last minute, approaching from our port side. She saw my bright red light on a

constant bearing. I stood in the cockpit ready to ignite a white flare while I wondered if I could swim ashore after the impact. Finally at the last minute the ship turned and gave way. As she passed near, inshore of us, her port bridge deck lights flashed on. A man walked to the searchlight and switched it on to see whom the red light belonged to. Oh! A sailboat! Satisfied, the officer snapped off the searchlight, walked back inside, the bridge deck lights went off, and the ship continued.

0610.   Hardly any steerageway. The oil platforms reek of sulfur. The fires are yellow and brown and red, and cumulous clouds form above them from the heat. Again I think of fire and brimstone and the devil when I look at the whole operation. Can oil be this important?

1000.   My first frigatebird, always the sign of the tropics. A slim black silhouette high against the blue of the sky, circling and gliding without the slightest effort. Long, narrow 8-foot wings and a pencil body with a forked tail. The real singlehander of the sky, eternally alert for a flying fish or ready to steal a meal from a booby.

The only two-masted yacht in the race was *Ecureuil-Poitou-Charentes* sailed by Isabelle Autissier. A slim aluminum hull, a yawl rig, and expert handling combined to give excellent performance even though *Ecureuil* lacked water ballast tanks. Here Isabelle starts north from Punta del Este in light airs.

<u>1216.</u>   Only 59 miles at noon. For the last 8 days our 24-hour average has been 134 miles, my all-time low.

Becalmed 7 hours since midnight. After thinking more about weather information I believe its first function is to keep a vessel out of calms, which absolutely ruin the time of a passage. Today's run is appalling. What can I do? I'm trapped in coastal calms.

<u>1425.</u>   Ships, helicopters, workboats, tugs pulling barges—all sorts of action. A merchant vessel arrived from the north headed SW, presumably for Cabo Frio. I was watching when suddenly the ship did a 180° turn and headed back north. Did someone forget something, or has the captain lost his marbles? In any case the container ship is disappearing northward.

The island of Fernando de Noronha is 1,200 miles north on a course of 047°—say 050° to clear the very dangerous Abrolhos Reef. A course of 055° would be better.

<u>1440.</u>   The circling ship is back again. She's gray with green bottom paint and LINEA MEXICANA on her side in large letters. Now she's headed for Cabo Frio.

<u>1641.</u>   We're 14 miles offshore. Finally a little wind (ESE 9 knots) and we're sailing at 5 knots. Wonderful!

<u>1817.</u>   Again I have put the latitude and longitude of a danger point in the GPS as a waypoint. By referring to the waypoint I know exactly where the danger is and the ship's relation to it.

<u>1824.</u>   Words to a song heard on the radio: "He's a wise man who quits when he's behind." Do I detect a persecution complex? Am I feeling sorry for myself?

<u>1928.</u>   I replaced the port running backstay recovery line. A problem with chafe against the lower block of the four-part vang tackle.

<u>2141.</u>   Wind SE 11 knots. Can this be the trade wind? The night descended half an hour ago, and I can see 8 offshore oil platforms, each with a weird deep-yellow glow. In addition, three merchant vessels and a tug pulling a barge are near us. The sea is flat, and we're going nicely. I'm steering 060° to get clear of the land, especially the Abrolhos.

<u>2220.</u>   Seven ships in sight, all headed in different directions.

<u>2306.</u>   Twelve knots of wind from the ESE. On course and going 7–8. I furled the genoa and set the jib. If only this wind will

last! It's handy to use the big electric lantern to check the sails. The traffic has thinned out because we're headed offshore.

APRIL 11, 1991. (THURSDAY). DAY 9.

<u>0656.</u>   Weather balmy and warm. A nicely curved sliver of moon with a few clouds drifting across it from time to time.

I've been up and down all night long. The wind didn't last, but veered to a little north of east where it is now. The best course I can do is 030° and even that is marginal. I'm so sleepy that I'd gladly welcome a stowaway if he (or she) would take over so that I could stretch out.

<u>0715.</u>   Some heavy dreams. One was about Kanga Birtles and his family who lived in a huge house.

<u>0745.</u>   This course is OK to north of Vitória, but then comes the problem of the Abrolhos. Perhaps by then we'll have a SE wind.

<u>0908.</u>   We're 30 miles offshore. A slight swell from the SE, and a 5-knot headwind. I'm groggy from being up and down all night. Yesterday I thought we had the trade wind and were off on 060°, which would have taken us clear of the coast. Maybe it'll happen today. Without hope, what's left?

<u>1110.</u>   Lots of big ragged-looking cumulus. I think we're going to have rain, which would mean a shower and clean clothes. The mountains around Vitória are ahead to port on the horizon. I'm concerned about the Abrolhos reefs and sufficient offing.

<u>1141.</u>   Headed by a north wind. Tacked and tacked back as the wind shifted under a band of cumulus. There are no clouds over the land or between us and the land. To seaward of us are small fleecy trade wind clouds. I think we're between the trade wind and the heating influence of the land.

<u>1213.</u>   A run of 86 miles at noon. Hand me the crying towel.

<u>1310.</u>   We're 33 miles offshore and becalmed again. Now and then a puff of wind. I've tacked twice since noon. I must remember to wear gloves to save my hands.

<u>1704.</u>   I just woke from a nap and have been sitting in the shade of the mainsail where it's cool. I have the genoa and mainsail carefully adjusted for a light easterly sea breeze. We're doing 6 knots in 7 knots of wind, close-hauled on a course of 042°M. A moment ago we glided past a small, bright yellow fishing boat with blue trim. Cheery waves from two Brazilians on deck.

This sailing is so peaceful. I wonder how many boat owners have ever known anything like this? To go along day after day in an engineless vessel with only the wind for propulsion is a marvel of transport. . . . The genie's magic carpet.

<u>1953.</u>   No big ships since this morning. It's good to be a little offshore and away from traffic.

APRIL 12, 1991. (FRIDAY). DAY 10.

<u>0221.</u>   The wind has veered so I have had to change my course from 060° to 020°, which has ruined my plan to get around the Abrolhos Reef. The wind strength has dropped from 11 knots to 2. We're essentially becalmed.

<u>0254.</u>   Tacked offshore, and we're doing fairly well. Amazing that I can roll up the big genoa, tack, and unroll the sail on the other side. Then deal with the running backstays. All in the dark. Actually, after a while I can see a little, and there's a bit of illumination filtering down from the masthead light. I'm watching a long, low line of cumulus off to the south (now starboard) that I don't like. No ships. One light from a nearby fisherman, but we should soon pass him. Then I can sleep.

My clothes are getting simpler. I'm wearing a T-shirt and some pajama bottoms. Barefoot. I have little appetite, but have been nibbling on crackers and canned luncheon meat. Yesterday my main meal was rice and a hearty soup—the U.K. Heinz products are excellent. The soup was goulash—thick and good. I drink a lot of milk from the special long-life one-liter containers. Funny how I've taken to milk, which I've hated for the last 30 years.

<u>0358.</u>   Going well. One southbound ship ahead two miles off the starboard bow. Sailing with the land and sea breezes is like following a piece of music.

There's a certain beauty and robustness to the sailing life. You accept what you find, and use your little ship as a tool to follow the wind. With patience it's surprising how successful you can become. It's no good fighting the elements. You must accept the winds and the life, and shape your course to use what you find.

<u>0928.</u>   Last night the wind was all over the place. It was tack and tack again. I've been trying to work offshore to get clearer air. My progress during the last five days has been disgraceful. There seems to be a pattern of NE winds in the morning. These breezes gradually back to the ESE or SE during the day. Now I'm north of 20°S., however, and should soon find the SE trades.

This morning we had a heavy rain shower, and I rushed out with a bar of soap. It felt good to wipe off with a towel and to put on clean clothes. Afterward there was a lovely rainbow. Only a partial one, but the colors—especially the greens—were vivid and intense.

<u>1002.</u>   Last night the course ahead looked clear. I was about to take a nap when I saw a tiny white light ahead. A fisherman. I took the greatest care to avoid the light. Isn't it amazing the respect we have for a light at sea? The light represents a person. The light is his spark of life, his spirit, and says "Look out for me. I'm here and doing my work." It may be a modest fishing smack or a giant ship, but the light says: "Please don't run me down."

<u>1109.</u>   The day is beautiful and clear after the rain. A golden sun and a bright blue sea and sky.

<u>1204.</u>   A run of 86 miles at noon. I think I've discovered a leak above the starboard chainplate. The area needs a knee or pair of knees bolted to the chainplate. I'm going to add a fastening.

<u>1341.</u>   I put a ¼″ bolt through the toerail, deck reinforcement, and the flange of the hull. The crack is a symptom of significant loads in the area. I also caulked the inside of the crack, which probably won't do any good. I'm surprised that this crack developed, since the shroud loads should be transmitted to the hull. The general design needs improving in this area, particularly with the loads of water ballast.

The weather is gorgeous, but the wind is trifling. I'm trying to work 90 miles east, to 38° west longitude if possible.

<u>2002.</u>   Amazing! A booby landed on the masthead in spite of the VHF antenna, the wind ribbon, B&G blades and cups, and the big navigation light fixture. Some flying skill. No amount of yelling or jerking the spinnaker halyards had any effect. The bird stayed an hour and then finally left of its own accord. This shows how smooth the sea is.

<u>2221.</u>   Wind ESE 13 knots. I rolled up the genoa and set the jib. I've been sitting in the dark in the cockpit enjoying the sailing. It's so delightful after all the calms.

<u>2301.</u>   I forgot to mention that twice this morning I saw tuna jumping and splashing. It's during calms that you become aware of life in the sea.

The radio says that Georgia has withdrawn from the USSR. I can imagine the ghost of Joseph Stalin writhing in his grave. I

CONTESTANTS (18) AT THE START OF LEG 4

CAPTAIN	COUNTRY	SHIP NAME
CLASS 1 (ten 60-footers)		
David Adams	Australia	*Innkeeper*
Christophe Auguin	France	*Groupe Sceta*
Isabelle Autissier	France	*Ecureuil-Poitou-Charentes*
Kanga Birtles	Australia	*Jarkan*
Nandor Fa	Hungary	*Alba Regia*
Alain Gautier	France	*Generali Concorde*
Philippe Jeantot	France	*Crédit Agricole IV*
Mike Plant	U.S.A.	*Duracell*
Bertie Reed	South Africa	*Grinaker*
José Ugarte	Spain	*BBV Expo '92*
CLASS 2 (five 50-footers)		
Jack Boye	U.S.A.	*Project City Kids*
Yves Dupasquier	France	*Servant IV*
Josh Hall	Great Britain	*Spirit of Ipswich*
Don McIntyre	Australia	*Buttercup* (renamed)
Hal Roth	U.S.A.	*Sebago*
CORINTHIAN CLASS (three entries)		
Robin Davie	Great Britain	*Global Exposure*
Minoru Saito	Japan	*Shuten-dohji II*
Paul Thackaberry	U.S.A.	*Volcano*

wonder about parallels between Kerensky (1917) and Gorbachev (1991)?

A doctor on the BBC spoke about salt in the human diet. By reducing the daily salt intake from 10 grams to 7 grams (which can easily be bettered), one person in five can be saved from stroke and one person in six can be saved from heart attack. The doctor said that you can soon become used to food without any salt at all, and he urged people to skip foods with heavy doses of salt.

APRIL 13, 1991. (SATURDAY). DAY 11.

<u>0235.</u>   Wind veering ESE to ENE. This puts us close to the Abrolhos Reef.

<u>0507.</u>   Wind veering steadily and lessening. Tacked to port and put up the genoa. Hard work. I'm puffing. No ships. To sleep.

<u>0753.</u>   The Abrolhos danger bears 007°. We're on 020°, so should be OK after a 2-hour tack eastward.

<u>1030.</u>   It's easier to furl and unfurl the headsails by hauling on the furling lines by hand than cranking on winches. At least in light airs. The furling line is very hard on the hands, however, so I try to wear gloves. I must watch my footing because if a line suddenly gives way when I'm pulling hard, I'm liable to fall backwards and crack my head on a winch.

<u>1055.</u>   We're 70 miles east of the Brazilian coast while we try to work around the Abrolhos Reef. The reef runs east for 38 miles from a headland that sticks out about 15 miles from the trend of the coastline. A mariner needs at least 53 miles of offing.

<u>1149.</u>   Wind NE 6–8 knots. We're headed north and making about 6 knots. There are two dozen cumulonimbus clouds around us—great soaring vertical cloud developments full of unstable air. We just passed a small fishing boat, 55 miles from shore. A crudely constructed wooden boat, rolling heavily, with a built-up roof to protect the fishermen from the sun.

Calms are more devastating than headwinds. With a headwind you can usually go one way or another and make some mileage. With calms you're dead.

<u>1348.</u>   A 108 mile-run at noon. I climbed to the top of the mast for a look and spotted the Abrolhos Lighthouse ahead to port. A huff and puff to get to the masthead. I can see 5 fishing boats and one merchant ship. We're in 7 fathoms depth.

<u>1513.</u>   I thought I could squeeze past the Abrolhos Reef and Lighthouse, but the cursed wind fell light. Where is the SE trade wind? We'll stay on this course—true east—for a while. Every time I tack in this heat the sweat pours off me.

<u>1909.</u>   A lovely east wind of 10 knots. I immediately tacked to the north. If the shift had come earlier it would have saved hours getting past the reef. My poor hands are like rough sandpaper even though I'm wearing gloves.

2015.   Dinner was a big success. Spaghetti with a sauce made of TVP (textured vegetable protein) with half a beef bouillon cube, a small can of tomato paste, pepper, and one chopped garlic clove. All heated for a few minutes. Delicious.

2056.   A lot of traffic along this coast. We usually have a ship and a fishing boat in sight. At night we certainly need a bright masthead light. Dinner was good tonight; the taste lingers.

2200.   I see the Abrolhos light (white, flashing 6 seconds) behind (at last) on the port quarter. The east wind is cool and steady, and we've been going well for four hours, a record for recent days.

2342.   We're a little overcanvassed, but going well. No clouds in the sky. The Big Dipper is upside down in the northern sky. The Southern Cross is south, Orion is in the west, and Scorpio is east.

APRIL 14, 1991. (SUNDAY). DAY 12.

0440.   Wind ESE 14 knots. I replaced the genoa with the jib. We're going better and not heeling so much.

1019.   A ragtag fishing boat is crossing in front of us. Our best route is 047°M., a straight line from our current position (16°04'S., 38°05'W.) to a point west of the island of Fernando de Noronha. This line goes close to Recife, after which we can sail more to the west, which should give us fair winds.

1210.   146 miles at noon.

1631.   We're north of the cumulonimbus towers that were all around yesterday. The sea is calm and a deep blue. I see low, small cumulus in every direction. The wind has freed a little so I put up a new red, white, and blue asymmetrical spinnaker. However I had trouble keeping the luff straight so I took the sail down after an hour. I think the wind is too light. The big genoa is more efficient and easier to handle.

2045.   I've been sitting on the weather side of the coachroof for the past hour admiring the water, the clouds, and the perfect sailing. The wind is ESE 9 knots, our course is 047°, and we're close-reaching at 7.7 knots, 66° off the wind.

   The mainsail is cut much too full without the long battens and has too much draft from half to three-quarters of the way up. What a pity the battens and batten hardware failed at the start of the race.

It's terrible that I'm so far behind in the race, but I've certainly been trying. I never recovered from the chainplate problems during Leg 1. During Leg 2 we had the jammed rudder, the deck cracks, the return to Cape Town, and the rollover. Then the calms of Legs 3 and 4.

I realize now that (1) high boat speed and (2) professional weather routing from shore are the keys to the race. All the leading Class 1 yachts have private routing, and Isabelle has been passing along her confidential routing advice to SERVANT IV in Class 2.

The yachts without weather routing tend to follow those who are ahead. David Adams on INNKEEPER, for example, told me that he watches the leaders, and when one of them makes a deliberate course change, David also changes his course and tries to cut the corner. As a whole, the fleet is largely directed from land.

The laggards, behind for one reason or another, have none of this expert guidance. The answer, of course, is to ban private weather routing from shore, which can cost from $8,000 to $36,000 for 100 transmissions. Plus a Standard C radio, an expensive computer, semi-custom software, a generator for power, and expensive air time. The bottom line is that the leaders are paying $35,000–$50,000 to have private weather assistance. This is crazy in a supposedly evenhanded sport.*

However that's all behind me now. No more complaints and whining. I must finish as best I can and try to beat some of the yachts to Newport. At least we're moving now. And some of those ahead may get becalmed.

APRIL 15, 1991. (MONDAY). DAY 13.

<u>0203.</u>   Being offshore means less shipping traffic, although I keep the masthead light on. Wind ESE 14 knots. I changed down to the jib and as usual we go faster. I think one reef in the mainsail is about due and might help the shape of the sail. We're 420 miles (on 049°M) from the Recife waypoint.

We're about to link up with our outbound track past Cabo de São Roque which will mean the completion of my third trip around the world.

---

*At a contestants' meeting after the race we asked the organizers to ban private weather routing from shore for two reasons: (1) Outside advice tends to interfere with a singlehander's peace of mind and his control of the enterprise. (2) Races should be between people, not checkbooks. New satellite receivers and other data collection devices can now be carried on board. Software can turn this raw weather data into (a) wind strengths and directions, and (b) assistance to avoid calms and severe storms.

<u>0417.</u>   A plane overhead. From São Paulo or Rio bound for Europe?

<u>0630.</u>   I've been reading under the cockpit shelter where it's cooler.

<u>0902.</u>   A little more wind and sea. One reef. Large cloud banks and giant cumulonimbus. Rain showers and one rainbow. The radio is filled with news of Kurdish refugees in Iran and Turkey.

<u>1011.</u>   A rain shower with a nice half rainbow with bright colors. A trace of a double rainbow.

<u>1209.</u>   A run of 160 miles at noon. I'm repairing burners on the cooking stove.

<u>1413.</u>   A small disturbance passed going westward. Half an hour of rain showers and a gusty north wind from a big cumu-

In the light weather zones of the tropics fierce squalls often threatened to destroy the sails and rig. Because the winds were so fleeting and variable I tried to keep sailing as fast as possible until the last minute. If the wind from a squall was fair we speeded up; if foul it was best to drop a big headsail. I attempted to judge the rotation of the winds and to change course so that I could use the squalls to make as much mileage as possible in the right direction. Sometimes, however, a dozen squalls surrounded the yacht, rain thundered down, and my progress was abysmal.

lonimbus cloud. Now we're back to full sail (wind ESE 8 knots). Stove working OK after switching a few burners. I'm sleepy.

<u>1844.</u> Wind SE 11–12 knots. Full main, full genoa, and water ballast while we close-reach at 8 knots on a smooth sea. Real progress now. If only the fleet weren't so far ahead! Will we be able to catch the yachts stalled in the doldrums?

I continue to read in Stuart Walker's *Wind and Strategy*, but I find the book hard going. Really a physics text on weather.

APRIL 16, 1991. (TUESDAY). DAY 14.

<u>0118.</u> Big black clouds. The trade wind is well into the SE (14 knots) so I rolled up the genoa and set the jib. The system is perfect with the two sails on rollers. I can see the loom of the lights of Aracaju on the Brazilian coast if I am in the cockpit in the dark for a while. We are 62 miles offshore and 250 miles from the waypoint offshore of Recife.

<u>0827.</u> Running a 25-watt bulb in the masthead tricolor light uses a lot of electricity. Plus the autopilot and B&G instruments. Fortunately the big alternator and regulator are working well.

<u>1005.</u> Busy working out courses to the finish line at Newport. Via Bermuda and Block Island. First we must get clear of the bulge of Brazil.

<u>1014.</u> We're 38 miles offshore and sailing at 8.25 knots with the full main and jib. I could put up the genoa, but I don't think it would help because the apparent wind angle is 80°. Once we get to Recife our sailing course will change, and the wind should be freer.

<u>1206.</u> When I checked around this morning I discovered an upper seam gone in the jib. I took down the sail and found the thread had given way, probably rotten. Never mind. That jib has done the work of Hercules since the first day of the race. I stuffed the jib down the forward hatch and put up a yankee from the 1986–87 race, a smaller sail with a high-cut clew. I had to move the sheet block a dozen places aft. A lot of hot work. I must have a little rest and some lunch. Hoisting a sail in the furling gear slot is a business. How did I do it so regularly in the 1986–87 race? I'm wringing wet.

<u>1210.</u> 189 miles at noon.

<u>1639.</u> In setting the genoa after some squalls, I noticed three small rips along the leech. Since the wind was light, I dropped the

sail, patched the rips with Dacron sticky-back tape, and then hoisted the sail. I had the usual hassle running back and forth between the extrusion at the stem, and the halyard winch at the mast. The bottom of the luff tape is worn, and I finally had to hoist the sail with the last of the luff tape outside the slot and put a tie around the extrusion and through a luff grommet near the tack of the sail. Meanwhile some wind had come up, and we were heeled a good deal.

2049.   Monumental rain squalls, one after the other. Wind up to 22 knots briefly, then no wind at all. I soaped up and am wonderfully clean, but one shower is enough. Three ships nearby.

2205.   No wind. Two ships inshore and many lights along the coast. I presume the trade wind will return. It's been a busy day with two sail problems and now all this rain. I got a set of Argos reports from WOM at 2100. It's pathetic how bad some of the operators are. Several seem hardly literate and have trouble reading a single page of names and figures. A sad commentary on American education. I would think that if a professional announcer read the same names night after night he would take the trouble to learn the pronunciation.

2350.   Can you believe a wind from the north? NNE 8 knots. Will it last? I'm drinking a marvelous cup of tea made with some of the rain water I caught. Good water makes a big difference.

APRIL 17, 1991. (WEDNESDAY). DAY 15.

0027.   Becalmed since midnight. The waypoint east of Recife is 88 miles on 052°M.

0503.   We're going 4.8 knots with a trace of the normal trade wind. The lights of Maceió are inshore. I'm just up from a good sleep which I desperately needed. Heavy dreams as usual. Margaret and I got to know Peter Blake and STEINLAGER and looked after the yacht for a few days while the crew went off for a rest. All utter fantasy of course, but dreams are often whimsical.

0557.   Earlier tonight I began to see the white blink of lighthouses from the shore, but I could make no sense of their characteristics. I saw lighthouses everywhere ("This coast must be dangerous."). Little by little I realized the lights were the single lights of fishermen, and that each flashing signal came from a small vessel bobbing up and down in the swells, which would cut off the visibility of a light for a few seconds.

<u>1105.</u>   I got out a bag of fruit from the forward cabin. Unfortunately the bag was plastic and allowed no air circulation, and many pieces of fruit were rotten. Not all, thank heavens. I've had the greatest trouble with this problem during the voyage. My fault entirely.

Yesterday was a mess with rain and upset winds. Today all the big cumulonimbus clouds are gone, and the breeze is steady and pleasant (SE 11 knots). Last night there were ships and fishing boats everywhere. Today no traffic at all.

I'm working hard to keep an offing from the Brazilian coast. We should be free of it in another day or so. The Brazilian charts are marked in degrees and tenths of degrees, which means a calculation to go from tenths of degrees to minutes.

<u>1205.</u>   A run of 135 miles at noon. We're 25 miles offshore. According to the U.S. Pilot chart we should have 0.8 of a knot of current with us.

<u>1703.</u>   Once again there are gigantic cumulonimbus towers around us. When I changed to a more northerly course at 1400 I put up the starboard spinnaker pole and set the genoa on it, but the wind is blocked by enormous clouds to windward.

<u>1746.</u>   The big cumulonimbus finally melted away, and the ESE breeze has come back. One ship to starboard.

<u>1843.</u>   Sail drill all afternoon. Genoa poled out. Genoa in. Reef in main. Reef out. Yankee out. Yankee in. Genoa poled to windward and yankee set to leeward. Both in. And so on. I've cranked the winches till I'm ready to drop.

I've been trying to check over the jib with the seam problem, but the sail—which is as stiff as sheet metal—takes up the entire forward cabin. I can't even find the seam. This job will have to wait. Just now we're going nicely with one reef in the main and the yankee to leeward with a beam wind (100° apparent). I cooked some rice and goulash soup and am about to have it in the shade of the mainsail. Then a nap.

<u>1935.</u>   Isn't reading amazing? Yesterday I read in Walker about cumulonimbus formation and dissolution. Today I watched what I read about yesterday.

<u>2152.</u>   Opposite João Pessoa and 25–30 miles offshore. Course changed to 010°M.

APRIL 18, 1991. (THURSDAY). DAY 16.

<u>0759.</u>   Becalmed from midnight to 0700. Then suddenly a swirling rain and an ESE wind.

<u>1054.</u>   I pulled the torn jib into the cabin and found that a seam about 7 feet long needs two rows of stitches. Also the sun cover and numbers need attention. I estimate 4–6 hours of sewing. I decided not to repair the sail, at least for the moment. I have a spare sail—not quite as good—which should get us to Newport, and I want to use my energy to sail the vessel. I should have had a new row of stitching put down each seam in Sydney, but there was no time. I have stuffed the torn sail back in the forward cabin. The cloth has become very stiff and hard from the sun, and I had to fist the sail and push it with my legs. I hate to think of the sails for a 60-footer.

     The calm last night lasted seven hours. Various clouds and rain showers simply blocked the trade wind. I got up each hour to check things. At 0200 I leaped up when the alarm went off, groped my way to the cockpit, and sat on the cockpit seat in the darkness while I tried to unmuddle my senses. I just couldn't wake up. There was no wind so I stumbled back to my berth and collapsed, still half asleep.

<u>1215.</u>   170 miles at noon. Wind east 10 knots.

<u>1300.</u>   Asymmetrical spinnaker up. A pretty red, white, and blue sail.

<u>1421.</u>   Two ships in sight. The sea is flat and we're going nicely. The sun is like a heat lamp.

<u>1648.</u>   Squally, so I handed the spinnaker. We're 20 miles offshore.

<u>2037.</u>   Wind ESE 11 knots, and aft of the beam a little. I've poled out the genoa to starboard. Very warm at 4°38'S. No signs of ships.

<u>2235.</u>   Going well with the genoa to leeward and eased. Wind a little more east.

APRIL 19, 1991. (FRIDAY). DAY 17.

<u>0813.</u>   The quietest and easiest night of the passage. Not much wind, but it was as steady as a train on a track. I must concentrate on

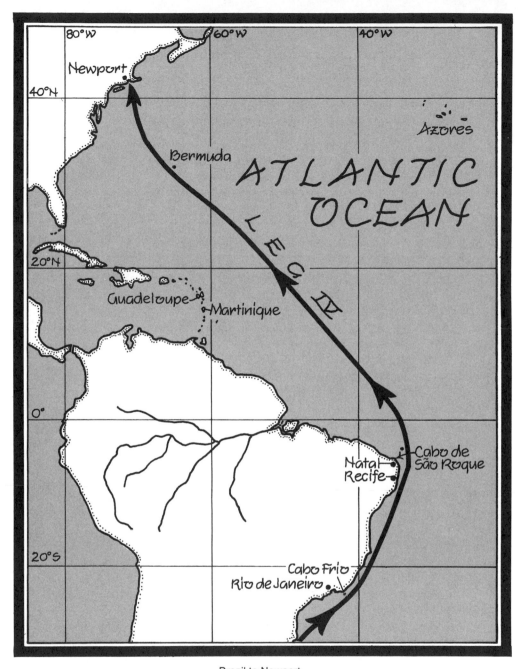

Brazil to Newport.

more sail area and more speed. According to the Argos reports, the first 13 yachts logged more than 200 miles yesterday (one did 306!).

1103.   Green and white spinnaker up. No great speed, but the wind is light. Today I am concentrating on staying out of the sun. I can't wait to cross the Equator which is 180 miles north. I am chasing SHUTEN-DOHJI II (125 miles ahead) and VOLCANO (323 miles ahead). I thought everyone would be stopped in the doldrums, but this gang presses on relentlessly.

1830.   The spinnaker sheet rubs the bottom of the boom as the clew of the spinnaker moves around. I have put a small snatch block on the sheet and snapped the other end around the mainsheet near one of the boom bales. This seems to have tamed the spinnaker sheet for the moment.

2104.   I've been watching the wind from several cumulonimbus clouds. I was all set to furl the spinnaker, but I wanted to hang on as long as possible because we were making good time, often 9 knots for long periods. Finally the wind increased slightly (to 15–16 knots true, say 8 or 9 apparent). As I went forward to pull down the spinnaker sock, the spinnaker blew out and ripped down the length of two sides. I had let the sheet and guy go so I pulled down the sock (empty except for the tapes) and then pulled the wreckage on the foredeck. My lovely green spinnaker! I blame the sailmaker for this because I specified 1½-oz. cloth, but was told I must have ¾-oz. cloth. ("With the reinforced clews, you'll never blow this out.")

2300.   Towering cumulonimbus in the moonlight.

APRIL 20, 1991. (SATURDAY). DAY 18.

0149.   Three large black clouds to windward. On the BBC a jazz orchestra is playing a blues number. I think it should be renamed "Lament for my Green Spinnaker" subtitled "Nothing Left but the Tapes."

0948.   Have we left the SE trades? There's a touch of north in the easterly. We are going smoothly with one reef in the mainsail and the full yankee.

My hands are in poor condition after all the sail drill yesterday. I can hardly open and close my fingers. I must try to minimize rope work today. I am still smarting over the spinnaker blowout yesterday. I will never have a ¾-oz. spinnaker again. The material is too flimsy for seagoing work.

I took a little video footage of some ominous-looking clouds this morning. Certainly the French term for the doldrums—*pot au noir*—is better than the English word.

1501.   Hooray! The GPS reads north latitude; we've crossed the Equator.

CHAPTER SEVENTEEN

The Light-Weather Chase

APRIL 20, 1991. (SATURDAY). DAY 18 (continued)

<u>1701.</u>   Wind ENE 17 knots. Barometer 1012 mb. Northbound ship to port. Sea rougher, and we're on the verge of needing a second reef. Again the automatic variation correction on the GPS doesn't work since we crossed the Equator.

<u>1948.</u>   A squall and rain from a cumulonimbus cloud. I rushed out, had a shower, dried myself, and put on clean clothes. Wonderful! Today has been easy, and I've hardly touched a sail. We're reaching along at 8–9 knots with the single-reefed mainsail, a full yankee, and a steady easterly wind (sometimes with a touch of north). The yacht is closed up to keep out spray, so I often sit in the cockpit under the shelter to protect me from the sun. A few days like this, and we'll be up with the fleet.

APRIL 21, 1991. (SUNDAY). DAY 19.

<u>0126.</u>   Hot and stuffy below with everything closed because of the spray. The rig seems strong and secure except for a little noise from the end of the main boom. The ship's log reads 113.1 at 0130, which gives 8.37 knots.

<u>0824.</u>   Just getting light. We're surrounded by rain showers.

<u>1034.</u>   Little by little the easterly wind is coming back. I had another wash this morning in a rain shower and collected 5 liters of water from the mainsail. With a few changes we could easily fill the water tanks directly from the mainsail. At last we're climbing the parallels of latitude to cooler weather.

<u>1203.</u>   A nice run of 201 miles at noon. We've done 772 miles in four days.

<u>1324.</u>   Wind east 20 knots. Very hard pressed. I found myself watching the starboard chainplates and wondering when (or if) the whole assembly would be ripped out of the yacht, along with the rig. Obviously it was time to put in a second reef. I did, and we're going along only a little slower (8.8 vs. 9.2), but life is more comfortable and safer. Also it's much easier on the autopilot and the captain's nerves. We have 2,841 miles to go to the finish line.

<u>1334.</u>   Up to 9.4 knots.

<u>1702.</u>   Earlier the wind increased to 21 knots. Now it's eased to 13-14, so I shook out the second reef. I'm trying to keep the speed above 8 knots. Quite hot, and the sky is overcast and gray.

<u>1930.</u>   Wind NE 20 knots. Second reef, and 3 rolls in the yankee.

<u>2045.</u>   I've been looking at three layers of clouds: cirrocumulus, altocumulus, and cumulus, one above the other. The layers are separated, and the setting sun has lighted them nicely. Only the lowest cumulus is moving with the brisk wind. The two higher cumulus formations appear stationary. I feel weary and can hardly be troubled to eat. We're over at 20° and going 9.2 knots at the moment.

<u>2200.</u>   A ship nearby with bright white lights topped with a quick flashing red light. A fishing boat? A factory ship?

<u>2243.</u>   Another ship. A big tanker or bulk carrier. Bound SE. The sea is rough, and I must hang on carefully.

<u>2300.</u>   The moon has made a ghostly white ring on a gossamer layer of wispy clouds miles up in the sky.

APRIL 22, 1991. (MONDAY). DAY 20.

<u>0529.</u>   Hard pressed. Another reef? The steps in the reefs in the new mainsail are gigantic. Maybe a few more rolls in the yankee.

<u>0639.</u>   Third reef in the mainsail. It's the first time I've reefed this sail so deeply. Amazingly we're still going 8.5 knots. The sail is a disaster in every way. Without the full-length battens, it has a shape like a paper bag. The spacing of the sail slides is so extreme that the luff between the slides vibrates in the wind and makes a terrible trembling noise. Just now when I reefed the sail I had to climb 12 feet up the mast to push part of the sail from behind a mast step because when I ease the halyard the wide spacing of the slides allows the sail luff to collapse and slip behind the mast steps. All this is enough to make a person weep with frustration.

0913.   We're hurrying along with about ¾ of the yankee and the triple-reefed mainsail, with the wind just forward of the beam. I can't believe we're going 8.45 knots with such little sail area. Water is flying all over the place, the yacht is mostly closed up, and it's warm and stuffy below.

I think we must have a small leak somewhere because we continue to fill half the bilge every day. Can the water be coming from spray that strikes the mast, goes inside the halyard exit slots and rivet holes, and then runs down inside the mast to the bilge?

More incredible dreams. Margaret and I were moving from one house to another. She went ahead on her bicycle. Somehow I got involved with an Italian family who ran a restaurant. There were prominent presidential-level politicians who were involved in a scandalous shakedown. I was taken to the home of the restaurant owner and shown his art collection. Excellent watercolors of his family. I can't forget the painting of his mother (a tough, corpulent, lovable Italian woman with wild black hair). And so on. All so vivid and real.

1010.   I've been studying the North Atlantic Pilot charts for April and May. Fascinating documents with wind roses (in blue), cyclone tracks (in red), current routes (in green) and ship routes (in black).

1100.   Less wind. Full yankee.

1217.   A good run of 217 miles at noon; 989 miles in 5 days.

APRIL 23, 1991. (TUESDAY). DAY 21.

0704.   I'm half hypnotized from all this fast sailing. It goes on day after day. How much longer to Newport and a walk ashore? GROUPE SCETA is supposed to arrive today, and the others will follow quickly. I still have 2,470 miles to go (to the NNW) which will take about two weeks. I predict I'll get in on May 7th.

0940.   The route north from Brazil across the trade winds seems endless. With the yacht shut up, the ventilation below is terrible. A single 12-volt fan would do wonders for the air circulation.

0950.   As the wind varies, I roll and unroll a reef in the yankee. This poor old sail has a lot of miles on it from the 1986–87 race. The upper leech is cupped and has some marginal-looking places, so I've decided to sew up the seam on the jib which is larger and in better condition.

1210.   Another good run—212 miles at noon. Bouncing around a lot. We've sailed 1,201 miles in six days. The three 60-foot French "superyachts" (GENERALI CONCORDE, GROUPE SCETA, and CRÉDIT AGRICOLE) are far ahead of the rest of the fleet and will finish in a day or two.

1519.   Trying to get a call through to Margaret and to Sebago's agency. Apparently no one hears me, although Portishead in England comes through clearly.

2211.   I've been sewing on the jib and worked through the afternoon until it got dark. The problem is getting at the seam. The sail takes up much of the cabin and the damaged seam is hard to align. If I could pin the panels then I could sew from one side. What I've done is to use a set of old needle holes to align the panels as I sew. However in order to use existing holes I have to sew from both sides. I reach through the yet-to-be-sewed seam and push the needle from underneath. The sun cover is another complication. I hope to finish the sail tomorrow.

2357.   The word from BOC headquarters is that GROUPE SCETA finished last night (a new record of 121 days for the four legs). GENERALI CONCORDE is still ahead on an overall basis. If Alain Gautier comes in within 21.5 hours he will win the race.

APRIL 24, 1991. (WEDNESDAY). DAY 22.

0738.   Still pitch black outside. I'm anxious to get on with the sail sewing. It's slow work because I have to pull the needle through with a pair of pliers for each stitch. Don McIntyre on BUTTERCUP said that he's been flying a spinnaker for three days. Don mentioned a lot of shipping.

1203.   A run of 220 miles at noon. 1,421 miles in seven days. Can I keep up this pace? We're at 11°13′N., 47°11′W. or about 765 miles east of the island of Tobago in the southern Caribbean.
    The yacht was a little underpowered with three reefs, so I shook out one reef. Now she's got a bit too much mainsail with two reefs. However we'll try it for a while.

1700.   Wind east 14–16 knots. Shall I shake out the second reef or put up part of the genoa? I still have some hours of sewing on the jib. I've finished one row of stitches, but the overlap is loose and the sun cover is torn.

2025.   I completed the jib repairs and kicked and shoved the sail into the forward cabin.

2205.   More breeze and we're heeled hard to port. Good speed, but we needed another reef. The third reef is too deep, but there's no other choice. Again, as soon as I eased the halyard, some of the sail—because of the extreme spacing of the luff slides—slipped behind several mast steps. I had to climb up half the mast to deal with this, which makes me furious. While I write I see that we're up to 9.47 knots, so the reef hardly slowed us.

APRIL 25, 1991. (THURSDAY). DAY 23.

0555.   Less wind. Two reefs out of the main.

0945.   Tearing along with the full yankee, one reef in the main, and a 16-knot beam wind. We're overloaded, but the speed is good. Meanwhile I'm cooking an omelet with cheese and onions.

1210.   Noon-to-noon, 213 miles.

1303.   A lot of sail up, and we're going fast for a wind just forward of the beam. I had a wash, shave, and put on clean clothes to celebrate crossing the 2,000-miles-still-to-go mark to Newport. The weather is fair and pleasant. When I run out of the east wind—at 23° north?—and have lighter weather I will put up the repaired jib.

1449.   I finally got WOM and a call to Potter Hazelhurst, Sebago's agency, which has made arrangements for me to visit several schools in Maine, and for five Maine teachers to come to Newport in connection with the Student Ocean Challenge program.

1454.   The air is clearer, and the sea seems bluer as we slowly climb northward from the steaming tropics. At the Equator the air was hazy, almost misty.

1701.   The port running backstay recovery line chafed through again. A trifling problem. I replaced the shackle holding the small block (aft of the shrouds) with a longer lashing so the line to the block will be clear of the offending vang tackle block.
     Wind east 14 knots. I now have the full mainsail flying. The next step is to use the genoa. The sea is quite calm, and I've opened the cabin hatch. The cool air below is wonderful. I saw a small grayish-white tern flitting about hunting for small fish. The first bird I've seen in some days.

1800.   Furled the yankee and set the genoa.

2115.   Too much wind for the genoa. I woke up from a nap to find water flying everywhere, and a speed of 9.2 knots. Back to the yankee.

2251.   Success with a spaghetti sauce made of a browned onion (sliced), TVP, tomato paste, a bouillon cube, water, and a garlic clove.

I accidentally punched the wrong button on the B&G computer and erased the daily log reading. Dumb!

APRIL 26, 1991. (FRIDAY). DAY 24.

0013.   I learned that GENERALI CONCORDE finished yesterday, but did not win the race. Alain Gautier split the lower part of his Kevlar mainsail and was forced to sail with two reefs. At the same time he ran into a disastrous calm. His speed fell from 13.5 knots on April 22nd to only 2.3 knots the next day. While Alain cursed the wind gods, his lead ran out, and he finished with a total time of 122½ days, good for second place. ("The truth is that *the race was decided in the last 200 miles,"* he said later. "Christophe took 20 hours; I took 45. It was a big difference.")

Both Christophe and Alain gambled everything to stay in the lead. Christophe said that between Bermuda and Newport the wind increased from 35 to 65 knots at one point, and he had GROUP SCETA's 83-foot mast in the water "for the first time in the race." Handling his enormous 1,615 sq. ft. mainsail must have been awesome. On his part, Alain reported: "I took a maximum of risks and flew a spinnaker in 40 knots of wind," a breeze that he normally would have sailed with deep reefs in the mainsail. Tough competitors!

0046.   Lovely altocumulus of evenly spaced puffs of cloud spread across the sky and backlighted by a waxing moon. It's a big effort to keep the vessel above 8 knots. I have tried again to get Norfolk weather charts. The weatherfax acts as if it is not connected to the antenna. The nights are a little cooler.

0718.   Scorpio high to port in a clear sky. Sea smooth with a swell of 1–2 meters. Less wind. I have set all of the yankee. I notice that BUTTERCUP did 118 miles in the last 24 hours, although Don McIntyre boasted of 12 knots with a spinnaker. Is he playing psychological warfare? Yesterday I spoke with Robin Davie, who was quite upset at the endless prattling of the ham operators involved with the race.

0958.   I finally received a Norfolk weather chart.

<u>1033.</u>   Since I accidentally switched off the ship's log yesterday, I've been wondering how far I've come. I got the idea of putting in yesterday's noon position as a waypoint, and the GPS tells me that we're now 203 miles away! These GPS devices are fantastic and a kind of navigational narcotic.

<u>1210.</u>   A good run, 217 miles at noon. That's 1,851 miles in nine days. Newport is 1,775 miles on 328°T.

<u>1423.</u>   Wind ENE 13 knots. Genoa up in place of the yankee.

<u>1600.</u>   A white-tailed tropicbird is alongside and is screeching like a metal bearing that needs a drop of oil.

<u>1730.</u>   We just passed a big clump of yellow gulf weed, which means we're near the Sargasso Sea and less wind. The yacht CITY KIDS was 858 miles ahead yesterday, although she owes me three days. To beat her will take some luck and cunning. I think I should leave Bermuda to starboard and steer low (south) of Newport because the Gulf Stream will carry me north. The worst case is that I'll be south of my goal which is better than being north. This means 335°M. instead of 340°. Currently a high is NW of us, which means our easterly winds should continue.

<u>2256.</u>   Wind east 11 knots. I changed course 5°, and we lost half a knot. The sail and steering adjustments are demanding. I'm steering 340° on a flat sea, and we're going 8.1 knots. I dumped half the water ballast. The moon is like an overhead street lamp. The Big Dipper is ahead, upside down, and the North Star is clearly visible about 20° above the horizon.

<u>2327.</u>   BUTTERCUP reported a broken genoa headstay tang, which means she can't use her big headsail. Bertie Reed said that his generator has been dumping its cooling water in the after compartment—all over his autopilot components!

APRIL 27, 1991. (SATURDAY). DAY 25.

<u>0710.</u>   Philippe Jeantot arrived in Newport yesterday. He was third, with a time of 129½ days. The Frenchmen have been supreme.

<u>0907.</u>   At dawn I sat in the cockpit drinking a cup of tea and savoring the warm and pleasant sailing. The tropics and the sweltering weather are behind me. Lots of gulf weed now. The easterly trade wind is about finished. My next goal is Bermuda. I would like to bend on the jib, but I need to inspect the repairs and maybe

put in another row of stitches. I must do some filming from the masthead with a spinnaker up when the weather is suitable.

1205.   We scraped through with a 201-mile day (2,052 miles in 10 days), but the wind has gone light. I'm afraid our high-speed run is over. To the west end of Bermuda is 972 miles; then 626 to the finish line in Newport. We've overtaken SHUTEN-DOHJI II so we're no longer in last place.

1326.   I hoisted an asymmetrical spinnaker in place of the genoa. Our speed increased only fractionally, from 5.2 to 5.4 knots although the wind (east 8 knots) is unsteady. The sail is easy enough to handle, but the tack arrangement is unsatisfactory because the tack line rubs on the bow pulpit. I would secure the tack to the pulpit, but I'm not sure how strong it is.

1505.   Reaching spinnaker down; genoa up. I headed up 10° to keep moving better. The wind is light for the running rig. With a conventional spinnaker I risk a wrap around the headstays.

1942.   Wind NE 7 knots. Going along surprisingly well with the full main and genoa. Lots of sail area is fundamental in such light weather. It's amazing that we're moving at all on this placid ocean, but we're logging 6–7 knots. The light genoa is completely satisfactory on the furling gear and is wonderfully easy to use. Much better than an asymmetrical spinnaker, which I think can be dispensed with. (I realize that I wrote the opposite several months ago!) I wonder if the genoa could be made of colored cloth—say 2.2-ounce nylon? I like brightly colored sails.

2148.   Very few birds since Brazil. One noddy, one tern, one tropicbird, and two or three solitary storm petrels.

APRIL 28, 1991. (SUNDAY). DAY 26.

0006.   We're almost to 21°N. latitude, and at night the weather is cool enough so that I need trousers and a jacket. It's absolutely beautiful outside as we glide along slowly with 8 knots of wind from the east. I must use every chance to work westward.

0024.   The wind worked a little aft, and I had the main and genoa trimmed in too tightly. As I eased the sheets I could feel the vessel magically pick up speed on the smooth sea. Maybe half a knot. I must watch the sail adjustments closely in these light airs.

0223.   Changed to the running rig. Wind aft 6–7 knots. We were doing 4.8 knots with the fore-and-aft rig.

<u>1000.</u>   Set the yankee to leeward. Over 2,000 sq. ft. of sail up.

<u>1100.</u>   I'm sanding the teak trim strip on the cockpit dodger.

<u>1208.</u>   Only 128 miles today. The great high speed run is over. However 2,052 miles in 10 days is a good mark. We're 849 miles from Bermuda.

<u>1300.</u>   Wind ENE 6 knots. Fore- and aft-rig again.

<u>1443.</u>   Gliding along on a slightly ruffled sea with the genoa way out. Patches of shimmering gulf weed. I varnished the trim strip on the cockpit dodger.

<u>2013.</u>   Only 26 miles since noon. A very light day with only a trace of wind from the east. The sea is smooth and deep blue. I've been switching back and forth between the fore-and-aft and running rigs.

The gulf weed is so pretty. I'd like to have a film sequence of me pulling some on board with the boathook (medium shots from ahead and aloft); then moving in to inspect the weed for crabs and inch-long fish (shot of man; then close-up of hands and gulf weed; finally extreme close-up of fingers and gulf weed). But filming by oneself with clamped cameras and self-timers is a hard business.

<u>2243.</u>   The leech and foot of the genoa are in poor condition. Brittle and with many short tears. Should the sail have been made of light Dacron instead of the Mylar-Dacron laminate? Early this morning I took a little video footage of the setting moon. Now it's already made a circuit of the earth and is back again. The full moon was a reddish ball as it lifted above the eastern horizon.

If the weather is light tomorrow I must patch the genoa and put up the jib. The reception of weather charts from Norfolk is poor. Tonight I couldn't read them. I must experiment with frequencies.

APRIL 29, 1991. (MONDAY). DAY 27.

<u>0618.</u>   The course to Newport is 341°M. We're steering 330°M., 11° low. I reckon the Gulf Stream will set us north. I will sail west whenever possible. Paul Thackaberry on VOLCANO was outraged at his poor winds and slow going when I spoke with him last night. He was thoroughly fed up.

<u>1057.</u>   I woke from a nap at 0900 to find the water as smooth as glass. The sea was rippled nearby, however, and we soon got a few puffs of wind. Many cumulus clouds around. Very white—

whiter than usual somehow. And a few budding cumulonimbus, my friends from the Brazilian coast.

1205.   A big job to fold the yankee by myself. Sweat is pouring off me. Come on wind! Only 91 miles in the last 24 hours.

1331.   Getting the jib out of the forward cabin was a project. During the repairs the three corners of the sail got twisted and fouled and practically tied in knots. The more I tugged the worse it became. I tried using a winch to pull a halyard tied to one of the corners but had no luck until I got inside the cabin and used my shoulder and fists. I finally heaved the unruly sail on deck and hoisted it.

The jib is a mass of wrinkles which I presume will gradually come out. I got so hot dealing with the sail I thought I would faint. I took off my clothes, hunted up a bucket, and poured seawater over myself. Bucket after bucket. Wonderful! Now I'm in the cabin about to have lunch. Texas chili and white wine.

We had a visit from six white-tailed tropicbirds, the "wide-awakes" of Bermuda. Noisy, squeaky birds with rapid wing flaps, so quick that I always worry that the birds will wear themselves out. The group of six circled around for about 15 minutes. I tried a few shots with the Sony video camera, but unfortunately I was busy bending on the jib at the time and failed to get anything good. Several times the birds fluttered quite close to me.

1713.   I'm exhausted. I've been on deck for hours gybing, fixing things, and running back and forth. I took the mast-end port spinnaker pole fitting to pieces to repair the latch. Then I radioed Nan Lincoln at the newspaper in Bar Harbor, Maine about a Student Ocean Challenge story.

2238.   Becalmed from 1800–2200. Two enormous rain showers several miles to port completely blocked our wind. Now we've got a couple of knots of wind from the NNE. I have a lot of sail up and must watch for squalls.

2322.   David Adams and Mike Plant arrived in Newport. So far, five Class I yachts have crossed the finish line. ALBA REGIA has lost her headstay and is sailing with her mainsail and a staysail and making poor time—only 36 miles yesterday.

APRIL 30, 1991. (TUESDAY). DAY 28.

0140.   A refreshing rain shower. 1,336 miles to Newport.

The outstanding Class 2 yacht was the 50-foot *Servant IV* designed by Jean Beret, which won all four legs of the race. This extremely light vessel (12,125 pounds) together with a simple rig, interior, and deck layout was expertly sailed by Yves Dupasquier.

<u>0904.</u>   Sail drill all night. Abysmal progress. We must slip through this dead area of rain showers, calms, and little wind.

<u>1057.</u>   The barometer has dropped a little (1015 mb.), and a line of rain showers has moved past us to the east. I can see bright purple, green, yellow, and orange bands on a rainbow. A second feeble rainbow parallels the first. Many strato-cumulus clouds. Can a weak front have passed? Will we have a steady west wind?

<u>1149.</u>   Bright and sunny with scattered cumulus clouds. One rain shower ahead but moving eastward. We're finally going well with a lot of sail up.

<u>1222.</u>   Only 68 miles at noon. The course to Newport is 342°M. We're steering 330°M.

<u>1428.</u>   Wind WSW 8–13 knots. Up and down. Filled the port water ballast tank when the wind came up after we crept past two rain showers. If the wind will only last!

<u>1540.</u>   Sails in, sails out, sails in, sails out. I'm dead.

<u>1630.</u>   First ship since Brazil.

<u>1810.</u>   Five more yachts finished the race: Isabelle Autissier on ECUREUIL; José Ugarte on BBV; Kanga Birtles on JARKAN; Bertie Reed on GRINAKER; and Yves Dupasquier on SERVANT IV. Yves did

particularly well, and not only triumphed in Class 2 in a record 141½ days, but won all four legs and frequently was ahead of one or two of the 60-footers.

2109.   We're sailing close-hauled with the full main and jib at 7 knots. I'm feeling a little blue. The long voyage is almost over, and I've done so poorly. Fifth in my class and not even close to the winner. I think I've sailed well, as my 10-day run of 2,045 miles attests. Yet everyone has beaten me. One must accept defeat with grace I suppose, but to lose by so much is humiliating.

I lost a lot of comradeship by not being with the others. I missed both their presence on the radio, and the weather and course information I could have learned. Rigging and weather forecasting problems (the terrible calms!) were my downfall. The yacht sails well, but needs a better captain.

2145.   For dinner I had a pouch meal of Salisbury steak in a nice sauce. I cooked ¼ cup of rice and put the sauce over the rice and the meat. Excellent. While I ate I listened to the reminiscences of violinist Yehudi Menuhin on the BBC. He seemed so happy and satisfied with his life. It was good to hear him.

2210.   Half a dozen squalls to the north. I see a sail ahead a little to port. Three or four miles away. It must be Minoru on SHUTEN-DOHJI II. I've been calling Minoru on two radios, but he must be asleep.

MAY 1, 1991. (WEDNESDAY). DAY 29.

0235.   The wind has veered to the NNE (10 knots). Tacked. Very groggy. I must sleep.

0447.   Wind NNE 16. Less sail. Bright moon on clouds. An upset night. A small flood in the head compartment because I forgot to shut off the freshwater line to the sink.

1033.   Bashing along in bright sunlight and a NE wind. Bermuda is 533 miles to the NNE.

1210.   A run of 169 miles at noon. Wind NE 16 knots.

1630.   A ship ahead to starboard crossed to the west. I took a series of bearings because I thought the vessel might be a factory fishing ship and stopped, but she slowly crossed in front of us and disappeared.

1939.   Wind ENE 12 knots. Debating whether to put up the

genoa. Lots of gulf weed, often in long streaks of yellow up to a quarter of a mile in length. We're at 26°N., the breeze is cooler, and I've put on a sweater.

<u>2341.</u>   A lot of impatience and complaining on the radio from SPIRIT OF IPSWICH and BUTTERCUP about no wind.

MAY 2, 1991. (THURSDAY). DAY 30.

<u>0539.</u>   Wind ENE 2 knots. The sea has even lost its ripples.

<u>0930.</u>   Replaced the forward burner in the Primus stove.

<u>1022.</u>   Becalmed since 0600. Now a few zephyrs from the north. The eastern point of Bermuda is 377 miles on 344°M.

<u>1204.</u>   Only 137 miles at noon. The sea has been calm since midnight. No clouds, and the sky is an umbrella of drab gray-blue, the color of leaves on an old olive tree. The only accents are bunches of bright yellow gulf weed. Occasionally a cat's paw of wind flickers across the water from the N or NE. We're as quiet as a glider in the sky.

<u>1350.</u>   I've just opened my last bottle of Uruguayan wine, which has not traveled well in the tropical heat and motion. Wretched sweet stuff that takes fortitude to drink. Nevertheless, to protect Margaret from this vile liquid I will have to drink it.

<u>1525.</u>   Becalmed again. Absolute silence. The only sound is the occasional growl of the autopilot. I've been sweeping up below and oiling the tools.

<u>2006.</u>   We've logged 15 miles in 8 hours, not all in the right direction.

<u>2146.</u>   Becalmed since 1600. Now 3 knots from the ESE. Absolutely quiet for minutes on end, then a gurgling sound of water along the hull.

I finished Stuart Walker's book *Wind and Strategy.* It's certainly an impressive study of dinghy racing by a real *aficionado.* I'm glad I read it. When I next see a dinghy race I hope the competitors are not as serious as Dr. Walker, who no doubt will be miles ahead of everyone else.

<u>2210.</u>   Earlier I put bedding compound on the SSB aerial and the GPS aerial where they go through the afterdeck. Plus a small patch on the foot of the genoa, which is in poor condition. I must

have run the genoa in and out a dozen times today as the winds rose and fell. The bearings are good, and the sail furls quickly.

2355.   I heard from SPIRIT OF IPSWICH that CITY KIDS had 70 knots of wind in the Gulf Stream and had to run off to the NE. She is having trouble with her headstay again.

MAY 3, 1991. (FRIDAY). DAY 31.

0046.   Newport is 989 miles to the NNW.

0800.   I am watching a ship to port. Yesterday we were becalmed for 9 hours. Earlier this morning we had no wind for 4 hours.

Nandor Fa in ALBA REGIA finished yesterday, so all 10 Class 1 yachts are in. I spoke with Minoru on SHUTEN-DOHJI II, who is always so cheerful and upbeat. Minoru kept asking about VOL- CANO and whether Paul Thackaberry has problems.

0905.   A triangular sail one or two miles to port.

0948.   I have been speaking with JAMBALAYA, a 35-foot French yacht (2 men aboard) sailing from Pointe-à-Pitre, Guadeloupe to the Azores. The crew is discouraged because of calms. I talked with the captain, Yves Jenorin, and gave him his position.

1210.   85 miles in the last 24 hours. West wind 4 knots.

1807.   Swell from the NW.

2300.   Although the wind is trifling and unsteady, we've logged 46.5 miles since noon. The sky is dotted with puffs of small cumulus clouds.

2323.   BUTTERCUP (Don McIntyre) and SPIRIT OF IPSWICH (Josh Hall) arrived in Newport. So far 13 of the 18 yachts have finished.

MAY 4, 1991. (SATURDAY). DAY 32.

0421.   Wind west 12 knots. I set the jib and filled the port water ballast tank. We're logging 8.3 knots. The swell from the NW seems to be gone. We're chasing GLOBAL EXPOSURE, although I think Robin Davie is too far ahead to catch after the disparity in our runs yesterday. (He did 179 on the Argos reports while I showed 117.)

The B&G speedometer stopped working, so I took out the impeller. It was fouled by gulf weed. To remove the impeller it's necessary to unscrew the housing and pull the impeller up and out from its through-hull fitting. Suddenly a 2″ dia. stream of water a foot high bursts into the cabin. You stop the flood by immediately jamming on a special cap. All this is pretty thrilling by yourself far out at sea. I always think of my friend Bob Van Blaricom, who shouts "pandemonium" when he does this little job.

I cleaned the impeller and replaced it. It's mind-boggling to think how many millions of times the impeller must have rotated during two circumnavigations.

<u>1123.</u>   Two hours of sail drill as a weak front passed, going SE. Sails in and out as breakfast started, stopped, re-started, and stopped again. We're now on the starboard tack (course 290°M. wind NNW 11 knots) which is better because the Gulf Stream current is on the lee bow.

<u>1203.</u>   We did 133 miles at noon. SEBAGO is 21 miles south of 30°N. According to the GPS, we're heading due west.

<u>1652.</u>   The mainsail is terrible. All it does is heel the yacht and give minimal drive. The camber in the sail is enormous.

<u>1659.</u>   A southbound bulk carrier. I'm trying to decide which tack is better.

<u>1831.</u>   Wind NNW 16 knots. Tacked to port. Course 025°M. The mainsail looks better reefed. I was ravenous after all the sail changing today. I had a big meal of spaghetti with the extra-good sauce (fortunately made yesterday when the yacht wasn't hopping around).

<u>1907.</u>   After being dead since the Equator, the automatic variation correction device on the GPS has suddenly begun to work. One less calculation to make.

<u>2243.</u>   Bang! Crash! We plow onward against a headwind. A layer of altostratus has cleared somewhat, and beautiful cirrus streamers wave high in the sky. In the west the setting sun is brushing the cloud banks with glimmers of orange and gold and polished brass.

It's wearying to poke along during the last miles. Only 759 miles left.

MAY 5, 1991. (SUNDAY). DAY 33.

<u>0320.</u>   A poor night. The wind veered and kept heading us. When we got to 050°M., I tacked to starboard. We're now sailing

310°, but the north wind is fluky and uncertain. At least the pounding has stopped. We should be heading 347°M. minus say 10° for the Gulf Stream. The nights are cooler, and I'm wearing a jacket. A southbound ship is nearby.

<u>0437.</u>   Much work in the dark. Genoa up and pulling nicely, but the wind hiccuped and went back to the NNW. I tacked and changed the water ballast. Time for a nap.

<u>1004.</u>   Two rips in the foot of the genoa. I rolled it up and set the jib. I'll patch the torn sail during the next calm. On the present course (022°M.) we'll pass well east of Bermuda, which is 68 miles north. We're sailing at 8 knots so we should be abeam of the island this evening.

Jack Boye and CITY KIDS arrived in Newport yesterday. Jack sailed a good race, but was plagued with rigging and mast spreader problems, especially on the second leg. The yacht is one of the fastest in Class 2, but the mast and rigging need improvements.

<u>1210.</u>   A run of 111 miles at noon. I stopped the yacht, unrolled the genoa, dropped it, and patched several long tears in the foot of the sail. As I've said before, it's tedious for one person to hoist a sail on a furling gear because you have to keep running back and forth between the mast winch and the stem to feed the luff tape into a groove on the aluminum extrusions on the headstay. The furling gear needs a feeder device of some kind. I noticed several broken rivets in the furling gear extrusions.

<u>1643.</u>   My wristwatch strap is defective, and my watch keeps falling off. Several times I just saved it from going over the side. The problem is the flimsy little pins with the spring-loaded ends that fit into holes in the watch casing and hold the strap to the watch. This is exactly how I lost the fine Seiko watch that Fos Whitlock gave me before the 1986 race.

<u>2250.</u>   I've been watching a fighter plane from Bermuda making contrails high in the sky. The barometer has been climbing (1023 mb.), not a good sign for wind. I must get clear of Bermuda.

<u>2316.</u>   A lighthouse on Bermuda bears 350°M. and flashes every 10 seconds. Gibbs Hill Light.

MAY 6, 1991. (MONDAY). DAY 34.

<u>0000.</u>   Gibbs Hill Light bears 010°M. It's chilly, and I'm wearing a sweater and my Musto jacket.

0118.   We're going west of Bermuda which is safer because of the reefs to the east. I'm watching Gibbs Hill Light, the GPS, the depth sounder, and all the lights of Bermuda, which are very close. I'd like to telephone Nicky and Bitten Dill whose house lights are twinkling there somewhere, but it's been a long day and I must use all my energy to sail and navigate.

0205.   Wind NNE 10 knots. We're gradually creeping out of soundings. I'm very sleepy.

0500.   Becalmed. The lights of Bermuda astern bear 100°M.

1051.   No wind. We're being slowly set WNW. No sign of the island which is 25 miles east and a little south of us.

1200.   Still no wind. In the last 24 hours we did 96 miles. SEBAGO is surrounded by dozens of small blue floating jellyfish called *velella spirans*. Each is 2–3 inches long and has a tiny sail or float that sticks a little above the surface of the water. The float is inflated by a gas that comes from a special gland. When the wind blows, the *velella* move, apparently without any control. Strange and curious creatures—sort of punctuation marks on the sea—that are low on life's scale.

1431.   Finally 2 knots of wind after nothing for 9 hours. I think I've repaired my watch. I found some needle-like $1/32''$ dia. stainless steel cotter pins, which I have put through the ears of the watch case and the strap ends. They should hold the assembly together. We'll see.

1551.   More genoa repairs while underway with the sail up. I leaned over the side (harness on) and slapped on a couple of sticky-back tape patches. Not neat, but the rips are covered.

1915.   Still more repairs. I dropped the sail halfway so I could haul the foot on deck (with sheet tension) and get at the leech and foot areas that needed patches. In half an hour I had it done and the sail back up.

1925.   A good nap. I must eat something, although I'm not a bit hungry. We've 592 miles to go. An excellent weather map from Halifax shows us in the middle of a 1029 mb. high with a big low coming from the NW.

2055.   I just spoke with Robin Davie on GLOBAL EXPOSURE and Minoru on SHUTEN-DOHJI II. Both reported SE winds, so I have set up my running rig, hoping that my weak ESE wind will strengthen.

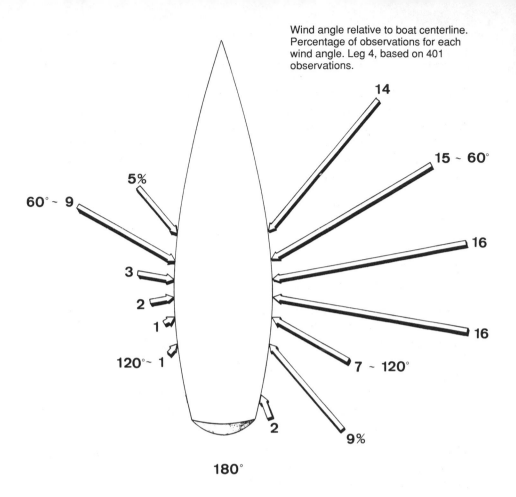

Wind angle relative to boat centerline. Percentage of observations for each wind angle. Leg 4, based on 401 observations.

14

15 ~ 60°

16

16

7 ~ 120°

9%

5%

60° ~ 9

3

2

1

120° ~ 1

2

180°

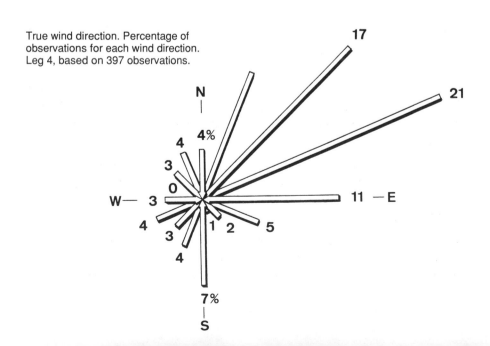

True wind direction. Percentage of observations for each wind direction. Leg 4, based on 397 observations.

17

21

N

4%

4

3

0

W — 3

11 — E

4

3

1   2   5

3

4

7%

S

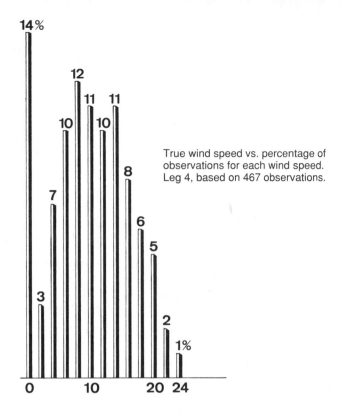

True wind speed vs. percentage of observations for each wind speed. Leg 4, based on 467 observations.

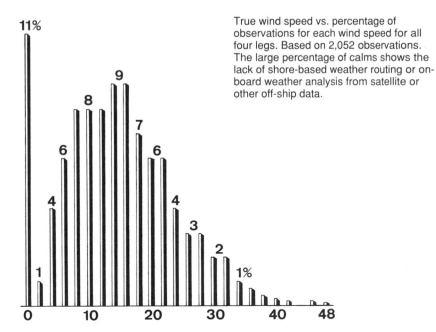

True wind speed vs. percentage of observations for each wind speed for all four legs. Based on 2,052 observations. The large percentage of calms shows the lack of shore-based weather routing or on-board weather analysis from satellite or other off-ship data.

MAY 7, 1991. (TUESDAY). DAY 35.

<u>0444.</u>   Bright loom of a ship to starboard. Probably a cruise ship on the New York-Bermuda run. Wind dead aft, so I changed course a little.

<u>0500.</u>   Northbound ship crossing ahead about 2 miles.

<u>0648.</u>   Gybed the running rig. Amazing that I can do all this in weak moonlight. I guess I know the lines.

<u>1210.</u>   A run of 108 miles at noon. Wind SW 12 knots.

<u>1325.</u>   The insolence of some ham radio operators is incredible. I was speaking with Robin Davie when a ham broke in and began talking to me in fatherly tones. If only these people would say something of merit instead of their endless clichés. Robin reported 30 knots of SW wind. "I'm roaring along like in the Southern Ocean only without reefs," he said. "I can't wait to get in."

<u>1355.</u>   I called Fred Cook at Schaefer with a report on the furling gear systems.

<u>1852.</u>   We're in that awkward range of sailing between the running rig and the fore-and-aft rig. I have the sheets well eased, but we tend to round up, and the autopilot is working hard. If I put the pole up and go to the running rig we'll need to head to starboard about 15 degrees to keep the poled-out headsail full and drawing, and not to backwind it. Normally I'd do this, but because the Gulf Stream is setting us north all this time, I prefer a course shy of the rhumb line.

<u>2030.</u>   Changed to the running rig. We're going 7.6 knots. A beautiful mackerel sky overhead which gives a heightened dimension to the sky. A nice feeling of space.

<u>2155.</u>   Wind SW 19 knots. Boatspeed 8.4 knots. I seem to be in a sort of narcotized fog today. I read a little, sleep a little, write a little, and look at the weather. I can't wait to get to Newport.

<u>2242.</u>   We were a little out of control so I put a reef in the mainsail. Gorgeous clouds in the west. Cirrocumulus, cirrostratus up high, and cumulus and stratus down low. A bit of pink sun winking through. A southbound ship nearby.

MAY 8, 1991. (WEDNESDAY). DAY 36.

<u>0101.</u>   Frustrating trying to get Argos reports. The radio people talk on half a dozen frequencies but seem to guard no single chan-

nel. I'm not sure what the weather will do. We're quite snug with the jib and the reefed mainsail. I put the port spinnaker pole and lines away.

<u>0610.</u>   Wind WSW 18 knots. We're going 8.9. A half tank of water ballast to weather and a reef in the jib did wonders. Just now we're even with Cape Hatteras on the U. S. mainland.

<u>1018.</u>   The front arrived at 0915 with the usual heavy rain and a wind shift from WSW 18 to NNE 24. I put on my oilskins for the first time in months. I tacked and fought the battle of furling the jib, changing the backstays, and switching the water ballast.

I just spoke to Minoru and told him about the weather.

<u>1149.</u>   Banging along. Better to ease off a little, I think. The main thing is that we're going roughly for the target. Lots of gulf weed.

<u>1203.</u>   A run of 167 miles at noon; 338 miles to go. The seas are rough with the NE wind against the Gulf Stream.

<u>1546.</u>   We're going west twice as fast as north. I finished Willard Bascom's book called *Waves and Beaches,* a sort of engineer's guide to the shoreline.

<u>1800.</u>   I've put up more sail because the wind is fluky and full of holes. The sea is choppy, and our course is not perfect. We're headed toward Atlantic City or New York. I'm a nervous wreck tonight. I must try to relax. Maybe it's time for a brandy.

<u>2143.</u>   Frustrating in the Gulf Stream. The wind backed a little so I tacked (runners, water ballast, sheets) only to have the wind revert. So back to the starboard tack. The seas were easier on the other tack, but I was headed for Greenland. I must get across the Gulf Stream and out of this area where the wind seems to pant and there are no birds.

<u>2113.</u>   I reckon I have one percent of the trip still to go (300 miles vs. 30,000).

<u>2301.</u>   Plenty of sail drill today. The sea has either calmed down or we're east of some of the upset waters of the Gulf Stream. Wind dying.

MAY 9, 1991. (THURSDAY). DAY 37.

<u>0147.</u>   A few light airs from the north, the direction we want to

go. I've been tacking back and forth, but we're only going 2-3 knots. Better than nothing.

<u>0619.</u>   A squall from the NNE. I rolled up the jib and put one reef in the main. A ship nearby.

<u>0729.</u>   Dark clouds and a slight wind shift. Tacked to starboard. We were taken aback and turned a complete circle. A nearby ship must have thought us crazy. The wind is unsteady in direction and strength.

<u>1206.</u>   Only 99 miles at noon. A lot of tacking yesterday. Wind NE 9 knots. At the moment we're going well on a flat sea.

<u>1310.</u>   A tremendous splash ¼ of a mile off the port bow. A dark brown whale with a roundish or small dorsal fin. I thought we were on converging courses, but I watched the whale's spout get smaller and smaller as the creature swam off to the west.

I've been putting more sticky-back tape patches on the genoa. I had a pleasant talk with Minoru Saito. Minoru is certainly upbeat. He has a nice infectious laugh and appears to be enjoying the race enormously.

<u>1900.</u>   Becalmed since 1600. Now a trace of wind from the NE.

<u>2025.</u>   We're in the Labrador Current. The water is much colder. I saw two storm petrels, the first birds since Bermuda.

The GPS device died. I got out old faithful, my Plath sextant. It was dirty, so I spent an hour cleaning the metalwork and polishing the brass scale. Then I shot a sun sight, which turned out OK. There's a big index error so I'll adjust the instrument tonight on a bright star if the sky is clear. The sextant and I have been through a lot together, and I have a great affection for this old brass instrument.

MAY 10, 1991. (FRIDAY). DAY 38.

<u>0049.</u>   Much colder. I am thinking of long underwear but resisting. The sea has the smell of life to it, an almost indefinable aroma of vegetation and growth. The slightest whiff of iodine. Yesterday I saw a whale, a few storm petrels, and one small fish which I think is following along under the hull.

Before it got dark I noticed stratus to the E and NE (some edges broken) and altocumulus to the west. We're almost to the latitude of Cape May and Delaware Bay. Our present course will take us to the middle of the south shore of Long Island.

<u>0507.</u>   The heck with being cold. I've put on a longjohn top and the light set of Musto foul-weather clothes.

Light fog or mist, and the wind is dying. Many bird sounds in the distance. Flashes of light in the water from a school of fish. My kingdom for a piece of fresh fish.

<u>1110.</u>   Finally 8 knots of wind from the ENE after being becalmed for 4 hours. Robin Davie on GLOBAL EXPOSURE sailed into Newport yesterday morning, the fifteenth vessel to complete the race. Robin sailed a good race in his 40-footer.

<u>1200.</u>   A run of 82 miles at noon; 159 miles to go. Cool, damp, and chilly. Low, well-formed stratus (some with fascinating swirls). A small tern is flitting about. I just had some hot tea and a bit of chicken and noodles after a nap.

The water is perfectly smooth, and SEBAGO is sailing nicely. The old genoa is pulling remarkably well, considering all the patches. The bottom panel is all distorted, but it seems to make no difference. I got a call through WOO in New Jersey on 8 mega-cycles to the BOC Committee in Newport and told Peter Dunning that I might arrive at 1400 tomorrow.

<u>1347.</u>   No wind. A solitary storm petrel nearby. Pleasant sit-ting in the cockpit writing in my journal. I wish I had a cod jig. Maybe I could catch a fish. No fruit, vegetables, bread, candy, or chocolate left. I'm eating up the cans one after another.

<u>1456.</u>   Two sonic booms from a Concorde. Back to the real world of business and commerce. Finally a little wind from the SSE. We've been becalmed 6 hours today.

<u>1520.</u>   A ship with an enormous white hull stacked high with containers passed going south. A small brown bird that looked suspiciously like a sparrow, whizzed into view, circled nervously, and disappeared.

<u>1621.</u>   White-bellied dolphins for a few minutes, jumping and splashing, and then gone. The new weathermap from Halifax shows us stuck in the NE quadrant of a 1026 mb. high with two 1029 mb. highs heading this way. Reports of heavy rain in Newport.

<u>1640.</u>   Minoru, 94 miles south, reports a NW wind of 13–18 knots. Paul Thackaberry in VOLCANO is back 207 miles.

<u>1750.</u>   I had just poled out the jib, after rolling up the genoa, when I heard thunder and saw lightning and dark clouds ahead. I

threw two reefs in the mainsail as rain came pouring down. I ducked below for oilskins and then tidied up the lines. The front amounted to nothing except for a backing wind.

1837.   Heavy rain. I caught four liters in a jug. I must have a nap. Only 130 miles to go. My next mini-goal is 100 miles.

2149.   Reefs out. A cold NE wind. Sun, some blue sky. Stratus to the NE. A seagull, a sign that we're nearing shore.

2301.   First fishing boat. Low clouds. A bank of stratus covers most of the sky. An orange hue from the obscured sun is filtering under the stratus from the west. The wind is cold. I must get out more warm clothing.

MAY 11, 1991. (SATURDAY). DAY 39.

0020.   Newport is 87 miles on 004°M.

0252.   Dense fog. No wind. No steerageway at all. I've been on deck listening to a ship sounding her foghorn and the heavy rumble of her engine. Louder and louder. Then gradually the sounds went away. Thank heavens.

0312.   Managed to get on course and set the genoa to starboard after a puff of wind, which died. Absolute stillness. Suddenly there was a splash nearby which scared me to death. A porpoise breaking the surface and breathing. Paaaaah! Since there's nothing I can do I'll sleep for an hour. Come on wind!

0400.   Becalmed for the last 2 hours. Now a little wind from the NW. Foggy. Birds squawking in the distance.

0633.   I discovered a chocolate bar and am having an orgy of gluttony.

0657.   Two fishing boats in sight. Sailing nicely at 6.8 knots in just over 5 knots of wind. Faster than the wind. About 60 miles to go.

0716.   One fishing boat has turned into a ship on a converging course.

0736.   The ship changed course.

0743.   Two ships and one fishing boat in sight. Depth 39 fathoms.

0751.   Sea perfectly calm. Genoa pulling nicely. The Big Dipper looks enormous and close off the port bow. The North Star is dead ahead. Scorpio with Antares is off the port quarter. The summer triangle of Deneb, Altair, and Vega is overhead, and Cassiopeia is off the starboard bow.

0800.   The palest orange-yellow sliver of a moon is rising in the east. It reminds me of the cover on my mother's piano sheet music of "Shine On Harvest Moon."

0856.   Just getting light. A dull orange streak in the east.

0944.   Going well. Strapped in, with a full tank of water ballast to port. The genoa is pulling hard with 16.4 knots of apparent wind. The sea is perfectly smooth, and we're on a weather shore. Will the sail blow out?

1210.   A run of 142 miles in the last 24 hours. I advanced my morning sun sight and crossed it with a timed sight at noon. Since I'm headed almost north, all I care about is longitude.

The wind is WNW 10 knots, and we're doing 8.3 knots. Four big party fishing boats in sight. We've had a little shore bird on board for a day or two. The size of a sparrow, very fat, with white and yellow streaks on his (her?) head, and bits of yellow on the body. Cheep-cheep, like a squeaky hinge. The bird is terrified of me and flies from one end of SEBAGO to the other.

1306.   The outline of Block Island is vaguely off to port. The sky is clearing, and the sun is shining on a blue ocean. The low line of the mainland is ahead in the distance.

1400   The wind continues to be light. WNW 6 knots. I've set the red, white, and blue asymmetrical spinnaker, which is pulling nicely. I'm beginning to recognize a few points on shore.

1537.   I crossed the finish line to the whistles and hoots of half a dozen spectator boats and the bang of a cannon. Everybody was waving. Somehow in the sun and on the smooth water it seemed like a Saturday afternoon sail, but it had lasted 30,146 miles and took 211 days. Did I really sail around the world or was it a dream?

It's all over.

*   *   *

I close my eyes and think of all the miles and all the things that happened. I see four images, four memories that I won't forget:

The first was last October in the South Atlantic in the middle of the night. I was running before a NE gale at 10–11 knots (sometimes surfing up to 14 or 15 knots for a few seconds) when the yacht broached violently. The mast was suddenly in the water,

Sebago crosses the finish line.

and all sorts of loose gear were airborne in the cabin. I became a weightless astronaut flying through the cabin. After the yacht righted herself and settled down, I got her going again at speed, and set the autopilot. SEBAGO immediately broached. I did it again and the same thing happened. I finally realized that the autopilot had died. I was already using the spare so I turned to the wind vane self-steering gear. But the bevel gears needed adjusting and I had to climb down on the transom with two wrenches and a flashlight in my mouth. It was a delicate moment . . .

My second recollection is in the Indian Ocean when a line got jammed between the rudder and the hull. After trying every remedy, I stopped the yacht, tied a couple of safety lines around myself, stuck the bread knife between my teeth buccaneer style, and jumped into the ocean. When I hit the 36° (F.) water, the shock was so great that I thought I'd been electrocuted. I'm not a complainer, but I had met my match. Certainly I was going to die. Yet what does one do but carry on? I adjusted my face mask and flippers and dove underneath SEBAGO to deal with the cursed line. I eventually climbed out of the sea, checked the movement of the rudder, and jumped in a second time to be sure that everything was clear.

The second dive was a big mistake, because I didn't realize how much the first dive had tired me. When I finished the second dive I barely had the strength to climb up on the steering vane at the transom. I lost one rubber flipper, but by desperately clawing at the steel pipes I managed to pull myself up on the vane framework. My strength was gone. I was sure I was going to slip back into the icy sea. Then I got my legs working and dragged myself over the stern pulpit to the deck where I lay quietly for a long time, the thought of a hot cup of tea somehow sustaining me. It had been a near thing.

The third incident was in the Indian Ocean on December 5th when I discovered the cracks in the deck around the new chainplates and realized that the mast might come down. Then the teeth-clenching moment when I decided to turn around and return to Cape Town which meant sailing back the 1,200 miles that I'd traveled in the Southern Ocean. Those miles were not nice.

The fourth thing, of course, was the January 11th rollover in the southeast Indian Ocean. My mind is filled with the vision of the blue keel pointing to the sky as I floundered in the water and the yacht lay upside down in the ocean. As I said at the time: "Jesus, what a moment!" Then dear little SEBAGO rolled halfway, her mast appeared, and I scrambled back on board. A minute later she rolled upright while water poured off the mast and headsail, and things crashed below.

Lots of experiences. Lots of drama. Was I lucky to get back? I guess so. Would I do it again? Why of course not. . . .

I finished the race on Friday. During an interview I said that the boat was uncompetitive, she was too small, and I really needed a 60-footer to make a dent in the competition. Besides, I was tired of the sea, and fed up with ocean racing, which was only for idiots and fools.

On Sunday, two days later, I was already planning for the next race and scheming how to raise the money, get the best design, and find a builder who could make something that was both light and strong. I have a few confidential ideas for the rig, and with a little luck I'm sure that the next time . . .

SAILING GLOSSARY

Afterguy. A controlling line that runs from the cockpit through the outboard or forward end of a spinnaker pole to the tack of a spinnaker or the clew of a headsail.

Alto. A prefix applied to a cloud type (stratus, cumulus) when the cloud type appears at middle altitudes.

Apparent wind. The strength and direction of the wind that occurs in a *moving* vessel. Or said another way: the wind you feel on your face when the ship is underway.

Argos, or Argos device. A location-transmitting instrument. In 1991 the usual apparatus carried on board round-the-world racing yachts was an Argos CML 86 location and data collection Platform Transmitter Terminal (PTT), a self-contained, watertight, space-age tracking device powered by a battery and solar cells. Such an instrument measures 16"x16"x6", weighs 17 pounds, and is mounted on deck or on the coachroof. The transmitter is put on board each yacht in a race and sends its position to shore stations at least six times a day via satellite. These positions are then given to the press, public, and contestants. The device also transmits barometric pressure and temperature from the yacht. In case of emergency, a switch can be thrown which sends a special signal. The daily Argos positions are important so each contestant can see how he's doing, and in planning tactical moves in relation to the other competitors.

Baby stay. A fore-and-aft piece of standing rigging that's connected to the foredeck between the base of the mast and the forestay, and typically about halfway up the front of the mast. The baby stay replaces the forward lower shrouds and works in connection with the two after lower shrouds to hold the bottom half (or third) of the mast securely in the grip of three wires spread at the deck in tripod fashion.

Back - veer. Meteorological terms used to describe the direction of wind shifts. In the northern hemisphere a veering wind moves clockwise when viewed from above. A backing wind moves counter-clockwise. Hence a veering west wind in New York moves northwest and then north. *In the southern hemisphere these terms are reversed.* For example, a veering west wind in Australia moves from west to southwest and then south. Expert sailors are fussy about how these terms are used.

Backstay. The piece of wire or rod standing rigging that runs from the top of the mast to the stern of the yacht and keeps the top of the mast from going forward.

Battens. Pieces of thin flexible wood, plastic, metal, or some combination that are inserted in a sailcloth pocket in a fore-and-aft direction in the leech of a sail to control the curvature (or sag) of the cloth. Around-the-buoys yachts typically have four battens spaced roughly equidistant along the trailing edge of a sail. Sometimes full-length battens support the cloth the entire distance from the leech to the luff of a sail. Battens often cause chafe of the sail, and batten pockets are usually heavily reinforced.

Brookes & Gatehouse, or B&G. A well-known English company that makes electronic instruments.

Chainplates. Superstrong metal or composite fabrications that are built into the hull-deck joint area (or a little inboard) to take the pull of the shrouds, which support the mast laterally.

Cirrus. Delicate, feathery, brush-like, high-altitude ice clouds (typically up six miles) that are fibrous, thin, and silky. The fallout from a cirrus head is a long streamer of ice crystals called a *fallstreak*. Cirrus clouds are often known as mares' tails.

Clew. The lower aftermost corner of a triangular or quadrilateral sail to which the controlling line (the sheet) is attached.

Cringle. A circular worked eye in a sail, often put through many thicknesses of material. A cringle is heavily stitched and is covered with a stamped-in grommet so that the reinforced eye can take a significant load at one of the corners of a sail or at a reef point along the luff or the leech.

Cumulus. Puffy, dome-shaped clouds occurring at middle altitudes. A heaped cloud.

Cumulonimbus. A towering, vertically developed cumulus, sometimes 1000 meters in height. Often called a thunderhead for good reason.

Cunningham. A stout cringle a foot or two above the tack of a sail and used to adjust the luff tension without stretching the entire luff which would make the sail exceed its measurement limits. Named for Briggs Cunningham.

Cutter. A single-masted vessel whose mast is located about 40 percent of the overall length behind the stem. The headsail area of a cutter is generally broken up into a staysail and a jib or a yankee.

Dacron. A proprietary polyester fiber introduced by Dupont in 1950 and widely used for sailcloth and cordage. Extremely tough and durable.

Foot (of a sail). The bottom (base) of a triangular or quadrilateral sail.

Foreguy. A line that runs from the cockpit to the foredeck and then up to the outer end of a spinnaker pole to help control the pole.

Forestay. A piece of standing rigging whose bottom end is secured to a point on deck generally half or more of the distance between the mast and the stem and whose top is fastened to the front of the mast at about three-quarters of its height. The luff of the fore-staysail is attached to this stay. The forestay is often called the midstay, which is a more descriptive term.

Gooseneck. A double pivoting metal connection between a boom (horizontal) and the mast (vertical). The gooseneck must be strong enough to withstand accidental gybes, the strains on the boom when the end of the boom drags in the water, and the loads imposed by a boom vang.

Grommet. A stout brass or stainless steel ring punched or sewn into a sail at one of its corners or in reefing rows at the luff or leech. A grommet generally is the finishing part of a cringle. There are also lightweight brass grommets that are punched into the corners and edges of canvas covers, bags, dodgers, and awnings to take tie-down and control lines.

Gybe. One of the two basic sailing maneuvers to bring the wind on the opposite side of the vessel (compare with tack). To gybe is to turn a sailing vessel so the wind passes across and *behind* the sail. Gybing a large sail in a strong wind must be done carefully to prevent damage to the sail, rigging, and mast. Generally the mainsheet is pulled in gradually until the mainboom is amidships, then the course is changed so that the wind comes from the other side of the sail when the mainsheet can be quickly eased on the new tack. It's also possible to gybe spinnakers and headsails, but since spinnaker poles are involved, the action is complicated (see entry under **sock**).

Halyard. A line or flexible wire attached to the head of a sail and led through a block or sheave up on a mast and then to the deck, so the sail can be hoisted or let down.

Heave-to. By adjusting the sails to give little or no forward drive and balancing this with opposite rudder, most of the forward motion of a sailing vessel can be stopped. This is often done in a heavy storm when a yacht is straining in big or dangerous seas, or for stopping to make repairs. Usually a headsail is backed in connection with a deeply reefed mainsail and opposite rudder. Modern racing yachts with narrow fin keels and spade rudders heave–to poorly and often continue to make 3-4 knots no matter what you do. Sailing vessels with long keels heave–to much better and can be very comfortable even in a heavy gale.

Headsail. The term given to all sails used forward of the mast.

Impeller. A small paddlewheel that sticks down into the water from the hull. Waterflow turns the paddlewheel, which sends electric impulses that are measured by a boatspeed instrument.

Ketch. A two-masted sailing vessel whose shorter aftermost mast is located forward of the rudder post.

Kevlar. A proprietary aramid fiber developed by Dupont in 1976 and used in sailmaking or line construction. The fiber is incredibly strong in tension but tends to be brittle in other directions. Because the fiber is so strong, lighter weight sailcloth can be used. Sailmakers are gaining experience with this specialized fiber and its use is increasing.

Lee cloth. A strong cloth, often about two feet high and four feet long, laced vertically to the inboard face of a bunk or berth to keep the occupant from falling out when the vessel is heeled. Sometimes this is made of wood (less comfortable) and called a leeboard.

Lee, leeward. Away from the wind.

Lee shore. A term used to describe land in relation to a vessel and the wind. When the wind is blowing from the vessel *toward* the shore, the land is called a lee shore. In a severe storm, this is a sailor's worst nightmare, and he always tries to keep an offing from a weather shore in case the wind changes.

Leech. The aftermost side of a triangular or four-sided sail, the part toward the stern of the vessel.

Luff. (noun). The forward, usually vertical or almost vertical edge of a sail. The part toward the stem of a vessel. When used as a verb, luff means to head into the wind so the sail shakes and is less efficient.

Mainsheet. The line that runs from the cockpit to the back lower corner of the mainsail (the clew) to control the mainsail. This is usually—not always—done via a multiple block attached to the main boom. Since the mainsail is large, this line often comes from a four- or six-part tackle (sometimes taken to a winch) so the person pulling or hauling on the mainsheet has increased power.

Mizzen. The small aftermost mast

on a ketch or yawl or the sail flown on this mast.

Navtec. A U.S. company that makes many special rigging parts and hydraulic controls.

Noddy. A dark brown or black pelagic tern of the tropical regions, often found far out at sea in dense flocks. The name comes from the birds' habit of bowing and nodding during courtship.

Offing. The distance a ship is away from an object, generally the land. Sometimes used to describe the distance a vessel is away or off a lee shore.

Padeye. A strong stainless steel or bronze fitting (usually through-bolted to the deck or coachroof) with an upstanding half loop to take a block.

Pennant. A long, narrow, often triangular small *flag* used for signaling or identification. Sometimes incorrectly used for pendant.

Pendant. A short length of wire added to the foot or head of a sail to position the sail vertically for various purposes. Also applied to a reefing line threaded through reefing cringles to pull down a reef in a mainsail or other sail. Not to be confused with pennant.

Pitch, pitching. The up and down movement of the bow and stern of a vessel pivoting about her athwartships axis.

Poled out. Description of a headsail held out with a spinnaker pole for downwind running.

Portlights. The ports or windows along the sides of the coachroof that let light and air (and water if left open at the wrong time) into the cabin. The term is generally preferred to ports or portholes, which are considered lubberly.

Preventer. A line from the end of the main boom forward to the stem to help control the boom,

particularly when running downwind to prevent an accidental gybe. Used in conjunction with a topping lift and mainsheet to hold the boom tightly.

Pulpit. A strong metal fence built above the deck at the bow and stern. The pulpits are connected to the deck stanchions with flexible cable to make up the lifeline structure. Generally a pulpit is two feet high (or a little more) and is welded together from 1″ dia. stainless steel tubing or pipe.

Reeve. A verb meaning to thread a line through various blocks, fairleads, or whatever.

Rod rigging. See **standing rigging.**

Roll, rolling. The rhythmical side-to-side motion of a vessel at sea pivoting back and forth on the longitudinal axis. Rolling is often prevalent downwind, and can be particularly violent if the mainsail has been lowered. Compare with **pitch** and **yaw**.

Running backstay. Either one of two major supports (one to port; one to starboard) between the afterdeck and the mast to keep the mast from moving forward. Often running backstays have two or three parts to give support to different areas of a mast. The bottom part of a running backstay generally meets the deck forward of the end of the boom which means that one backstay must be slacked and eased so the boom can swing across when tacking or gybing. Meanwhile the other backstay is tightened to give support to the mast.

Running by the lee. The dangerous moment when the wind gets behind or is about to get behind a sail and cause it to gybe accidentally.

Running rigging. All movable parts of the rigging such as halyards, sheets, guys, lifts, downhauls, pendants, and ties, which are made of flexible line or cable. Distinguished from **standing rigging** which is generally stiffer and more permanently fixed. Running rigging controls the sails.

Schooner. A two-masted sailing vessel whose taller rear mast (the mainmast) is aft of the shorter forward mast (the foremast).

Self-tailer. A patented labor-saving device on top of a winch which holds and automatically keeps tension on a line as it peels off the winch. With a self-tailer you don't have to hold the line with one hand while you crank with the other, and you can use two hands to turn the winch crank. Self-tailers are extremely helpful on shorthanded sailing vessels.

Sheave. A roller or wheel with a grooved rim over which a line runs to change its direction of pull. Pronounced *shiv*.

Sheets. The control lines that run from the cockpit to the back lower corner (the clew) of the jib to control the sail. There are usually two sheets, one to port and one to starboard. *To ease the sheets* or *haul in on the sheets* on a sloop generally means to slacken or tighten the jib sheets and mainsheet. Dealing with the sheets on a sailing vessel is an almost constant chore.

Shrouds. The heavy wires (part of the standing rigging) that run from the chainplates on the sidedecks outboard of the mast up to various points high on a mast to give it lateral support. The shrouds, together with the various headstays and backstays support the mast.

Slat or slatting. When a vessel is becalmed in a swell, or a swell is running at an angle to the wind, a yacht often gets a rolling, back-and-forth motion that causes the sails to bang on the rigging—first on one side and then on the other. The noise is hard on a sailor's nerves and can cause severe wear or chafe on the sails and running rigging. Slatting can be lessened by suitable rigging adjustment or sometimes by lowering a sail.

Sloop. A single-masted vessel with the mast located about one-third of the overall length aft of the stem. A sloop generally carries a single large headsail. (Compare to **cutter.**)

Sock. A device to help handle and control large lightweight running sails. A very long, narrow, circular sock of light material (the same length as the sail measurement from head to foot) is pulled down and around a sail to keep it from opening and billowing out. The sail (inside the sock) is hoisted up the mast and made fast. Then when the controlling lines at the foot of the sail are ready, a sock lifting line is pulled. This raises the sock to the top of the sail and allows it to billow out and be set. To douse the sail, the control lines at the foot are eased and the sock is pulled down, gathering up the sail into a compact, sausage-like roll.

Spreaders. Carefully streamlined metal, wood, or plastic fabrications placed at almost right angles to a mast or boom to hold the shrouds away from the mast and give them more effective angles for opposing the bending loads applied to the mast.

Squall. A brief, sudden, and violent windstorm, usually demanding a quick reduction of sail.

Stanchion. Vertical fenceposts spaced about every two meters along the deck to hold the lifelines, which run to the pulpits at the bow and stern.

Standing rigging. Heavy permanent wires or rods which support a mast and are infrequently adjusted. Standing rigging on sailing yachts is often made of nineteen strands of stainless steel wire suitably laid up into a single spiral form, called 1x19. Rigging can also be made of single wires or rods. Each system has various advantages and special problems.

Staysail. A small sail set ahead of a mast. Properly, the staysail is given a prefix depending on which mast the sail is set forward of (in the case of more than one mast). On a yawl or ketch, a sail set forward of the mizzen mast is called a mizzen staysail. On a schooner you have a main staysail or a fore-staysail.

Stratus. Low, spread-out, uniform, gray clouds. With rain, status is called *nimbostratus*. When wind rips stratus apart (often with ragged, torn-looking bottoms), the clouds are called *fracto-stratus*.

Tack (noun). The lower forward corner of a triangular or quadrilateral sail. The word *tack* is also used with port or starboard to describe the side of the vessel over which the wind is blowing. Sailing on the starboard tack, for example, means that the wind is passing over the vessel from the starboard side.

Tack (verb). One of the two basic sailing maneuvers that takes the bow of a vessel through the eye of the wind so that the driving wind force is changed from one side of the sails to the other. Compare with **gybe.**

Tie rods. Stout, solid rigging rods that tie heavily loaded deck rigging fittings to strong points down on the hull.

Topping lift. A controlling line from a block or sheave high on the mast down to the end of a pole or spar. (1) Used in conjunction with a foreguy and an afterguy to control the outer end of a spinnaker pole. (2) To control the end of the main boom (with the mainsheet and a preventer line) when running. (3) To support the weight of the main boom in port or when the mainsail halyard is slacked for reefing.

True wind. The true direction or speed of the wind without any allowance for the movement of the vessel. (Compare to **apparent wind.**)

Vang. A mechanical or hydraulic device used to pull down the main boom for sail control and adjustment. Vangs are often rigged between the foot of the mast and a point on the bottom of the boom about 25-35 percent of the boom length aft of the gooseneck. Vangs typically put severe bending loads on the boom and often cause breakages. An alternate scheme is to use a block-and-tackle purchase arrangement, which will generally break *in extremis.*

Veer - back. See back - veer.

Weather shore. Land in relation to a vessel and from which the wind is blowing *toward* the ship. The opposite of lee shore.

Windward. Toward the wind.

Yankee. A special jib with a high-cut clew.

Yawl. A two-masted vessel with the after mast—the mizzen—located aft of the rudder post. The mizzen sail of a yawl is smaller than the mizzen of a ketch.

About the Author

Hal Roth is one of America's best known sailing writers. He enjoys a large following here and abroad. He has sailed around the Pacific, cruised to Cape Horn (where he survived a wreck), and circumnavigated the world three times.

He twice participated in the BOC Challenge round-the-world single-handed race. *Chasing the Long Rainbow* chronicled the 1986–87 race, and *Chasing the Wind* is Hal Roth's very personal account of the challenges he faced in the 1990–91 event.

He has written some of the finest books on sailing and the sea, among them *After 50,000 Miles, Two Against Cape Horn,* and *Always a Distant Anchorage* (about his and his wife Margaret's experiences in their 35-foot sloop *Whisper*). Hal Roth is also an accomplished photographer and has produced two documentary films about sailing.